Nature, Man, and Society in the Twelfth Century

Nature, Man, and Society

in the

Twelfth Century

ESSAYS ON NEW THEOLOGICAL
PERSPECTIVES IN THE LATIN WEST

M.-D. CHENU, O.P.

with a Preface by
ETIENNE GILSON

Selected, Edited, and Translated by
JEROME TAYLOR and LESTER K. LITTLE

The University of Chicago Press
CHICAGO AND LONDON

Originally published in 1957 as
La théologie au douzième siècle
© *1957, J. Vrin*

The University of Chicago Press, Chicago 60637
The University of Chicago Press, Ltd., London

© 1968 by The University of Chicago
All rights reserved. Published 1968
Midway reprint 1983
Printed in the United States of America

ISBN: 0–226–10256–4
LCN: 68–15574

TRANSLATORS' NOTE

The nine essays translated in this book as well as the preface by M. Gilson and the author's own introduction represent a selection from *La théologie au douzième siècle* (Paris: J. Vrin, 1957), by Père M.-D. Chenu, O.P. Both the selection and the translation were undertaken with the author's permission and with his ready and gracious cooperation as particular problems arose. Only one paragraph of the original has been changed by him; the change occurs in the first paragraph of the sixth essay, and its purpose was to supplant a contemporary reference which, for an audience outside French-speaking Europe, might have had less meaning than he wished to convey. Where shortcomings remain in the translation, some are doubtless due to differences in language which elude resolution—at least our own; some, perhaps, to limitations in our understanding, of which we remain imperfectly aware; none to limitations in the thought or the helpfulness of Père Chenu, veritable *magister magistrorum* in our time.

The order of the essays corresponds to chapters 1, 5, 7, 9, 3, 10, 11, 15, and 19 in the French original. Chapter 3, it will be noted, has been transposed. Dealing as it does with historiography, with "Theology and the New Awareness of History," it both bridges and unites in a special way the intellectual considerations on the one hand, and the institutional or social developments on the other, which the first and the last four essays respectively emphasize.

Père Chenu's chapters, however, do not unfold a single linear story, a tightly sequential argument, destroyed by omission or transposition of any one of its parts. Their relationship is better depicted by an image of concentric circles, each delimiting one area in unique fashion, while all having a common focal point. Individually and collectively they demonstrate that the study and the history of man's intellectual life may not properly be fragmented into dissociated disciplines or traditions, truncated into historical periods, or divorced from the external culture within which it grows, by which it is influenced, and which it informs. If Père Chenu considers "history of theology" to be the central concern of this collection, it is because he conceives of theology as an all-encompassing science, one which reflects the comprehensive unity of intellectual life as that develops within a culture. Literary history and criticism, cultural history, philosophy, biblical exegesis, historiography, ecclesiastical and social history, the history of education—all these and more are here involved, in their interdependence. The essays from the original volume not included in our translation add little to this range, though much to the understanding of yet other, perhaps more specialized topics.

Documentation from the original has been preserved, with, however, correction of errors in the printed text and with several additions. Thus, for convenience to some readers, we have supplied editions of Latin or vernacular texts cited only by title in the French work. Old editions there cited, for example those of the *Patrologia Latina*, we have replaced where possible or supplemented with more recent and accessible ones. We have added or expanded Latin texts not quoted, or not fully quoted, in the notes of the French work; all quoted texts have in any case been checked and if necessary emended to conform with the editions cited. We have replaced Latin quotations in the body of Père Chenu's work with English, and placed the Latin originals in the notes.

With similar convenience in mind, we have also added references to published English translations of both Latin and vernacular works and after every Latin quotation have supplied in parentheses an English rendering, either as published or else as corrected or supplied by us. Having once mentioned such editorial procedures as these, we feel it unnecessary to give special indication of them in the notes. When, however, we have in rare instances added a footnote, or have occasionally introduced into an existing note a fact or reference that has appeared since 1957, or have ventured to call attention to a few older materials that seemed to us to give particular support to a point, we have placed such intrusions within brackets.

We gratefully acknowledge the hospitality and helpful advice of the author's colleagues at Le Saulchoir, particularly of Père H. D. Saffrey, who as *bibliothécaire* opened the resources of the library to us. We are also grateful for secretarial and financial assistance, particularly a Willett Faculty Fellowship, provided by the College of the University of Chicago. Thanks are equally due to the John Simon Guggenheim Memorial Foundation and the Danforth Foundation for a fellowship year, part of which was used toward the completion of the project.

J. T.
L. K. L.

Preface

BY ETIENNE GILSON

The unity of conception guiding the work which we have the privilege of welcoming into this series[1] is so evident that it would be superfluous to enlarge upon the point. The precise subject of the studies contained in this work and the spirit in which that subject has been studied, the author himself has discussed with such clarity and energy that one could only weaken his words if one sought to paraphrase them. On these points, one can only send the reader to the author's introduction and urge that he read it with attention. What Père Chenu there says, in the intricate and highly personal language one associates with him, concerning the definite historical reality he has sought to identify, to comprehend, and to describe, reveals to plain view the underlying conception of his research. One can add nothing to what he himself has said.

Perhaps, however, it will not be without value to say a few words about the origin of this volume. For several years past we have pursued Père Chenu for permission to assemble in one or more volumes the numerous scholarly articles which, thanks to his generous industry, have appeared in many different journals in France and other countries. Our wish was wholly self-interested, and yet we excused it by reflecting that such a project, highly useful as it would be for us, would realize the hopes of others besides ourselves. Very few historians, professors, or readers have at hand those collections of

---

[1] [*La théologie au douzième siècle* forms vol. 45 in the series *Etudes de philosophie médiévale*, ed. Etienne Gilson.]

ix

journals necessary if one is to have access to the numerous studies by Père Chenu, studies important to consult or to cite.

The collection which we sought with an insistence that only friendship could excuse, Père Chenu never quite granted or quite refused. And, in fact, we still do not have it, for there yet remain in French, Italian, English, and German journals many historical studies by him which have not been gathered into this book.[2] Let us not cease to hope that they will one day be brought together into other volumes which will complement the present one. The point we should like to stress here, however, is that in not granting us precisely what we had asked for, Père Chenu has given us not less but much more and, to tell the truth, something quite different and at a cost of which something should be said.

From his available published works, our historian chose those that bear upon the theological ferment of the twelfth century; in so doing he assured to the collection a material unity indicated by the book's title. These articles the author submitted to careful revision, occasionally changing them, often enriching them with considerable additions. Finally and more importantly, to the selection of already published articles he added a second series of unpublished studies bearing upon the same general subject but investigating certain of its aspects not yet considered. What we have here, then, is a work that is really new in overall conception and in content as well.

Every reader of this book will find in it things that his own particular interests—historical, philosophical, theological—lead him to look for; but beyond these exists a general lesson which all will benefit by learning. One of the scourges of history is the obligation weighing heavily upon every historian to specialize and particularize. The medieval period has suffered from this obligation at least as much as other periods; but it is a matter of grave concern that in the case of the medieval era, scholars hesitate to correct too radically the accepted points of view lest, in so doing, they should lose as much truth as they gain. Many recent studies urge that one soften the sharp distinction, traditionally marked by volume 217 of Migne's *Patrologia Latina*, between the end of the late patristic period and

---

[2] [Chenu's publications between 1922 and 1963 are listed in his *La parole de Dieu*, vol. 1: *La foi dans l'intelligence* (Paris, 1964), pp. 397–411.]

the beginning of the great scholastic theology whose works fill the thirteenth and fourteenth centuries. Very rarely does such accumulated evidence fail to contain some truth; or, to put it somewhat better, vary rarely does it fail to be fundamentally true. No one thinks of rejecting the evidence, but it is equally the case that the effort to give such distinctions a meaning as precise as possible often hardens them beyond all reason.

If one were not sensitive to this danger, one might well miss the full import of the studies contained in this book. By the entire cast of his thought as well as by his religious vocation, Père Chenu finds himself naturally at home in the realm of Thomistic theology. Those whose allegiances are to other traditions have difficulty grasping the extent to which the theology of St. Thomas concentrates within itself all the responses which one and the same mind can expect to experience on all levels of man's intellectual life. Especially for a son of St. Dominic, what men call "Thomism" is integrally and indivisibly a philosophy, a theology, a spirituality, and a mysticism born in its entirety from the word of God, nourishing itself on that word and illuminating it in turn with its own light. But that which is one in life necessarily becomes divided in teaching and, too often, becomes fragmented in history. It appears that in his principal works Père Chenu is led by the desire to preserve the unity of Thomistic theology, and not without good reason, since to permit it to be resolved into separate disciplines is to permit its destruction. In fact, the theology of St. Thomas is not a constellation of diverse disciplines. Rather, it eminently embraces them all within its transcendent unity and is, as the magnificent phrase of the master himself has it, "in effect the expression of the divine knowledge, which is the law, one and simple, of all things" (*velut quaedam impressio divinae scientiae, quae est una lex simplex omnium*).

Père Chenu has emphasized that unity, under all its aspects, in his masterly *Introduction à l'étude de Saint Thomas d'Aquin*,[3] but it is not impossible that the present studies of theology in the twelfth century should aid in the comprehension of a further trait which, in the eyes of the author, is inseparable from genuine Thomism.

---

[3] [A. M. Landry and D. Hughes, tr., *Toward Understanding St. Thomas* (Chicago, 1964).]

It has often been observed that elements of scholasticism already exist in twelfth-century theology. It is likewise important to note that patristic elements still exist in the scholasticism of the thirteenth century. Let us rather say that the whole of the patristic theology of the twelfth century, presented in a new form, and more besides, passed into the great doctrinal syntheses of the following century. The studies comprising this volume often suggest to the reader the picture of a scriptural theology which, precisely because it presages in many ways the work of the great scholastics, insinuates itself in advance into that great fabric. Nothing could afterwards pluck it out.

In still larger perspective, it seems certain, in consequence, that one must renounce that long accepted historical schematization: end of the patristic era, scholasticism, Renaissance. Not that this schematization is false, but it is oversimplified. In many respects the twelfth century stands forth as a time of vast theological activity, certain lines of which continue to develop within scholasticism, while others, overwhelmed by the extraordinary richness of thirteenth-century theology, fall into a sort of half-sleep, or simply become less prominent while awaiting the aggressive return they will make in the fourteenth century. There can, in our view, be no doubt that the *devotio moderna*, which owed its novelty to the stand it took against the scholasticism of the thirteenth century, simply continues an older trend opposed in advance to theological methods whose future development, even toward the end of the twelfth century, was not yet foreseeable.

O that they would employ such effort in the improvement of their lives as they spend in studying far into the night!

O that they would grow as pale from desire for their heavenly home as they do from intense intellectual effort, wasting as they do both time and youth in altercations over words!

Subtleties which they cannot compass they wish wholly to comprehend. . . .

O vanity of vainglory! O snare of praise! O useless curiosity.[4]

---

[4]   O si tantam diligentiam adhiberent morum aedificationi quantam apponunt nocturnae lucubrationi!

O si ita pallerent prae desiderio patriae caelestis quantum pallent pro vehementi animi applicatione, dum circa verborum cavillationes tempus et aetatem consumunt!

Subtilitates quas assequi nequeunt, examussim comprehendere volunt....

O vanitas ostentationis! O laudis ambitus! O inutilis curiositas!

Who speaks in this vein? It is not the author of the *Imitation of Christ;* it is merely Alexander Neckham, whose treatise *On Nature* stands athwart the end of that century in which the theological activity here described by Père Chenu took place. Thus, as if to compensate for the precise discriminations he must make, the historian rediscovers the continuity of actual history without sacrificing any of its diversity.

Let us add that in this context the word "history" must not delude us. Thanks to the word of God on which it lives, theology escapes from time in a manner analogous to that *scientia Dei* of which it is, in man, the image. Informed minds will not for an instant lose sight of this truth while reading studies striving so profoundly to tie sacred doctrine to the social contexts which carry and influence that doctrine through their aspirations even as they are instructed and directed by it. What is always at stake in the history of theology is theology itself. This, indeed, is why the lessons we draw from the history of theology are valid for all times.

Introduction

Half the studies presented in this book have seen publication before; they are collected here to satisfy the confident wish of insistent friends. This confidence, however, has itself spurred me on not only to revise the original versions closely but to follow up the thread of these original investigations with an equal number of closely related essays in order to give more substance to my interpretation of the history of theology in the twelfth century.

We have here, in one sense, only a collection of monographs; they do not pretend to constitute an organic history of a century great in its theology. Nonetheless, all the essays share in a project which unifies them closely—the project of identifying systematic procedures and, beneath the procedures taught, those implicit intellectual perspectives which, more than systems and controversies, determined the course of a century universally acknowledged to be the turning point of the Middle Ages in the West, both in institutions and in religion.

My determination to hold to this design carries over into the very wording of the essay titles, none of which alludes to any of the masters of that time, from Abelard to William of Auxerre, from St. Bernard to Joachim of Floris, nor yet to any of the major controverted doctrines, from Christological nihilism to the definition of the sacraments, from the dispute over universals to the condemnation of Amaury of Bène. It must be said that these essays could not have appeared had it not been for the remarkable efforts of scholars who, especially by going back to manuscripts still buried in libraries, have reoriented the field of theology and its philosophical underpinnings since World War I. The reader must have constant recourse to the great scholarly enterprises of Landgraf and Lottin, of Gilson and Leclercq, without forgetting the pioneer of literary history, Ghellinck.

This resolute design, moreover, resists any simple division of labor. History, I am convinced, must reach the root causes that underlie texts, controversies, systems—indeed that underlie great minds, if it is true that a genius is one whose words have greater import than he alone could have given them. To be worthy of its subject, all the more if that subject is the thought and life of the Christian people, history aspires to isolate the internal forces which determine the climate of an age and the belief of the faithful. It lays bare, within that climate and within that belief, those collective insights which transcend the most marked diversities and so achieve the unity and the tensions of generations at work. Geological deposits with different effects upon plant life do not each produce some separate species of plant from the soil in which they coexist, but together they account for the total native fertility and diverse productivity of that soil.

Surely one must not underestimate in any way the role that genius, with its highly personalized insights, plays in the origination of systems and of institutions. The conversion of St. Bernard is, even for theology, a major event to the extent that theology is fortified by the power of faith and to the extent that the Cistercian order, apart from its influence upon the salvation of many individuals, gave direction to the history of the church. But these very masters of thought, these very founders, are themselves to be understood only within their contemporary contexts; or, since we are here concerned with theology, only within the ecclesiastical society which produced them. The historian cannot see his task as a matter of pitting great personalities successively one against another; he aspires to lay hold upon total social entities and upon the factors, mental or institutional, which condition their operation. It is the whole social body of the church which, in the twelfth century, penetrates the Christian mystery by renewed study of the gospel; it is the entire body of the clergy which, in the unprecedented rise of urban schools, provides doctrinal and moral elaboration to the substance of the word of God through newly self-conscious reliance upon a symbolism that formed an integral part of biblical interpretation and patristic tradition.

Precisely in the twelfth century we find ourselves in an age when, in the West, Christian people, thanks to the spread of culture and thanks even more to a sensational apostolic awakening, became collectively aware of their environment and sought to rationalize it. Controversies no longer had to do with the dogmatic formulation of this or that mystery as they had in the fourth century, but with intellectual or institutional behavior. It was not Abelard's mistakes concerning appropriation within the Trinity or concerning the absolution of penitents that St. Bernard combatted; it was the proud pretension that divine mystery can be penetrated by dialectical procedures. If the disciples of Gilbert of La Porrée encountered opposition from Augustinian masters, it was because the West recoiled instinctively from the cosmology and anthropology of the Greek fathers—a contest of preferences more decisive in their consquences for Christian thought than the events of the Council of Reims. The formation of evangelical brotherhoods, at once so distinctive and so much alike, whether one thinks of Peter Waldo or Francis of Assisi, marked an event in the history of theology of a quite different importance from that of the condemnation of Christological nihilism by Alexander III. The joy of St. Francis had more influence than King John's oath of fealty to the pope, not only upon the prosperity of the church but also upon men's progress in the knowledge of Christ.

Thus, I regard institutional history and intellectual history proper as closely interdependent. Events are pregnant with ideas; ecclesiastical events more so than others since, insofar as they are authentic, they are expressions of the word of God. Theology attests freely and fruitfully to the organic interdependence of the phenomena of civilization because its divine subject is given, developed, and sanctioned by a church, a society incarnate in a visible institution. Moreover, it is a commonplace that the evangelical awakening exemplified by the mendicant brotherhoods is set within the human context of rising guilds and religious confraternities, of new generations of city-dwellers who are the objects of their ministry and the source of their recruits, of university schools in which the leading lights of the orders take their seats as masters of science and apostles of catholicity. The peculiar spirituality and the institutional problem associated with the poverty of St. Francis cannot be defined except as intrinsic to a social evolution which tends to render obsolete the ancient monastic poverty tied up with the feudal regime. The symbolism found in scriptural interpretation and the liturgy would remain a closed book to one who had not experienced for himself the vision of the cosmos introduced into men's minds by the diffusion of Dionysian concepts that went beyond the classical morality of St. Gregory. The figure of God posed as artisan of the cosmos as one sees it on the portal of Chartres would be inconceivable in a society that believed in the eternity of essences; and in that same place of spiritual and esthetic eminence, man portrayed as Christ's double, affords a daring plastic translation of that *imago Dei* which scripture intruded into an otherwise cold Platonic cosmogony.

Even literary forms acquire significance in this season of methodological renewal. The revival of Platonic dialogue is not without meaning, however mediocre the achievements were. As to the development of the *quaestio* and the employment of dialectic which it permits, it is evident that these dominate all the forms of expression appropriate to that divine "science" which will turn into scholastic theology.

Finally, fields which historians have too long divided into the history of theology on the one hand and the history of spirituality on the other should be reintegrated. To be sure, these fields employ different techniques, each has a "style" different from the other, and the same men are not always masters in both. Even so, it would be senseless to reconstruct the history of theology without speaking of the Spirituals, to consider Richard of Saint-Victor as a "mystic" in a pejorative sense, to measure the influence of St. Bernard by his slight contribution to scholasticism, to treat Abelard as a dialectician while ignoring his spiritual dialogue with Heloïse. And how can one write the theological history of the church without attending to the history of the gospel within the church?

These various undertakings, considering the unity proper to a history and especially to a religious history, obviously oblige one to go beyond mere study of texts or recital of events. Nothing would exist without such study or such detailing of events; fidelity and exactitude in these tasks is the elementary condition of historical truth. But historical understanding strives for an interior comprehension of events and of texts beyond what even the authors of these explicitly saw or said at the time. Positivism has been given fair trial in history as in other disciplines, and the end result was to downgrade understanding in a factual pastiche, supposedly objective.

For the sake of such interior comprehension, I have deliberately attempted an interpretation of events and of texts, not, to be sure, by making some ideological imposition upon them in subservience to some thesis or system, but by making an impassioned search for internal points of contact, for half-conscious relationships, for determining factors of institutional or spiritual character. Things themselves, whatever the originality of the minds that handle them, have their own determining character: once the concept of "nature" had been put into circulation at Chartres and afterwards in the groundswell of Aristotelianism at the end of the century, the consequences were there to pay, for good or ill, whatever the outcome and whatever the confusion. This sort of thing leads one to pursue texts and events with an inquiring eye, even when they have already been analyzed dozens of times by qualified scholars.

One always runs the risk of a subjective interpretation which imputes unverifiable and possibly imaginary relationships to the reality being described. But this risk is worth running if it is true that the task of the historian is to construct and not simply to recover. Nor can his task be anything else. The positivist historians interpreted unconsciously in using the mental categories of the Enlightenment which proscribe the irreducible integrity of the phenomenon of religion. The Middle Ages suffered among the most from such interpretation. We have not yet quite recovered from it, and the learned conscientiousness of a Prantl or an Hauréau maintains an uncomprehending view—that is the least one might say of it—of medieval doctrines. Our understanding of the twelfth century has been distorted by the rationalist prejudices of Enlightenment philosophy; we should heartily concur in its celebration of Abelard, whom it naïvely treated as its forerunner, but we should firmly maintain against this philosophy and its adherents that symbolic methods of religious expression have at least as much importance and certainly more Christian efficaciousness than dialectical methods. In proceeding differently from the positivists, after all, we run only such risks as arise from an appreciative understanding of the course of that history—which we will have studied first, to be sure, by reading the documents as they stand and by analyzing the techniques employed in them.

More than other forms of history, the history of theology calls for such knowledge to the extent that this history involves a communion of faith, above all to the extent that it has for its object a living tradition. In a way, the history of theology falls within theology itself. A perfect history of theology, if one existed, would yield a theology of history.

Western theology in the twelfth century affords an admirable subject for this kind of history. Granted that among the great minds of this century one does not find genius comparable to that of the doctors of the thirteenth century; granted that in the thick undergrowth of its literature one cannot descry schools from which great systems of thought grow to lofty heights. Nonetheless, it is filled with a sap that presses upwards into new tissues; many of its attempts will be aborted or yield doubtful results; but the intuitions in which these are rooted retain their vitality, and this will not always be true of the literature and teaching of the great century to follow. The general history of the period confirms the view of the historian of theology.

It is irrelevant to a project such as this to summarize the latest findings of work that has been in progress during recent decades, even under the pretext of providing a complete inventory of that work. To do so would involve quite a different sort of project, and therefore, within limits, I have resisted this temptation and preserved the essay character of the collection. Customary bibliography, which readers will be able to find in competent reference works, likewise seemed out of place here, and it has been my practice, when documenting a significant point, to cite a single apposite scholarly article without feeling obliged to refer as well to major works that are well known. Once and for all, let me here refer the reader to existing literary histories, treatises on doctrines, and monographs on institutions and major figures.

Contents

✣

1

Nature and Man
The Renaissance of the Twelfth Century

IN VIEW OF its dominant position in our history of western civilization, the term "Renaissance" calls for a rigorous examination that will set it free from historical dogmatism on the one hand and from facile overgeneralization on the other. Created in the service of theoretical presumptions regarding the evolution of culture in the West and arising from a fixed conception concerning the role played by "Antiquity" in this evolution, the term "Renaissance" required that the bridging concept of "Middle Ages" be invented. Since the definitions of Burkhardt and Voigt, however, the term "Renaissance" has been subjected to a searching criticism, especially by those whose improved knowledge of the thousand years of the "Middle Ages" awakened in them serious doubts concerning the whole conception. The fact that they have lifted the term and applied it in some fashion to important episodes within the "Middle Ages" themselves—one hears of a "Carolingian renaissance," then of a "renaissance of the twelfth century," and finally that the "Middle Ages" were destined to play their role in a three-stage renaissance of Antiquity of which the Italian quattrocento was simply the completion[1]

---

[1] The historical view of the Middle Ages as progressively assimilating ancient culture has been put forth by Mandonnet, Gilson, Haskins, and Paetow and has displaced the conception of the Renaissance popularized by Burckhardt (1860) and Voigt (1859). One finds a presentiment of the new view in J.-J.-A. Ampère, *Histoire littéraire de la France avant le douzième siècle,* III (Paris, 1840), 33: "I maintain that there were three renaissances: the first dates from Charlemagne; the second, which falls at the end of the eleventh century, initiates the Middle Ages; the last is the great renaissance of the fifteenth and sixteenth centuries."

—leads us today to go beyond this rather too handy and factitious periodization and to seek a deeper understanding of what was peculiar to the various epochs to which the common term "renaissance" has been applied in so equivocal a manner.

Medieval men themselves, insofar as they were conscious of their place in the ferment of history, furnished justification for the idea of successive stages of renaissance. They characterized their cultural heritage as a *translatio studii* (transmission of learning) which, like the *translatio imperii* (transmission of empire) in the political sphere, pointed to the source of their spiritual capital.[2] The modern term "Middle Ages," however, set up as a foil to the "Renaissance" and lexically suggesting little more than a dead center, stripped such transmissions of their responsiveness to evolving conditions; indeed, it sold short the very concept of "renaissance," for this term now no longer expressed the capacity for continual renovation characteristic of western Christendom, except as comprised within some external imitation of Antiquity.

If we turn our attention to the development of religious knowledge in its different forms, literary and doctrinal, and particularly if we turn our attention to the development of the theological disciplines, we find it surprising that the term "renaissance" was ever used to mark the rhythm and stages of an evolution whose course was obviously set from within the faith. A literary or philosophical rebirth of Antiquity should affect Christian belief, one would think, only by providing the tools with which it can work. And even then one can foresee that religious inspiration will modify intrinsically, will in some sense transubstantiate, the materials taken from Antiquity—even where imitation of Antiquity is most alluring and fully approved.[3]

---

[2] See below, chap. 5, and Etienne Gilson, "L'humanisme médiéval," in *Les idées et les lettres* (Paris, 1932), pp. 132–85.

[3] One must observe, further, that the concepts of "Antiquity" and the "Middle Ages" involve a near-sighted concentration upon Europe alone and a hasty oversimplification of the complexities even of Europe's development. They force us to exclude from purview whole blocks of significant human activity that are properly part of civilization. Ibn Khaldun, fourteenth-century Muslim historian, clearly showed a more realistic grasp of things when he noted that the geohistorical evolution of the ancient world, whether in Egypt

"Renaissance" is not reducible to impassioned imitation of the literary, artistic, scientific, or philosophical masterpieces of Greco-Roman antiquity—to imitation which sees archeological reconstruction as the furthest bound of its ambition. It literally involves new birth, new existence in all the changed conditions of times, places, and persons; it represents an initiative all the more irreducible to the ancient materials it uses because it is a spiritual initiative. Imitation is subordinate to inventiveness even when providing it with material. The particular value of the advances made in the course of such an awakening is traceable, as the historian must acknowledge, to geographical, economic, social, political, and religious contexts. These are not merely external conditions permitting a restoration in the simple and obvious sense given to the word in political affairs; they are intrinsic guarantees that a discovery hitherto unimagined will be made.

The school of Chartres provided, during the "renaissance" of the twelfth century, a ready-made case in point, if it is true that there the study of Euclid and the translation of the *Almagest* were touched off by a native interest in the scientific exploration of the universe and not by the curiosity of some librarian lovesick for the past; if it is true that there courtly love expressed a new sensitivity to the power of passion, and that Ovid's *Art of Love* was only its handbook; if it is true that there the commentaries upon the *Timaeus* were the means of satisfying minds eager to know the origin of the universe, not just to devote their energies to scholarly annotation. Curiosity about literature, together with all its apparatus, is ever able to serve the discovery of nature and of man. Return to the ancients always

---

or Chaldea or the Mediterranean basin, depended radically upon interaction between nomadic shepherds and sedentary farmers. [See Muhsin Mahdi, *Ibn Khaldun's Philosophy of History: A Study in the Philosophic Foundation of the Science of Culture* (Chicago, 1957).] On "renaissance" as a historical category, see W. K. Ferguson, *The Renaissance in Historical Thought: Five Centuries of Interpretation* (Boston, 1948); on application of the term to the twelfth century, a résumé of the controversy will be found in E. M. Sanford, "The Twelfth Century—Renaissance or Proto-Renaissance?" and U. T. Holmes, Jr., "The Idea of a Twelfth-Century Renaissance," both in *Spec.*, XXVI (1951): 635–42, 643–51. [Further discussion in Erwin Panofsky, *Renaissance and Renascences in Western Art* (Copenhagen and Stockholm, 1960).]

begets a historically oriented humanism, to be sure; philology becomes its instrument, and the human sympathy we derive from such
study is not without a certain aristocratic distinction. But Antiquity
can be evoked under other skies than its own and, though it might
be at the price of historical accuracy, it can be reborn in a spiritual
assimilation which keeps the ancient materials intact within a new
organism. The bringing to light once more of the ancient materials
is by no means the sufficient cause or the characterizing mark of
such an advance in culture; it is an effect incidental to a hunger of
spirit. It is within the spirit that the joyous rebirth takes place; the
sources just discovered had perhaps long been accessible but had
long remained unproductive for want of some spirit to breathe upon
the waters.

To broaden a too narrow conception of the reactivation of ancient
values, whether in the twelfth century or in others, all one needs to
do is to evoke the cathedral being built at the shrine of Chartres in
a burst of creative zeal and decorated with the most realistic scenes
from contemporary life at the very moment when Gilbert of La
Porrée was at work glossing Boethius; or the lofty theme of the
Grail as handled by Chrétien of Troyes, who was also curious about
ancient things; or the rise of communes and corporate urban society,
the leaders of which were to give a prompt and eager reception to
the *Politics* of Aristotle; or, in the case of John of Salisbury, to take
into account the crucial role of his very modern political experience
as well as the ancient ingredients with which the immense erudition
of his *Policraticus* abounds.

The Discovery of Nature[4]

The discovery of nature: we are not now concerned merely with
the feeling for nature which poets of the time evinced here and
there in fashionable allegorical constructions, nor are we concerned
merely with the plastic representations of nature that sculptors fashioned at the portals and on the capitals of cathedrals. Rather, our

---

[4] On this matter consult the full and well-documented account of Tullio
Gregory, *Anima mundi: la filosofia di Guglielmo di Conches e la scuola di
Chartres* (Florence, 1955), chap. 4, "L'idea di natura," pp. 175–246.

concern is with the realization which laid hold upon these men of the twelfth century when they thought of themselves as confronting an external, present, intelligible, and active reality as they might confront a partner (and in fact they personified this partner in their allegories) whose might and whose decrees called for accommodation or conflict—a realization which struck them at the very moment when, with no less a shock, they reflected that they were themselves caught up within the framework of nature, were themselves also bits of this cosmos they were ready to master.

Merely to mention the new and fresh perceptions that writers, artists, and sculptors offered to the sensibilities of their contemporaries, or the secular shape that men of politics and affairs were giving to institutions hitherto sacramentalized, is to suggest, as one must, which way the wind was blowing—blowing over all of nature, from flora and fauna to the shape given the human body, from erotic impulses to the behavior patterns of corporate life. One finds the strophe of William of Aquitaine on springtime, and the voluptuous Eve on the lintel of the north portal at Autun; the sketchbooks of Villard of Honnecourt, and the erotic casuistry of Chrétien of Troyes; the small tradesmen set in the stone of capitals, and the realistic sense of man's destiny among the great chroniclers; the political psychology of John of Salisbury, and the anticlericalism of the second part of the *Roman de la Rose;* the limitation of certain secular rights of the clergy by Philip Augustus or St. Louis, and recourse to rational proofs in courts of law instead of the mystical expedient of trials by ordeal. The whole world of pseudonature, which had long cast its deluding shadow over things and men, was fading from men's imaginations; it was by quite other means than imagination that nature, discovered now in its earthly reality, would acquire its religious significance and lead men to God.

And how did theologians participate in this critical development? The simplest but not the least significant evidence of this discovery of nature was their perception of the universe as an entity. One recalls that this was a cardinal point with the ancients, and it was now revived. The unmistakable sign of this was the spread of the word *universitas* employed independently and as a concrete noun (not *universitas rerum*) to designate the universe in descriptions or in systematic treatises. Doubtless this usage was stimulated by the reading of John the Scot, who characteristically used the term in this way.[5] But precisely because the usage is traceable to him, one is compelled to distinguish the cosmic sense of *universitas* from numerous contemporary usages semantically at variance with it—from logical, juridical, social, and intellectual senses of the term. In the history of knowledge, this is not the first time that the idea of a single integral world arises within and because of a religion. To conceive the world as one whole is already to perceive its profound structure —a world of forms transcending the medley of visible and sense-perceptible phenomena. The whole penetrates each of its parts; it is one universe; God conceived it as a unique living being, and its intelligible Model is itself a Whole.[6]

Bernard Sylvester's title, *De mundi universitate* (*On the Universe of the World*),[7] employed the full sense of the term. Honorius of Autun provided expected evidence of the use of *universitas* to mean universe.[8] The word came spontaneously into use whenever men were thinking of the homogeneity of natural phenomena, as one sees

---

[5] John the Scot *De div. nat.* ii. 1 (*PL*, CXXII, 524: ". . . omne enim quod in ipso [Deo] et ex ipso est, pie et rationabiliter de eo praedicari potest—sed intelligibili quadam universitatis contemplatione—universitatem dico Deum et creaturam" (everything that exists in God or comes from God can piously and reasonably be predicated of God—but only if we are looking at the universe from the standpoint of intelligibility—and by "universe" I mean God and creation). *Expos. in Hier. coel.* iv. 6 (H.-F. Dondaine, ed., *AHDL*, XVIII [1950–51]: 264): ". . . dum ceteri auctores . . . quinquiformem universitatis condite dividunt modum [entia, viventia, sentientia, rationabilia, intellectualia], . . . iste magister quadripartitum definit modum . . ." (while all other authors offer a fivefold division of the created universe [beings, living beings, sentient beings, beings capable of reason, intellectual beings], . . . this master sets up a fourfold mode of division).

[6] Cf. Plato *Tim.* 30d. 2–5: "Then God, having decided to form the world in the closest possible likeness to the most beautiful of intelligible beings and to a Being perfect in all things, made it into a living being, one, visible, and having within itself all living beings of like nature with itself."

[7] [Barach-Wrobel, ed.; the title used by this old edition is actually the subtitle, as is demonstrated by A. Vernet in a study and new edition of the work that he is about to publish. The original title was simply *Cosmographia*.]

[8] *Liber XII quaest.* ii, iv, xii (*PL*, CLXXII, 1179, 1180, 1184, 1185) (see n. 16, below); *Expos. in Cant.* v. (*PL*, CLXXII, 432): "Et sicut angelus in universitate habet suum locum ita homo in universitate habet suum" (And just as the angel has its place in the universe, so man has his).

in Gerhoh of Reichersberg,[9] Hugh of Saint-Victor,[10] Arnold of Bonneval,[11] Adam of Dryburgh,[12] and others.[13]

Because it is a single whole, the harmony of this universe is striking, despite the extreme diversity of the beings that compose it. "The world is an ordered aggregation of creatures."[14] The *universitas* is

---

[9] *De aedificio Dei* i (*PL*, CXCIV, 1193): ". . . tota universitatis structura convenienter ornatur" (the whole structure of the universe is suitably equipped).

[10] *Expos. in Hier. coel.* iii (*PL*, CLXXV, 980): ". . . nihil in universitate est, quod a summo bono participationem non trahat" (there is nothing in the universe that does not participate in the Highest Good); *ibid.*, iv (*PL*, CLXXV, 1003): "Hoc autem diligenter attendendum est, quod non singulis quibusque, sed hierarchiae, idest universitati, bona illa manifestata dicuntur, ita tamen ut a singulis in universitate imitationis studio exerceantur. . . ." (It must be carefully noted that not to any individual being but to the entire hierarchy, that is, to the universe, are those goods revealed, but in such a way that they are exercised through zealous imitation on the part of each being in the universe.) *De sacr.* i.2.2 (*PL*, CLXXVI, 206; Deferrari, p. 29): "Rerum omnium ordo dispositioque a summo usque ad imum, in universitatis hujus compage ita . . . prosequitur, ut omnium quae sunt, nihil inconnexum aut separabile natura externumque inveniatur." (The ordered disposition of things from top to bottom in the network of this universe . . . is so arranged that, among all the things that exist, nothing is unconnected or separable by nature, or external.) Cf. *ibid.* i.1.2; i.1.24, i.2.2, i.6.1 (188B, 202D, 207B, 264B). *De arca Noe morali* iv. 6 (*PL*, CLXXVI, 672; CSMV, p. 138): "Sicut duo opera, id est opera conditionis et opera restaurationis distinximus, ita duos mundos esse intelligamus, visibilem et invisibilem. Visibilem quidem hanc machinam universitatis quam corporeis oculis cernimus. . . ." (As there are two works, the work of creation and the work of restoration, so there are two worlds, visible and invisible. The visible world is this machine, this universe, that we see with our bodily eyes.)

[11] *De operibus sex dierum* (*PL*, CLXXXIX, 1516): ". . . sub distinctionibus et formis universitatis implexio indissolubili connexione in illa mente divina, ab aeterno astricta" (under the distinctions and forms of the universe exists a bond eternally tied within the divine mind by an indissoluble knot).

[12] *Epist. ad Praemonstr.* (*PL*, CXCVIII, 793D).

[13] Pseudo–Hugh of Saint-Victor *Quaest. in Ep. Pauli*, ad Rom., q. 34 (*PL*, CLXXV, 440): "Nota, in magnitudine universitatis notatur divina potentia, in pulchritudine sapientia, in utilitate bonitas. . . ." (Take note, in the hugeness of the universe is recorded the divine power, in its beauty the divine wisdom, in its serviceableness the divine goodness.) *Liber de stabilitate animae* (monastic provenance, about 1130; *PL*, CCXIII, 917): "Cum enim universitatis pulchritudinem, caeli terraeque machinam, opus mirabile delectabileque homo inspicit. . . ." (When man beholds the beauty of the universe, the intricate contrivance of heaven and earth, this marvelous and delightful work.)

[14] William of Conches *Glossa in Timaeum* (Parent, p. 146; Jeauneau, p. 103, cf. p. 125): "Et est mundus ordinata collectio creaturarum."

a cosmos; its contemplation is a source of delight.[15] When one considers the laws proper to each being, even the antinomy between matter and spirit, the universe resembles an immense zither whose strings produce an astonishing harmony for all their differences of sound:

The supreme artisan made the universe like a great zither upon which he placed strings to yield a variety of sounds, for he divided his work in two—into two parts antithetical to each other. Spirit and matter, antithetical in nature yet consonant in existence, resemble a choir of men and boys blending their bass and treble voices. . . . Material things similarly imitate the distinction of choral parts, divided as things are into genera, species, individuals, forms, and numbers; all of these blend harmoniously as they observe with due measure the law implanted within them and so, as it were, emit their proper sound. A harmonious chord is sounded by spirit and body, angel and devil, heaven and hell, fire and water, air and earth, sweet and bitter, soft and hard, and so are all other things harmonized.[16]

Doubtless such considerations might never rise above banality and commonplace. Here, however, through the firmness of the formulation, through the allusions to Platonic idealism, and through the free options exercised in interpreting the universe of Genesis for example, these considerations evinced an optimistic rationalism that was not banal in the vision they afforded of the order of the world. Arnold, abbot of Bonneval near Chartres, friend of St. Bernard, re-

---

[15] Honorius of Autun *Elucidarium* i.12 (*PL*, CLXXII, 1117; Lefèvre, p. 373): "Omnis itaque Dei creatio consideranti magna est delectatio, dum in quibusdam sit decor, ut in floribus; in aliquibus medicina, ut in herbis; in quibusdam pastus, ut in frugibus; in quibusdam significatio, ut in vermibus et avibus." (All of God's creation gives great delight to anyone looking upon it, for in some things there is beauty, as in flowers; in others healing, as in herbs; in others food, as in produce; in others meaning, as in snakes and birds.)

[16] Honorius of Autun *Liber XII quaest.* ii (*PL*, CLXXII, 1179): "Summus namque opifex universitatem quasi magnam citharam condidit, in qua veluti varias chordas ad multiplices sonos reddendos posuit: dum universum suum opus in duo, vel duo sibi contraria distinxit. Spiritus enim et corpus quasi virilis et puerilis chorus gravem et acutum sonum reddunt, dum in natura dissentiunt, in essentia boni conveniunt. . . . Similiter corporalia vocum discrimina imitantur, dum in varia genera, in varias species, in individua, in formas, in numeros separantur: quae omnia concorditer consonant, dum legem sibi insitam quasi tinnulos modulis servant. Reciprocum sonum spiritus et corpus, angelus et diabolus, coelum et infernus, ignis et aqua, aer et terra, dulce et amarum, molle et durum, et sic caetera in hunc modum."

sponsive to the influence of Chartres and to the beauty of nature, displayed his fascination for the lofty theme of cosmic unity in the following excursion upon the first chapter of Genesis:

God distributed the things of nature like the members of a great body, assigning to all their proper places and names, their fitting measures and offices. Nothing is confused in God, and nothing was without form in primordial antiquity; for physical material, as soon as it was made, was forthwith cast into such species as suited it. . . . He encloses all things, strengthening them from within, protecting them from without, nurturing them from above, supporting them from below, binding contraries with perceptible art, joining opposites into one and with marvelous moderating power enjoining peace upon them, holding down lightweight things lest they fly off, holding up ponderous things lest they crash downwards. . . . By God's moderating rule diverse and contrary things meet in the unity of peace, and static and erratic things are brought into orderly line; huge things do not swell larger, and the smallest things do not disappear. The entire fabric of the world—consistent though made of such dissimilar parts, one though composed of such diverse things, tranquil though containing such opposed elements—continues in its lawful and ordered way, solid, harmonious, and with no dread prospect of ruin.[17]

Arnold had come to the point of refusing to imagine a primitive chaos. He espoused the opinion vigorously expressed by William of Conches in protest against those who, under pretext of exalting the power and wisdom of a God who imposes order upon the universe at will, detracted from the simple play of the laws of nature, sufficient in themselves to explain that order. The disagreement was basic. It was by no means a quibble between exegetes over a verse in the Bible; it was the clash of two mentalities, on the one hand the naturalistic idealism of Chartres instinctively picking up the outlook of

---

[17] *De operibus sex dierum*, prol. (*PL*, CLXXXIX, 1515–16): "Et [Deus] quasi magni corporis membra, rerum naturas, distinguens propria loca et nomina, congruas mensuras et officia assignavit. Nihil apud Deum confusum, nihil informe in illa antiquitate fuit, quia rerum materia, ubi facta est, statim in congruas sibi species est formata. . . . Complectitur omnia, intra solidans, extra protegens, supra fovens, infra sustinens, arte investigabili ligans diversa, temperatura mirabili astringens in pacem et in unum jungens contraria, premens levia ne effluant, sustinens ponderosa ne ruant. . . . Cujus moderamine diversa et contraria in unitatem pacis conveniunt et immobilia et errantia ad certum ordinem revocantur; nec intumescunt maxima nec minima consumuntur: nec tota illa mundi fabrica sine ulla ruinae formidine ex tam dissimilibus partibus uniformis, ex tam diversis una, ex tam contrariis quieta, et solida et concors in sua lege perseverat et ordine."

9

the *Timaeus*,[18] on the other hand Hugh of Saint-Victor with his practical sense of a historical order in which divine and human liberties were at play, over and above any natural determinisms.[19]

The proof that the naturalistic view of the world went beyond mere poetic or rhetorical commonplace is that it was coupled with an increasingly active scientific curiosity in the centers where it was entertained. To be sure, there was not yet the ferment produced at the end of the twelfth century and in the thirteenth by the discovery of Aristotelian and Islamic science; but already men were at work studying what the ancients had said about nature, living nature as well as the nature of the stars; and we know that at Chartres the *quadrivium*, the instructional framework for what we call the sciences, received equal attention with the *trivium*, the instructional framework for what we call letters. Absalom of Saint-Victor, a perfect representative of the surge toward mysticism in his abbey, would later denounce this prying into "the composition of the globe, the nature of the elements, the location of the stars, the nature of animals, the violence of the wind, the life-processes of plants and of roots." If the creators of monstrous symbolic bestiaries were now rivaled by naturalistic artists who from this point on sculpted little scenes of animal or human life on the capitals of cathedrals, it was because in the schools and in the streets and fields men's minds had already been awakened to an attentive observation of reality.

Histories of the different sciences furnish detail on what men were reading at this time (for example, the *Quaestiones naturales* of Seneca, a book first put into extensive circulation by William of Conches and a copy of which John of Salisbury left to his church in Chartres) and on the new works that drew upon this reading (such

---

[18] Cf. *Tim.* 30a, where anthropomorphism governs the narrative: "Taking hold of the visible mass in its native state, that of a chaos shaken with convulsive and disordered movements, the Demiurge caused it to pass from disorder to order." Cf. Festugière, vol. 1, p. 11: "The world is eternally a *cosmos*, an order; the chaotic state of the visible mass before God set it in order is suppositious." It was because of the epic manner, the narrative method he chose, that Plato presented his exposition in the form of a cosmogony implying movement from chaos to order.

[19] Cf. M.-D. Chenu, "Nature ou histoire? Une controverse exégétique sur la création au XII⁴ siècle," *AHDL*, XX (1953), 25–30 [Cf. Taylor, p. 227, n. 3, where successive texts from William of Conches and Hugh of Saint-Victor document the outline of the controversy.]

as the *Imago mundi* of Honorius of Autun). What it is important to notice here is what motivated men over and above their reading. These men were bent upon a search for the causes of things—the most keen and arduous as well as the most typical of the activities of reason when, confronting nature, men discovered both its fecundity and the chains of necessity by which it is bound; an activity proper to science, and one which clashed violently with religious consciousness, which when it was yet inexperienced and immature, was willing to engage in its characteristic activity of looking immediately to the Supreme Cause, at the expense of disregarding secondary causes. St. Thomas would react firmly against this dissociation of religion from natural science: "To slight the perfection of created things is to slight the perfection of divine power." This is literally what William of Conches had said,[20] and the shock it produced among men of the twelfth century was no less great. With bitter irony William protested against those who condemned the search for causes:

Ignorant themselves of the forces of nature and wanting to have company in their ignorance, they don't want people to look into anything; they want us to believe like peasants and not to ask the reason behind things. . . . But we say that the reason behind everything should be sought out. . . . If they learn that anyone is so inquiring, they shout out that he is a heretic, placing more reliance on their monkish garb than on their wisdom.[21]

---

[20] *Philosophia mundi* i.22 (*PL*, CLXXII, 56): "[Dicet aliquis] hoc esse divinae potestati derogare. . . . quibus respondemus e contrario id ei conferre, quia ei attribuimus et talem rebus naturam dedisse, et sic per naturam operantem corpus humanum creasse." (Someone will allege that this is to derogate from the divine power. . . . To such we shall reply that, on the contrary, it adds to the divine power because to that power we attribute not only the giving of a productive nature to things but the creation of the human body through the operation of such nature.) *Glossa in Boetium* (MS Troyes 1381, f. 60r; cited in Parent, p. 92): "At dicet aliquis: Nonne hoc est opus Creatoris quod homo ex homine nascatur? Ad quod respondeo: Nihil detraho Deo. . . ." (But someone will say, Isn't it the Creator's work that man is born from man? To which I reply, I'm not taking anything away from God.) Cf. St. Thomas Aquinas *Contra gentiles* iii.69 (Aquinas, *Opera omnia*, V, 211 ff.; Aquinas, *S. Gent.*, III, pt.l, pp. 165–72).

[21] *Philosophia mundi* i.23 (*PL*, CLXXII, 56): "Sed quoniam ipsi nesciunt vires naturae, ut ignorantiae suae omnes socios habeant, nolunt eos aliquid inquirere, sed ut rusticos nos credere nec rationem quaerere. . . . Nos autem dicimus, in omnibus rationem esse quaerendam. . . . Sed isti, . . . si inquirentem aliquem sciant, illum esse haereticum clamant, plus de suo caputio praesumentes quam sapientiae suae confidentes."

To appeal to the omnipotence of God is nothing but vain rhetoric; naked truth requires a little more sweat.[22] To one who objects by pointing to the metaphors found in the biblical account of man's origin, William replies: to search out the "reason" of things and the laws governing their production is the great task of the believer and one which we should discharge together, bound by our curiosities into a fraternal enterprise.[23] Moreover, it is not the task of the Bible to teach us the nature of things; this belongs to philosophy.[24] It is the nature of things, as Honorius of Autun had already declared,

---

[22] *Ibid.*, ii. praef. and 3 (*PL,* CLXXII, 57–8): "Sed, quamvis multos ornatum verborum quaerere, paucos veritatem scire cognoscamus, nihil de multitudine, sed de paucorum probitate gloriantes, soli veritati insudabimus: Maluimus enim promittere nudam veritatem quam palliatam falsitatem. . . . Miseri! Quid miserius quam dicere istud, est! quia Deus illud facere potest, nec videre sic esse, nec rationem habere quare sic sit, nec utilitatem ostendere ad quam hoc sit. Non enim quidquid potest Deus facere, hoc facit. Ut autem verbis rustici utar, potest Deus facere de trunco vitulum: fecitne unquam?" (Although we know that most men are bent upon a splashy prose style and few of them have got hold of the truth, we ourselves, ignoring the multitude and glorying in the uprightness of those few, will sweat on after truth alone. We prefer to present the naked truth, not some dressed up falsehood. . . . Wretches! Could anything be more wretched than saying that something exists because God *can* make it, and yet not seeing that it does not exist, or having any reason why it should exist, or showing the usefulness for which it would exist? God does not do everything he is able to do. To use a peasant's words, Can God make a calf from a tree trunk? Has he ever done it?)

[23] *Ibid.*, i. 22 (*PL,* CLXXII, 56): "Sed isti vicinos multos habentes domui suae conjunctos, ex superbia nolunt aliquem convocare: maluntque nescire, quam ab alio quaerere. . . ." (But those fellows, although they have plenty of neighbors nearby, out of pride won't call on a single one of them; they prefer to remain ignorant rather than to ask someone else.)

[24] *Glossa in Boetium* (MS Bibl. Mun. d'Orléans 27, f.20a): "Sed dum moderni divini hoc audiunt, quia in Libris ita scriptum non inveniunt, obstrepunt statim, hoc ignorantes quod auctores Veritatis philosophiam rerum tacuerunt, non quia contra fidem, sed quia ad aedificationem fidei, de qua laborant, non multum pertinebat; nec volunt quod aliquid supra id quod scriptum est inquiramus, set ut rusticus ita simpliciter credamus." (But when modern divines hear this, they hoot at it right away because they don't find it like this in the Bible. They don't know that the authors of Truth are silent on matters of natural philosophy, not because these matters are against the faith, but because they have little to do with the upbuilding of such faith, which is what those authors are concerned with. But modern divines don't want us to inquire into anything that isn't in the scriptures, only to believe simply like a peasant.) Cf. remarks and texts cited by Charles Jourdain, "Des commentaires inédits de Guillaume de Conches et de Nicholas Triveth sur la Consolation de la Philosophie de Boèce," *Notices et extraits des manuscrits de la Bibliothèque Impériale,* Tome XX, 2e partie (Paris, 1862), p. 12.

that illuminates for us the way in which the universe (*universitas*) is put together.[25]

At the same time, Adelard of Bath, inspired by the knowledge and the spirit of his Muslim masters, made the same pronouncement in the same terms. In his *Quaestiones naturales* he professed with the same vigor, as against the pretensions of intellectual authoritarianism, the power of human reason to discover the internal laws of things and claimed indeed that it is this power that makes us men.[26] Were we to neglect coming to know the admirable rational beauty of the universe in which we live, we would deserve to be cast out from it like guests incapable of appreciating a home in which hospitality is offered to them.[27]

---

[25] *Libellus VIII quaestionum* v (*PL*, CLXXII, 1190): "Porro natura rerum exigit, ut quae in universitate discrepantia, per sibi contrarium vel simile fiant consonantia." (Indeed, the nature of things demands that whatever is at variance in the universe be brought into harmony by its contrary or by something similar to it.)

[26] *Quaest. nat.* iv (Müller, p. 8): "Deo non detraho. Quidquid enim est, ab ipso et per ipsum est." (I do not derogate from God, for whatever exists comes from him and exists through him.) *Ibid.*, vi (Müller, p. 11)—that tirade that Roger Bacon will later echo: "Ego enim aliud a magistris Arabicis ratione duce didici, tu vero aliud[;] auctoritatis pictura captus capistrum sequeris. Quid enim aliud auctoritas dicenda est quam capistrum? Ut bruta quippe animalia capistro quolibet ducuntur, nec quo aut quare ducantur, discernunt restemque, quo tenentur, solum sequuntur, sic non paucos vestrum bestiali credulitate captos ligatosque auctoritas scriptorum in periculum ducit." (I learned one thing from my Arabian masters with reason as guide; you, however, have learned another; captured by the pretensions of authority, you are led by a bridle. For what else should authority be called but a bridle? Just as brute animals are led around by any bridle at all, not knowing where or why they are being taken and plodding after the rope that holds them, so many of you, reduced and bound by an animal's credulity, are being led into peril by the authority of things you read.) [For a complete English translation of Adelard's *Quaestiones naturales*, see Gollancz, pp. 85–161.]

[27] *Astrolabium* praef. (MS Cambridge, Fitzwilliam Museum, McClean 165, f.81, as cited by C. H. Haskins, *Studies in the History of Mediaeval Science* [Cambridge, Mass., 1924], p. 29): "Dicis enim ut in domo habitans quilibet, si materiam eius et compositionem, quantitatem et qualitatem sive districtionem ignoret, tali hospicio dignus non est, ita si qui in aula mundi natus atque educatus est, tam mirande pulcritudinis rationem scire negligat, post discretionis annos indignus atque si fieri posset ejiciendus est." (You say that if anyone living in a house is ignorant of what it is made of and how it is made, of its size and quality or layout, he is unworthy of its shelter; and that just so, if anyone born and educated in the residence of this world neglects learning the plan underlying its marvelous beauty, upon attaining the age of discretion he is unworthy and, were it possible, deserves to be cast out of it.)

This desacralizing of nature—and of the outlook men brought to nature—produced an unmistakable crisis both in the recourse to symbolist interpretation which a certain way of looking at nature invited, and in the limitations now placed upon the preternatural. Criticism of symbolism, necessarily felt throughout speculation on the sacraments, was in fact largely impeded by literary and liturgical conformism, all the more so since the radical distinction between a causal explanation and an interpretation of "meaning" in discussions of natural phenomena remained unclearly drawn; it was not to be much more clearly drawn even in the middle of the thirteenth century. On the other hand, criticism of the preternatural, whether in nature or in everyday life, continued to grow from this point on, despite the permanent attraction that the marvelous held for men. Scholars have not yet delineated the various strands found in this development in mental attitude, but moral and political anti-clericalism were surely involved. It would be extremely enlightening to discriminate among the various strands. One of the masters at Chartres was not attacking strawmen when he denounced the impiety of "certain men" who were denying that God could modify the workings of the laws of nature.[28] In one of his letters John of Salisbury questioned the motives of those who described the miracles of Thomas Becket as "men's fantasies."[29] Amaury I, King of Jerusalem (1162–75), asked William of Tyre for rational proofs of the immortality

---

[28] *Liber de eodem secundus* (Parent, p. 213): "Nemo itaque impie cogitet, sicut quidam impii cogitaverunt, nihil contra naturam, scilicet contra solitum cursum naturae, provenire posse, cum ex quibusdam causis occultis, quae in mente creatoris ab aeterno sunt absconditae, ad ostensionem gratiae Dei multa contra solitum naturae cursum proveniant, non contra naturam, quae est voluntas Dei. . . ." (Let no one impiously think, as certain impious men have, that things contrary to nature—that is, contrary to the accustomed course of nature—cannot occur; for, from certain mysterious causes hidden in the mind of the Creator from eternity, many things contrary to the accustomed course of nature occur to show men the grace of God, and these are not contrary to nature, which is the will of God.) [For a recent critical edition of this text and discussion of its provenance and import, see Nicholas Haring, "The Creation and Creator of the World according to Thierry of Chartres and Clarenbaldus of Arras," *AHDL*, XXII (1955), 137–216.]

[29] Raymonde Foreville, "Une lettre inédite de Jean de Salisbury, évêque de Chartres," *RHEF*, XXII (1936), 179–85.

of the soul, since scriptural testimony did not satisfy him.[30] The chronicle of Laon made light of the original vision that sparked the formation of the *Capuciati* at Le Puy about 1170.[31] And at Paris, Bishop Manasses II of Orleans, in a scene that smacked of light opera, bluntly announced that he had his doubts about the relics of St. Genevieve (1162). Abelard, one recalls, was driven from Saint-Denis for having expressed some reservations about whether the body of the Areopagite venerated at the abbey was actually what it was thought to be.

Apart from such toughening in personal views, one can observe in theology itself the progressive elaboration of the essential distinction between preternatural events and the supernatural order of grace, the latter of which has nothing to do with marvels. The masters of the thirteenth century would be able to establish this distinction firmly when, thanks to a knowledge of Aristotle, the concept of nature achieved full development. St. Thomas would elaborate his entire treatise on "the divine governance," as men called it then, without attending to the sphere of the miraculous, a sphere relegated to the fringes of the normal laws governing the conduct of the world and, indeed, of the church. No one in the twelfth century, whether philosopher, historian, or spiritual writer, had gone this far.

---

[30] William of Tyre *Historia rerum in partibus transmarinis gestarum* (*L'Estoire de Eracles empereur*) xix. 3, in *Recueil des historiens des croisades, Historiens occidentaux*, tome I, IIe partie (Paris, 1844), pp. 886–88; E. A. Babcock and A. C. Krey, tr., *A History of Deeds Done beyond the Sea, by William, Archbishop of Tyre* (New York, 1943), II, 298–300. As late as the thirteenth century, Roland of Cremona, first Dominican master at the University of Paris (before 1230) observes: "Quoniam multi sunt qui credunt animam humanam esse corruptibilem et simul mori cum morte sui organi, necnon plerique qui hoc dubitant, nonnulli vero qui in suis cordibus hoc esse impossibile dicunt sola fide suffulti, alii vero et ratione, idcirco visum est nobis utile . . . philosophiae ponere rationes. . . ." (Since there are many who think that the human soul is corruptible and dies simultaneously with the death of its organ, the body, and many who doubt this but who say in their hearts, some of them, that it is impossible and rely on faith alone, while yet others rely on reason as well, it has therefore seemed to us useful to set forth the reasons that philosophy gives.) *Expos. in Job* i (MS Paris, B.N., lat. 405, f.1.)

[31] *Chronicum anonymi Laudunensis canonici, HF,* XVIII (Paris, 1822), 705–6. Guyot de Provins exploits this satire in his *Bible* at the beginning of the thirteenth century.

The same apperception was even more operative in scriptural exegesis, if not in the account given of the history and economy of salvation, at least in the account given of nature. The creation narrative in Genesis was interpreted as recounting the natural play of the elements, which by themselves explain the emergence of the world; to be sure, God was not absent, but it is the very laws of nature that reveal his presence and his action. The *De mundi universitate* of Bernard Sylvester merely reworked in a personal manner the method invariably employed by the masters of Chartres within the framework of their commentaries; and Alan of Lille, entirely abandoning the form of the hexameral literature, would express the role of nature more boldly still.[32] The letter in which Abbot William of Saint-Thierry complained to St. Bernard about William of Conches is famous. This innovator with his "new philosophy," William of Saint-Thierry complained, sees the first man as coming "not from God but from nature, from spirits and stars." As to the creation of woman "from the rib of Adam," the Abbot continued, William "holds the authority of sacred history in contempt . . . ; by interpreting that history from the point of view of physical science, he arrogantly prefers the ideas he invents to the truth the history contains, and in so doing he makes light of a great mystery."[33] Here indeed was conflict between natural science and symbolism.

Such conflict, however, was not exclusive to the school of Chartres. At this very time Abelard too was proposing a rigorous distinction between the properly creative act of God and the forces of nature; these forces, without prejudicing God's creative activity, but also without any miracles being involved, operate autonomously.[34]

---

[32] Cf. R. de Lage, chap. 3, "Nature, son aspect cosmologique."

[33] *De erroribus Gulielmi de Conchis* (*PL*, CLXXX, 339–340): "Deinde creationem primi hominis philosophice, seu magis physice describens, primo dicit corpus ejus non a Deo factum, sed a natura, et animam ei datam a Deo, postmodum vero ipsum corpus factum a spiritibus, quos daemones appellat, et a stellis. . . . In creatione vero mulieris palam omnibus legentibus est, quam stulte, quam superbe irridet historiam divinae auctoritatis; scilicet excostasse Deum primum hominem, ad faciendam de costa ejus mulierem. Et physico illud sensu interpretans, nimis arroganter veritati historiae suum praefert inventum, parvipendens magnum illud sacramentum. . . ."

[34] *Expos. in Hexaemeron* "De secunda die" (*PL,* CLXXVIII, 746): "Forte

At Saint-Victor, Andrew declared that before hasty recourse to miracles (*ad miracula confugere*) one must exhaust all the possibilities of natural explanation—a venerable Augustinian principle, but one which from now on men became newly fascinated to apply, as Beryl Smalley observes.[35] Thus do we see in the hexameral literature of the time a constant recurrence to cosmological theories, and the most outrageous impositions of physics upon scripture serve only to emphasize the naturalism of the exegeses.

The mention of Andrew of Saint-Victor invites us to recall, in line with our inquiry, the central role he played in "naturalistic" exegesis, which demands that history too, and not merely nature, be taken at face value and read literally.[36] In Andrew we meet the influence of Hugh of Saint-Victor and his historicist reaction against too hasty allegorization of scriptural texts, his fundamental premise being that the literal or historical level of scripture is the foundation upon which all further treatment of the Bible must rest. Though standing poles apart from the platonizing idealism of the cosmologists of Chartres, Andrew sounds a comparable note of naturalism. He accepts the slow appearance of natural species from primitive chaos; against the ancient tradition of simultaneous creation, he espouses

---

et hoc aliquis requirit . . . qua vi naturae id factum sit. Ad quod primum respondeo nullatenus nos modo, cum in aliquibus rerum effectis vim naturae vel causas naturales requirimus vel assignamus, id nos facere secundum illam priorem Dei operationem in constitutione mundi ubi sola Dei voluntas naturae efficaciam habuit in illis tunc creandis. . . . Deinceps vim naturae pensare solemus . . . ut ad quaelibet sine miraculis facienda illa eorum constitutio vel praeparatio sufficeret." (Perhaps someone will ask, too, by what power of nature this came to be. First, I reply that when we require and assign the power of nature or natural causes to certain effects of things, we by no means do so in a manner resembling God's first operation in constituting the world, when only the will of God had the force of nature in creating things. . . . We go on to examine the power of nature . . . so that the constitution or development of everything that originates without miracles can be adequately accounted for.)

[35] Latin text and English translation in Smalley, pp. 144, 388–9: "Verumtamen in scripturarum expositione cum secundum naturam res de qua agitur nullatenus fieri potest tunc demum ad miracula confugienda noverit." (But he should realise this: in expounding Scripture, when the event described admits of no natural explanation, then and then only should we have recourse to miracles.)

[36] *Ibid.*, chap. 4, "Andrew of Saint-Victor."

the idea that the cosmos developed in successive stages through time.[37]

Dame Nature

Under the pressure of such influences and in the enthusiasm of men's new awareness, the concept of nature acquired an unprecedented sophistication, and the direction even of men's religious curiosity shifted. It was no longer the extravagant occurences that interested them, those marvels which entranced their forebears and rapt them into a world all the more real in their eyes for its very capriciousness. On the contrary, they were interested in regular and determinate sequences, especially in the area of vital activity. *Nature* existed—and one must take care to spell the word with a capital letter, for Nature became personified and as such, by a fashionable literary fiction of the time, became a goddess. But the fiction in this case had real philosophical worth.

O Child of God and Mother of things . . .

So began the ode, as if it were a hymn, of Alan of Lille. Bernard Sylvester, in his *De mundi universitate*, had already allegorically portrayed Nature as the partner of Noys in the ordering of chaos; Alan developed this allegory in the pedantic imagery of his *De planctu Naturae (The Complaint of Nature)*, the reputation of which would survive the flood tide of Aristotelianism as it would the advance of poetry in the centuries ahead. Its reputation would survive because his literary conceits did not date or render obsolete the genuine comprehension for which they served as vehicle—that wonderment experienced by minds which, as they raised their eyes from the marvels

---

[37] Hugh of Saint-Victor *De sacramentis* i.1.3 (*PL*, CLXXVI, 188; Deferrari, pp. 8–9): "Nobis autem videtur (excepto eo quod nihil in hac re temere diffinire volumus) omnipotentiae Creatoris in nullo derogari, si per intervalla temporis opus suum ad consummationem perduxisse dicitur; . . . in eis omnibus faciendis illum praecipue modum servare debuit [Deus], qui ipsius rationalis creaturae commoditati ac causae magis congruus fuit." (It seems to us—though we do not wish to make any rash definition on the point—that it takes away nothing from the Creator's omnipotence if one says that he brought his work to completion across intervals of time; . . . in all the things God proposed doing, he must have kept especially to that mode of action which best served the need and convenience of his rational creature.)

of their bestiaries and lapidaries and moved out of the social and intellectual immaturity of serfdom, discovered life's ordered energies, its instincts, its laws and its freedom, the rhythmic movement of the seasons and the recurrent life-cycles of living beings:

> O Child of God and Mother of things,
> Bond of the world, its firm-tied knot,
> Jewel set among things of earth, and
> > mirror to all that passes away,
> > Morning star of our sphere;
>
> Peace, love, power, regimen and strength,
> Order, law, end, pathway, captain and source,
> Life, light, glory, beauty and shape,
> > O Rule of our world![38]

Beneath the pagan overtones of Alan's fable there lay a validly religious perception. To thus exalt these powers of Nature was not at all to detract proudly from the omnipotence of God, as we have already heard William of Conches claim in self-defense; and Alan's Nature was herself made to proclaim this fact with a lyricism to which metaphysics lent precision and feeling:

His working is one, whereas mine is many; his work stands of itself, whereas mine fails from within; his work is a thing of wonder, mine shifting. He is without origin, whereas I was brought forth; he is a maker, I made; he is the workman behind my work, and I am the work of that workman; he makes his work out of nothing, I beg mine from some source; he works in his own name, and I in his. . . . And, in order that you may recognize that my power is powerless in contrast to the divine power, know that my effect is defective and my energy cheap.[39]

---

[38] Alan of Lille *De planctu Naturae* (*PL*, CCX, 447):
> O Dei proles, genitrixque rerum
> Vinculum mundi, stabilisque nexus,
> Gemma terrenis, speculum caducis,
> > Lucifer orbis.
> Pax, amor, virtus, regimen, potestas,
> Ordo, lex, finis, via, dux, origo,
> Vita, lux, splendor, species, figura,
> > Regula mundi.

[39] *Ibid.*, 445: "Ejus operatio simplex, mea multiplex; ejus opus sufficiens, meum deficiens; ejus opus mirabile, meum opus mutabile. Ille innascibilis, ego nata; ille faciens, ego facta; ille mei opifex operis, ego opus opificis; ille operatur ex nihilo, ego mendico opus ex aliquo; ille suo operatur nomine, ego operor illius sub nomine. . . . Et ut, respectu potentiae divinae, meam potentiam impotentem esse cognoscas, meum effectum scias esse defectum, meum vigorem vilitatem esse perpendas."

A whole century later, this conception of Nature would animate the *Roman de la Rose* of Jean de Meun and keep the same religious intensity, though by then Aristotelian philosophy would have strengthened the concept and taken away its mystical content.[40] Such persistence suggests that this view of Nature was not the work of a few scholars; it was the collective acquisition of a whole generation and those that followed.[41]

The long entry devoted to the word "Nature" in the theological dictionary of Alan of Lille testifies as explicitly as possible to the doctrinal profundity of such literary uses of the concept.[42] The eleven meanings he assigned to the content of the term pertained to wholly diverse intellectual contexts which are revealed by the ideological sources he cites, from Boethian metaphysics to medical terminology to the religious vocabulary of St. Paul. This assembling of meanings was no mere technical exercise; instead, an underlying consistency of emphasis and outlook reveals that the "naturalism" of Alan belonged rather to the whole cast of his mind than to a theoretical analysis that fits into a perfected system of thought.

With this general philosophical profundity one must associate the peculiar success enjoyed for some fifty years by the theory of the world soul, a theory adduced to subserve the lofty conception of

---

[40] See G. Paré, *Les idées et les lettres au XIIIᵉ siècle: Le Roman de la Rose* (Montreal, 1947).

[41] Not, to be sure, without great virtual differences varying with the acceptance given to the formulas of Augustine or, even more, to concrete states mentioned in Biblical history and anthropology. The mixture is seen in the analysis of "natural" found in a gloss on the Sentences of Peter of Poiters, II, 19 (MS Erfurt, Amplon., cod. Q, 117): "Nota: Naturale multipliciter dici. Naturale, quod a prima infuit conditione, ut innocentia in Adam. Naturale: sine quo non potest homo subsistere, ut ratio, memoria. Naturale: sine quo non potest diu subsistere, ut spirare, comedere. Et hoc quandoque a natura corrupta, sicut nos; quandoque a natura non corrupta, ut Adam. Quandoque naturale, quod non est contra usum, ut coitus maris cum femina; innaturale, quod est contra usum." (Note: "Natural" is said in many senses. "Natural": what was present from original creation, as innocence in Adam. "Natural": that without which man cannot exist, as reason, memory. "Natural": that without which man cannot long exist, as breathing, eating. The word is sometimes used of corrupt nature—ours; sometimes of uncorrupted nature—Adam's. Sometimes "natural" means "not contrary to use," as intercourse between husband and wife, and "unnatural" means "contrary to use.")

[42] *Distinctiones* (*PL*, CCX, 871).

Nature, for the universe too has its animating principle, its "entelechy."[43] The school of Saint-Victor distrusted, and Cîteaux denounced, this pagan idea. But the masters of Chartres found great inspiration in Plato's world-soul and, despite their shifting explanations of it, gave new life to the cosmic and religious vision of the *Timaeus*. Of this vision Festugière writes:

> No longer is there a radical opposition between the sense-perceptible and the intelligible. The concrete world is joined to the world of ideas by the intermediary of the world-soul. The world, as a vast living thing, is possessed of self-movement, and this presupposes a soul. And the motion of the world, at least in the celestial regions, is a regular motion which reveals a design, a rationale; and this fact invites the inference that the soul that moves the universe is an intelligent soul. In fact, the world-intelligence contemplates the beauty of the ideal realm, and it is in virtue of this contemplation that it imposes upon the universe the ordered movement we see. In consequence, the world is truly an "order," a *kosmos*. To be sure, disorder is found within it, not, however, as an essentially evil thing but only as a lesser good. There could be no "order" without a multiplicity of beings, each consequently limited; or without a diversity of beings, each consequently endowed with a greater or smaller share of goodness. If, therefore, one considers only a part of the whole, one necessarily discovers limits or privations of goodness, disorders. But this is precisely because one is looking only at a part, not the whole. If one makes the effort to comprehend the whole in a single view, the disorder disappears; it becomes explicable within the whole and becomes absorbed into the total order. Always look to the whole—such will be the rule of this self-consciously optimistic philosophy.[44]

If Festugière sees this Platonic vision as the key to what was intelligent and great in the mediocre Hermetic sects of the Hellenistic period, we in our turn can recognize the same vision as the ever-fertile soil from which the masters of Chartres and Paris, in the cloisters of their cathedrals and before the turbulent student throngs

---

[43] Gregory, p. 152, justly emphasizes the connection between the idea of nature and that of the world-soul. Men of the Middle Ages had made the same observation; see Herman of Carinthia *De essentiis* (Manuel Alonso, ed. [Comillas (Santander): Universidad Pontificia, 1946], p. 63): "[Naturam] eodem nomine vocare possumus, quo Plato significans mundi animam vocat." (We are able to call Nature by the same name that Plato used in speaking of the world soul); John of Salisbury *De septem septenis* vii (*PL*, CXCIX, 962), where John compares the *natura* of Hermes Trismegistus, the *anima mundi* of Plato, and the *divina dispositio* of theologians.

[44] Festugière, vol. 2, pp. xii-xiii.

frequenting the communal city schools of the twelfth century, could bring to fruition their own discovery of nature and man. Neither the literary uses to which this vision was put among medieval Christian authors nor the shakiness in the philosophical substructure of their works should obscure our sense of the fascination which held them as it did the sculptor at work upon the cathedrals (think of the depiction of Christ, Savior of the World, on the portal of Chartres) and which occasionally inspired in them profound apperceptions regarding God's relations with the world and God's scheme for the world as seen even in the world's disorder.

It occasions no surprise to find here in the twelfth century this doctrine of the world-soul, the essential element of the cosmic philosophy of the *Timaeus*. We find its original import hallowed, brought into relationship—a fairly uncertain one, to be sure[45]— with the Christian conception of the presence of the Holy Spirit in the world. Even a Hugh of Saint-Victor or an Arnold of Bonneval, though they rejected the errors of "the philosophers," recognized that "mysterious power of nature, which invisibly feeds and fosters all things."[46] In fact, the connection made between the world-soul

---

[45] William of Conches recorded the various efforts and interpretations in his *Philosophia mundi* i.15 (*PL*, CLXXII, 46). For the history, contexts, sources, and variants of this doctrine in the twelfth century, see Gregory, chap. 3.

[46] Hugh of Saint-Victor *Hom. in Eccles.*, hom. 2 (*PL*, CLXXV, 136) commented as follows on the phrase *mens agitat molem* from Vergil *Aeneid* vi. 688: ". . . in his verbis illum potius errorem probare videatur, qui mundum hunc sensilem quasi anima constans ex anima et corpore, ipsamque ejus animam spiritum esse cuncta moventem asseveret. Sed, quomodolibet opinio errantium exponatur, nos sano intellectu 'spiritum pergentem in omnia et in circulos suos revertentem' occultam naturae vim accipere possumus, quae universa invisibiliter nutrit et vegetat." (In these words Vergil seems rather to approve of the error that asserts that this sense-perceptible world is composed, as it were, of a soul and body and that its soul is a spirit imparting motion to everything. But however one may explain this erroneous opinion, we, with sound understanding, can take the words "spirit moving outward upon all things and returning upon itself in circles" as designating a mysterious power of nature, which invisibly feeds and fosters all things.) Arnold of Bonneval *Liber de operibus cardinalibus Christi* xii (*PL*, CLXXXIX, 1672): "Hanc vitam, hunc motum, hanc rerum essentiam, animam mundi philosophi vocaverunt. . . ." (This life, this movement, this essence of things philosophers have called the world-soul.) Abelard made the same comparison, but with the same reserve; see *Introd. ad theol.* (*PL*, CLXXVIII, 1024, 1080); in this

and the Holy Spirit was wholly superficial and could not stand up under the critical investigation of physicists or theologians. And yet there persisted the idea of a world-soul, an intelligence interior to the cosmos, an agency energizing the physical world and, as it turned from its contemplation of the Good, conferring upon that world its truth, its order, its beauty, and its goodness. The optimistic intellectuality of Chartres stood at the opposite pole from a mechanistic interpretation of the universe.

At the very time that the concept of a parallelism between man as microcosm and the universe as macrocosm was coming newly to the fore, the Dionysian and Erigenist theme of a "continuity" between man and the cosmos was about to emerge to qualify the Platonic concept. Here we have a theme that springs not from an archaic and animistic physics but from a metaphysical and mystical preoccupation quite differently oriented—the preoccupation with hierarchy of pseudo-Dionysius. From the middle of the century on, the "hierarchical" conception of the universe would cast over men's minds a spell comparable to that cast by the scientific *mythos* of evolution in the nineteenth century. The key to the understanding of the universe, and of man in the universe, was taken to be the ordered, dynamic, and progressive chain of all beings—a chain in which causality and meaning fall together, and in which each being is a "theophany," a revelation of God. The schematization, though richly suggestive, was dangerous, for it followed only one of the two ways in which understanding could be sought: through it, symbolism would be deployed on a cosmic scale and the universe would again take on a sacramental character at the risk of telescoping the distinction between explanation as produced by the scientific discovery of causes, and signification as delivered through symbols. Here we are no longer at Chartres but within the ambiance of those centers in which pseudo-Dionysius and his successors became influential—particularly, Saint-Victor—and we shall see that the microcosm delineated by Godfrey of Saint-Victor reveals an inspiration

---

matter as in others St. Bernard pushed his criticism of Abelard too far (*De error. Abel.* iv. 10; *PL*, CLXXXII, 1062), and the Council of Sens did not sustain his accusation.

quite different from that of Bernard Sylvester. Nonetheless, the Dionysian vision of hierarchy was to contribute in its way to the growing awareness of nature and natures. Whatever the obscurities from which that awareness might yet suffer, as we move closer to the end of the century, a developing syncretism among divergent approaches extended the resources that could be brought to bear upon men's encounter with nature.

Man as Microcosm

The universe, then, is an admirably ordered unity (recall what was said above of the use of the word *universitas* beginning with John the Scot). The integration—at once ontological and noetic— of all the beings it contains in its hierarchical order implies a "continuity" that is at once dynamic and static in principle. Between each of these beings in their separate ranks exists an intimate bond: the greater intensity of the superior being exerts an attractive force upon the one next below it and draws it upward toward its own higher level; and out of this attraction arises the fulfillment of the lower being, or, if it is a spiritual being, its happiness. We are far from a discontinuous universe in which each being possesses its dynamism and intelligibility wholly and only within itself. Man may break out of the material universe in the metaphysical part of his nature, but biologically speaking he remains in continuity with it. Such continuity in the universe does not compromise the intrinsic law operative at each level, the proper autonomy of each being; it does not infringe the purity of natures, of essences. A century later, St. Thomas would construct his *Summa theologiae*, no less, along lines determined by this Neoplatonic vision, and the result would be to open up the Aristotelian universe ("essences are just like numbers") to the transcendence of God, to the free play of grace, to the historical actuality of the economy of salvation, and to a cosmic view of man. The *imago mundi* of all the thirteenth-century masters would follow essentially the same lines, however different from one another their formulations appear.[47]

---

[47] St. Thomas was influenced as much by the Muslim philosophers as by pseudo-Dionysius. See *De verit.* q.2; q.6; q.10, a.5; q.14, a.1, *ad* 9; q.10, a.1.

With respect to man, we see here that his animal and sensuous powers were considered to be undergoing an attraction upwards, a progressive sublimation that was not merely the effect of any moral and psychological asceticism. Indeed, human nature was defined in terms of matter and spirit, sense and intelligence, and was located, as regards its metaphysical constitution, at the point where these two worlds meet, long before the psychological problem of human liberty was posed in an Augustinian manner. It is fascinating to watch the Augustinian Hugh of Saint-Victor at work commenting on the *Celestial Hierarchy*:[48] not only did he have to purge from it all taint of emanationism, but he made a desperate effort to hold on to the ontological naturalism found in the work while at the same time preserving a personal, free, and freely given relationship between the soul and God as envisioned in Augustinian theology with its "inward" emphasis.

If Hugh of Saint-Victor corrected John the Scot's interpretation of pseudo-Dionysius with a firm hand, it was the followers of Gilbert of La Porré, the *Porretani*, who, also against John the Scot, would carry the pseudo-Dionysian cosmogony to its rational consequences. Under the influence of Platonic ambivalence prone to see matter as an unmitigated force of disorder, John the Scot supposed that God had not originally intended his creative power to descend as far down the scale as corruptible matter, and that the subsequent descent of that power followed upon a defeat or fall. Man had been intended to have a spiritual body only, without animal needs. As against this projection of sin onto the cosmos, the masters of the twelfth century, resting their case on the interpretation given the *Timaeus* and the pseudo-Dionysian hierarchy at Chartres, proclaimed that the possibility of participating in the divine reality belonged expressly to matter as well as to everything above it; that the immense unity of all things was knotted up together in man who stands at the paradoxical borderline of matter and spirit. The human *compositum*, men would say later on, solemnizes man's union with the universe. It is in the *nature* of man to include matter. It is even for this purpose that he was created. "For it was fitting," says Alan of Lille in answer-

---

[48] *PL*, CLXXV, 923–1154.

ing the question why man was created, "that corporeal as well as incorporeal nature should come to participate in the divine goodness, should relish that goodness, and live in joy."[49]

It comes as no surprise that Honorius of Autun was the proponent of this naturalistic thesis as against one of the spiritualist themes of monastic theology.[50] Again and again, tenaciously, he denounced the strained traditional reasoning stemming from St. Gregory. For Honorius, creation comes to fulfillment in a universe in which natures of diverse character insure an over-all harmony; it is in the integration existing among these that the greatness of God's plan lies. Honorius was quite carried away by this vision which rested, for him, upon a valid syncretism in which the pseudo-Dionysian "hierarchy" and, possibly toward the end of the century, the influence of the Hermetic writings[51] confirmed not only the "continuity" among all beings but their natural autonomy as well. Matter has significance in the Christian universe, and it is man that gives it that significance. The Platonic ambivalence was removed, and the spiritual inquietude of Augustine was surmounted.

Man, then, who exists within Nature, is himself a nature. The fact that he is spiritual, that his nature is in consequence endowed with liberty, and that he is thus caught up in the history of salvation in which his own liberty encounters that of God, does not undermine the fundamental condition in which he was created. The very

---

[49] *Contra haereticos* i.14 (*PL*, CCX, 319): "Decens enim fuit, ut tam corporea quam incorporea natura divinae bonitatis particeps fieret, et ea frueretur, et feliciter viveret." Alan's statement comes at the end of a limited but very revealing controversy, belonging to the early decades of the century, over why man was created. [Cf. M.-D. Chenu, "*Cur homo*? Le sous-sol d'une controverse au XIIe siècle," *MSR*, X (1953), 197–204, re-edited and republished in Chenu, *TDS*, chap. 2, pp. 52–61.]

[50] See his *Elucidarium* i.11 (*PL*, CLXXII, 1116); *Liber XII questionum* i (*PL*, CLXXII, 1178); *Liber VIII quaestionum* (*PL*, CLXXII, 1185); *Expos. in Cant.* v (*PL*, CLXXII, 432). Rupert of Deutz, who had just taken part in the controversies then in course at Laon in 1117, reported the problem at length: *In evangelium sancti Joannis commentariorum libri* XIV.ii (*PL*, CLXIX, 265).

[51] Hermes Trismegistus, at the beginning of the Latin *Asclepius* 2 (A. D. Nock, ed. *Corpus Hermeticum*, II [Paris, 1945], 298), starts his discussion from the principle of "continuity" among all the kinds of beings in the universe.

play of his liberty is meshed with the laws of nature: *Natura* is not only mistress of the universe and of all generation that takes place within it; she is also moderatrix of virtue. Does she not weep over men's infidelities to the ideal she teaches in her laws? In his *Complaint of Nature*, Alan of Lille extended his doctrine concerning Nature into the moral universe. "Alan's apotheosis of the perfect man is blended with his glorification of Nature and of the Virtues who construct that human hero."[52] The moral life of men is a particular instance of life as found in the universe; the universe of human liberty presupposes the universe of Nature, and it fulfills the promise of that universe of Nature.[53]

However original Alan's extension to the moral order of the cosmological philosophy of Chartres, it nonetheless shared some common elements with the ongoing evolution of Christian thought and indeed played its own part in that evolution. One can observe this evolution by noting the elaboration, side by side with supernatural morality, of a secular moral science based on natural law, in intellectual circles and in the schools. At their different extremes, Abelard and William of Conches gave evidence of the development, and so too did the diffusion of the works of the pagan moral philosophers.[54] One can observe this evolution by noting, too, the way in which classifications of the virtues now came to be derived from philosophical categories while the evangelical virtues of humility, chastity, piety, and poverty were relegated to spiritual and indefinable upper reaches or, as by Alan of Lille, reduced to natural classifications—chastity to temperance, humility to fortitude, piety to Cicero's definition of it.[55] One can see the evolution in the attempts,

---

[52] R. de Lage, p. 85.

[53] Thus, in the century following, the moral philosophy of St. Thomas would be conceived within a cosmic perspective, not bent in upon man alone. Cf. Jacques Maritain, *De Bergson à Thomas d'Aquin* (Paris, 1944), p. 60.

[54] See the studies of Philippe Delhaye, especially: "La place de l'éthique parmi les disciplines scientifiques au XII⁰ siècle," *Miscellanea A. Janssen*, I (Louvain, 1948), 29–44; "L'enseignement de la philosophie morale au XII⁰ siècle," *MS*, XI (1949), 77–99; "Une adaptation du 'De officiis' au XII⁰ siècle: Le 'Moralium dogma philosophorum,'" *RTAM*, XVI (1949), 227–58; XVII (1950), 5–28.

[55] Cf. R. de Lage, p. 86. An examination should be made of the organizing principle and inspiration of treatises *De virtutibus et vitiis*.

if not to displace the biblical classification of history into ages, at least to reintroduce the non-sacred categories of world history into it, whether through employing ancient sources or through new attentiveness to the actual unfolding of recent events.[56] One can see it again in a natural dimension given to eschatology, as when the coming of Christ is seen as described in Vergil's "golden age," in which the "new man" will come to birth.[57] And one can finally see it, this new mental outlook, transforming treatises on the moral education of princes. From Carolingian times such treatises were strung together from texts borrowed from the Bible and the fathers; now, more and more, they came to have recourse to the profane authorities of antiquity as did the *De instructione principum* (*On the Education of Princes*) of Gerald of Wales (Giraldus Cambrensis), the first part of which appeared between 1177 and 1180, and the *Policraticus* of John of Salisbury, which already at this early date propounded an entire political philosophy.

To be sure, men were still far from a detailed theology of the relations between nature and grace in human action, and none of these masters, Alan of Lille included, questioned the great Augustinian propositions concerning the necessity of grace and the debased condition of human nature. However, they fortified their Augustinianism, even at Saint-Victor, with a more or less independent investigation of the resources and the behavior in which grace finds its matter.

It was within the context of such renaissance, such rebirth—in which inspiration dominated imitation, and in which ancient resources nourished the initiatives of a new spirit—that the theme "man is a microcosm," with all that it implied for the relationships of man and nature, received literary, esthetic, and doctrinal elaboration. One is immediately struck by the apparently sudden but in any

---

[56] One thinks of the famous remark of Bernard of Chartres: "Like dwarfs standing on the shoulders of giants, we see farther than they," reported by John of Salisbury *Metalog.* iii.4 (Webb, p. 136; McGarry, p. 167), and of the various "states" of Christendom discerned in relation to historical events; for example, by Anselm of Havelberg in his evolutionist theory; see his *Dialogi* i.2 (*PL*, CLXXXVIII, 1144; datable between 1136–49) and the general discussion of historical literature at the time in Ghellinck, *Essor*, II, 39–103.

[57] So Alan of Lille in his *Anticlaudianus.* Cf. R. de Lage, p. 98.

case widespread diffusion of the theme in the first decades of the twelfth century.[58] It is true that in the ninth century John the Scot gave forceful expression to this theme for men in the West, and we shall have to account for his interest in it. But in this as in so many other matters, John the Scot stood alone in that gateway to the Middle Ages, that first so-called Carolingian renaissance, as if his greatness had ripened too early among men as yet unprepared to assimilate his metaphysics of the divine. In the generations immediately following him we find vital traces rather of his polemical writings on predestination or on the eucharist than of his profound and lofty philosophy.[59] Yet it was precisely through him, thanks to the active interest inspired by certain elements of his philosophy at the outset of the twelfth century, that the theme of man-as-microcosm came into decisive prominence. The mysterious Honorius of Autun is the first notable witness to the diffusion of this theme in his youthful work, the *Elucidarium*, translated into eight or ten languages, including Middle English after 1125, and influential in preaching, sacred art, and poetry.[60] The novelty of the *Elucidarium* will strike us if we reflect that the conception of man-as-microcosm is absent from the writings of St. Anselm, the venerable teacher of these generations, and from the school of Laon, where John the Scot had formerly taught and which remained one of the great centers of learning.

---

[58] One could doubtless collect a list of texts on man-as-microcosm from the tenth to the twelfth century; but these represent the summary and passive handing on of a commonplace, unconnected with philosophical or religious reflection and not nurturing any fresh contemplation of nature—the mere passing along of a *topos* from Christian writer to Christian writer, as in Gregory *Hom. XXIX in Evang.* (*PL*, LXXVI, 1214).

[59] The hold of certain Erigenist themes is evident in John the Scot's own generation. On the theme of the microcosm see Almantius (died about 889), disciple and possibly the pupil of John the Scot (cf. A. Wilmart, "La lettre philosophique d'Almanne," *AHDL*, III [1928], 285–319; esp. pp. 300, 314), and Remigius of Auxerre (died about 908), who attended to the likeness between microcosm and macrocosm throughout the long course of his writings—his commentaries on Prudentius, on Genesis, on the *Consolation of Philosophy* of Boethius (cf. P. Courcelle, "Etude critique sur les commentaries de Boèce," *AHDL*, XII [1939], 15, 42, 60).

[60] *Elucidarium* i.11 (*PL*, CLXXII, 1116; Lefèvre, p. 371); cf. *Liber VIII quaestionum* (*ibid.*, 1185C, 1186B–D, 1189C–D, etc.). The unedited *Clavis physicae* of Honorius plagiarizes the *De divisione naturae* of John the Scot.

It was another center of learning, Chartres, which would long remain the fertile soil in which this conception would grow, and this the more as the *Timaeus*, itself constructed upon the parallelism between microcosm and macrocosm, became a central preoccupation of teaching at Chartres. This was the first age, the golden age, of Platonism as such in the West, an age which found in the *Timaeus* an entire physics, an anthropology, a metaphysics, and even a lofty spiritual teaching. An inventory is still being made of the numerous commentaries on the *Timaeus* inspired in their treatment of this point as of others by the commentary of Chalcidius.[61] The best known among them was that of William of Conches (died about 1154), who gave explicit, personal, and long valued service to this commentary tradition.[62] Gilbert of La Porrée, who taught at Chartres from 1124 to 1137, gave attention to the theme in his *Liber de sex principiis* (*Book of the Six Principles*), a work destined to have great future influence and to become a standard text in the faculty of arts at Paris throughout the thirteenth century.[63] Between 1145 and 1153, Bernard Sylvester composed his tribute to Nature, the *De mundi universitate*, the two parts of which set forth respectively a description of the universe as macrocosm and of man as microcosm.[64]

One would be surprised to find a physics based on the microcosm in Cistercian centers far removed from Chartres were one not acquainted with the work of William of Saint-Thierry, who became a Cistercian in 1135 and died in 1148. The adversary of William of Conches and of Gilbert of La Porrée, he made frequent and profitable use of Origen and Gregory of Nyssa and from them derived the inspiration for the use he made of the theme in his *De*

---

[61] Wrobel; Mullach.

[62] Cf. Parent, chap. 3, "Les gloses de Guillaume de Conches sur le *Timée*," pp. 137–77, for discussion and extracts. [For new and complete edition of William's commentary, with introduction and notes, see Jeauneau.]

[63] From his work the theme passed into vernacular literature, e.g. *Le roman de Fauvel*, vv. 1837 ff. (Artur Långfors, ed., [Paris, 1914–19], pp. 69, 107).

[64] Barach-Wrobel, pp. 5 and 64. Cf. E. Gilson, "La cosmogonie de Bernardus Silvestris," *AHDL*, III (1928), 5–24. [For later and differing interpretations, see Theodore Silverstein, "The Fabulous Cosmogony of Bernardus Sylvestris," *MP*, XLVI (1948–9), 92–116, and views cited.]

natura corporis et animae (*On the Nature of Body and Soul*).[65]

The new generation of writers that appeared about 1150 took up the theme in a decisive and vital manner. To be sure, Peter Lombard, focusing his attention upon an Augustinian theology little concerned with the value of the cosmos, failed to treat man-as-microcosm in his *Sententiae*[66] and in consequence provided no occasion for scholastic and official discussion of the theme in the commentaries on his book during the centuries that followed. Nonetheless, the geographical spread of the theme quickly assured its influence in all cultural centers and upon all intellectual outlooks. At Saint-Victor, where Master Hugh (died 1141) did not make much use of it, Godfrey, who entered the abbey between 1155 and 1160 and died in 1195, produced a full and original treatment of the theme in his *Microcosmos*, written, it may be, outside the abbey which was at this time dominated by the anti-intellectualism of its prior, Walter.[67] The extraordinary nun, Hildegard of Bingen, who died in 1179, utilized this physics of the macrocosm and the microcosm, which lent itself well to all kinds of symbolism, in the construction of her imagery and in the theological explanation she made of her visions.[68] Herrad of Landsberg, who died as Abbess of Saint-Odelia in 1195, illustrated the theme, even pictorially, in her *Hortus deliciarum* (*Garden of Delights*).[69] That the *Porretani* also took it up and exploited it will hardly come as a surprise considering the capital use made of it at Chartres, whence the *Porretani* derived rich inspiration for their "naturalism." As for Alan of Lille (died 1203), good

---

[65] *PL*, CLXXX, 695–726. Cf. J. M. Déchanet, *Oeuvres choisies de Guillaume de Saint-Thierry* (Paris, 1944), p. 60. Hugh of Fouilloy, prior of this abbey near Corbie in 1153, was very close to William in sources and perhaps in formulation as well; cf. his *De medicina animae* (*PL*, CLXXVI, 1183–1202).

[66] Neither is the theme treated in the *Glossa ordinaria* nor in Gratian. The exclusively western orientation of these three basic school texts stands opposed to importations from Greek theology.

[67] See Delhaye, *Microcosmos*.

[68] Cf. H. Liebeschütz, *Das allegorische Weltbild der hl. Hildegard von Bingen* (Leipzig, 1930), chap. 2, on her use of the theme.

[69] Delhaye, II, 165, points to the clear relationship between the text of Honorius of Autun and the picture (miniature reproduced) constructed by Herrad.

disciple of William of Conches, Bernard Sylvester, and Gilbert of La Porrée that he was, his reading of the Latin *Asclepius* could only bring the reinforcement of Hermetic tradition to those elements he drew from the *Timaeus* or from John the Scot's *De divisione naturae* (*On the Division of Nature*).[70]

This brings us to the thirteenth century. Here the tide of Aristotelianism would submerge not only the Platonism of the *Timaeus* but also the metaphysics of John the Scot, the symbolism of Saint-Victor, and the revelations of Hermes Trismegistus. The theme of the microcosm would survive—it would even find some explicit support in Aristotle[71]—but it would be associated with a physics and a naturalistic anthropology of a quite different orientation. One will find it among such theologians as Albert the Great, Bonaventure, Thomas Aquinas, and in French vernacular literature as well, Jean de Meun affording a good example.[72]

This is not the place to analyze the sources used by all these authors. Having called attention to them in passing, let us merely record the fact that in the course of the twelfth century the philosophical capital provided by the ancient classical authors was enriched by a new draft from the works of John the Scot, by a reading of the Greek fathers (among others, of Gregory of Nyssa, already used by John the Scot), and finally by the Hermetic writings—all these closely woven into a texture as bewildering to the historian to disentangle as it is significant in itself. The ancient classical heritage, philosophical in content, was repeatedly invested with a religious character which, even in pre-Christian times, had caused it to issue into a cosmic spirituality,[73] and which, in the Christian West, would develop into a humanism looking both to nature and to God with

---

[70] Among his other works, see his theological dictionary, the "summa" *Quot modis* (*Liber in distinctionibus dictionum theologicalium*), under *Mundus* (*PL*, CCX, 866).

[71] *Phys.* viii.2.252b26.

[72] *Roman de la Rose* vv. 19041–53. Cf. Paré, p. 75. (Ernest Langlois, ed., *Le roman de la Rose par Guillaume de Lorris et Jean de Meun*, IV [Paris, 1922], 253; Harry W. Robbins, tr., *The Romance of the Rose by Guillaume de Lorris and Jean de Meun* [New York, 1962] p. 404).

[73] Cf. Festugière, Vol. II; and P. Allers, "*Microcosmus* from Anaximandros to Paracelsus," *Trad.*, II (1944), 318–407.

an ambivalence found in all humanism. Man encompasses an anti-nomy—he is seen as simultaneously an image of the world (as philosophy would have it) and an image of God (as Genesis declares). It is precisely these two extremes that the twelfth century brought together, with the different schools entertaining different views as to man's exact composition and orientation, and with spokesmen for Augustinianism—Hugh of Saint-Victor, Peter Lombard—resisting the effort.

The first attempts to construct the parallelism between microcosm and macrocosm were rational, let us even call them scientific, in type. Like the cosmos, man is made of the four elements, and their placement, at creation, within the superior structure of the human body did not alter their native physical character or operation.[74] Learned lumber of poor quality, this science, despite its basic reflection of Platonism![75] But there was enough in it to excite the interest of William of Saint-Thierry as well as of the masters of Chartres; and, even under the daunting allegories of Bernard Sylvester and Alan of Lille, it afforded a vision of man's place in the world capable of giving birth alike to science and to contemplation. Henceforth Christians would direct interested attention upon the world; they would judge that in exercising such an attention they were fulfilling at least some part of their destiny, on the supposition that man is a being consecrated to the world and that in coming to know the world he comes to know himself as well.[76]

---

[74] Cf. Honorius of Autun *Elucidarium* i.11 (*PL*, CLXXII, 1116; Lefèvre, p. 371): "Unde corporalis [substantia in hominis creatione]? De quatuor elementis, unde et microcosmus, idest minor mundus, dicitur: habet namque ex terra carnem, ex aqua sanguinem, ex aere flatum, ex igne calorem." (Whence came the corporeal substance used in man's creation? From the four elements, and for this reason man is called a microcosm, that is, a lesser world; for from earth he has his flesh, from water his blood, from air his breath, and from fire his warmth.)

[75] Cf. *Platon, Oeuvres complètes* (Collection des universités de la France publiée sous le patronage de l'Association Guillaume Budé), vol. 10: *Timée-Critias* (Paris, 1925), ed. and tr. Albert Rivaud, introduction, pp. 2–120, esp. p. 7. [Cf. F. M. Cornford, *Plato's Cosmology. The* Timaeus *of Plato Translated with a Running Commentary* (London, 1937).]

[76] Cf. St. Thomas *Summa Theol.* i, q.96, a.2 (Aquinas, *Opera Omnia*, I, 382; Aquinas *Summa*, III, 322): ". . . in homine quodammodo sunt omnia [=microcosmus]; et ideo secundum modum quo dominatur his quae in seipso

In any case, a complete psychology rooted in the study of the composite elements of the world now began to arise. The numerous treatises "On the Soul" which appeared in the twelfth century, however much they might yet retain of the "inwardness" of Augustinianism, incorporated these physical principles and this "materialist" outlook. In an effort to pin-point the development of physiological categories used to classify the faculties of the soul, it has recently become possible to fix 1130 and 1150 as the dates between which anatomical and physiological ideas first appeared in the writings of the Cistercian mystic, William of Saint-Thierry, and of that philosopher of Chartres, William of Conches, and so gave physical basis and substance to the mere moralizing analysis in which spiritual writers typically took refuge. Even more, John of Salisbury, the most discriminating among the scholars of Chartres, expressly brought together the philosophical tradition of the ancient classical writers and the teachings of the fathers, particularly the *De natura hominis* (*On the Nature of Man*) of Nemesius, which Bishop Alfanus translated before his death in 1085.[77]

These resources supplied by natural reason from the realms of physics and metaphysics were peculiarly exploited and given a symbolic turn. Philippe Delhaye, who has recently reconstructed for us the life and work of Godfrey of Saint-Victor, has with keen insight

---

sunt, secundum hunc modum competit ei dominari aliis." (all things exist, in a certain manner, within man; and for this reason it is fitting that he should govern other things in the manner that he governs what is within himself); also at the outset of a political treatise, the *De reg. prin.* i.12 (Aquinas, *Opera omnia*, XVI, 235): "in homine, qui ob hoc minor mundus appellatur, quia in eo invenitur forma universalis regiminis. . . ." (in man, who is called a lesser world because the form of universal governance is found within him.)

[77] *Metalogicon* iv.20 (Webb, p. 187; McGarry, p. 234): "Qui vero naturam anime diligentius investigare voluerint, non modo Platonis, Aristotilis, Ciceronis, et veterum philosophorum scripta revolvant, sed Patrum qui veritatem fidelius expresserunt. . . . Quod si quis non potest evolvere, vel *Premnonphysicon* legat, librum de anima copiosissime disputantem." (If anyone wishes to investigate the nature of the soul thoroughly, led him read not only the writings of Plato, Aristotle, Cicero, and the ancient philosophers, but those of the fathers, who set forth the truth very faithfully. . . . But if anyone cannot do this, let him at least read the *Premnon physicon*, a book which discusses the soul most fully.) Alfanus entitled his translation *Premnon physicon* because, he says, the study of man's nature is the root or stock (*stipes naturalium*) from which all the natural sciences have sprung.

protested against likening the microcosm drawn by the Victorine poet to the cosmogony of the masters of Chartres: "In his *De mundi universitate*, Bernard Sylvester starts with a cosmology and ends up with an anthropology; Godfrey starts with a psychology and ends up with a theology."[78] Godfrey did not fail to notice the relationship of man's body to the world, but his outlook was not that of a physicist or student of nature; it was that of the fathers, for whom, thanks to the intimate bond between the fate of the universe and the destiny of man, a favorite theme of the Greek fathers, the world symbolized spiritual realities. To be sure, Bernard Sylvester had used allegory and had used it beyond all measure. But symbolism is something quite different from allegory, in the kind of literary construction it promotes as well as in intellectual outlook. Allegory is a fine-spun intellectual production, neither popular nor religious save possibly in the myths that sustain it. The symbolism in vogue at Saint-Victor, on the other hand, whatever awkwardness or contamination it might have involved, provided for the spirit an immediate nourishment drawn from the sacramental character of the universe; for, even before men contemplate it, the sacramental universe is filled with God. Indeed, natural science, despite its hostility to any symbolic interpretation of reality, expands into obscure zones of cosmic and human reality in which symbolism is the means taken over to express what remains mysterious. The optimism of Godfrey, which was of a piece with accepted trends at Saint-Victor, made clear that in a milieu wholly different from that of Chartres he had grasped and given expression to values arising from the parallelism between the soul of man and the cosmic order.

Comparably, the extravagant visionary temperament of Hildegard of Bingen transformed the learned physical science she used as the stuff of her symbolism and made it express rather the developing history of Christianity than the static universe of the Greeks. In like manner had her contemporary, Hadewych of Antwerp, transposed the themes of courtly troubadour poetry into Christian mysticism.[79]

---

[78] Delhaye, II, 148.

[79] Hadewych of Antwerp, *Poèmes des Béguines*, tr. J.-B. Porion (Paris, 1954).

We turn, finally, to entirely religious considerations. Here we run into the ambiguity, of a Platonizing syncretism once again rife in Christian thought, a syncretism wherein Platonic concepts were applied to Genesis to explain creation; for the speculative focus of this syncretism was directed not upon the gift of grace but upon the act of creation, both of them being gratuitous on God's part but entailing quite different conceptions of the divine liberty. Bernard Sylvester affords a perfect example of the kind of ambiguity involved. Historians, as is well known, disagree on the proper interpretation of his work. Some, like Curtius, see in it pagan thought gaining sway over Christian conscience, and others, like Gilson, see in it an intrepid biblical faith ingeniously utilizing the ancient cosmogony to promote understanding of the faith.[80]

But granting this ambiguity, the theme of the microcosm is quite capable of nurturing authentic religious values and constructions. The fathers—Origen, Gregory of Nyssa, Nemesius—demonstrated this within the Christian ambiance, as had philosophers during the course of the Hellenistic age. Plato will always beget a truly religious philosophy. In the twelfth century, not only William of Saint-Thierry, who stood too much on the fringes of the optimistic Platonism of the *Timaeus*, but above all the *Porretani*, thanks to their kinship with Chartres, were proponents of a theology and a spirituality which, under diverse forms, have always had free run in the West. The Christian contemplating the world is torn by a double attraction: to attain God through the world, the order of which reveals its creator, or to renounce the world, from which God is radically distinct. Disciples of Plato had already been caught up in this dialectic: the *Symposium* sets forth the dualistic conception, the *Timaeus* the monistic one, "monistic in the sense that God is there more or less identified with the world; optimistic in the sense that since the world is good, contemplation of this good work leads to knowledge of the Workman."[81] The world, filled with divine ideas, is for that very reason filled with God; and this God is great, is true. The remarkable "definitions" which the twenty-four philosophers placed under the

---

[80] [See n. 64, above.]
[81] Festugière, II, 585.

patronage of Hermes Trismegistus, like the system of axioms proposed by Alan of Lille to define the economy of the Christian faith, belong to great theology.[82]

The Platonism of the masters of Chartres, of Gilbert of La Porrée and his followers, indeed that of Saint-Victor, was, in the medieval West, the fine product of that intellectual mysticism which, in its optimistic naturalism, can threaten the balance of a Christian conscience, can threaten even its orthodoxy, but which leads to a high wisdom. Equipped with the tools of Boethian logic, infatuated with formulas and with mathematical analyses (an altogether Platonic trait), expressed now with the conciseness found in a sequence of axioms and now in interminable allegorical imagery, this wisdom did not attain its full stature in the twelfth century when the wisdom of Augustine commingled with that of Aristotle. Yet it cut an impressive figure—indeed a beautiful figure in those pictorial representations in which God was shown in the guise of Philosophy.[83]

Man as Master of Nature—Art and Nature

It was not only the theologians in their schools who were the proponents of this intimate physical and spiritual relationship between man and his universe, this new balance between grace and nature. They announced the laws of the new relationship, the new balance, only after the twelfth-century church had undertaken the reconstruction of its spiritual and pastoral existence in new forms and new states of life. The famous quarrel between the monks and the regular canons and, surpassing the canonical reform, the apostolic movements inspired by the pure gospel implied not only new institutions but unprecedented attitudes in that struggle between the world and

---

[82] Cl. Baeumker, "Das pseudo-hermetische 'Buch der vierundzwanzig Meister,'" *Studien und Charakteristiken zur Geschichte der Philosophie*, in *BGPM*, XXV, i (Münster, 1928), 207–14; Alan of Lille *Regulae theologicae* (*PL*, CCX, 622–84).

[83] Such representations constituted a new step in the long history of iconography in the West; from the time of Alcuin and John the Scot, the Wisdom of God was commonly presented under the appearance of the *Philosophia* of Boethius. See M.-Th. d'Alverny, "La sagesse et ses sept filles: recherches sur les allégories de la philosophie et des arts libéraux du IX⁰ au XII⁰ siècle," *Mélanges F. Grat*, I (Paris, 1946), 245–78.

the gospel within which the tensions of the interior life of the Christian take shape. In a twofold yet unique impulse, the return to the primitive apostolic life, ignoring monastic feudalism, demanded and obtained the Christian's presence in the world. No longer was it a question of polarizing the perfect life through the monastic ideal and creating on earth an adumbration of the city of God; rather was it a question of casting the evangelical leaven into a world in which a new civilization was rising out from under the oppressive weight of feudalism. Mere moral purification inspired by a zeal for personal reform was not by itself enough—the twelfth century already abounded with that; wanted now was the refraction of the gospel's truths throughout a determinate social structure; wanted was the church's encounter with the world, an encounter to be accomplished by a pure and forthright witness, but one sensitive to the values of the new society, rather than by the apparatus of a Christianity powerful—and compromised—by its establishment. It will surprise no one to discover that in the generations to follow, the ranks of evangelically-minded men supplied the theologians for this new Christianity in which reason itself, that sensitive summit of human nature, would enter into the construction on earth of the science of God. Scholasticism, as men would say later, is the highest expression of the axiom, "Grace does not vitiate nature, it perfects it."

Arising from an apostolic consciousness of the world, this new sensibility carried the discovery of nature into the domain of societal life and developments. Before analyzing the effect of this and turning our attention to realities in the world order,[84] let us peer into the modest and hidden details of daily life. The encounter between man and nature becomes complete only when man has subdued nature to his service; the order of nature demands man's mastery and, for the Christian, so too does the command given man by the Creator on the first pages of the Bible. The twelfth century followed this command.

In his history of technology, Lewis Mumford speaks appreciatively of the first efforts of mankind before the modern period and underlines the importance of the progress accomplished in the Mid-

---

[84] See below, pp. 202–38.

dle Ages. He opens his account of that progress by sketching the time when, with senses awakened to nature, artist and artisan were one:

> By a slow natural process, the world of nature broke in upon the medieval dream of hell and paradise and eternity. In the fresh naturalistic sculpture of the thirteenth-century churches one can watch the first uneasy stir of the sleeper, as the light of morning strikes his eyes. At first, the craftsman's interest in nature was a confused one. Side by side with the fine carvings of oak leaves and hawthorne sprays, faithfully copied, tenderly arranged, the sculptor still created strange monsters, gargoyles, chimeras, legendary beasts. But the interest in nature steadily broadened and became more consuming.[85]

I concur with the suggestive picture Mumford gives, as do art historians. The rise of new techniques both betokened and promoted a true discovery, an active discovery of nature; and man advanced toward self-discovery as he came thus to master nature. The self-discovery may have been unconscious at first, but it showed itself soon in the eager curiosity that arose when physical tasks and laborious enterprises modified men's intellectual life and restored sanity and balance to their obsession with dialectic or illusory cerebration.

In this respect, too, the twelfth century was a turning point in medieval civilization; so marked was the transformation that took place in the material conditions of life that it has been possible to speak of a "technological revolution." Encouraged by the breakup of the feudal monopoly of the soil, by the economic and political emancipation of urban artisans organized into guilds, and by the active mobility of men and goods in a market economy, the use and spread of new techniques of production and commerce profoundly altered not only the material side of life but also the modes of perception, sensibility, and representation that pertain to the life of the spirit. Did not Aristotle base his analysis of change and becoming upon the analogy of the artisan and his work?[86]

"Can one consider things manufactured by man—footgear, cheese, and like products—as works of God?" wondered Master

---

[85] *Technics and Civilization* (London, 1934), pp. 28–29.

[86] For the analogy between τέχνη and φύσις see *Phys.* ii.1,193a32–36, and ii.2,194a21.

Gilbert. It was a theological question, not a matter for philosophical deliberation in the fashion of Aristotle. Beneath its artless phrasing the question revealed a dawning awareness of the part to be played by man's productive pursuits in the religious scheme of things. Thus the question was of greater import than Gilbert's answer, though the answer too is not without interest. In it Gilbert distinguished three aspects to the great work of God: the divine creative action, the operations of nature, and the things made by men—all three being parts of the divine "governance" of the world.[87]

This was no incidental observation of Gilbert's but an integral and deliberate part of a religious metaphysics which defined man as artisan (*homo artifex*) in relation to God's creative work (*opus Creatoris*) and the work of nature (*opus naturae*). The relationship to God's creative work conferred a religious significance upon human productive activity; the relationship to the work of nature

---

[87] *Notae super Johannem secundum magistrum Gilbertum* (MS London Lambeth Palace 360, f. 32ʳb) : "De artificialibus quaeritur utrum a Deo facta sunt, sicut caseus, et sotulares, et hujusmodi quae dicuntur esse opera hominis non Dei.—Omnia quidem a Deo facta sunt tanquam ab auctore; quaedam tamen ejus opera dicuntur, sicut sunt, illa quae per se operatur ita scilicet quod nec naturae similitudine, nec alicujus ministerio, ut caelum et terram. Alia dicuntur opera naturae, quae a Deo ita creantur quod ad alterius similitudinem, ut quod grana ex granis, et equus ex equo, et similia ex similibus. Alia quae hominis ministerio facit, hominum dicuntur. Unus ergo omnium auctor Deus, diversae tamen operandi rationes, et auctoritatis et ministerii, quorum alterum homo dicitur auctor, alterum vero Deus. Similiter usualiter dici solet de aliquo divite quod multa fecit edificia, quae eadem singulariter fecit et carpentarius, sed alter auctoritate sola et jussu, alter ministerio." (It is asked whether artificial things—footgear, cheese, and like products, which we say are works of man and not of God—have been made by God.—Indeed, all things have been made by God as their author; but certain things are called God's works just as they are, namely those which he makes by himself and neither after some resemblance in nature nor through the intermediary service of someone else, as he makes heaven and earth. Others are called works of nature, and these are created by God after some natural resemblance, as a seed from other seeds, a horse from other horses, and similar things from their similars. Others which he makes through the intermediary service of man are called works of men. God, therefore, is the sole author of all things; but there are different ways of making, both as to authority and as to intermediary service, such that on the one hand man is said to be the author, and on the other hand, God. In a similar manner we customarily say that some rich man has built many buildings which in fact a carpenter has built, but the one has built them only by his authority and command, the other by his service.)

provided such activity with its earthly standard of truth. The three-fold distinction was drawn from the commentary of Chalcidius upon the *Timaeus*: "All things that exist are the work of God, or the work of nature, or the work of a human artisan imitating nature."[88] But the distinction was amplified until it furnished a complete vision of the world and a definition of man, and even the guidelines for man's productive activity. Thus, William of Conches wrote:

Having shown that nothing exists without a cause, Plato now narrows the discussion to the derivation of effect from efficient cause. It must be recognized that every work is the work of the *Creator,* or the work of *nature,* or the work of a human artisan imitating nature. The work of the Creator is the first creation without preexisting material, for example the creation of the elements or of spirits, or it is the things we see happen contrary to the accustomed course of nature, as the virgin birth and the like. The work of nature is to bring forth like things from like through seeds or offshoots, for nature is an energy inherent in things and making like from like. The work of an artisan is a work that man engages in because of a need, as making clothes for protection against cold or a house against bad weather. But in all that he does, the artisan imitates nature, for when he makes clothes he fashions them after the natural disposition of the body's members; and when he makes a house he remembers that water that collects on flat surfaces makes wood rot, whereas it flows down off slopes and cleanses them, so he makes his house peaked.[89]

In this distinction between three types of activity—itself characteristic of the masters of Chartres—it is important to recognize the full significance of the difference between works that are properly divine, such as creation and miracle, and works that belong to the natural order, divine too in their supreme or ultimate source, but effected in accordance with the laws of an order autonomous in its consistency. The diffuse Christian spirituality hitherto dominated by the Augustinian view of the universe had seen the omnipotence of God revealed as plainly by the buds of spring as by the flowering of Aaron's rod, as much by the squeezing of wine from grapes as by

---

[88] Chap. 23 (Wrobel, p. 88; Mullach, p. 85): "Omnia enim quae sunt vel opus Dei sunt, vel naturae, vel naturam imitantis hominis artificis."

[89] *Glossa in Timaeum*, ad 28a (Parent, p. 148; Jeauneau, p. 104). Cf. *Dragmaticon* (ed. Guil. Gratarolus [Argentorati, 1567], p. 31). The threefold distinction is found also in Augustinian ambiance; cf. Robert of Melun *Sententiae* i.1.21 (Martin, I, 224–7) [and Hugh of Saint-Victor *Didascalicon* i.9 (Buttimer, p. 16; Taylor, p. 55)].

the miracle at Cana, as much by the daily birth of infants as by the raising of a dead man to life. This constricting religiosity, under-valuing secondary causes, had operated within a symbolic vision of the world which tended to let slip the explanation of phenomena by reference to immediate causes and to stress the meaning such phenomena might acquire *sub specie aeternitatis*—a practice as legitimate in the realm of sacred value as it is in that of poetry. The various forms of Neoplatonism then prevalent lent to such meditations the substance found in philosophical reflection of high quality, despite occasional childish lapses. We touch here upon a doctrinal development that we shall examine in another connection.

John of Salisbury, more sociologically than theologically oriented, took account of the place which workmen occupy in the human community whether agricultural workers or craftsmen; their growing specialization, while it advanced the common good, hardly gave the legislator authority to outline directions for the conduct of their innumerable tasks.[90] Alexander Neckham (died in 1217), successively master in law, medicine, and theology and aware of the different methodological principles appropriate to the different branches of knowledge, composed, in addition to his *De naturis rerum* (*On the Natures of Things*), a sort of dictionary of domestic tools and equipment, the *De nominibus utensilium* (*On the Names of Utensils*),

---

[90] *Policraticus* vi.20 (Webb, II, 20; Dickinson, p. 243): "Qui sint pedes reipublicae et de cura eis impendenda.—Pedes quidem qui humiliora exercent officia, appellantur. . . . quidem agricolarum ratio vertitur qui terrae semper adhaerent sive in sationalibus sive in consitivis sive in pascuis sive in floreis agitentur. His etiam aggregantur multae species lanificii artesque mechanicae quae in ligno ferro ere metallisque variis consistunt. . . . Haec autem tot sunt ut respublica non octipedes cancros sed et centipedes pedum numerositate transcendat. . . . tam variae figurae sunt ut nullus unquam officiorum scriptor in singulas species eorum specialia praecepta dederit." (Of those who are the feet of the commonwealth, and of the care which should be bestowed thereon. —Those are called the feet who discharge the humbler offices. . . . Among these are to be counted the husbandmen, who always cleave to the soil, busied about their plowlands or vineyards or pastures or flower gardens. To these must be added the many species of cloth-making and the mechanic arts, which include work in wood, iron, bronze, and the different metals; . . . All these different occupations are so numerous that the commonwealth in the number of its feet exceeds not only the eight-footed crab but even the centipede. . . . they are of so many different varieties that no writer on the subject of offices or duties has ever laid down particular precepts for each special variety.)

which applied the contemporary taste for lexicography to the mechanical arts.[91]

But the rise of technology surpassed quantitatively and qualitatively the still elementary awareness that professional or religious men had of the role technology was to play. The production of energy made enormous strides with the perfecting and spread of machines to harness waterpower and to produce circular motion; mill wheels; hydraulic wheels, which enabled one horse to do the work that formerly required twenty-five; windmills, first used in Europe in 1105; machines that could store power through a system of weights and geared wheels; new armaments that made the old mounted warrior obsolete (the second Lateran Council in 1139 prohibited the arbalest which had just recently made its appearance). New means of transport and travel gave men increased freedom: the early invention of the draft collar for horses or oxen transformed rural life; the use of the keel and rudder dates from 1180; and the compass allowed long voyages by sea, fostered a commercialism in which the middle-class merchant acquired ascendency over the excluded noblemen, and helped displace commerce from the Mediterranean to the Atlantic. In 1188 the bridge at Avignon was built with its eighteen arches of stone. The mechanical clock began to rationalize time, its regularity measuring out a mechanized civilization; for, as Lewis Mumford observes,[92] its pendulum not only kept track of the hours but also synchronized the actions of men, and the bells of the clock tower dominated urban life. The new gadget was everywhere and cast a new aura around existence, which was governed now not by rhythms natural to human life but by a mechanical time. The rich ornamentation of the clocks gave expression to the new compulsion engaging the spirits of the populace.

In this mechanism-minded world, man moved away from a confused trial-and-error approach, became objective and impersonal in his efforts, and grew aware of the complex structures of realities governed by natural laws. Order was no longer merely the scheme

---

[91] Thomas Wright, ed., *A Volume of Vocabularies* (London, 1857–73), I, 96–119. Cf. Haskins, *Studies*, pp. 359–63.

[92] [*Technics and Civilization*, pp. 12–18; cf. Lynn White, Jr., *Medieval Technology and Social Change* (Oxford, 1962).]

proposed by aesthetic imagination or religious conviction; it was experimentally ascertained and systematically verified, for nature was seen as penetrable and predictable. The knowledge to which man could attain included the knowledgeable mastery of nature. The *quadrivium*, directed to knowledge of things, had an educative value no less than that of the *trivium*, directed to knowledge of words—and productive of too many rhetoricians and dialecticians. Gilbert of La Porrée advised students who had become fanatical about dialectic "to pick up the baker's trade." And the artisans working on the cathedral of Chartres, were they not cut from the same cloth as Abelard?[93] Hugh of Saint-Victor gave an important place to the mechanical arts in his *Didascalicon*: "cloth-making, armaments and architecture, navigation and commerce, agriculture, hunting and food preparation, medicine, theatre and the arts of entertainment" (leisure hours were not overlooked in this happy economy!).[94] Godfrey of Saint-Victor, in drawing up a chart of trades according to their function in society, took exception to the definition long given of the mechanical arts and derived from a false etymology; an etymology that survives in classical French: *Scientiae mechanicae, idest moechiae seu adulterinae* (The mechanical sciences, that is, the prostituting or adulterate sciences)—the view having been that these adulterate the spiritual dignity of man by associating it with matter.[95]

Henceforth, the new *homo artifex*, maker of shapes and forms, distinguished between the animate and the mechanical, rid himself

---

[93] John of Salisbury, *Metalog*. iii.10 (Webb, p. 161; McGarry, p. 198), reports William of Conches' comparison between the efforts of the dialectician and those of one Ascelin, master smith of some fame: "Hescelinus faber, sicut magister Willelmus referebat, illorum morem sequebatur, qui nichil in disputationibus certum appetunt, et sic rem fabrilem, sicut hii expediunt dialecticam, exercebat." (Ascelin the artisan, as Master William used to say, followed the practice of those who have no settled objective in their disputations and so exercised his craft as they do dialectic.)

[94] ii.20–27 (Buttimer, pp. 38–44; Taylor, pp. 74–79). Hugh's interest results rather from his open-mindedness and his bookish cultivation of the ancients than from watching artisans of his own time at work.

[95] *Microcosmus* 55–57 (Delhaye, I). Cf. Delhaye, II, 115, where the import of this humanist interest in technology is justly characterized, and M.-D. Chenu, "Arts 'méchaniques' et oeuvres serviles," *RSPT*, XXIX (1940), 313–15, where the relationship of feudal serfdom to this conception of work is discussed.

of the childish fancies of animism and of the habit of seeing divinity in the marvels of nature. The sacred realm which he secularized by this process no longer possessed any properly religious value for him. He knew its place in the universe better than that. This new breed of medieval man was taken up with the machine, which so usefully freed men from countless humdrum activities. Man's growing control over matter, moreover, lifted this dense and lifeless stuff into an economy which, at its final term of development in the "new heavens and new earth" promised after the last judgment, would confer divinity upon the natural universe, this time for good. Alan of Lille explicitly professed this belief, though for him it was an *a priori* deduction.[96] So too the Ionians, thinkers and artisans of an earlier day, far advanced beyond the gods of Hesiod, made for themselves a new cosmogony in which intelligence and technology laid nature open to plain view.

Art and nature—Aristotle would provide the thirteenth-century masters with an exceedingly rich philosophical formulation of the two, a formulation which their dialectic would not thoroughly explore, one must add.[97] But the masters of the twelfth century, their reflections less confined by classroom exercises, had already perceived all that art, by directing nature, could bring out in man; at the same time, their discovery of nature gave substance to their metaphysics of the universe and to new ways of thinking.

Art and nature—already the two stood opposed to each other, however, and the contest between them began. Man, confronting the universe, did not merely accept this external world; he changed it and, with his tools, sought to make of it a humanized world. Moreover, he did not merely accept his animal needs; he denied them after a fashion, at least he denied them free rein, in order to train and ed-

---

[96] [*De arte seu articulis catholicae fidei* ii.12 (*PL*, CCX, 607–8). On ascription of this work to Nicholas of Amiens, whom Chenu here names instead of Alan of Lille, see M. Grabmann, *Die Geschichte der scholastichen Methode,* II, 431–34, 452–76; on its restoration to Alan of Lille, see C. Balić, "De auctore operis quod 'ars fidei catholicae' inscribitur," *Mélanges de Ghellinck,* II (1951), 793–814, and M.-Th. d'Alverny, *Alain de Lille* (Paris 1965), pp. 68–69. Cf. below, p. 279, n. 30].

[97] These masters, whether their interest lay in natural science or in letters, were also very aware of the limitations of the arts and crafts in comparison to achievements of nature. Cf. Paré, pp. 65–68, on Jean de Meun.

ucate them (*ars* as *disciplina*). There was thus a double contest, a contest quickly couched in Christian terms, whether those of Genesis or those of Pauline mysticism, which equally assume a sinful world that man can no longer easily govern. Nature entered actively into history. The other branch of ambivalent Platonism also became actively influential, though after some serious modifications. Augustine had tied procreation, Nature's great work, to original sin and had said nothing of Nature's other works.

In isolating the influences behind the gradual emergence of the idea of nature, I have deliberately confined the discussion to the external reach of these doctrinal and spiritual tides in the twelfth century; but the same influences exerted continual, spontaneous, and healthy pressure upon men's "interior life." For the intellectual and technological enterprise trained upon the macrocosm called forth an interior life in the microcosm in the name of its very nature too. St. Bernard was scarcely aware of the parallelism, but William of Saint-Thierry understood how to make the Cistercian grace by which he had been touched benefit from an anthropology enriched not merely by Augustine but by the Greeks' sense of the cosmos; and his *Physica animae*,[98] a treatise on the image of God in man, went beyond advocacy of self-knowledge to an investigation, as its title suggests, of the "physics" of the soul as discussed by natural philosophers and doctors of the church, principally Gregory of Nyssa, whose *De hominis opificio* had been translated by John the Scot.

Such blending of diverse elements made for unstable compounds but very significant ones. More and more of it took place; and with the appearance of Avicenna at the end of the century a new element was introduced which, for a brief time, looked as if it might be capable of synthesizing the influences stemming from pseudo-Dionysius and John the Scot, from Augustine, and from Aristotle.[99] Significant blending of diverse elements—not only the combination of heterogeneous source materials, not only the continuing interaction among contrasting currents of thought, but an interior and authentically

---

[98] Forms the second part of his *De natura corporis et animae* (*PL*, CLXXX, 695– 726).

[99] Cf., for example, the tentative synthesis afforded by the *Liber de causis primis et secundis*. [See below, "The Platonisms of the Twelfth Century," pp. 53 and 89ff.]

Christian union between two such disparate values as those entailed in the discovery of nature on the one hand and contempt for the world on the other. The tension between these two not only defined the state of the Christian in the world but also dominated his theological labors and his personal life. Inevitably and quite normally this tension led to different choices and emphases in theological reflection, in spirituality, and apostolic enterprise. Time and again, one can be sure, Cîteaux would oppose the masters of Chartres publicly, and the *Porretani* would point accusingly at the weaknesses of the Augustinian Peter Lombard. When he was not under the spell of the myth of nature, Alan of Lille himself pronounced the formulas of Augustine on original sin. He found man's nature insufficient by itself to provide a definition of man either in his existence or in his conduct; human nature is rooted in historical conditions (historical states, Augustine called them), and these a philosophy of essences ended up ignoring; for, ignorant of history, it could not deduce them from nature.

Every "philosophy of the world" (think of William of Conches' *Philosophia mundi*) aims legitimately to comprehend the whole of its object; and it would be a mistake and a blunder to preserve some zone of mystery, some sanctuary for the sacred, to the detriment of such a philosophy and for the pretended benefit of the religious soul. All of nature belongs to secular science, but all of nature is sacred as well. It is merely one's perspective that changes, and science and mysticism ought naturally to complement one another. The exaltation of Nature meant, it is true, putting an end to one particularly Christian conception of the universe, just as the ideological and political struggle against the Holy Roman Empire meant putting an end to one peculiar form of Christendom.[100] The years of the twelfth century saw just such a two-pronged operation (actually one operation was under the surface); and John of Salisbury, for all his violent partisanship of Thomas Becket, stood like a preamble to the whole proc-

---

[100] [For the work of twelfth-century lawyers and the growing conception of the natural foundations of independent sovereign political communities, see G. Post, "The Naturalness of Society and the State," chap. 11, *Studies in Medieval Legal Thought* (Princeton, 1964), pp. 494–561. Cf. B. Tierney, "*Natura Id Est Deus:* A Case of Juristic Pantheism?" *Journal of the History of Ideas*, XXIV (1963), 307–22.]

ess. Laicism and scientism afflicted those years like a malignant fever; but it proved in the end to be benign, and its crisis signaled growth. Christ remained on the portal of Chartres as the savior of his creation.

Theology, too, benefited by the crisis, for its rational character was strengthened within the very framework of its guiding faith. It was none other than Alan of Lille, that advocate for Nature, who elaborated the theoretical "rules for theology," that is, who defined the method according to which faith-knowledge, like any other intellectual discipline, was organized and built upon internal principles which gave it a scientific turn and value.[101] Alan did not regard reason as opposed to faith any more than he regarded secular as opposed to sacred; he distinguished between them, but only to unite them. "We have to do with diverse, not adverse, things," Alan made Dame Nature say in her concern to maintain the supreme dignity of Lady Theology.[102] Certain "spirituals" would become worried about such confidence in reason; the century of Albert the Great, of Bonaventure, and of Thomas Aquinas would prove them wrong.

Thus we see that without any weakening of the contempt for the world exercised at Cîteaux or of the monastic theology that supported it, and without the benefit of any genius to give final expression or complete balance to the new ideas, the twelfth century featured an essentially religious discovery of the universe through a discovery of Nature—Nature which, as the earthy and impious Jean de Meun puts it, is "God's chambermaid." And Alan of Lille, one notes, was to end his days at Cîteaux—at the very moment that St. Dominic relieved the faltering Cistercians by taking pastoral charge of a new civilization, which Thomas Aquinas was to portray theologically and humanly.

---

[101] *Regulae theologicae* (*PL*, CCX, 622–84).

[102] *De planctu Naturae* (*PL*, CCX, 446): "Nec mirum si in his theologia suam mihi familiaritatem non exhibet, quoniam in plerisque non adversa sed diversa sentimus. Ego ratione fidem, illa fide comparat rationem; ego scio ut credam, illa credit ut sciat; ego consentio sciens, illa sentit consentiens; . . ." (It is not odd that Theology does not exhibit any kinship to me in these matters, since for the most part we have to do with diverse, not adverse things. I supply faith with reason, she furnishes reason with faith; I know in order that I may believe, she believes in order that she may know; I consent when I know, she knows when she consents.)

2

The Platonisms of the Twelfth Century

PERHAPS ONE COULD measure the power of a mind by observing the varied systems of thought which its own intellectual constructions have more or less directly inspired in the course of history. Aristotle inspired Themistius, Averroes, and Thomas Aquinas; Descartes inspired Malebranche and Comte; Hegel nurtured Marx and Croce; in theology, Augustine was authentically represented in the quite different thought of Bonaventure and Thomas and compromised in that of Jansenius. That one man's thought should bring forth such varied progeny will seem less paradoxical if one reflects that master-insights never find complete expression in a single conceptual system and consequently they lend themselves readily to further adaptation, even to frank distortion that nonetheless preserves an undeniable kinship with the original.

Plato affords the major instance of this phenomenon, and historians have some difficulty in sorting out the currents of thought traceable to him. These Neoplatonisms that recur century after century comprise a family with little coherence, despite the profound perceptions radically common to them all.

Precisely in the area of Plato's influence, the twelfth century furnished a spectacle of the clearest debt yet with the most tangled lines of descent; an undeniable core of common perceptions did not inhibit a certain amount of picking and choosing, and the resulting systems of thought represented incompatible and bewildering syncretisms. Moreover, with religious values, themselves highly diverse, intruding into these syncretisms as they already had into the Platonism of ancient times, it becomes impossible to lay out a complete intellectual map of the developments. Alan of Lille, disciple of Gilbert of La Porrée, took intellectual nourishment from the *Timaeus* and from Proclus at the same time, but finished his days as a Cistercian and a spiritual son of St. Bernard. The course of his life encountered several "conversions." From the thought of Hugh of Saint-Victor to the tightly articulated system of Thomas Aquinas, the Neoplatonism borrowed from Augustine remained incompatible with that taken from pseudo-Dionsysius, and even more incompatible with that of Avicenna, despite the ingenious attempt of Duns Scotus to combine them.

Two characteristics were common to the thinkers of this time. In the first place, all of them must be linked with the family of those whom historians have called Neoplatonists. To be sure the *Timaeus* provided the strong nourishment of Plato's own text for certain of these thinkers—those of Chartres; but even these men, whether by recourse to Macrobius or by recourse to the synthesis of Aristotle and Plato propounded by Boethius, encountered Plato's thought in different contexts. The resulting distortion is the more evident since apart from the *Timaeus* and a few other fragments, as we have seen, the Plato of history, the Plato of the *Symposium* and the *Laws*, of the Good (*Republic* vi), and of the One (*Parmenides*) remained unknown throughout the century. For the most part Platonic tradition came to these men from authors of the late empire and above all from the doctors of the church.

Derivation from Christian sources greatly strengthened the second principal trait of this Neoplatonism—its religious orientation, which among non-Christians had taken the form of theurgy. Indeed, the principal reason for the innate prestige which all forms of Platonism enjoyed among Christians was their capacity for expressing religious values of moral thought and action, even those proper to the Christian religion. Testimony to this capacity had been given—and continued to be given in the twelfth century—by Augustine's confession of faith under the spell of the Platonists and by the affinities, spontaneous or cultivated, between mystics and pseudo-Dionysius.[1]

---

[1] Plato's prestige was everywhere paramount in the twelfth century: Adelard of Bath *De eodem et diverso* (Willner, p. 4) and John of Salisbury *Policraticus* vii.6 (Webb, II, 111; Pike, p. 233) called him the *princeps*

These two characteristics can be seen in certain governing ideas that recurred in twelfth-century teachings, or rather in intuitions that were commonly accepted and that underlay all ultimately divergent elaborations of thought. One can find these ideas, these intuitions, everywhere—from Chartres to Cîteaux, from Toledo to the schools of Paris, not to mention Byzantium—in commentaries upon pseudo-Dionysius and in expositions of the *Timaeus*. They include the opposition between the intelligible and the sense-perceptible worlds; the transcendence of the Demiurge as creator; the presence of that Demiurge in all reality, in its very being; man's progressive assimilation to God as his goal, as the summit of human activity; and in written discourse, the image of light everywhere zealously employed,

---

philosophorum (prince of philosophers); John praised his doctrine, *ibid.* vii.5 (Webb, II, 104–11; Pike, pp. 227–33), though he also admitted that Aristotle *nomen philosophi pre ceteris meruerit* (merited the title of philosopher before all others), *Metal.* iv.7 (Webb, p. 171; McGarry, p. 213)—the admission signals a new era as the full penetration of Aristotle begins; Abelard *Theologia christiana* i (*PL*, CLXXVIII, 1144A) called him *ille maximus philosophorum Plato* (Plato, that greatest of philosophers) and in *Dialectica* pars i, lib. 2 (V. Cousin, ed. *Ouvrages inédits d'Abélard* [Paris, 1936], pp. 205–6) that *primum totius philosophiae ducem* (supreme commander of all philosophy); Isaac of L'Etoile *Sermones* 24 (*PL*, CXCIV, 1679C) exalted him as *magnus ille gentium theologus* (that great theologian of the gentiles). At Cîteaux, however, Plato, like Aristotle, was slighted by the anti-philosophical spirit; cf. St. Bernard *In festo Apost. Petri* sermo i, 3 (*PL*, XLXXXIII, 407): "Quid ergo docuerunt vel docent nos apostoli sancti? Non piscatoriam artem. . . , non Platonem legere, non Aristotelis versutias inversare." (What, then, did the holy apostles teach us? Not the art of fishing. . . , not to study Plato, not to turn Aristotle's subtleties inside out.) Richard of Cluny, in his *Chronica*, circulated the legend that Plato's body had been found in a tomb and bore on its breast a golden tablet inscribed, "I believe in the Christ who will be born of a virgin"; the legend is referred to by Martin Polonus (*MGH, Scriptores,* XXII, 461), by Roger Bacon *Metaphysica, sive de viciis contractis in studio theologiae* (ed. Robert Steele [Oxford, 1905], p. 9) and by St. Thomas *Summa theol.* IIª IIᵃᵉ, q.2, a.8, ad 3 (Aquinas, *Opera omnia*, III, 15; Aquinas, *Summa*, IX, 45). The title "theologian" had commonly been given to Plato by Christian writers, as in the letter of Theodoric (=Cassiodorus) to Boethius: *Plato theologus, Aristoteles logicus* (Plato the theologian, Aristotle the logician)—a division of titles disputed in the last third of the century upon the discovery of the *Liber de causis*, attributed to Aristotle [see below, n.66]. Cf. C. Baeumker, "Der Platonismus im Mittelalter," in *Studien und Characteristiken zur Geschichte der Philosophie insbesondere des Mittelalters* (*BGPM*, XXV, 1–2), p. 147. On Christian Neoplatonism as a whole—its content, tendencies, variants—see R. Arnou, "Platonisme des Pères" *DTC*, XII, 2258–2392.

as well by mathematicians as by men of literary bent.[2] To these one must add the constant effort demanded by Christian orthodoxy against two problematic themes found in all Neoplatonisms: the need to limit the role accorded to beings intermediary between God and man, and the need to affirm the absolute character of creation as against the alleged eternity of matter.

It will be necessary to survey the common reactions to the latter two problematic themes—reactions traditional in Christian ambiance but now expressly elaborated—before turning our attention to particular characteristics of each of the several currents of Platonism as revealed in highly significant stages of their influence. For, as Gilson has observed, "All forms of Platonism are closely related to each other. Exchanges between distinct currents are not rare, but to distinguish these currents from one another would be a step forward."[3]

Common Christian Reactions to Neoplatonism

First of all, there was the rejection of intermediary beings—not of the *logoi*, spirits, and powers of middle Platonism unknown to men of the Middle Ages, nor of the *logos* as conceived by Origen,

---

[2] The image of light was far more than a literary figure; it was the consistent effect of the metaphysics of emanation, which saw not only intelligences but nature itself as filled with the light of the supreme and motionless One and as becoming assimilated to the One through conscious or unconscious contemplation of it. Whether in St. Augustine or pseudo-Dionysius, in Alexandrian theology or the liturgy, one of the best established commonplaces of Christian thought is the connection seen between such "light" and Biblical uses of the image, all the way from religious exaltation of the sun in the Old Testament to the concept of the Logos, light of men. The entire stock of such commonplaces was common during the Middle Ages. Cf. R. Bultmann, "Zur Geschichte der Lichtsymbolik im Altertum," *Philologus*, XCVII (1948), 1–36; F. J. Doelger, *Sol salutis: Gebet und Gesang im christliche Altertum* (Münster, 1925); O. Semmelroth, "Gottes ausstrahlendes Licht: zur Schoepfungs- und Offenbarungslehre des Ps.-Dionysius Areopagita," *Schol.*, XXVIII (1953), 481–503.

[3] Etienne Gilson, *La philosophie au moyen age* (Paris, 1944), p. 380. It is both such distinctions and such shared exchanges that I should like to observe here, rather within the twelfth century than in the original constitution of the different Platonisms. Cf. M. de Gandillac, "Le platonisme au XIIe-XIIIe siècle," Association Guillaume Budé: Congrès de Tours et Poitiers (*3–9 septembre 1953*) (Paris, 1954).

but of those ranks of beings found in Plotinus. Once men became caught up in the dialectic between the One and the many and conceived of the One as an inviolable and unchanging absolute, they could only envisage the relationship between these as a graded emanation in which both immediate creation and, in the other direction, man's immediate assimilation to God were compromised. What had happened in Plotinus happened again in the twelfth century, especially when some contamination from Hermetic writings or influences from Muslim philosophy were also present.

The pseudo-Dionysian "hierarchy," given the prestige of its author, provided an even more dangerous temptation. But as a safeguard against possible heterodoxy here, it sufficed to bring forward the interpretation already advanced by John the Scot; namely, that the "hierarchy" did not involve a hierarchy of beings but a multiplication of "formative" activities. By the 1140's commentary on the famous definition of "hierarchy" (*Hier. cael.* iii) had been fixed in an impeccably orthodox and classic manner by Hugh of Saint-Victor.[4] There was no more problem.

Platonic emanationism as filtered through Muslim philosophy called forth a more energetic resistance. Had not Gundissalinus yielded to it in his *De unitate?*[5] The *Liber de causis primis et secundis* (*Book concerning the First and Second Causes*) was soon to adopt the Avicennian version of emanation without sufficiently critical dis-

---

[4] *Expos. in Hier. Cael.* iv (*PL*, CLXXV, 992). From the outset, the characteristically pseudo-Dionysian concept of *formatio* (formation) enters into the commentary and is invested, moreover, with an Augustinian sense typical of Hugh. Cf. *ibid.* ii ad init. (*PL*, CLXXV, 937): "Propter hoc ergo unum lumen in multa se lumina participatione profundit, ut multos illuminatos ad unum lumen reformaret, ut dum illud participando multi acciperent, in illius forma omnes unum apparent." (Hence, therefore, the one Light, through participation, shed itself upon the many in order that it might reform the many, so illuminated, towards the one Light; so that the many, while receiving that Light through participation, might all appear one in its form.) Here one sees a fidelity to the original doctrine of pseudo-Dionysius. Cf. R. Roques, *L'univers dionysien* (Paris, 1954), Chap. 3, "L'activité hiérarchique."

[5] "Prima enim et vera unitas, quae est unitas sibi ipsi, creavit aliam unitatem, quae esset infra eam." (For the first and true Unity, which is Unity in and of itself, created a second unity below itself.) P. Correns, ed., *Die dem Boethius falschlich zugeschriebene Abhandlung des Dominicus Gundissalinus De Unitate* (*BGPM*, I, 1), p.5.

crimination.[6] Alan of Lille, like the writer of the *Liber xxiv philosoph-orum* (*The Book of the Twenty-four Philosophers*), placed at the head of his *Regulae caelestis iuris* (*Rules of the Celestial Law*) axioms concerning the supreme Monad. "Unity brings forth unity from itself," he wrote, doubtless influenced by the Hermetic terminology then current. But he immediately sidestepped emanationist implications. First, he imitated the accommodation to the Trinity formerly made by the doctors of the church: "The Father (*Unitas*) brings forth the Son in equality (*aequalitas*)"; from this idea Alan developed, with fine metaphysico-mathematical fulness, his resources for explaining the dogma, drawing upon an Augustinian formula as he did so.[7] Second, he analyzed the movement from the One to the many, basing his analysis upon the difference between *alteritas* (twoness), in which movement and a certain changeableness were present (case of the angels), and *pluralitas* (manifoldness), in which every sort of multiplicity was present (case of the terrestrial beings).[8]

---

[6] The text is edited by R. de Vaux, *Notes et textes sur l'avicennisme latin aux confins des XII–XIII⁰ siècles* (Paris, 1934); see esp. chap. 4, "Quod primum causatum est intelligentiam" (That Intelligence is the first caused), pp. 97–102.

[7] "Unitas de se gignit unitatem, de se profert aequalitatem. Sic Deus a nullo, quilibet ab ipso; sic gignit alterum se, idest Filium; de se profert aequalem sibi, idest Spiritum Sanctum." (Unity begets unity from itself, from itself produces equality. So God exists from nothing, and each person exists from him; so he begets a second self, that is, the Son; and from himself he produces one equal with himself, that is, the Holy Spirit.) *Regulae caelestis iuris* reg. i (*PL*, CCX, 623 [on correction of the title of this work from *Regulae theologicae*, see M.-Th. d'Alverny, *Alain de Lille* (Paris, 1965), pp. 66–68]). Cf. reg. iv (*PL*, CCX, 625): "In Patre Unitas, in Filio Aequalitas, in Spiritu Sancto Unitatis Aequalitatisque connexio." (In the Father is Unity, in the Son Equality, in the Holy Spirit the bond of Unity and Equality.) Except for the concluding word, the statement is taken from St. Augustine *De doctr. christ.* i, 5 (*PL*, XXXIV, 21). We have here another instance of the formulae and the reasoning used at Chartres to explain temporal evolution in terms reflecting the eternal production of the first Unity: emanating beings exist and acquire their form, their *aequalitatas essendi*, in a fashion modeled after the divine Wisdom, the Word, the *aequalitas Unitatis*. St. Augustine's account of appropriation within the Trinity here found an unexpected adaptation to the cosmos, one which shocked William of Saint Thierry; cf. his letter to St. Bernard against William of Conches (*PL*, CLXXX, 333–40, and Parent, pp. 55 and 76–78).

[8] *Reg. cael. iur.* reg ii (*PL*, CCX, 624): "In supercaelesti unitas, in caelesti alteritas, in subcaelesti pluralitas. . . . Caeleste est angelus, in quo primo est

Here, under the Boethian vocabulary, one recognizes the emanation of the First Intelligence, which had within itself a principle of division, since on the one hand it was an intellectual nature participating in a certain way in God's necessity through knowledge of Him, and on the other hand it was a created nature and therefore, in itself, only a "possible" being. The theory of the First Hypostasis (Plotinus *De causis*; later taken up by Avicenna) was here Christianized with little cost.

On this point all twelfth-century authors benefited by St. Augustine's own vigorous reaction, which was not only protective of orthodoxy but derivative from a spiritual life dominated by ineffable intimacy between God and the soul. This intimacy would have been jeopardized by any intermediary whatever, above all by a cosmic intermediary. The immediate vision of God was the sole object of Augustine's hope. Cistercians, Carthusians, Victorines, all shared and felt even more intensely this unrelenting and holy demand of their common master.

The problem of the creation of matter was no less crucial for Christians than the immediacy of man's relationship to God; at the same time it lay closer to the heart of the Platonic system and its radical obscurities. The ancient commentaries, from Chalcidius through the Hermetic writers, had all run afoul of the ambiguous *hyle*, or primordial matter; and medieval thinkers had the same difficulty, intensified by the rigorous inquiries constantly made into their orthodoxy.[9] They countered with an explicit answer to the

---

alteritas, quia est primus a Deo creatus, et primus post Deum mutabilis factus; hic tamen non tantam dicitur habere varietatem, quantam habet subcaeleste. Unde quia alteritas prima est pluralitas, in eo non dicitur esse pluralitas, sed sola alteritas." (In the supercelestial is Unity; in the celestial, twoness; in the subcelestial, manifoldness. . . . Celestial being is the angel, in whom twoness is first to be found, because it was the first being created by God and, after God, was the first being made subject to change, though it has less variety than the subcelestial order. For this reason, it is only twoness and not manifoldness that is predicated of the angel, though twoness is the first order of manifoldness.)

[9] Adelard of Bath speaks of the difficulty experienced by his contemporaries; cf. *Quaestiones naturales* (Müller, p. 69): "In hac enim difficultate tractandi de deo, de noy, de yle, de simplicibus formis, de puris elementis disserendum est, quae sicut simplicitate propria naturam compositorum excesserunt, ita et

weighty problem imposed on them by the system, but not without laborious and revealing efforts.

The system as it reached them had been stylized and took no account of divergent forms of Platonism; it proposed three coeternal principles to explain the origin of the world—God, matter, ideas. Apart from the identification of the Demiurge (*Opifex*) with God, this was authentically the Plato of the *Timaeus*, free of the Plotinian conception of the One. With this proposition there was categorical disagreement. "On this point our authors differ from the philosophers," Hugh of Saint-Victor declared, "namely, the philosophers claim that God is only an *opifex*, a shaping agent, and that there are three ultimate principles—God, matter, and archetypal ideas; our authors, on the other hand, claim that there is but one ultimate principle, and that this is God alone."[10] About the same time, Hugh of Rouen observed: "There were men . . . who said that there are three coeternal things—God, matter, and all forms—and they thought that God was not the creator but only a shaper who had by no means created either matter or the forms but merely knew how to join and fit them to one another."[11] Peter Lombard settled Plato's case for the following centuries when he wrote: "Moses says that the world was made by God as creator, and he avoided the error of certain men who supposed that many first principles existed without a first principle. For Plato thought there were three sources of things, namely God, an exemplar, and matter, with matter being

---

de eis disputatio alias omnes dissertationes et intellectus subtilitate et sermonis difficultate praecellit." (In this difficulty of treating God, noys, hyle, and simple forms, one must discuss pure elements; and, as these in their native simplicity lie beyond the nature of composites, so too does disputation concerning them reach beyond all other discussions and understandings in subtlety and difficulty of discourse.)

[10] *Expos. in Heptateuchon* iv. (*PL*, CLXXV, 33): "In hoc differunt auctores nostri a philosophis, quod philosophi Deum opificem tantum, et tria ponunt principia: Deum, materiam, et archetypas ideas; nostri vero unicum ponunt principium, et hoc Deum solum."

[11] *Tract. in Hexameron* i, 10 (*PL*, CXCII, 1251): "Fuerunt homines . . . tria esse coaeterna dicentes, Deum scilicet, atque materiam, et formas omnes, Deum non creatorem sed opificem aestimantes, qui materiam et formas minime creasset, sed conjungere nosset et simul aptare potuisset." The whole paragraph in the source should be read.

uncreated and without beginning, and God a sort of artisan, not a creator."[12]

Alan of Lille reacted with more spirit: "Obsessed by this madness, Plato declared that some sort of disordered matter existed before the beginning of the world." Alan denounced "certain modern authors" who claimed that primordial matter, although proceeding from God, exists eternally.[13] Abelard had already rebuked a contemporary theologian for asserting that, temporally speaking, God did not exist before the world.[14]

Thus, in the midst of the Christian Middle Ages we find again that historic controversy provoked throughout the course of earlier Platonizing centuries by *Timaeus* 28b[15]—a passage that, taken together with its entire context, tends to view matter as a principle separate from the action of the Demiurge and in consequence eternal. Galen and Proclus, for example, held that the material world had a cause, but not an origin in time. Philopon had opposed Simplicius on the point. At Chartres, clearly, men were aware of the problem. Bernard and Thierry of Chartres rejected the proposition that matter is coeternal with God. William of Conches, in his commentaries on the *Timaeus* and on *The Consolation of Philosophy*, presented a remarkable analysis of the various modes of duration and, at the end of a cautious examination of Plato, proposed to ex-

---

[12] *Quatuor libri sententiarum* ii, d. 1, c. 1 (*PL*, CXCII, 651): "Moyses . . . a Deo creatore mundum factum refert, elidens errorem quorundam plura sine principio fuisse principia opinantium. Plato namque tria initia existimavit, Deum scilicet, exemplar, et materiam, et ipsam increatam sine principio, et Deum quasi artificem non creatorem."

[13] *Summa 'Quoniam homines'* (Glorieux, pp. 128–9): "Item qua insania ductus Plato asseruit quandam inordinatam materiam mundi prevenisse exordium."

[14] *Theol. christ.* iv. (*PL*, CLXXVIII, 1286).

[15] ["Now everything that becomes or is created must of necessity be created by some cause, for without a cause nothing can be created. . . .Was the heaven then or the world . . . always in existence and without beginning? or created, and had it a beginning? Created, I reply. . . . But the father and maker of all this universe is past finding out; and even if we found him, to tell of him to all men would be impossible. And there is still a question to be asked about him: Which of the patterns had the artificer in view when he made the world —the pattern of the unchangeable, or of that which is created?" B. A. Jowett, tr., *The Dialogues of Plato* (New York, 1937), II, 12–13.]

culpate him from the errors commonly charged against him, by applying to the problem of the eternity of matter Boethius' distinction between "perpetuity," which belonged to the material world, and "eternity," which was reserved to God.[16] In so doing, he was running counter to Chalcidius, the established commentator on the *Timaeus,* who even at Chartres was the determining influence upon the exegesis of several masters and had led them to accept the idea that matter is both created and eternal at the same time.[17] The author of an anonymous gloss on *The Consolation,* for example, wrote: "The term 'eternal' applies to things existing before time, with time, and after time; that is, to things which never had a beginning and will not have an end; of this sort are God, father and ἀγαθόν; the νοῦς or mind; and that matter from which the world was made. . . . According to the philosophers, the world is eternal in its matter but perpetual in its form."[18] Among these masters we should perhaps include Bernard Sylvester; in his *De mundi universitate* he was silent about the creation of matter in a context which would otherwise have called for explicit mention of the point, doubtless because he

---

[16] Cf. Boethius *De cons. phil.* v. pr. 6 (Peiper, pp. 139, 141) and, for the vocabulary, Proclus *In Tim.* (Diehl, III, 1–3). A nice instance of the operation of Platonic sources and the interplay of diverse systems is provided here: (1) The *Timaeus*—William handles his exegesis adroitly; his method is to preserve Plato's point of view while giving it a favorable interpretation in which, by using subtle distinctions (e.g., creation not *in tempore* but *cum tempore*), William denies the actuality of imaginary time antecedent to creation; (2) *Boethius*—whereas Boethius saw Plato favoring the eternity of the world, the scholars of Chartres took advantage of the distinction between *eternitas* and *perpetuitas* which Boethius had borrowed from Proclus and which had become decidedly classic; (3) *Augustine*—ultimately, Augustine's biblicist emphasis upon the historical order took precedence over the Greek unconcern for time and was placed in an ideological and technical framework taken from the Platonism of Boethius.

[17] Chalcidius *Comm. in Timaeum* xxiii (Mullach, p. 185): "Et mundus sensibilis opus Dei. Origo igitur ejus causativa, non temporaria. Sic mundus sensibilis, licet corporeus, a Deo tamen factus atque institutus, aeternus est." (The world is God's work in the sensual order. Its origin is thus causative, but not temporal. The sensual world, although physical and made and instituted by God, is eternal.) Cf. Boethius *De cons. phil.* v, pr. 6.

[18] "Eterna vero dicuntur ante tempus et cum tempore et post tempora, idest que nunquam habuerunt principium nec finem habebunt, sicut Deus pater tagaton, et noys idest mens, et materia illa unde factus est mundus. . . . Mundus autem dicitur eternus secundum philosophos quantum ad materiam, perpetuus vero quanto ad formam." (Quoted in Parent, p. 98, n.1.)

judged the eternity of matter consistent with its having been created.[19]

In his own way John of Salisbury testified to these instances of audacity; after setting forth the position of his master, Bernard of Chartres, "the most perfect Platonist among all the Platonists of our age," in favor of the creation of matter *ex nihilo* as Augustine had taught, he let it be known that there were others who accepted the existence of matter *ab aeterno*.[20] Perhaps these others also admitted that matter, like ideas, was *ab aeterno* but not "eternal" in the sense of possessing immutable life in its fulness.[21]

Underlying the verbal subtlety at work here was a valid intellectual inquiry. Aimed at bridging the chasm that separated Greek thought from the biblical mentality, St. Thomas, as is known, made the same effort with means other than those used by the masters of Chartres, but not without the same active opposition from his peers. For the Greeks, the problem of the origin of things was posed in terms of a dualism between matter and idea: idea or form organized primitive chaos into a cosmos; time played no part in this organizing activity as such. For the Hebrews, for Old Testament metaphysics, if one may so call it, the world was not envisaged as an analogue of a work of manual art; the problem of the relations between form

---

[19] On these positions, tendencies, and variations among the scholars of Chartres, see, together with primary texts there cited, Parent, pp. 40–43 ("La création de la matière par Dieu") and chap. 6 "Création et temps," esp. pp. 99–106. [On Bernard Sylvester in particular, see above, p. 30, n. 64.]

[20] *Metalogicon* iv. 35 (Webb, pp. 204–7; McGarry, pp. 258–61).

[21] *Ibid.* (Webb, p. 207; McGarry, p. 261): "Quidam tamen, licet ab eterno concedant esse vera, ea tamen negant esse eterna, dicentes nichil esse eternum, nisi quod vivit, eo quod eternitas, teste Augustino, status est interminabilis vite." (Others, however, though they admit that things 'from the eternal' are true, will not call them 'eternal,' for they say that nothing is eternal except that which lives, since eternity, as Augustine declares, is a state of interminable life.) Bernard [following John the Scot] called the ideas eternal but not *co*-eternal with God; *ibid.* (Webb, p. 206; McGarry, p. 260): "Ideam vero, quia ad hanc parilitatem non consurgit, sed quodammodo natura posterior est et velut quidam effectus, manens in archano consilii, extrinseca causa non indigens, sicut eternam audebat dicere, sic coeternam esse negabat." (The 'idea,' however—because it does not attain such parity [as exists among persons of the Trinity] but is somehow a posterior nature and like an effect that resides within the divine mind without needing an extrinsic cause—he dared to call eternal but denied that it was coeternal.)

and matter did not arise; the notions of cosmos and of nature were missing. Creation was not a making, a fabricating, nor was it the blazing forth of the ideal One in the material many; creation implied the passage of time. The Hebrew concept of becoming, precisely the opposite of the Greek concept of becoming, required the coexistence of time and eternity. The creator had need of nothing, and he alone stood eternal in his complete self-sufficiency; but the divine eternity did not do away with time any more than time did away with the truth of things. It ran counter to the biblical sense of history when thirteenth-century metaphysicians separated time from creation in order to admit the possibility of a creation *ab aeterno*. It also ran counter to the biblical sense of history when John of Salisbury warmly accepted, almost with religious fervor, the Platonic and Augustinian view that only eternal realities were true and truly were —those realities, namely, which were "untroubled by invasion or passion or injury to their power or by the passage of time, but which ever persevere in the vigor proper to their condition."[22] The ambiguity of Bernard Sylvester's *De mundi universitate* came from the same opposition, and his Platonic rationalization of the book of Genesis was a paradoxical undertaking even though theologically legitimate.[23] Outside Chartres, all the masters of the twelfth century held to the historical reality of creation as essential to creation *ex nihilo*, including the creation of matter.

The Enduring Influence of Augustine's Platonism

In order to lay bare the hidden contours of the evolution of theology in the twelfth century, we must not only be alert to the various kinds of Platonism, all highly volatile and constantly emerging at this time; we must be no less aware of the enduring influence of Augustine's Platonism as the common ingredient of all these syncretistic forms. Such was the force of his prestige that it did not

---

[22] ". . . que nec incursionum passionumve molestiam metuunt, non potestatis injuriam, non dispendium temporis, sed semper vigore condicionis sue eadem perseverant." *Metalogicon* iv. 35 (Webb, p. 204; McGarry, p. 258).

[23] Gilson [see ref. cited above, p. 30, n. 64] stresses the basic Christianity that underlies the paganism of the work's form. [Cf. Parent, pp. 16–17.]

enter the mind of any of the masters or the "spirituals" of this century, as it did the minds of men in the thirteenth century, to discriminate within the thought of this Christian doctor between things original with him and those deriving from the direct influence of pagan philosophers, and therefore allowing room for questioning. Thus, what has earlier been said of Augustine's religious prestige is equally true of his philosophic prestige. It was only when the followers of Gilbert of La Porrée undertook a critique of the theory of ideas in the second half of the century that the way was prepared for such discrimination. Alan of Lille, in order to relieve Augustine of any discreditable subservience to Plato, proposed that there are five ways of speaking which are not all equally employed in one's references to another's thought.[24]

To be sure, the influence of Augustine was very unevenly distributed. Peter Lombard retained only vague, general perspectives from the "philosophy" of his master, whereas the *De causis primis et secundis* expressly and systematically integrated fundamental ideas from Augustine into its Avicennian synthesis. St. Bernard, imbued as he was with Augustinian thought, allowed its outlines and even its vocabulary to become blurred by his own personal experience, whereas William of Saint-Thierry preserved the features of Augustinian thought more carefully, even when making the most original adaptations of it. Almost universally, except among the followers of Gilbert of La Porrée, there was an unconscious absorption of Augustine's Platonism, which bound together the most incompatible pseudo-Dionysian and Augustinian elements, to the enrichment of the latter. The *causae primordiales* (primordial causes) of pseudo-Dionysius, lifted from context, were bracketed with Augustine's *rationes aeternae* (eternal ideas), as John the Scot had wanted them to be. The cosmic symbols of pseudo-Dionysius were mixed in with the imagery of the African rhetorician. Bernard Sylvester wove together texts from Augustine's works on Genesis and texts from the *Timaeus*. It was only toward the end of the century that, without always admitting it, theologians who had grown increasingly sensitive to intellectual techniques and structures and to ways of stating

---

[24] Glorieux, p. 129.

problems were driven to perceive certain incompatibilities between aspects of Greek thought and of Augustine's Latin mentality.

The wide acceptance of Augustine's philosophical vocabulary was likewise a matter of note. In varying degrees, as their individual cast of mind and the work upon which they were engaged suggested, writers of the twelfth century employed such Augustinian terms as *mundus intelligibilis* (the intelligible world), *rationes aeternae* (eternal ideas), *mens* (mind, with all the profundity Augustine attached to this term), or *formatio* (formation) to convey the dialectic at work in the genesis of beings as well as in the laws governing man's mind and his knowledge of God. The very term *philosophia*, whether in Abelard or St. Bernard, retained the comprehensive extension to all of Christian wisdom which Augustine had given it—this, despite different emphases attending its use and despite the already detectable tendency to secularize it.[25]

The philosophical themes of Augustine's Platonism, which constituted the common property of theologians in this period, are readily recognizable in their syncretistic writings: all things comprised an order (totally different from the pseudo-Dionysian "hierarchy")[26]; the key to this order was at once the distinction and the intimate relationship between the intelligible and the sense-perceptible worlds into which the universe was divided. True reality belonged to the intelligible world, which alone was unchanging and which alone, therefore, was true. (Thus, both nominalists and realists could claim dependence upon Augustine.) God, author of this universe and this order, was the source of all reality and of all truth; as such he was transcendent, and it was his very transcendence which underlay his omnipresence. Man was composed of a body and a soul, and through these he entered into the two worlds. The soul, in itself, was one, substantial, reasonable, and individual, even when it was ruling a body. (This definition prevailed throughout medieval philosophy, despite the success of Aristotelianism.) Man's dualism had implications for the ways and means by which he knew; the soul had two

---

[25] Thus the term *philosophi*, in contradistinction to *philosophia*, designated the pagan philosophers.

[26] See below, pp. 79–88.

faces, one turned toward the intelligible world, the other toward the
sense-perceptible world. (Christian experience continued to favor
the Augustinian theory of knowledge over Aristotelian "novelties.")
Cultivation of the interior life was the supreme goal of man's perfection and happiness, even if physical existence thereby became
enigmatic, and even if man's openness to society and nature were
thereby compromised. Evil was rooted in the original nonbeing of
the creature; only the unchangeable Being was true and good;
change, or becoming, was a defect in truth and in goodness; this
was equally true of man, for whom such evil in his will became sin.

Although Augustine came to Platonism through Plotinus, he did
not organize the Platonic elements of his thought around speculation upon the One but around the theory of ideas. Though these
ideas were unified in God, in the word of God, and though he expressly identified oneness and being, Augustine's metaphysical preference in this tie between the One and the ideas to which all thinkers
held[27] was less a philosophical choice than an expression of his personal religious temperament—a temperament ultimately at variance
with another type of mind and temperament, equally Platonic, but
attracted rather to the mysticism of the One. Pseudo-Dionysius and
his followers implicated the cosmos in the special dialectic by which
man achieved ecstasy beyond the intelligible order; but Augustine,
attracted by the Christian emphasis upon man's inner life, abandoned
Plotinus at this point and reversed the process of ascent toward God,
whom he himself was to find in the intimate depths of his own mind
as it became freed from the scattered condition native to creatures
and from the anguish of becoming. For Augustine, *mens* (mind)
was not the Greek νοῦς of the *Timaeus* or of pseudo-Dionysius.

---

[27] Not until after the surge of Neoplatonism in the middle of the twelfth
century did the scholars of Chartres become concerned with the relationship
of the ontology of the One and of Being. For a later exploration of this relationship, see the treatment of God as *unitas* and *esse* in the commentary of
Boethius *De Trinitate* excerpted by Parent, pp. 183, 195; cf. Wilhelm Jansen,
ed., *Der Kommentar des Clarenbaldus von Arras zu Boethius De Trinitate*
(*Breslauer Studien zur historischen Theologie,* Band VII, Breslau, 1926), pp.
9–10 [later treatment by N. M. Haring, "The Creation and Creator of the
World according to Thierry of Chartres and Clarenbaldus of Arras" (study
and texts), *AHDL*, XX (1955), 137–216].

Augustine's orientation toward an interior life that took external objects as mere occasions for its enrichment favored a theology of grace which provided for the free play of divine benevolence through personal encounter between God and man, irrespective of the order or disposition or intelligibility of nature; nature became thereby a mere field for man's interior experience. Platonic dualism, by this route, came to foster a distinction between grace and nature far different from the pseudo-Dionysian conception of the supernatural. In the same way, Augustinianism instilled into Christian spirituality the radical indifference of the Platonic οὐσία (essence) to the world of concrete things in which men presently live. The biblical feeling for historical actuality, more keenly felt by the evangelical reformers at the end of the century, ran counter to all this; and it joined forces, curiously, with an Aristotelian outlook readily critical of the Platonic ideas. The realism of the incarnation was to favor the restoration to theology of secondary causes in both time and space.

The Platonism of the Timaeus and of Boethius

The more one observes how Augustine put the resources of Platonism to work in the service of Christian grace, the more curious one becomes about other elements of Platonism which, even before the rediscovery of Aristotle, were to encourage theologians to develop an awareness of nature and natural causality operating under the free play of divine grace. The time had arrived when the opposition, found in all Platonism, between the unknown, mysterious God and the cosmic God was going to worry the most evangelical Christian thinking, strained as it already was by the quite different emphases and viewpoints of the two creation accounts in the opening pages of the Bible (Gen. 1, 2). The text of the *Timaeus* furnished the literary and doctrinal source for this opposition, which Boethius had already imported into the Latin tradition in contradistinction to the experience of Augustine.

The intimate connection established between the *Timaeus* and Boethius in one of the most lively areas of twelfth-century philosophy was not a matter of chance. Was not the much admired poem found in Book III, metre 9 of the *Consolation* regarded as a summary, in twenty-eight verses, of Plato's whole treatise? Moreover, ancient manuscripts of the Latin version of the *Timaeus* contained numerous passages from Boethius in their margins. The masters of Chartres were to find in both texts not only their common inspiration but the scholarly authority upon which they based their teaching. Anticipating the curricula of thirteenth-century universities, they commented at the same time upon the Platonic dialogue, the *Consolation*, and besides these, upon Boethius's *opusculum*, the *De Trinitate*.[28]

a. The Platonism of the *Timaeus*

Chalcidius, through his translation, had long made the *Timaeus* accessible to the Latin West; and from it men of the Middle Ages nourished their admiration for Plato, since his other works were practically unavailable to them.[29] In the twelfth century, this dialogue was everywhere found in monastic and episcopal libraries; it was cited by Abelard, the masters of Saint-Victor, John of Salisbury, and Alan of Lille; Adelard of Bath consciously took from it the title of his *De eodem et diverso* (*On the One and the Many*). But since Chalcidius's translation omitted that part of the dialogue concern-

---

[28] Reference might often be made to the valuable account, based on unpublished manuscript materials, of Tullio Gregory, "Note e testi per la storia del platonismo medioevale," *GCFI*, XXXIV (1955), 346–84, as well as of Parent. On the abundant commentary literature on the *Consolation* and the *Timaeus* see Pierre Courcelle, "Etude critique sur les commentaires de la Consolation de Boèce (IXe–XVe siècles)," *AHDL*, XII (1939), 6–140; and R. Klibansky, *The Continuity of the Platonic Tradition during the Middle Ages* (London, 1939) [see also his "The School of Chartres," in Marshall Clagett, Gaines Post, and Robert Reynolds, eds., *Twelfth-Century Europe and the Foundations of Modern Society* (Proceedings of a Symposium Sponsored by the Division of Humanities of the University of Wisconsin and the Wisconsin Institute for Medieval and Renaissance Studies, Nov. 12–14, 1957; Madison, 1961), pp. 3–14].

[29] The translation by Cicero (W. Ax, ed., *Timaei translatio* [Leipzig, 1938]; Mullach, pp. 157–76) which St. Augustine used seems not to have been current in the twelfth century. [The translation by Chalcidius has appeared in a new edition which supercedes those of Wrobel and Mullach, hitherto standard: J. H. Waszink, ed., *Timaeus a Calcidio translatus commentarioque instructus* (Corpus Platonicum medii aevi—Plato Latinus, Vol. IV: London: Warburg Institute, 1962). See also R. Klibansky, "Plato's *Parmenides* in the Middle Ages and the Renaissance. A Chapter in the History of Platonic Studies," *MRS*, I (1943), 281–330.]

ing man (it contains only sections 17–53), it shifted the emphasis of the work toward cosmology and made it appear to be a study of the origins and the order of the world. "Thus, we can say," said William of Conches at the beginning of his commentary, "that the matter of this book is natural justice or the creation of the world."[30] This narrowed even further men's view of Plato's thought; but even so, there was enough here to furnish sustenance to minds newly responsive to nature as well as to the problems posed by nature's creation and its relationship to God.

The commentary Chalcidius wrote, like all commentaries, can strike one as uninspired; yet, for all its run-of-the-mill knowledge, it conveys precious information about the fruitful history of Plato's treatise (Chalcidius drew upon the commentary of Iamblichus and even more upon that of Porphyry, who died in 305 A.D.), and it provided effective lexical tools for a period in which a new philosophical vocabulary was being invented. Furthermore, it is important to note that Chalcidius did not employ the forms and method characteristic of Plotinian thought, but rather the Hellenistic conception of the world based upon a search for cosmic harmonies—one thinks of Posidonius, another commentator on the Timaeus, whose philosophy embraced not only the dynamic continuity among things but the harmonies of man and nature. Throughout the twelfth century, then, Chalcidius's translation and commentary constituted a major part of the basic Platonic deposit underlying successive inundations of Neoplatonism.[31]

---

[30] "Unde possumus dicere quod materia huius libri est naturalis iusticia vel creatio mundi" (Parent, p. 142, Jeauneau, p. 59). On William's story concerning the translation's having been undertaken by the "archdeacon" Chalcidius at the request of Bishop Osius, see Jeauneau, p. 63, or PL, CLXXII, 247–8 (text mistakenly attributed to Honorius of Autun).

[31] Consult B. W. Switalsky, *Des Chalcidius Kommentar zu Platos Timaeus,* in *BGPM,* III (Münster, 1902). Note that in and through St. Augustine the Middle Ages received elements that derived from an earlier Platonism, antecedent to Neoplatonic developments; pre-Neoplatonic elements are found in some works of the Cappadocian fathers as well. As a result, in the Middle Ages the term *platonici* ("Platonists") complicated the confusion between original Platonism and Neoplatonism; bit by bit, it seems, the term came to designate philosophers who favored "separate Ideas."

Of the same sort was Macrobius (end of the fourth century), zealous student of both the *Enneads* and the *Timaeus* as commented by Porphyry, whom he followed with the veneration of a disciple. An author of secondary rank, his commentary on Cicero's *Somnium Scipionis* (ed. Franciscus Eyssenhardt

Let us summarize the main features of this Platonism as elaborated by William of Conches among others. William, however, produced no vague commentary upon the doctrine in general but a literal explication that kept close to the text:[32] The world was order and beauty; in all its multiplicity and for all its successive generations, it constituted a *whole*. (Boethius reinforced this idea, foreign to Aristotle; and the frequent use of the term *universitas* in the twelfth century showed the idea's currency).[33] The world was necessarily pat-

---

[Leipzig, 1893]; tr. William Harris Stahl, *Macrobius' Commentary on the Dream of Scipio* [New York, 1952]) nonetheless provided an important source for medieval Neoplatonism. Its importance derived from its definitions of the soul (i.XIV.19) and statements concerning the soul's immortality and incorporeality. Abelard included Macrobius among those pagans whose works [interpreted *per involucrum*] contained Christian revelation [see Taylor, p. 182, n. 26, for brief discussion and bibliography on such interpretation; cf. Edouard Jeauneau, "La notion d'integumentum," *AHDL*, XXIV (1957), 35–100, and M.-D. Chenu, "*Involucrum*: le mythe selon les théologiens médiévaux," *AHDL*, XXII (1955), 75–79]. Macrobius was drawn upon to support personal immortality against Avicenna, as by William of Auvergne. He was among the authorities used to support the conception of a world soul; he transmitted Pythagorean ideas on the properties of numbers (In *Somn. Scip.* i.V–VI); he made known and propagated the Plotinian analysis of the development of virtues used by theologians in their accounts of spiritual experience.

[32] He distinguishes expressly between "commentary" *solam sententiam exequens* (expounding the thought only) and "gloss," which attends to *continuatio litterae* (the literal statement): ". . . quia commentatores litteram nec continuantes nec exponentes soli sententiae serviunt" (for commentators, neither following through nor explicating the literal sense, want the underlying thought only); cited in Parent, pp. 19, n. 3, and 138, n. 1, and Jeauneau, p. 57.

[33] The conception of the world as a *whole* was not incidental but essential to the Platonic world view; cf. *Timaeus* 33A: "and so the Demiurge put the whole together in order that, first of all, the whole should be as perfect a living being as possible, formed of perfect parts; and in the second place, that it should be one." The medieval commentator was aware of the centrality of this conception; cf. William of Conches' statement, cited in Parent, p. 65, n. 2: "Plato enim non de creatione alicujus rei in mundo contente egit sed de ipso universo in quo omnia continentur. Unde per 'hoc omne instituendum' nec hoc nec illud voluit significare, sed ipsam universitatem que in suo genere id est in genere rerum sensibilium optima est et perfectissima." (Plato did not treat the creation of any object contained in the world but the very universe in which all things are contained. Hence by 'put the whole thing together' he did not mean this or that particular thing but the very universe, which, in its genus—that is, in the genus of sensible objects—is best and most perfect.) *Ibid.*, p. 149, and Jeauneau, p. 127: "Dixit [Plato] 'omne,' quia mos fuit antiquorum mundum quoddam 'omne' vocare." (Plato says 'whole' because it was the custom of the ancients to call the world a certain 'whole.')

terned upon a model, a changeless and eternal exemplar, a self-subsistent Living Being comprehending in itself the natures of all things. (It is well known what varied adaptations this great Platonic theme has undergone.) The world's construction (its creation, as Christian commentators called it) was the work of an Artisan, Efficient Cause, or Demiurge, who acted out of self-diffusing goodness. (Twelfth-century commentators did not find emanationism in their text; that was the product of influences from pseudo-Dionysius and John the Scot.) The world had a soul, the ordered principle of its movements and cause of life. Underlying the organization of the world was matter (itself also created, said Christian commentators). Man, center of this universe, reflected in himself all its elements and was a "microcosm" in order that he might dominate it all by his intelligence. (Their Christian belief led commentators to alter this theme profoundly in the direction of Augustine's *imago Dei*.) Finally, the *Timaeus* furnished twelfth-century authors with assorted elements of physics—the heavenly spheres, the elements, the concept of space—which provided competition for the Ptolemaic ideas that translators had been bringing into circulation since the beginning of the century.

Apart from the theory of ideas, there were three other problems around which discussion centered in the schools:

First, identification of the Platonic demiurge (*opifex*) with God. This completely destroyed the balanced structure of the Platonic system, as men of the time well knew and clearly said when they outlined and rejected out of hand the theory of the three coeternal principles. The identification of God with the *opifex* of the *Timaeus* made for some interesting speculative possibilities; but it also entailed equivocal points that the criticism of Simon of Tournai, among others, sought to resolve.

Second, when one superimposed the *Timaeus* upon Genesis, how could one picture the actual unfolding of creation? Respectfully but firmly both Hugh of Saint-Victor and the masters of Chartres, and surely Peter Lombard himself, discarded Augustine's idealist view that the successive "days" had only a logical significance; the Bible's historical orientation and Plato's realistic physics worked against such a view. Moreover, as to the construction of the cosmos, a sharp and very revealing controversy arose over primitive chaos, some authorities basing their contentions on the text of the *Timaeus* and Chalcidius's interpretation and advocating an initial disorder, others (especially William of Conches) adopting a decided naturalism and teaching that from the beginning the laws of nature operated according to an intrinsically determined order and not according to some arbitrary benevolence on the part of the Divinity.[34]

Third, the theory of the world soul. Accepted by Abelard and his disciples and by all the masters of Chartres with a range of interpretations that William of Conches classified neatly,[35] it was very quickly discarded, possibly not so much through Cîteaux's abrupt rejection of it[36] or through narrow-minded attackers as through the mature reflection of theologians. In fact, this was one of the pagan ideas most difficult to reconcile with the biblical outlook to the extent that it reduced the Holy Spirit's role in history to presiding over cosmic evolution. Augustine, however, had not rejected it; and Basil had accepted the identification of the Holy Spirit with the world soul—so seductive did Plato prove as a means of understanding Christian mystery.

But apart from any fallacious attempt to harmonize the three hypostases of Plotinus with the three persons of the Trinity, the experimental identification of the Holy Spirit with the world soul being the third of these, Plato presented certain distinct intellectual advantages as against Aristotle. As Emile Bréhier remarks, "Aristotle, in a sense, expunged the soul from his image of the universe; the primary moving principles of the heavens are minds; the soul appears only in living sublunar bodies, as bodily form, and is a wholly intellectual concept formulated by a physiologist in search of the

---

[34] See M.-D. Chenu, "Nature ou histoire? Une controverse exégétique sur la création au XIIe siècle," *AHDL*, XX (1953), 25–30.

[35] *Philosophia* mundi i.15 (*PL*, CLXXII, 46; false attribution to Honorius of Autun). Three interpretations: it was a natural energy given things by God; it was an incorporeal substance animating the universe and present in its parts; it was the Holy Spirit. See Gregory.

[36] Arnold of Bonneval (friend of St. Bernard) *De operibus sex dierum* (*PL*, CLXXXIX, 1515); *Disputatio altera adversus Abaelardum* (*PL*, CLXXX, 321–2; not by William of Saint-Thierry but by a Benedictine abbot at the request of Hugh of Rouen).

principle of corporeal functions; the soul as the seat of destiny has disappeared."[37] Platonists, on the other hand, believers in the substantial unity of the cosmos and in the mutual sympathy of its parts, saw souls as having a cosmic function: they were destined to play the same role in the moment-to-moment governance of small things that the world soul played in the whole. Soul was the intermediary between the intelligible world and the world of sense perception. The fathers, no less, had severely criticized Aristotle's definition of the soul. Pseudo-Gregory of Nyssa (Nemesius) was the source of such criticism in the Middle Ages. Aristotle's definition, he held, seriously imperiled the substantiality of the soul and thus its immortality.[38] The rising influence of pseudo-Dionysius, whose hierarchy provided no place for the world soul, preserved to advantage these Platonic values of the cosmic interrelationship of souls. In adopting them, St. Thomas broke with Aristotle's view of the structure of the cosmos.

In all the interpretations made of the *Timaeus* and in all the uses made of it in theology, two features of Plato's method caused problems. One was a literary feature, but of great importance philosophically; namely, the use of fables or myths, and above all of the cosmogenetic myth involving the demiurge, which accounts for the ambiguities of what men commonly call Plato's theology. Twelfth-century thinkers took judicious stock of the role of myth. William of Conches, after having observed its use by Boethius, proposed to explain its further use by Plato.[39] Abelard saw myth as a necessity for philosophy when it came to the discussion of mysterious realities.[40] Alan of Lille saw "colors" (the term applied to these *integu-*

---

[37] Emile Bréhier, *Histoire de la philosophie* (Paris, 1948), I, 458; tr. Wade Baskin, *The History of Philosophy*, Vol. II: *The Hellenistic and Roman Age* (Chicago, 1965), p. 190.

[38] *De natura hominis* (*PG*, XL, 560).

[39] *Comm. in Boet. de Consol.* (MS. Orléans 274, f. 37a): "Quod Plato voluisset omnes animas simul creatas fuisse, nusquam invenitur; sed impositas esse stellis et descendere per planetas, hoc quidem invenitur. Sed dictum est hoc in *O qui perpetua* per integumentum, et hoc idem ostendemus, Deo annuente vitam, super Platonem." (That Plato intended all souls to have been created at once is nowhere found; but that they had been placed upon stars and descended through the planets, this one does find. The same point was made allegorically in the poem 'O qui perpetua' [*De cons.* iii.m.9] and, if God grants me life, I shall show that the same is true in Plato.)

[40] *Introd. ad theol.* i.19 (*PL*, CLXXVIII, 1022): "Semper philosophia arcana sua nudis publicare verbis dedignata sit, et maxime de anima et de diis

menta in rhetoric) as arising from a necessary intellectual modesty.[41] But none of these men measured the role of Platonic myth with any profundity. Abelard, wishing to free Plato from gross animism, saw mere metaphor in this *involucrum*.[42] At Chartres, myth was converted into decorative allegory; the commentator interested in ideas was consequently led into making tendentious interpretations that pretended to find in the text a purely reasoned solution to the problem of the world's origin.[43]

The second feature is still more important, touching on the very

---

per fabulosa quaedam involucra loqui consueverat." (Philosophy always disdains publishing its secrets in plain words; especially concerning the soul and the gods, it covers up what it has to say under fabulous disguises.) Cf. H. Ostlender, ed., *Peter Abaelards Theologia* "Summi Boni" in *BGPM*, XXXV, ii-iii (Münster, 1939), 14.

[41] *De planctu Naturae* (*PL*, CCX, 452); "Nolo enim ut prius plana verborum planitie explanare proposita, vel profanis verborum novitatibus profanare profana; verum, pudenda aureis pudicorum verborum phaleris inaurare, variisque venustorum verborum coloribus investire." (I do not wish, as before, to expose my designs on the open surface of words, or to violate unholy things with novel and unclean words; rather to overlay shameful things with the golden adornments of chaste words and to clothe them with the contrasting colors of beautiful words.) Nature's interlocutor questions her about the substance of metaphors which do not satisfy him (*ibid.*, 454): "Quamvis enim plerique auctores sub integumentali involucro aenigmatum, ejus naturam depinxerint, tamen nulla certitudinis nobis reliquerunt vestigia." (Although a good many authors have represented its nature under the enveloping concealment of figures, yet they have left us no roads to certitude.)

[42] *Intro. ad theol.* i.20 (*PL*, CLXXVIII, 1023): "Clarum est quae a philosophis de anima mundi dicuntur, per involucrum accipienda esse. Alioquin summum philosophorum Platonem summum stultorum reprehenderemus. Quid enim magis ridiculosum quam mundum totum arbitrari unum animal esse rationale, nisi per hoc integumentum sit prolatum." (Clearly, what philosophers say about the world soul must be taken under a figurative veil. Otherwise, we should despise that greatest of philosophers, Plato, as the greatest of fools. For what could be more ridiculous than to suppose that the entire universe is one big rational animal, unless by this a figure were expressed?) Cf. Ostlender, *op. cit.*, pp. 15–16 [and articles by Jeauneau and Chenu cited above, n. 31].

[43] Boethius had already done the same; so had Proclus in his commentary on the *Timaeus*. In Plato, the gods belonged to the order of myth and of existence; they were causes of 'becoming.' Thereafter, the Good, the Ideas (creative), and Being itself acquired the status of causes of essence or nature, above nature but part of its dialectical extension and in line with it. Boethius was to use abstract language on such points, and his figures were to be no more than allegorical. So it developed throughout the Middle Ages. The cosmogony of Bernard Sylvester did not escape from this fate which Platonism had undergone. Alan of Lille provided a perfect example of it in his allegorical description of Nature and Love.

inspiration of Plato, on what we might call his "Socratism." Under-lying Plato's thought was the intellectual orientation of his master, and it lent to his thinking, if not to his system, a moral bias, a re-sponsiveness to values, an existential character—resources that would have made him receptive to the idea of creation despite all else, and that Aristotle did not preserve. Medieval thinkers were ignorant of the genius of Socrates and of his orientation of philosophy toward human values and problems. Augustinianism did not succeed in making up for this lack, whether in philosophy or in intellectual life. Faithfully and single-mindedly, commentators on the *Timaeus* de-veloped their "philosophy of the world;" and their knowledge of physical things did not inspire them to any significant reflection upon themselves or to any progress in self-knowledge. The omnipresent God, that *forma essendi* (form of existence) of every creature, whom one finds in Thierry of Chartres' teaching, or, later on, the One of Gilbert of La Porrée's followers—none of these shared the quali-ties of Augustine's God in the *Soliloquies*. Of Augustine they read and reread his various treatises on Genesis, preserving in their har-monizing endeavors. Their schematization of the *modi universitatis* (modes of the universe) included Augustine's *seminales rationes* (seminal causes), and their *possibilitas absoluta* (absolute possibil-ity) defined his *materia informis* (matter without form). But Pla-tonic though both vocabularies were, they were obviously different.[44]

b. The Platonism of Boethius

Though one can speak of the Augustinianism of Boethius, and though the author of the *Consolation* contributed to an Augustinian reading of the *Timaeus* of which the terminology just mentioned pre-serves traces, it is nonetheless true that he read the works of Plato with other eyes than Augustine's, with greater scholarly fidelity and without that religious and philosophical transformation to which the Christian doctor subjected them. In truth, Boethius, even in his lofty

---

[44] The combination of these two vocabularies—Augustine's and Boethius's terms for Platonic concepts—is evident in various works of Chartrian prov-enance; e.g., see Wilhelm Jansen, ed., *Der Kommentar des Clarenbaldus von Arras zu Boethius De Trinitate* (Breslauer Studien zur historischen Theologie, Band VII; Breslau, 1926), p. 64; cf. Parent, pp. 207–13.

spiritual aspirations, remained a man formed by the school—the school of Ammonius of Alexandria, which made him a follower of Proclus as distinct from other strains of Neoplatonism[45]—and he retained the learning, the techniques, and the methods of the school. Yet he was far from being weak in personality; he showed this in his curiosity, his preferences, his interiorized convictions, his nobility. His extraordinary success throughout the Middle Ages testifies indisputably to his personal appeal.

Here, in brief, are the elements and qualities that he contributed to the Platonic syncretism of the twelfth century and, beyond that century, to the whole outlook of medieval philosophy:[46]

1. First of all, there was his express purpose to reconcile Aristotle and Plato—even though the realization of this purpose was cut short by his death. He wished "to bring the thought of Aristotle and Plato somehow into harmony" and to show that "these two philosophers are not at odds in everything as a great many persons suppose, but that they agree in a very large number of points, including the most important points in philosophy."[47]

We have here the resolution of a disciple who, in his admiration for two masters, was unwilling to choose between them, between the two truths they propounded. But we have also a modest mind's expression of two intellectual needs which were as imperious as they were in fact irreconcilable in the conceptions they produced of the universe. According to the one the truth about the universe was to be found in unchanging and identical essences distributed among a multiplicity of individuals, while according to the other that truth was to be found in the concrete particular realities which we experience and which alone exist. Bernard of Chartres approved of Boe-

---

[45] See Pierre Courcelle, *Les lettres grecques en occident de Macrobe à Cassiodore* (Paris, 1948), "L'Orient au secours de la culture profane: Boèce," pp. 257–312, where both the dependence of Boethius upon Ammonius and the original features of his Neoplatonism are clarified.

[46] [For a detailed consideration of the influence of Boethius by Chenu, see *TDS,* Chap. VI, "Aetas Boetiana," pp. 142–58.]

[47] ". . . Aristotelis Platonisque sententias in unam quodammodo revocare concordiam, eosque non ut plerique dissentire in omnibus, sed in plerisque et his in philosophia maximis consentire demonstrem." *De interpretatione, editio secunda,* ed. Carolus Meiser (Leipzig, 1880), p. 79.

thius's project; but John of Salisbury, whose keen perceptiveness was greater than his powers of intellectual construction, observed with wry humor that it would be rather difficult to reconcile after death two men who had managed to disagree with one another all their lives.[48]

In fact, Boethius platonized. While he remained faithful to Aristotle in logic and in the systematizing of knowledge, he yielded to a metaphysical realism in which the Aristotelian philosophy of substantial forms reverted to the sole truth of pure essences.[49] It is significant that the agent intellect was not recognized by Boethius. Twelfth-century schools and masters who, following Boethius, ignored this faculty all perpetrated the same distortion even though they opposed each other as nominalists and realists—such was the startling ambiguity of Boethius's system. Gilbert of La Porrée and

---

[48] *Metal.* ii.17 (Webb, p. 94; McGarry, p. 115): "Egerunt operosius Bernardus Carnotensis et auditores eius ut componerent inter Aristotilem et Platonem, sed eos tarde venisse arbitror et laborasse in vanum ut reconciliarent mortuos qui, quamdiu in vita licuit, dissenserunt." (Bernard of Chartres and his students labored strenuously to compose the differences between Aristotle and Plato, but I think they arrived on the scene too late and labored in vain to reconcile two dead men, who, as long as they were alive and could have agreed, disagreed.) In the thirteenth century the ascendancy of the works of Aristotle arrested but did not destroy this ambition to reconcile the two ancient philosophers, a persistent idea of the twelfth century. Herman of Dalmatia noted the disagreement between their two definitions of the soul but, in his *De essentiis*, sketched a plan for coordinating them (cited in Haskins, *Studies*, p. 61); Hugh of Saint-Victor, in his *Didascalicon* (ii.1 [Buttimer, pp. 23–25; Taylor, pp. 61–63]) combined the Platonic division of the sciences, as rendered by Boethius, with that of Aristotle. Augustine, following Porphyry, had already believed confidently that philosophy was one: ". . . non defuerunt acutissimi et solertissimi viri, qui docerent disputationibus suis Aristotelem ac Platonem ita sibi concinere, ut imperitis minusque attentis dissentire videantur; multis quidem saeculis multisque contentionibus, sed tamen eliquata est, ut·opinor, una verissimae philosophiae disciplina." (There has been no lack of most keen and skillful men who have taught that Aristotle and Plato so cooperate in their disputes that to unskilled and inattentive minds they appear to disagree. Many have been the centuries and many the contentions; but, as I think, a single discipline of philosophy most true has filtered through). *Contra academicos* iii.19.42 (*PL*, XXXII, 956).

[49] William of Conches had observed this point well: "Boethius vero in utroque fuit nutritus: in aristotelica, in dialectica et logica; in platonica, in philosophia." (Boethius, however, was nurtured by both systems: by the Aristotelian in dialectic and logic; by the Platonic in philosophy); *In Boetium de Consol.* (2nd version), MS Paris BN lat. 6406, fol. 9ᵛ.

his followers handled Boethius with the most faithful respect and managed to preserve a large measure of Aristotelianism, even though substantial intrusions of Neoplatonism of Proclus's type were to invade their early syncretism. Gilbert's speculation about the Trinity unmistakably revealed the determining influence of Boethius's conception upon theology itself.

Among spiritual writers the absolute primacy of Augustine left little room for Boethius and his school training. Only here and there did Boethius contribute a few elements of vocabulary or definition to a certain conceptualism which introduced a humanistic strain into their mystical thought. So it was with Alcher of Clairvaux and above all with Richard of Saint-Victor. But the "philosophy" of Boethius's *Consolation* could only strike these monastic authors as too profane —a view with which the evangelicals at the end of the century effectively agreed.

2. The immediate effect of this yoking together of Plato and Aristotle was to divide the life of the mind into two levels, irreducible despite their permanent connection. Platonism itself had already promoted such bifurcation by defining ultimate reality as independent of those limited forms in which the mind knows objects. But for the Middle Ages Boethius was the author of one of the most widely accepted formulations of this noetic dualism. He held that there were two orders of object—*intellectibilia* (intellectible objects), which included only the Divinity, ever one and identical, inaccessible to all approach through the sense-perceptible world; and *intelligibilia* (intelligible objects), which included created spirits, among them the human soul, accessible through their introduction into the world of sense. To these two orders corresponded two types of knowledge, one rooted in the *intellectus* (intellect), the other in the *ratio* (reason); Aristotelian noetic took over in the latter. Spiritual writers joined the masters of the schools in following Boethius's dualism in order to give account of their mystical experiences. The numerous treatises *De anima*, Cistercian or other, introduced these Boethian categories into their diverse vocabularies. Richard of Saint-Victor based his analysis of the degrees of contemplation on the Boethian distinctions. For Thierry of Chartres, the understanding that was derived from the intellect had religious value in itself; it alone made

proof of God; it was the properly theological faculty, while reason was the faculty that dealt with predicamental and quantified being.

3. The influence Boethius exercised upon metaphysics was still more decisive. Some of his propositions became so classic that often a later writer such as St. Thomas was unable to reject them out of hand but had instead to adapt them. In fact, before Aristotle became influential (the text of his *Metaphysics* began to circulate about 1240), Boethius reigned in schools wherever metaphysical analysis of creation nourished the contemplation of God, as it had in his theological *opuscula*. The composite condition of created beings, the simplicity of the divine Being—here was the central theme, Neoplatonic insofar as it stressed the primacy of the One, but Aristotelian in its treatment of everything involving form. God was pure form; other beings were composed of form, their *quo est* or *esse* (that *by which* they exist, their *being*), and the subject possessing this form, the *quod est* (that which *exists*, which *has* being). A realist interpretation of this distinction was to lead Gilbert of La Porrée beyond the Boethian exegesis of kindred spirits at Chartres and to upset, if not the orthodoxy of his theology, at least the balance of his teaching on the Trinity. Although God was the *forma essendi* (form of the being) of every creature—and on this point Gilbert mixed Boethian propositions with Augustinian ideas—nonetheless created beings were only incarnate reflections, epiphanies of God, belonging to the intelligible order. They had their own integrity; and the divine activity did not substitute itself for their own any more than the divine form substituted itself for their form, united to matter. One sees here the influence of the Aristotelianism of Boethius, even in the affirmation that God is ontologically present in created beings. Without excluding the Platonic ideas or forms from his thought, Gilbert had overcome the radical separation of the Platonic *ousia* from the everyday world of concrete actualities in which we live. John of Salisbury was to perceive very clearly this movement in the direction of Augustinian Platonism.[50] It was not a philosophical operation

---

[50] See, e.g., his observations in *Metal.* ii.20 (Webb, pp. 115 ff.; McGarry, pp. 118 ff.). [On Gilbert of La Porée's commentaries on Boethius, see the editions of N. Haring in *Trad.* IX (1953), 117–211; *AHDL*, XXI (1954), 241–357; and in *Studies and Texts,* vol. I: *Nine Medieval Thinkers* (Toronto, 1955), pp. 23–98.]

only, but the basis of a wholly new religion, theology, and spirituality. As to the pantheism of Amaury of Bène, decked out as it was in a whole panoply of Boethian terms, it was possible only through the gross wrenching of these terms from their original meaning.

4. Boethius gave the natural sciences their statute of autonomy. He was, and right up through St. Thomas he would remain,[51] the great authority for a systematization of knowledge differentiated according to its objects. He saw theology, its transcendence assured, as making use, in its constructive task, of rational concepts which retained their proper validity in the sphere of faith and which were adequate to the formulation of theological problems. Here too, following upon a century of commentators, St. Thomas drew heavily upon the work of Boethius; and the celebrated axiom, "Authority is the weakest source of proof,"[52] repeats Boethius's own standard of judgment. It was not simply as a logician that Boethius formulated a number of concepts destined to common currency among theologians—such concepts as "nature," "person," "substance," "eternity," "providence"—but as a religious thinker who trusted the work of man's reason. The *Consolation*, deliberately constructed upon a purely rational foundation, is an extreme instance of theological reliance upon reason. It was not at all a "profane," a "pagan" work; no medieval writer, not even the most anti-intellectual among them, would ever have taken it for that. From this point of view and on this ground, Boethius was the first of the scholastics—a title one would not think of bestowing upon Augustine. He succeeded in using the logic of Aristotle in a domain of inquiry to which it could claim no special right of entry—the domain of the First Being and of pure spirits.

Such, then—and very different from that of Augustine—was the Neoplatonism of Boethius. The distinction between the two reached stealthily but effectively into the twelfth century and was revealed in even such a mild dispute as the exchange of letters between Nicho-

---

[51] Thomas Aquinas *Comm. in Boetii De Trin.* qq. 5, 6 (Aquinas, *Opera omnia*, XVII, 379–96).

[52] "Locus ab auctoritate est infirmissimus," *Summa theol.* I, Q.1, a.8, ad 2 (Aquinas, *Opera omnia*, I, 8; Aquinas, *Summa*, I, 13) [cf. Boethius *In Topica Ciceronis commentaria* vi (*PL*, LXIV, 1166 ff.) and *De differentiis Topicis* iii (*ibid.*, 1199C)].

las of Clairvaux and Peter of Celle about the primacy of unity (as conceived by Plato) and simplicity (as conceived by Augustine).[53] The audiences to which Boethius and Augustine appealed were quite different. The Augustinianism of Boethius, including that of his *De Trinitate*, which theologians read side by side with Augustine's *De Trinitate*, echoed not so much the personal reflections of Augustine as certain Neoplatonic commonplaces suggestive of Proclus. Attempts to harmonize Boethius and Augustine were legitimate but not wholly successful. Boethius's philosophy of liberty and his theology of divine foreknowledge were taught in the schools; and St. Anselm, anticipating many others, utilized the famous passage on contingency from Boethius's commentary on chapter 9 of Aristotle's *Peri hermeneias* (*On Interpretation*), in rivalry with Augustine, in his *Concordia praescientiae Dei cum libero arbitrio* (*Harmony of the Foreknowledge of God with Free Will*).[54] But Boethius's philosophy and theology could never match the Christian flavor or spiritual quality of Augustine's *De gratia et libero arbitrio* (*On Grace and Free Will*), used by St. Bernard in his work of identical title.[55]

Of the *Timaeus*, which helped form his thought, Boethius achieved one of the most intelligent adaptations in the long history of the work. Not only did he take over, as did all Christians, the three principles discussed above, but he pushed far along the Christianization of the providence of the God-demiurge. The famous metre, *O qui perpetua*, of *Consolation* III, m.9, possessed great religious depth, despite the ostensible naturalism of its terminology.[56] Among

---

[53] See M.-D. Chenu, "Platon à Citeaux," *AHDL*, XXIV (1954), 99–106.

[54] *PL*, XLVIII, 507 ff.

[55] *PL*, CLXXXII, 1001–1030 [English translation with valuable notes by W. Williams, *Concerning Grace and Free Will* (London, 1920)].

[56] "O qui perpetua mundum ratione gubernas" (O thou who governest the world by thine Eternal Thought). The *ratio perpetua* is the eternal reason of God and the supreme model of all the beings of the world, governing them by its thought; for this model is the life of the world. Eternal preexistence in the divine exemplar gives meaning to terrestrial existence, a reflection of true existence. Its philosophical character admitted, the *Consolation* was nonetheless subject to increasingly Christian interpretation, certainly by John the Scot and by twelfth-century commentators; see Pierre Courcelle, "Etude critique sur les commentaires de la Consolation de Boèce," *AHDL*, XII (1939), 5–

Neoplatonists his stress upon the divine unity placed him in a tradition different from that of Augustine, who stressed the divine ideas— a tradition that exercised a recurring influence upon theologians and mystics and was soon reinforced by the influence of pseudo-Dionysius.[57]

Finally, Boethius was a man of the Latin West, whereas pseudo-Dionysius, also a disciple of Proclus, was subject to the alien culture of the East. The Platonism of Boethius tended toward abstraction; it excluded the symbolism and myth equally to be found in Plato and favored the conceptualized dialectic congenial to the schools of the Middle Ages, where the science of theology had to become more and more cognizant of metaphor, including the "divine names" which it found in the Bible and was prone to treat as common anthropomorphism. Western theology was to nurse a continual mistrust of the East; and the allegorizing which western theology came to cultivate to excess in its biblical exegesis, in its liturgy, in its analysis of the sacraments, and in its pastoral efforts was only an intellectualized and aristocratic distortion of the symbolic mysteries of Christianity.

The Introduction of Pseudo-Dionysius

The One, the Good, Being—it is in their different handling of these three inseparable denominations of the supreme reality that the

---

140. Its inspiration has justly been recognized in Alan of Lille's fine poem on Nature, even in the form of the opening line: "O Dei proles, genitrixque rerum" (See above, p. 19, and n. 38).

[57] The mystical theme of god's solitude was nurtured by the metaphysics of the One. Cf. Bernard Sylvester *De mundi universitate* (Barach-Wrobel, p. 61): "Unitas non inceperat: simplex, intacta, solitaria, ex se in se permanens, infinibilis et aeterna." (The divine Unity had no origin: simple, integral, solitary, it endures in and from itself, endless and eternal.) The undeniable religious depth of such a statement springs from the Boethian metaphysics of the school of Chartres. Cf. Gilbert of La Porrée *Comm. in lib. de Trinitate* (*PL*, LXIV, 1269): "Vere est [Deus] unum, et adeo simplex in se, et sine his quae adesse possunt solitarium, ut recte de hoc Uno dicatur quod de ipso principio cujus ousia est dicitur, scilicet est id quod est." (Truly is God one, and so simple in himself, and so solitary without added attributes, that we rightly say of this One what is said of the very principle of which he is the existence, namely: He is that which is.)

varieties of Neoplatonism are to be distinguished. The terms continually slip, so to speak, and the resulting syncretism lessens the hard and fast supremacy of the One over Being upon which Plotinus had insisted.[58] The masters of Chartres, following Boethius and before the new translations of Boethius had appeared, devised a number of excellent formulas which with greater or less deliberateness combined the themes of the One and Being. The study of pseudo-Dionysius, which became quite intense starting in the second third of the twelfth century, introduced an original treatment of the doctrine of the One and the Good into the store of ideas already twice translated into Latin by Augustine and by Boethius. A tone hard to define, an extravagant vocabulary, and highly attenuated concepts of cosmic import were brought in from the world of Proclus, a world vastly different from that of Augustine with his sensitivity to the interior movements of the soul and his resonant spiritual rhetoric. "Contemplation" as hitherto understood in the West took on the mystical dimension of *theoria*; "ignorance" came to suggest the darkness of the negative way; "mind," for all its original profundity, became charged with the sacred connotations of the untranslatable νοῦς. In his characteristic manner, Hugh of Saint-Victor witnessed to these changes from the first. Within the constraining limits of his textual commentary on *The Celestial Hierarchy*,[59] he not only rejected and imputed to John the Scot one or another doctrine that he judged heterodox, but he constantly adapted terms, concepts, and whole sets of ideas within the Augustinian categories that provided his enduring frame of reference.

The concept of "hierarchy" was the keystone of the system of pseudo-Dionysius; it dominated and supported everything else within that system and accounted for its spirit. *Ordo sacer* (sacred order) —this Latin rendering of the term conveyed very little of the meta-

---

[58] Boethius inspired equally the traditions stressing the One or the Good. In his *De hebdomadibus* he calls the genesis of beings a "fluxus a prima bonitate" (outflow from the First Good) (*PL*, LXIII, 3111); but one of his first axioms is: "Omne quod est idcirco est quia unum est." (The whole that exists, exists because it is One.) (*PL*, LXIV, 83). In taking its place with the opuscula of Boethius, the *De unitate* of Gundissalinus weighted the tradition in favor of the One. Alan of Lille's *Regulae* had the same effect.

[59] *Expositio in Hierarchiam coelestem* (*PL*, CLXXV, 923–1154).

physical and religious richness of the original concept,[60] which, despite this weakening and despite the loss of fundamental features, was to exercise an astonishing attraction. Communication of divinity

---

[60] *Ordo* and *hierarchia*—we have here an example of completely different terms—in origin, conception, social and ideological reference—even when they are interchanged. Both were rich terms, unhappily impoverished by legalistic handling. Their difference may be schematized thus:

Implications of *ordo:*

—order of the state with particular reference to justice; general social structure.

—order as a framework established by law in the public interest or domain (*res publica*); so used in Roman legal terminology.

—order as an institutionalized group—political, economic, religious (*ordo militaris, ordo equester*).

—order in reference to offices performed, or to prerogatives, rights, and franchises enjoyed in virtue of *status* (position) in feudal or communal law (cf. St. Thomas *Summa theol.* I. q. 108. a. 2: "Diversitas ordinum secundum officia").

—order as the intrinsic discipline of a rule (*ordo regulae, ordo disciplinae*).

—order as used by the church of functions and ministries (*ordo monasticus, ordo canonicus*, the sacrament of major orders or the order of priesthood).

—order as used of ceremonies or rites (*ordo missae, ordines et consecrationes*, conferring the order of knighthood through the order or ordination of dubbing).

Implications of *hierarchia:*

—hierarchy as a first principle having sacred value (literally ἱερά ἀρχή, sacred beginning).

—hierarchy in virtue of emanation from the divinity.

—hierarchy as implying ontological value; natural, rather than by will or juridical fiat of men.

—hierarchy as expressing an order, a τάξις or arrangement, primarily in a mystical sense: a holy disposition on the part of God, a "super-essential harmony."

—hierarchy as dynamic in character.

—hierarchy to suggest a religious sense extending beyond the juridical, or when the divine disposition exceeds moral and social laws.

In Aristotelian philosophy of nature, the term "nature" acquired new meaning. It designated an "order" in nature's striving for perfection (*ordo ad finem*), its determined forms, its laws. *Hierarchia* lost its pseudo-Dionysian meaning from the thirteenth century on, even in a sacred context. Augustine, and many following him, remained Roman even in religious uses of *ordo*. Note that neither *ordo* nor *hierarchia* is of New Testament origin or tone. See R. Roques, *L'univers dionysien. Structure hiérarchique du monde selon le pseudo-Denys* (Paris, 1954), esp. chap. 1: "Le monde comme ordre: vocabulaire et sources"; and H. Krings, *Ordo. Philos.-histor. Grundlegung einer abendländische Idee* (Halle, 1941). [See below, pp. 225 ff., for *ordo* and social *status*.]

along a descending scale, along an emanation of the multiple forms of being, rank on rank, all participating directly but differently in God, whose fulness was thus manifested through them (the provision for direct participation avoided the emanationism of Proclus but not the peril of a theory of intermediaries): such was the grand vision which intoxicated pseudo-Dionysius and provided the master plan within which the universe and man, God and Christ, the sacraments and contemplation, body and soul, light and shadows, symbols and negations all found a sublime explanation. In our time, the analogue of this total hypothesis is the theory of evolution.

The concept of hierarchy clearly presupposed the classic Platonic thesis of two worlds, the worlds of intellect and of sense; but it altered this thesis profoundly by taking the sense-perceptible world as a field in which symbols were in play. To be sure, this approach to the world was native to Platonism, but its wholesale extension transformed the basic character of the system and, when blended with the symbolism of the Christian sacraments, gave it a religious profundity as potentially fruitful as it was ambiguous. This symbolism screened divine truths from the eyes of the throng, the uninitiated. The "sign" of Augustine and the "symbol" of pseudo-Dionysius belonged to two quite different Platonisms.

Pseudo-Dionysius remained entirely faithful to Neoplatonism, which was essentially a method of approach to intelligible reality, not an explanation of the world of sense by means of that reality. But for him this method was to be conceived as an ascent that began from the lowest material level, on which the mind of man found its connatural objects—objects whose value for knowledge, for sacred knowledge, lay not in their own coarse material natures but in their symbolic capacity, their "anagogy." "Anagogy" was not only wholly different from the technique of metaphor employed by scripture or the poets;[61] philosophically speaking, it was also totally different from the Augustinian (later, the Cistercian and Victorine) "image"

---

[61] Pseudo-Dionysius was not touched by poetry or rhetoric. He treated scriptural images as ontological symbols, not as literary figures subject to grammatical and psychological analysis. He was thus profoundly different from the humanists of western monasticism, who taught the seven liberal arts as propaedeutic to scriptural interpretation.

and from Aristotelian abstraction from sense-perceptible particulars. Both of the latter were to make pseudo-Dionysian "anagogy" and "theophany" almost unintelligible to men of the West.

This anagogy, this ascent or conversion, this hierarchial activity took place through three distinct but simultaneous operations: purification, illumination, perfection. The popularity and success of this doctrine and formula are well known. Both became commonplace among theologians and even more among spiritual writers. But the doctrine lost its proper shape when translated into the Latin tongue, which often reduced the operations of pseudo-Dionysian "initiation" to moral activity on the part of *incipientes, proficientes,* and *perfecti* (beginners, proficients, the perfected). The very terms lacked sacred character and turned what was properly a transcendent divine operation into a matter of ascetic law; indeed, the words νόμος (arbitrary enactment) and θεσμός (law) were both rendered by *lex* (law) in Latin. The price paid for such success, however, did not vitiate the functional analysis through which pseudo-Dionysius had built the religious potentialities of Proclus's philosophy into an integrated doctrine.

Increasingly important as a challenge to the Aristotelian concept of "substance," the concept of "hierarchy" shattered the metaphysical scheme which locked up each nature within its own ontological perimeter. This concept entailed natures so universally and normally open to causal influence from the being above them that the action of that superior being was intimately involved in their own natural acts. This "sympathy," this *continuatio* as it was translated in Latin, was of·a piece with the Plotinian idea of "participation"; it clothed reality with qualities deriving from a mysterious kinship and invested the unitary order of the universe, emanating from the One, with a religious value.

From this conception of "hierarchy" derived the sacredness of knowledge, which, submissive to the laws of hierarchy, was the proper possession of the "perfect." The Greek idea of ἐπιστήμη (certain knowledge), as typically happened in Neoplatonic tradition, was realized through the cathartic and mystical operation of a θεορία (contemplation), a term which Latin spiritual writers, though not the scholastics, took over bodily and contrasted to *scientia* (scientific or demonstrable knowledge), which for them usually retained a secular meaning. A great many spiritual writers placed confidence in such contemplative understanding, for it breathed an optimism quite unlike the ascetical empiricism of certain reformers. If this process of contemplation divinized men, it was because it showed them the theophanies truly found in all beings and revealed in the universe a cascade of illuminations descending from God who nonetheless remained invisible in himself. This was not at all a matter of pantheism but of mystical emanation with an undergirding of agnosticism, and it was to become the most seductive and disruptive of the original expressions of the philosophy of "participation" found in Christendom.

The most prominent trait of this "hierarchy"—one which Christianized the structure of Neoplatonism but at the same time limited the originality of the Christian world view—was its mingling of cosmology and soteriology, its combining of God as creator and God as savior into one. In western tradition, thanks in large part to Augustine, the two had been kept separate; and their separateness was reflected in the major distinction between nature and grace. It is not that pseudo-Dionysius was at all infected by naturalism or that he linked the divinization of man to progress or evolution in the cosmos. Quite the contrary, even in underlying moral outlook, he was wholly theocratic and seemed to transplant into Christendom the theurgic prayer of Iamblichus. But the law of divinization impinged upon the interior life and liberty of men's souls only in and through the objective order and from outside the activity of the hierarchy; the divinely willed predeterminations provided for within this system had nothing in common with the impromptu character of grace as Augustine conceived it. Here one sees an ingenious translation of the Platonic metaphysics of participation into a Christian structure. In the course of this translation the concept of "analogy" was forged—a new and sensitive concept in later ideological syncretism, which threatened the vision of pseudo-Dionysius with devaluation, with invasion from Aristotelian conceptualism and Augustinian supernaturalism at the same time. Moreover, the psychological reality of grace and of free will, of the two liberties, God's and man's, which the Pelagian controversy established for good in the West, could not easily be fitted

84

into the closed system of action required by the hierarchical destiny of created beings. On this point the Christianity of pseudo-Dionysius yielded to Neoplatonism and its restraining interventions from above. John the Scot was the scapegoat who ran away with this stubborn point, over which no one felt free to attack the prestige of pseudo-Dionysius.

Where pseudo-Dionysius broke with Proclus and reverted to the personal God of Christianity, it was out of a just conception of the incommunicable transcendency of the supreme principle which was simultaneously One, Being, Life, and Intelligence. "The One, whom we may still not call 'being' . . .," Iamblichus had said. The emanationism and the *henads* of Proclus were eliminated. There was a decisive effort on the part of all Christian Neoplatonisms to this end. Among the transcendentals, "the Good" became the supreme qualification; God was pure and simple ἔρως (love) who extended his action to the very last and least of beings and drew them toward himself. *Bonum est diffusivum sui* (Good is self-diffusing): the Latin axiom everywhere testified to the influence of pseudo-Dionysius—a decidedly Christian influence, for grace ruled over his system; and such knowledge as one could have of it came from a revelation, from the wisdom of God which was the only true "philosophy." Apollophanes the Greek was right to call pseudo-Dionysius a parricide who had dispossessed the Greeks of their wisdom.[62]

On the other hand, in the contemplative understanding taught by pseudo-Dionysius, Neoplatonism threatened the basically Christian originality of the incarnation by tracing it to the procession of the many from the One in the generous self-diffusion of the Good; it threatened all elements of the "mystery" by viewing the sacraments, even the eucharist, less as participations in the humanity of Christ than as rites symbolic of union with the Perfect One; it threatened to reduce the religious history of sinful man to a fall into multiplicity followed by a return to divine unity.

All this is the antithesis of what one finds in Augustine, whose

---

[62] See the letter of Dionysius to Polycarp, *Epistola* VII (*PG*, III, 1080). [The letter Dionysius supposedly wrote to Apollophanes, *Epistola XI* (*PG*, III, 1119), is a medieval forgery based upon the former.]

Christian conversion had nothing in common with Plotinian conversion or even with the "hierarchical" conversion of pseudo-Dionysius. Here now was an interior experience which Latin writers would associate with the *pati divina* (divine undergoing) of which pseudo-Dionysius spoke to Hierotheus in a magnificent but solitary passage. Moreover, the *anagogia* (ascent, or return) of pseudo-Dionysius developed within a metaphysical order and within a symbolic play from which literal history, even sacred history, was dismissed as beneath notice and which no longer served to provide men with strings of facts but rather to "initiate" them, through its symbols, into the τελέωσις (consummation, perfection) of the Divine Life. The second generation of Gilbert of La Porrée's followers, who drew upon pseudo-Dionysius to fortify the Neoplatonic doctrine on the One that they had received from Boethius, manifested the contempt felt by all Platonists for contingent events, even sacred events, of history. This contempt underlay their impatience with the skimpy Augustinianism of Peter Lombard.

Boethian humanism—logic-oriented, academic, Aristotelian—was alien to the spirit of pseudo-Dionysius. For Boethius the human sciences had their own independent purport apart from the hierarchical analogy, or ascent, for which they might prove a sound propaedeutic. In an effective encounter, however, his philosophy of the One was to help gain acceptance for the pseudo-Dionysian "One" and for the axioms deriving from it. Furthermore, critical analyses of the Platonic ideas and of the "divine names" combined Boethian epistemology fruitfully with the negative theology of pseudo-Dionysius—a feat which established syncretism as something more than facile harmonizing.

Pseudo-Dionysius's critical analysis of the divine names was, without a doubt, his most admirable Christian adaptation of Neoplatonic method. In this analysis he remained at the same time the faithful disciple of his Greek masters and the creator of a Christian theology. The *via negativa* (way of negation) of his treatise *On the Divine Names* brought into the West, especially through his ceaseless efforts to create new terminology, the entire store of Platonic dialectic concerning the ineffable, the ἐπέκεινα τῆς οὐσίας of *Republic* 509b which Plotinus and Proclus had already echoed. For three centuries, generation after generation of schoolmen drew upon this treatise—from John the Scot to St. Thomas, from Hugh of Saint-Victor to Eckhart —giving it expression within extremely varied systems, even including it within a modification of Aristotelian logic, which originally did not allow for the transcendent. In itself this fecundity testified at the same time to the religious greatness of pseudo-Dionysius, to the effectiveness of a Neoplatonic problematic in Christian theology, and to the ability of a full-grown faith to express itself in an authentic human culture and take root in an authentic system of human thought.[63]

This is the place to call attention to the infiltration of Hermetic thought that enriched this mystical concept of an unknown God and that belonged to the general stream of Neoplatonism, though to a different current. The first evidences of this infiltration were to be seen in the anonymous *Liber de sex rerum principiis (Book Concerning the Six Principles of Things)*,[64] produced between 1135–47. Hermetic influences here were as yet tenuous, confused, mixed with elements of Muslim astrology, and indebted to the works of "a certain natural philosopher" (Adelard of Bath). Bernard Sylvester and John of Salisbury were later to draw upon this work. Around 1160 the presence of Hermetic influences became more pronounced in precisely those centers which had been inspired now by Boethius, now by pseudo-Dionysius, but which remained reserved toward Augustine. Examples are to be found in the *Liber xxiv philoso-*

---

[63] E. von Ivanka, "La signification historique du Corpus Areopagiticum" *Rech. SR*, XXXVI (1949), 5–20.

[64] Theodore Silverstein, ed., "Liber Hermetis Mercurii Triplicis de VI rerum principiis," *AHDL*, XXII (1955), 217–302, where, along with the text, there is an analysis of its sources, content, and influence. Traces of it are found in Bernard Sylvester *De mundi universitate* and John of Salisbury *De septem septenis (PL*, CXCIX, 960–2). [On correspondences between this text and details of Hugh of Saint-Victor's *Didascalicon*, see Taylor, introduction, III: "The Readaptation of Heterodox Cosmological Texts and Themes" (pp. 19–28); cf. pp. 188–9, nn. 52, 53, 55, and p. 208, n. 8.] Roughly of the same period were Hugh of Santalla *Hermetis Trismegesti Liber de secretis naturae et occultis rerum causis ab Appollonio translatus* (MS Paris BN lat. 13951, fol. 1–31; analyzed by F. Nau, *Revue de l'Orient chrétien*, XII [1907], 99–106; traces in Herman of Carinthia *De essentiis*) and Adelard of Bath *Liber prestigiorum Thebidis secundum Ptolemeum et Hermetem* (see Haskins, *Studies,* p. 30); but these contain derivative and scattered astrological elements of Hermetic philosophy.

phorum (*Book of the Twenty-four Philosophers*) and the *Summa* of Alan of Lille.

Once again a metaphysics of the One was emphasized, but with accents peculiar to the *corpus Hermeticum*. There was a keen perception of the transcendent as rooted in the One. In its total and adequate awareness of itself, the One was an Intellect (νοῦς), a *movens immobilis* (immovable mover). As Being and Cause, it was Life. As Intellect and Life, this One engendered within itself as through a divine birth-process—something quite different from the production of beings through emanation. In this feature, medieval thinkers were pleased to recognize a presentiment of the Christian Trinity. Mathematical expressions and figures (the circle, the sphere, the point) were favorite means for describing emanation from the Monad. Delight was taken in epigrammatic formulas and axioms in repetitive and even alliterative chains; the *Book of the Twenty-four Philosophers* was not wide of the mark in attributing its remarkable definitions of God to Hermes Trismegistus. The most metaphysical expressions were charged with a religious character.

The mysticism of regeneration, of knowledge through introversion, of an aristocratic piety tied to a theurgic type of salvation, did not derive from Hermetic sources.[65] This was because the Hermetic writings did not have any systematic coherence. Unlike those of pseudo-Dionysius and Boethius, therefore, they did not circulate except in excerpts lifted from context rather as propositions that had been taught than as accounts of experience.

Finally, in line with Neoplatonic tradition, Hermetic authors did not distinguish between God as principle of the cosmic order and God as supreme idea and sole true reality; instead, they combined the two to support an idealist theology of creation and a lofty conception of transcendance paradoxically consistent with immanence.

The Introduction of Muslim Neoplatonism

A new tributary was to swell the stream of Neoplatonism still further. Heir and depository of Greek science and philosophy for

---

[65] See Festugière, vol. 4: *Le Dieu inconnu et la gnose.*

three centuries, the Muslim world was to pour its riches into the Christian West, which, though on crusade against Islam, was aware, at least in frontier regions such as Sicily and Spain, of the wealth and truth possessed by the adversary. The basic homogeneity of the Neoplatonic inspiration showed itself once more, this time in the contribution—as yet rudimentary but already important—which it made through Muslim culture to the converging influences of Augustine, pseudo-Dionysius, John the Scot, and Boethius. In the last third of the twelfth century, the first lot of Muslim works passed through the scriptorium of the Toledo translators and added yet another metaphysical and religious variant to the shifting forms of Neoplatonism already existing in the West. Thus began a protracted period of crises that was to end only at the beginning of "modern times," after the Middle Ages, through repeated struggles, had absorbed Muslim thought. The condemnation of 1210 revealed, in a manner as confused as the thing it denounced, a keen awareness of this ideological invasion, at the heart of which, it seems, lay a Muslim emanationism Neoplatonic in character.

a. The *Liber de causis*

The little treatise *De causis* (*Concerning Causes*), destined to have a great future, came into circulation toward the 1180's. It was a Latin translation made by Gerard of Cremona (died in 1187) from an Arabic text, probably of the ninth century. A concise and original reworking of the *Elementatio theologica* of Proclus, it circulated under the title *Liber Aristotelis de expositione bonitatis purae* (*The Book of Aristotle Concerning the Pure Good*)[66]—a title which gave further evidence of the guise under which Aristotle made his appearance at this moment in the West after having been considered a mere logician in the early Middle Ages. There were as yet only a few traces of the use of the *De causis*—in Alan of Lille; in the *De fluxu entis* (*On the Outflow of Being*), also entitled *De causis primis et secundis* (*On the First and Second Causes*);[67] in the *De*

---

[66] O. Bardenhewer, ed., *Die pseudo-aristotelische Schrift über das reine Gute, bekannt unter den Namen Liber de Causis* (Fribourg, 1882). It is improbable that the Arabic *De causis* was the work of a muslimizing Christian of Toledo in the twelfth century, as Théry and Alonso have suggested.

[67] See above, n. 6.

statibus hominis interioris (On the States of the Interior Man);[68] and in the *Speculum speculationum (Mirror of Speculations)*, written by Alexander Neckham between 1204–13. Despite its limited use at this early period and despite a syncretism that restricted its originality, the *De causis* had an influence worthy of careful description upon doctrine and literature. One had to wait for St. Thomas to solve the enigma of its origin and to perceive the framework of its thought.[69] Nonetheless, from 1180 on men recognized the resources it offered to a Christian seeking a way to purge the metaphysics of the One of emanationism. For that matter, it was itself clearly the product of a mind that wished to bend Proclus's hypostases to the service of the Judaeo-Muslim doctrine of a creator-God.

As its first resource, the *De causis* offered a complete and systematic explanation of the world in a series of theorems compact in their formulation, delightful to the mind, and exhibiting a real genius for metaphysics in their analysis of such great categories as the one and the many, the unchanging and the changing, cause and effect, whole and part, being, and intelligence. Not since Proclus had a Neoplatonic manual followed a method so deductive and so consistent in its idealism.

Obviously, the concept of causality was most fully exploited and developed with a metaphysical richness that neither Augustine nor even pseudo-Dionysius in his "way of causality" had achieved. Whereas in pseudo-Dionysius the Neoplatonic system was vitalized by a dynamic hierarchy that provided an ontological law and a religious thrust, here in the *De causis* the levels of being remained fixed and self-enclosed, with each reality deriving its participation in higher realities from within. Furthermore, the book preserved the integrity of the spiritual life, which had been central for Plotinus but which had disappeared in Proclus. It did so by affording a profound meditation upon eternity and by asserting the immanence of the First Cause in its effects and the presence of these, in turn, in the

---

[68] This is the title supplied for the anonymous and anacephalic treatise on the spiritual and cosmic journeys of the soul; text edited and analyzed by M.-Th. d'Alverny, *AHDL*, (1940), 239–99.

[69] See H. D. Saffrey, ed., *Sancti Thomae de Aquino super Librum de causis expositio* (Fribourg-Louvain, 1954), introduction.

First Cause. The treatise *On the States of the Interior Man* profited by these considerations in its description of the soul's pilgrimage toward beatitude. In the *De causis*—this Muslim adaptation of Proclus's *Elementatio theologica*—God existed, and not merely the One with its henads. While concentrating the transcendental realities within himself, He became, if not a person, at least an existence, an *esse*. This is a long way, however, from the "definitions" of God in the *Book of the Twenty-four Philosophers*, an admirable expression of the mystical metaphysics of the twelfth century.

However, it was in its adaptation of the concept of "procession" to creation that the *De causis* opened up traditional Neoplatonism to theologians. The First Cause, now including the fulness of transcendental perfections—one, good, intelligence, soul, the one supreme and universal form—was the creating cause as well. The fourth proposition of the *De causis* became classic—*Prima rerum creatarum est esse* (the first of created things is being)—and this *esse*, as the first form of all reality, defined the radical dependence of that reality upon the *primum esse* (First Being). But twelfth-century masters, completely dominated by the notion of "formation" typical of Platonic idealism not only in the *De causis* but in Augustine and Boethius or Proclus and Avicenna, were as yet unable to isolate "creation" properly so called, namely as the cause of total existence. The treatise *On First and Second Causes* prepared the way for their discernment of creation[70] but did not itself depart from the thesis of the *De causis* that several creative principles, each according to its own formality, came together in the production of beings. In this matter the Aristotelianism of Boethius would seem to have offered greater stimulus to metaphysical reflection by providing beings with an ontological constitution of their own without excluding, indeed right *within*, their participation in the transcendent.

b. Avicenna

Acquaintance with Avicenna, who was just being made known to the West by the Toledo translators, strengthened the hold that this

---

[70] See de Vaux, *op. cit.,* pp. 124–5.

same metaphysical structure—its problems and solutions—had upon men. Knowledge of Avicenna was as yet mostly sketchy. If Gundissalinus, given the advantage of his situation in Toledo, had a good view of the totality of Avicenna's thought, those who made use of that thought in other centers took from it, apart from certain Neoplatonic commonplaces, only the most conspicuous elements of his cosmology and psychology. No doubt it is with these first infiltrations of Avicenna that one must identify the *commenta Aristotelis* (comments upon Aristotle) that were denounced in 1210 and associated with Amaury of Bène.[71]

Except in Gundissalinus, the influence of Avicenna brought "the Cause" to greater prominence than "the One" and "the Good" in ongoing Neoplatonic tradition. One sees this in the later disciples of Gilbert of La Porrée, for instance, in Ralph of Longchamp's commentary on the *Anticlaudianus* of Alan of Lille, about 1205; in the treatise *On First and Second Causes*, which attempted without much success to combine Augustine, John the Scot, and the *De causis* with Avicenna; and in the treatise *On the States of the Interior Man*, which was textually closer than others to Avicenna and faithful to his hierarchy of beings.

Twelfth-century authors as yet made no use of Avicenna's famous thesis concerning the accidental quality of existence or of his metaphysics of essential, not merely temporal, contingency. In the fragments of the *Shifa* that they read, they did not avail themselves of its meticulous analysis of the creative act, tied as this analysis was to subtle Arabic terminology untranslatable in stiff and plain Latin phrases. Thus it was in quite elementary fashion that they, above all Amaury, handled the concept of *esse* (being) which Avicenna had subjected to the classical dialectic of Neoplatonism in the style of the *De causis*.[72] And yet, thanks to Avicenna, they began to recog-

---

[71] [See Cl. Baeumker, *Contra Amaurianos. Ein anonymer, warscheinlich dem Garnerius von Rochefort zugehöriger Traktat gegen die Amalrikaner aus dem Anfang des XIII Jahrhunderts* (*BGPM*, XXIV [Münster, 1926], 5–6); C. Capelle, *Autour du décret de 1210: Amaury de Bène, étude sur son panthéisme formel* (Paris, 1932); and M.-Th.d'Alverny, "Un fragment du proces des Amauriciens," *AHDL*, XVIII (1950–1), 325–66.]

[72] A jamming together of the technical terminology of Boethius and that of Avicenna on *esse*—"forma," "quo est"—worked against the originality of

nize that the diversity of beings sprang not from a limitation inseparable from emanation as such, but from the conscious intention of
the First Cause; this recognition gave a setback to pure emanationism
by providing for the ultimate will of the creator.

The *De immortalitate animae* (*On the Immortality of the Soul*)
of Gundissalinus, the *De anima* (*On the Soul*) attributed to him, and
the treatise *On the States of the Interior Man* first introduced the
West to Avicenna's metaphysics of the soul and his related analysis
of the theory of knowledge. The whole was framed within a cosmology featuring the stars, animate heavens, and the like, which struck
men's imaginations, if one may judge by graphic representations that
accompany the manuscripts.[73] Here again, certain curious points of
contact with the accounts of the soul given by Christian spiritual
writers, even at Cîteaux,[74] allowed for some contribution to the syncretism of these thinkers; one such involves the doctrine of the two
"faces" of the soul, which, preserving its Augustinian character in
Gundissalinus, is found in the distinction between *intellectus* and
intelligentia (intellect and understanding) in the treatise *On the Soul*
attributed to him.

Those who gave or were yet to give a religious cast to their transcendental dialectic likewise drew upon Avicenna with good reason.
The Muslim philosopher was of a completely different stamp from
Proclus, whose theurgic piety was excluded from his manuals of
metaphysics. Avicenna was a mystic, and his philosophical concepts
were not divorced from his mystical experience. Even when William
of Auvergne would denounce Avicenna's *deliramenta* (mad ideas),
he could not have escaped from the religious influence of one whom
he called "so great a philosopher."[75] Moreover, the *theoria* of pseudo-

---

the Muslim philosopher, even in Albert the Great. St. Thomas reversed that
influence, both in terminology and in doctrines, to the benefit of Avicenna.

[73] See illustration reproduced in M.-Th. d'Alverny (cited above, n. 68), p.
268.

[74] See de Vaux, *op. cit.*, pp. 172, 175; striking likenesses are to be found
between Gundissalinus's *De anima* (last chapter) and Isaac of L'Etoile.

[75] *De legibus* (see the Orléans, 1674 ed., of William's works: Vol. I, p.
54a): "Cujus damnatio tanto justior quanto ista deliramenta tantus philo-
sophus magis videre potuit et videre neglexit." (His condemnation is the more
just because of those mad ideas which so great a philosopher could more
easily have judged and which he failed to do.)

Dionysius blended well with the vision of things in God evoked by Avicenna's analysis of their subtle being. This was not the case with the *De causis.*

Conclusion

Were these Neoplatonisms of the Middle Ages anything more than sketchy and confused offshoots of the great works of Plato, of Plotinus, of Avicenna? Ignorance of a great part of the work of these men, indirect and fragmentary transmission of their texts and teachings, independable translations and the poverty of the Latin vocabulary, an experimental syncretism which picked apart the best constructed systems—all of these seriously restricted the authenticity and the quality of these Neoplatonisms. At the same time, scholars have justly reacted against an earlier and excessively harsh judgment which concealed the originality of this Latin Platonism of the twelfth century and refused to see in it anything more than a patchwork product.[76] To be sure, no genius rebuilt, from within, a new system based upon Plato's inspiration, as St. Thomas was to do with Aristotle in the following century. Even less was this a renaissance, a rebirth, in the manner provided by the historical reconstruction of the Quattrocento. Nonetheless, the intellectual curiosity and the protracted labors of the twelfth-century masters gave both unity and character to the Platonic materials with which they dealt, whether in their schools or in their meditations.

As Christians, as students of the Bible, as theologians, these masters tried to overcome the antagonism they endlessly encountered between Semitic religion and Hellenic intellectualism, between the gospel and Greek naturalism, by a convinced determination to harmonize them. The fathers had certainly pointed the way. Philo among the Jews and Avicenna among the Arabs had anticipated the effort made by twelfth-century masters to bring together the God of nature with the God of history and of the Bible. After much fumbling and many setbacks, they raised their endeavors to the level of theological knowledge, the great task of which is precisely to use

---

[76] See Klibansky, *Continuity of the Platonic Tradition* (cited above, n. 28).

the resources of reason to build up faith in the mystery of God from within the faith itself. The task remains and is renewed from century to century, and it finds its unity and its validity less in its philosophical materials than in its confronting these materials with the same promises and the one light of Christian revelation. The masters of the twelfth-century were intellectually and institutionally theologians, not philosophers. The historian of philosophy cannot give them full treatment. To de-existentialize creation, to lift the history of individual souls into the eternal order of things, to fill up the chasm dividing an essentialist Platonic ontology from a theology of history —to these immense tasks five generations devoted themselves with tenacity; and ancient Platonism, already prolific in countless ways, found a new fruitfulness in their works. Testimony to its vitality is found in the very opposition the enterprise encountered, not only from the monastic theology of a Rupert of Deutz or from Cîteaux, but from certain professional experts in theology as well. Robert of Melun, one of the adversaries of Gilbert of La Porrée at the Council of Reims, denounced its contaminating effect upon doctrine and even upon biblical language: "As for that quotation I gave you— 'the causes or reasons of things are inferior to the creator but superior to the creature'—I have never heard anyone cite any passage of scripture where this quotation can be found or clearly implied, nor can I find it in scripture myself, no matter how hard I try. Indeed, these words—'the causes or reasons of things are inferior to the creator but superior to the creature'—smack more of Platonic thought than they do of the Church's."[77] It was necessary to bring in either Augustine, with his transformation of Neoplatonism through his own brilliant experience, or pseudo-Dionysius, with the reputation his mysticism and his legend enjoyed. Peter Lombard, insensitive to Neoplatonism, ignored pseudo-Dionysius and impoverished Augustine.

---

[77] *Sententiae*, i.XI.12 (Martin, II, 269): "Quod autem dixi scriptum esse *Rationes rerum infra creatorem esse et supra creaturam,* nec scripturam in qua hoc reperiri possit aut certo vocabulo designari audivi, nec in aliqua scriptura, in quantum valeo, legi. Verba vero haec *Rationes rerum infra creatorem sunt et supra creaturam,* platonicam disciplinam magis redolent quam ecclesiasticam."

In this fashion, then, and bending before the necessities which always dominate even the most flexible accommodations, Christians of this century revived various tensions internal to Platonism itself: the tension between the cosmic God of the *Timaeus* and the hidden God of Plotinus and Hermes Trismegistus; between an optimistic vision of the world and a pessimistic dualism of matter and spirit; between a rational theology and theurgic mysteries; between the way that leads from the many to the One and that leading from the One to the many. Alan of Lille was the best witness of these tensions. The realism of Christian history, the inevitable personalism of grace, the inviolable mysteries of the divine plan—these both illuminated and screened the Platonizing in which theology deliberately engaged. Augustine and pseudo-Dionysius could not easily be reconciled; Boethius seemed too pat. Some refused Platonism as too rational; others were led astray by it into heresy. Plato led some to scorn the world of sense, others to rejoice in exuberant contact with nature and to become interested in the sciences and arts. All accepted the duality of the human mind, its face turned upwards toward ecstasy; and thus they deviated from the biblical monism, in which man was caught up in the drama of sin and grace in all his concrete reality, and in which God's action became incarnate in order to make contact with creation precisely in its physical reality.

But whatever the variants of Neoplatonism, it remained, as Emile Bréhier called it, "a description of the metaphysical landscapes through which the soul is transported as it undergoes what might be described as spiritual training."[78] It was precisely its religious character that attracted men of this time. In their schools or in their cells, it was for them a means of access to the intelligible Reality. Despite its awkward conflation of disparate elements, the treatise *On First and Second Causes* was a theological work, not a venturesome sortie into metaphysics. Moreover, they considered knowledge, or contemplation, as having an ontological worth—what an exaltation of faith! Here we are far from Aristotelian intellectualism, from Plato himself. The concept of creation was a religious one;

---

[78] *Histoire de la philosophie*, I, 450; tr. Baskin, II, 182 (cited above, n. 37).

God was no mere architect. By itself, metaphysics could only lay hold upon the paradoxes attending this concept; it was peculiar to Hebraic thought.

Yet, many, though nourished by the *Consolation of Philosophy* and closer to the *Timaeus*, used this supreme intelligible Reality to explain the sense-perceptible world and not merely to mount toward Being that is self-existent and divorced from the world. The followers of Gilbert of La Porrée combined the cosmic mysticism of the Greek fathers with the epistemological rationalism of Boethius. Hugh of Saint-Victor, faithful Augustinian that he was, drew up an *ordo disciplinae* (order of study or discipline) which soon entered into the Aristotelian naturalism that characterized medical studies from 1200 on. And yet the appearance of Aristotle was to provoke a violent reaction not only from the orthodoxy but from the sensitivities of Christians.

Was Platonism, then, to be the only philosophy congenial to the theologian? St. Thomas showed that it was not. In his work, faith in search of understanding had recourse to Aristotle—to his anthropology, his metaphysics, his method—in order to build itself into a "science," a project which neither Platonic inspiration nor Platonic techniques could authorize.[79] Strange outcome, this, for the genius of Aristotle, which had never taken the transcendent as its object. Yet it provided the means for estimating the scope and establishing the methods proper to man's earthbound reason, if only to permit its attaining to the First Being, whereas Platonism impugned these for the sake of methods independent of the structures of man's intelligence.[80]

---

[79] Cf. Etienne Gilson, "Le christianisme et la tradition philosophique," *RSPT*, XXX (1941–42), 249–66; on the double polarity of Christian theological traditions, see A. von Ivanka, "Aristotelismus und Platonismus im theologischen Denken. Westliche und östliche Theologie," *Schol.*, XIV (1939), 373–96.

[80] See L. B. Geiger, *La participation dans la philosophie de saint Thomas d'Aquin* (Paris, 1942), p. 449: "If men went beyond Aristotle here, Aristotle was not betrayed. One may go so far as to say that Aristotle's logic, just as he elaborated it, remained intact, for it was still the only logic having empirical and rigorous worth and did not stretch beyond the world of sensible substances for which Aristotle himself used it. What St. Thomas added to it was not a new logic; it was a new use of the unique logic of Aristotle in a negative

A rarified outcome as well, for Aristotelianism did not destroy Platonic "spiritualism," to which Christians still turned spontaneously, though not without some handicap to their appreciation of the spirit of the gospel, to their appreciation of historical reality, to their worldly effectiveness. Nor did Aristotelianism diminish in any way the nobility and the truth of twelfth-century Neoplatonism —a fact that rules out any simplistic contrast between "the Aristotelianism of the scholastics" and "the Platonism of the fathers," a distinction which represents a historical error and a misunderstanding of theology.

---

form in a domain it had not penetrated—that of pure spirits and the First Being.

"But since this was an extension made negatively, Aristotle's logic was not totally abandoned. It was retained as the permanent basis of the boldest efforts to express the nature of separated substances and of God: negative knowledge, as St. Thomas understood it, far from denying the primacy, *quoad nos,* of man's apprehension of the sensible world and his rational knowledge, implied that such primacy was its most essential character."

In consequence, the laws, the very existence, of such negative knowledge of the mystery of God are not simply an outgrowth of the affective side of human nature but a structural necessity imposed by the rational struggle of the theologian to lay hold upon the divine object. The too hasty syncretism of Neoplatonists in the twelfth century arrested this process only momentarily.

3

The Symbolist Mentality

"**P**OETRY'S LYRE RINGS with vibrant falsehood on the outward literal shell of a poem, but interiorly it communicates a hidden and profound meaning to those who listen. The man who reads with penetration, having cast away the outer shell of falsehood, finds the savory kernel of truth wrapped within."[1] Thus does Alan of Lille declare the principle of his art, which uses metaphor and, even more, myth—the myth of Nature, the myth of Fortune, the myth of Venus, which support the play of his art through a long narrative—not as mere literary devices or tropes to give a poet's touch to some intellectual reality, but as consistent means for signifying the inner substance of things. They are not therefore part of a psychological game played by an esthete, even though literary elegance—*elegans pictura* —is also involved; at stake is the discernment of the profound truth that lies hidden within the dense substance of things and is revealed by these means.

One might have taken the same sort of declaration from a professor of the "arts of poetry" in the schools or, better still, from the works of Chrétien of Troyes or from Arthurian romance—did not

---

[1] "At, in superficiali litterae cortice falsum resonat lyra poetica, sed interius, auditoribus secretum intelligentiae altioris eloquitur, ut exteriore falsitatis abjecto putamine, dulciorem nucleum veritatis secrete intus lector inveniat"; Alan of Lille *De planctu naturae* (*PL*, CCX, 451C). This statement on the use of myth, Alan puts into the mouth of Dame Nature. Cf. R. de Lage, p. 117: "One surmises that this author found pleasure in the difficulty of working out a metaphor, and one can judge him successful. His ingenuity does not entitle one to lavish praise upon the ease and inventiveness Platonism afforded him; selection and arrangement would have been a crushing task for a twelfth-century author. Yet one must grant Alan of Lille a certain talent for the difficult art he chose as a vehicle for his ideas."

the quest for the Holy Grail supply this art with its most beautiful theme? I take the principle, however, from a theologian and philosopher—one, to be sure, who wrote allegorical poems on the side and who was disposed by his profession to inquire into the profound reasons of things and to assess special instances of human behavior even when he wrote in literary forms invented by human art. Alan of Lille defined the end and the means of the poetic art that dominated the great works of the century. Undoubtedly one can disagree with this conception of art—use of poetic fiction to express intellectual truth, so that art becomes a minor branch of man's quest for truth. But at least one should see this conception as the result of a world vision comprehending two levels, with the second level lying beneath the surface and becoming accessible through transposition, via imagery, onto the first. Such symbolic transposition was the admirable means of penetrating the mysterious material density of things—natural objects or historical personages, Biblical or profane —and of getting, "through the shell, to the savory kernel of truth." Poetry was in the service of wisdom—of philosophical or theological wisdom.[2]

---

[2] Authors of the twelfth century explicitly drew the consequences that followed from subordinating "the young boys' cradle of poetic discipline" to "the adult exposition of philosophy"—the terms are Alan of Lille's (*De planctu naturae, PL,* CCX, 451C): "Nonne ea quae in puerilibus cunis poeticae disciplinae discutientur, altiori distinctionis lima, senior philosophiae tractatus eliminat?" (The things left cluttered in the young boys' cradle of poetic discipline—does not the adult exposition of philosophy, with its filing edge of analysis, eliminate them?) "Poetry's lyre" plays in the name of truth, while the fictions (*figmenta*) of poetry, lovely without question, are lies that move us to relish truth for its full worth. Poets are liars, and "the lies of poets are in service of truth" (*mendacia poetarum serviunt veritati*), said John of Salisbury *Policraticus* iii.6 (Webb, II, 186; Pike, p. 167). Aquinas would later repeat it as a common proverb; see M. R. Cathala and R. M. Spiazzi, eds., *In duodecim libros Metaphysicorum Aristotelis expositio* (Turin, 1950), comm. 63, and John T. Rowan, tr., *St. Thomas Aquinas, Commentary on the Metaphysics of Aristotle* (Chicago, 1961), I, 26: ". . . poetae non solum in hoc, sed in multis aliis mentiuntur, sicut dicitur in proverbio vulgari" (poets lie not only in this matter but in many others, as the common proverb says). Cf. also John of Salisbury *Entheticus de dogmate philosophorum* 183–8 (*PL,* CXCIX, 966):

                    . . . Insta
        Ut sit Mercurio Philologia comes,
        Non quia numinibus falsis reverentia detur,

If in what follows I attend simply to the philosophical import of the literary and artistic forms of the twelfth century, it is because it is not my task here to describe such forms in and for themselves; for this, one must go to literary historians and the historians of the representational arts. It is necessary to keep these art forms before us, however, because the symbolist methods we are going to examine, whether used in the exploration of natural phenomena or in the reading of sacred texts and the interpretation of the liturgy, become historically understandable only in the context of the poetry and visual art of the century. The same men read the Grail story and the homilies of St. Bernard, carved the capitals of Chartres and composed the bestiaries, allegorized Ovid and scrutinized the typological senses of the Bible, or enriched their christological analyses of the sacraments with naturalistic symbols of water, light, eating, marriage. To be sure, they did not confuse either their levels of operation or their objects; but on these different levels they benefited by common recourse to the subtle play of analogies drawn from the mysterious kinship between the physical world and the realm of the sacred. How can one write the history of Christian doctrines, let alone that of theological science, without taking into consideration this recourse to symbols—to symbols drawn from nature, from history, from liturgical practice—which continually nourished both doctrine and theology?

Thus it is appropriate to take stock of the techniques characteristic of this symbolism, unique yet markedly versatile in its application in many fields, and first, of the linguistic side of this symbolism—its vocabulary, its literary or didactic genres, its maxims, its divisions and subdivisions, its "topics," in short, the whole of its school-taught

---

Sed sub verborum tegmine vera latent.
Vera latent rerum variarum tecta figuris,
  Nam sacra vulgari publica jura vetant.
[Insist that Philology is consort to Mercury not
because reverence is paid to false deities but
because truths lie under the cloak of words.
Truths lie covered by the figures of various
things, for public laws forbid sacred things
to the crowd.]
Is this a degradation of Platonic forms and method? Symbols, if metaphor is not operative, are only empty contrivances and betray reality.

apparatus.[3] From this we shall pass on to what we have called a "mentality": a permeating influence, of which men were more or less aware, upon their ways and turns of thought; a cast or coloration given to even their commonest notions; a body of assumptions rarely expressed yet accepted everywhere and by all and very difficult to uncover.[4] Masters in the schools, mystics, exegetes, students of nature, seculars, religious, writers, and artists—these men of the twelfth century had in common with all other men of the Middle Ages the conviction that all natural or historical reality possessed a *significatio* which transcended its crude reality and which a certain symbolic dimension of that reality would reveal to man's mind. This conviction, enforced by the context of their lives, dominated their judgment by supplying it with an intrinsic set of categories and values. Giving an account of things involved more than explaining them by reference to their internal causes; it involved discovering that dimension of mystery.

The Extension of Symbolism

While historians of rationalist orientation—even historians of theology—have noted and valued the rise of dialectic under Abelard's influence, they have shown some contempt for those areas of literature which used symbolism as a method of inquiry and formulation. This adverse judgment, which even the worst excesses of

---

[3] Lacking a comprehensive treatment of these features, one may consult particular studies which, apart from creations used in the plastic arts, analyze the literary forms and techniques of Bernard Sylvester's *De mundi universitate,* the poetic works of Alan of Lille, romances of the various cycles, philosophical cosmographies, typological exegeses of the Bible, liturgical works, and pastoral homilies with their *artes praedicandi.* For a few elemental categories, see E. R. Curtius, *European Literature and the Latin Middle Ages* (New York, 1953), esp. chap. 7, "Metaphorics" [discussion of Bernard Sylvester and Alan of Lille in chap. 6, "The Goddess Natura," pp. 106ff. and passim], and for primary sources, Edmond Faral, *Les arts poétiques du XIIe et du XIIIe siècles* (Paris, 1923).

[4] Ranging beyond languages and literary techniques as it obviously does, the "mentality" of an age nonetheless does not completely reveal the "spirit" of the age, even when conveying it. One cannot reduce the irreducible message of a St. Bernard or a Gilbert of La Porrée to a category of mental behavior. I resort to these historical categories as they are formulated by J. Guitton, *Le temps et l'éternité chez Plotin et Saint Augustin* (Paris, 1933).

allegorism do not justify, cannot in any case conceal that vast literature with its extraordinary diversity of product, from mirrors of the cosmos to biblical typologies. In the whole range of its culture, the medieval period was an era of the symbol as much as, indeed more than, an era of dialectic. As for dialectic, so for symbolism, as we have already remarked, there arose an apparatus of expressions, of technical terminology, which provided the tools common to this mode of thought; and one can observe side by side with the logical methods elaborated by the *Analytics* and the *Topics* extremely varied forms of reasoning which lay at the basis of symbolic treatment. "A symbol," said Hugh of Saint-Victor, "is a juxtaposition, that is, a coaptation of visible forms brought forth to demonstrate some invisible matter."[5] The play of this sort of reasoning did not constitute proof. Hugh's "demonstration" was hardly that of Aristotle, and it ought rather to be rendered as "display"; to think the opposite would be seriously to confuse two distinct modes of thought to the detriment of both. To bring symbolism into play was not to extend or supplement a previous act of the reason; it was to give primary expression to a reality which reason could not attain and which reason, even afterwards, could not conceptualize. Moreover, these symbols claimed to disclose certain intimate relationships—ranging from the psychological import of colors to the sublimated religious value of social acts or to revelations of the divine in nature—which the art of ascertaining multiform truth could not fail to take into consideration. The growing discredit of symbolic modes of thought and of the role of metaphor in religious knowledge of the world provided, without doubt, the basic motive for the conservative reaction against the seductions of dialectic and the spread of Aristotelian logic in the twelfth century and after. Abelard was the contemporary of Rupert of Deutz (died 1138), known for his systematic allegories, and of Hildegard of Bingen (died 1179), whose cosmology was permeated with symbolic soteriology.

This later discredit of symbolic modes of thought obscures for us

---

[5] *Expos. in Hier. cael.* iii, *ad init.* (*PL*, CLXXV, 960D); ". . . symbolum, collatio videlicet, id est coaptatio visibilium formarum ad demonstrationem rei invisibilis propositarum."

even today the extent and quality of that immense field within which, in the twelfth century, symbolism progressed without any break with earlier centuries from childish utilization of a rudimentary knowledge of nature, to the valid poetico-theological "demonstrations" of Hugh of Saint-Victor; from idealization of the "lady" in courtly love, to the metaphors with a liturgical reference found in the quest for the Grail; from the eschatological imagery of Joachim of Floris, to the evangelical world of the first Franciscans.

The most rudimentary material utilized at this time came from the lapidaries and bestiaries. This literary genre goes back to pagan antiquity, and its materials provided a miserable substitute for men's ignorance of the laws of animate and inanimate nature. Under color of reference to spiritual values, the properties of things ceased to be objects for scientific study and were taken as images of human virtues and powers; so earth, rock, soil, and of course light, shadows, and stars; so grass, the spike of grain, straw, and seed; so the lion, the wild ass, the sparrow, and the scorpion. At its farthest reach, symbolism was carried away by its game and indulged in allegory. For its own pleasure it created mythic beings—the griffin, the phoenix, the unicorn—and, in these contrived beasts, nature with its attendant meanings was no longer present.[6] For living beings in particular, the *Physiologus*, composed in Alexandria in the second century, remained the classic source book, one already given currency by Isidore's *Etymologiae*. The old reserve of the *Decretum Gelasianum*, which classed the *Physiologus* as apocryphal (the term was

---

[6] Here we do no more than call to mind, in their range, the vast fields covered by an overgrowth of symbols. Among many such, see, for the field of letters in France, C. V. Langlois, *La vie en France au moyen âge* (4 vols.; Paris, 1926–8), and for the arts, Emile Mâle, *L'art religieux du XIIIe siècle en France* (Paris, 1902; published in 1913 as *Religious Art in France of the Thirteenth Century*, reprinted [New York, 1958] as *The Gothic Image*), bks. 1–4, "The Mirror of Nature," "The Mirror of Instruction," "The Mirror of Morals," "The Mirror of History." [On the use of such materials in poetry, see, e.g., Léopold Hervieux, ed. *Les fabulistes latins depuis le siècle d'Auguste jusqu'à la fin du moyen âge*, 5 vols. (Paris, 1884–99), and on a modern approach to medieval poetry through attention to such materials, D. W. Robertson Jr., "The Doctrine of Charity in Mediaeval Literary Gardens: A Topical Approach through Symbolism and Allegory," *Spec.* XVI (1951), 24–49, with discussion of dangers and problems in Dorothy Bethurum, ed., *Critical Approaches to Medieval Literature* (N.Y., 1960).]

originally applied to a work of unknown authorship and on that account suspect), was repeated by Hugh of Saint-Victor[7] but without effective detriment to the work's fame. At the beginning of the century the Anglo-Norman poet Philip of Taon translated it into French, as did William of Normandy a century later. Hugh of Fouilloy used it expressly in his *De natura avium* (*On the Nature of Birds;* about 1166); biblical glosses on the names of animals copied from it, and so did sermon literature.

At Chartres, the study of nature was tied to symbolist traditions in letters as in the plastic arts. The allegorical formulations of Bernard Sylvester in his *De universitate mundi* were at one with the cosmogony of Thierry of Chartres and contemporary with the lifelike fauna and flora carved on the capitals of the cathedral. Alexander Neckham, in his *De naturis rerum* (*On the Natures of Things*)[8] did not reject the world as seen by Rhabanus Maurus; and, if he profited by the rise of naturalism and valued the true properties of

---

[7] *Didascalicon* iv.15 (Buttimer, p. 91; Taylor, p. 117). [Detailed history of the original Greek *Physiologus* and medieval Latin and vernacular translations in Florence McCullough, *Medieval Latin and French Bestiaries* (Chapel Hill, 1960); bibliography, pp. 205–10. Latin text of one version in Francis J. Carmody, ed. *Physiologus latinus: éditions préliminaires, versio B* (Paris, 1939), and another by the same editor in "Physiologus Latinus Versio Y," *Univ. of California Publications in Classical Philology*, XII (1941), 95–134; English trans. by the same, *Physiologus. The Very Ancient Book of Beasts, Plants and Stones* (San Francisco, 1953). On relationship between the *Physiologus* and a Latin work mistakenly attributed to Hugh of Saint-Victor, see Carmody's *"De Bestiis et Aliis Rebus"* and the Latin Physiologus," *Spec.,* XIII (1938), 153–9.]

[8] Thomas Wright, ed. *Alexandri Neckam De naturis rerum libri duo* prol. (Rolls Series, vol. 34 [London, 1863], p. 2): "Decrevit itaque parvitas mea quarumdam rerum naturas scripto commendare, ut proprietatibus ipsarum investigatis ad originem ipsarum, ad rerum videlicet opificem, mens lectoris recurrat, ut ipsum admirans in se et in creaturis suis, pedes Creatoris, justitiam scilicet et misericordiam, spiritualiter osculetur. Nolo tamen ut opinetur lector me naturas rerum fugere, volentes investigare velle philosophice aut physice, moralem enim libet instituere tractatum." (My poor ability has set me the task of writing about the natures of certain things, so that when their properties have been explored, the reader's mind may hark back to their source, namely the Maker of things, and, admiring that Maker in Himself and in His creatures, in spirit kiss His feet, that is, His justice and His mercy. But I do not want the reader to think I am shirking the natures of things, for it is agreeable for those who wish to investigate them philosophically or physically to subject them to moral treatment.)

things, he nonetheless made his own the metaphysical and symbolic perspective which thrived on using natural objects to elevate the mind to their Creator.

Among all the realities of nature, color has always been a suitable vehicle for some supraphysical meaning out on the spiritual borderline. Commonplace in all times, color symbolism was utilized even more by liturgists than by poets in the twelfth century. Innocent III afforded a classic instance of this in his *De sacro altaris ministerio* (*On the Sacred Ministry of the Altar*).[9]

Numbers were like the thoughts of God, and in decoding their meaning one discovered the secret of a world whose harmony derived from "measure and number and weight" (Wisd. 11:21). Here as elsewhere, it was Isidore of Seville who had assembled the traditional materials in his *Liber numerorum* (*Book of Numbers*).[10] To gather together the number allegories of Hugh of Saint-Victor is to reconstitute almost the whole of Augustine's speculations on numbers.[11] Sacramentaries and biblical commentaries put together numbers with no less subtlety than satisfaction. Odo of Morimond composed an *Analytica numerorum in theographiam* (*An Anatomy of Numbers for Divine Writings*).[12] All knew that they were exploiting a vein worked by the "philosophers," that is, the pagans; but they loaded their neo-Pythagorean speculations with biblical arithmetic and their calculations on the cosmos were shot through with Christian mystery and so sanctified.[13] The Trinity provided notable occa-

---

[9] i.32: "De quatuor coloribus" (On the Four Colors; *PL*, CCXVII, 786).

[10] *Liber numerorum.qui in sanctis scripturis occurrunt* (*Book of Numbers that Occur in Sacred Scripture; PL*, LXXXIII, 179–99).

[11] [Cf. his peculiar numerological interpretation of the soul and the body in *Didascalicon* ii.4–5 (Buttimer, pp. 27–29; Taylor pp. 64–67), and his traditional view of mathematics as a *doctrinalis scientia* (doctrinal science), *ibid.* ii.3 (Buttimer, pp. 25–27; Taylor, pp. 63–64, and esp. p. 196, n. 7).]

[12] See the notice in *PL*, CLXXXVIII, 1643.

[13] So Rupert of Deutz *De divinis officiis* vii.14 (*PL*, CLXX, 194): "Ternarius numerus, qui apud saeculares quoque philosophos insignis habetur, pro eo quod imparium, et eorum qui praeter unitatem nullam aliam recipiunt sectionem, primus est numerorum, apud nos longe amplius praeclari nominis, imo primae ac divinae est auctoritatis, tam propter ipsam essentiam sanctae et individuae Trinitatis, quam pro eo quod salvator noster tertia die resurrexit a mortuis." (The number 'three,' revered among pagan philosophers because it is the first of odd numbers and numbers that cannot be divided by any except

sion for such speculation, and so did the number seven; septenaries kept on multiplying, and the seven sacraments, the seven virtues, the seven gifts of the Holy Spirit, and the seven capital sins joined the seven planets, the seven celestial periods, and the seven musical tones of the *pervirgo septenarius*.[14] Ralph Glaber spoke of the "divine quaternity" of the four gospels, the four elements, the four principal virtues, and the four senses.[15]

It was known that the "philosophers" had regarded names too as signs that revealed the realities they stood for (think of the *Cratylus* of Plato). Here again Semitic belief as found in the Bible joined hands with a thesis of the Greeks, and men of the Middle Ages developed the whole thing into a system enriched by the "etymologies" of Isidore. The pseudo-Dionysian theory of analogies promptly conferred a quasi-metaphysical importance upon the grammatical operation of *denominatio*, the giving of names to things. The alphabet itself, as found in the letters of a name, was used: "Adam," according to the numerical values of the Greek letters, added up to forty-six, the number proper to the perfect man[16]; and the *Semina scripturarum* (*Seeds of the Scriptures*) attributed to Joachim of Floris[17] includes a complete symbolism of the alphabet.

Man himself, his history and destiny, would seem at first blush to be little susceptible of symbolic interpretation. But in all civilizations myths have formed the collective expression of symbolic views of history as well as of basic religious categories; their subsequent

---

'one,' is even more revered among us as of prime and divine authority, both because of the essence of the holy and individual Trinity and because our savior rose from the dead on the third day.) [For an arithmological treatment of the procession of the divine Wisdom from the Father, and of creation itself, see Thierry of Chartres *De sex dierum operibus,* Haring, cited above, p. 63, n. 27.]

[14] [See, e.g., the *De quinque septenis seu septenariis* (*On the Five Sevens or Septenaries; PL*, CLXXV, 405–14) ascribed to Hugh of Saint-Victor, and the *Liber de septem septenis* (*Book of the Seven Sevens; PL*, CXCIX, 945–64) ascribed to John of Salisbury.]

[15] *Historiarum sui temporis libri quinque* I.1: "De divina quaternitate" (*PL*, CXLII, 613–14; Prou, pp. 2–7). From the extraordinarily large list of available studies on number symbolism in the Middle Ages, see V. F. Hopper, *Medieval Number Symbolism* (N.Y., 1938).

[16] Honorius of Autun *Sacramentarium* (*PL*, CLXXII, 741D).

[17] MS Vat. lat. 3819, f. 1–10.

naturalistic interpretation, as in the case of euhemerism, might ruin their claim to religious value, but it then turns about and confers upon mythic episodes a moral significance. The Christian Middle Ages, following the example of the fathers who had played Euhemerus against the false gods, used the mythographers, whose prototype they took to be Fulgentius with his *Mythologiae*, dating from the second half of the fifth century. Sigebert of Gembloux perfectly described the mechanism at work in Fulgentius[18]; and Alexander Neckham, in his *Scintillarium poetarum* (*Glimmerings of the Poets*), or *Mithologie*,[19] clearly took up the mythography of Fulgentius for his own purposes. Martianus Capella's *De nuptiis Mercurii et Philologiae* (*On the Marriage Feast of Mercury and Philology*),[20] the basic textbook of medieval instruction in the seven arts, popularized the method while totally depriving mythology of any pagan character, for its allegory rested upon no believed-in events or personages. No more than Remigius of Auxerre, commentator on Martianus in the ninth century,[21] did Bernard Sylvester and Alan of Lille and others of their later time have the least belief in Minerva, in Venus, or in Fortune; it was their metaphysical inventiveness that created and exploited myth, under however mediocre an allegory.

The same procedure came into play in personification of the vir-

---

[18] *Liber de scriptoribus ecclesiasticis* xxviii (*PL*, CLX, 554): ". . . hic certe omnis lector expavescere potest acumen ingenii ejus, qui totam fabularum seriem, secundum philosophiam expositarum, transtulerit vel ad rerum ordinem, vel ad humanae vitae moralitatem." (Here, surely, every reader can tremble before the power of his [Fulgentius's] genius, for he has applied the entire series of fables, philosophically explained, either to the order of nature or to the moral order of man's life.) [For text and study of Fulgentius, see Rudolfus Helm, ed. *Fabii Planciadis Fulgentii . . . opera* (Leipzig, 1898) and H. Liebeschütz, *Fulgentius metaforalis; ein Beitrag zur Geschichte der antiken Mythologie im Mittelalter,* Studien der Bibliothek Warburg, iv (Leipzig, 1926); see also J. D. Cooke, "Euhemerism: A Mediaeval Interpretation of Classical Paganism," *Spec.* II (1927), 396–410, and for discussion of the tradition in art, Jean Seznec, *The Survival of the Pagan Gods* (New York, 1961), with references to studies by Bezold, Liebeschütz, Panofsky, Saxe, and Adhémar on p. 3, nn. 2,3.]

[19] [On the ascription of this work to Neckham, see Max Manitius, *Geschichte der lateinische Literatur des Mittelalters,* III (Munich, 1931), 793.]

[20] Ed. Adolfus Dick (Leipzig, 1925).

[21] [Ed. Cora E. Lutz, *Remigii Autissiodorensis commentum in Martianum Capellam* (Leiden, 1962).]

tues and vices, of which Prudentius with his *Psychomachia*[22] was the acknowledged master as the *Physiologus* had been for natural symbolism. Poets and sculptors, moral philosophers and theologians one after the other used such personification ceaselessly, even though they altered and construed it in a special way, combining it with the theme of Jacob's ladder,[23] or the tree of the virtues,[24] or the cosmic voyage,[25] metaphors palpable enough to allow all abstract moral clichés to be brought to life.

From all this was born a method of exegesis for use in reading the ancient poets, whose idolatrous or licentious content would have been unacceptable. To read into them lessons of morality presented figuratively was to save them. So already the Stoics had done. Ovid was the special object of such "moralization" by Arnulf of Orléans and by many others after him[26]; Dante so read Vergil, as Bernard

---

[22] Latin ed. with English trans. in H. J. Thomson, *Prudentius*, 2 vols. (Cambridge, Mass., 1949–53).

[23] So Honorius of Autun *Scala coeli minor, seu de gradibus charitatis opusculum* (*The Little Ladder to Heaven, or Essay on the Rungs of Charity; PL*, CLXXII, 1239–42); same image developed in his *Speculum ecclesiae*, sermon for quinquagesima Sunday (*PL*, CLXXII, 869–76).

[24] So Hugh of Saint-Victor *De fructibus carnis et spiritus* (*On the Fruits of Flesh and Spirit; PL*, CLXXVI, 997).

[25] So Alan of Lille *Anticlaudianus* v–vi (*PL*, CCX, 529–50).

[26] [See, in general, E. K. Rand, *Ovid and His Influence* (London, 1925); L. P. Wilkinson, *Ovid Recalled* (Cambridge, 1955), esp. pp. 366–444; S. Battaglia, "La tradizione di Ovidio nel Medioevo," *Filologia romanza*, IV (1959), 185–224; and L. K. Born, "Ovid and Allegory," *Spec.*, IX (1934), 362–79. On Arnulf of Orléans, see Fausto Ghisalberti, "Arnolfo d'Orléans, un cultore di Ovidio nel secolo XII," *Memorie del R. Istituto Lombardo di Scienze e Lettere*, classe di Lettere, Scienze e morali storiche, XXIV (Milan, 1932), 157–234; on commentators after Arnulf, see further Ghisalberti's *Giovanni di Garlandia, Integumenta Ovidii, Poemetto inedito del secolo XIII* (Milan, 1933); "L' *Ovidius moralizatus* de Pierre Bersuire," *Studj Romanzi*, XXIII (Rome, 1933), 5–136; and "Giovanni del Virgilio, espositore delle Metamorfosi," *Giornale Dantesco*, XXIV (Florence, 1933), 1–110. For brief accounts of twelfth-century commentators on Ovid, see Ghellinck, *Essor*, pp. 433–4 (on Baudri of Bourgueil), 284–5 (on Arnulf of Orléans), and 471–2 (on John of Garland), with slighter mentions of Pierre Bersuire and John Ridewall (see index). For the works of Baudri (*c.* 1065–1130), whose interest in Ovid considerably antedated Arnulf's, see Phyllis Abrahams, ed., *Les oeuvres poétiques de Baudri de Bourgueil* (Paris, 1926), and for the growth of the tradition after two centuries, see C. de Boer, ed., *"Ovide moralisé," poème du commencement du quatorzième siècle, publié d'après tous les manuscrits connus*, vols. 1–5 (Amsterdam, 1915–38); cf. Joseph Engels, *Études sur l'Ovide moralisé* (Gröningen, 1945).]

Sylvester had done before him.[27] The success of such exegesis sustained and extended its practice into and beyond the Renaissance. It had, moreover, a specific name: it was the method of *integumentum* or *involucrum*, and its applicability to myths made the very name of the method suspect in other domains. "Integument," Bernard Sylvester says expressly, "is the kind of demonstration that wraps the thing that is understood under a fabulous narration of the truth, and for this reason it is also called an *involucrum*, or envelope."[28] Thus literary expositors compiled their *Integumenta Ovidii*, their *Integumenta Virgilii*. One may go so far as to presume that typological interpretation of the Bible encouraged, by contagion, the allegorization of the pagan texts, just as moralization in turn established itself in both writing and teaching as an authentic genre of biblical exegesis. Erasmus would still combine the two.[29]

Consideration of sacred history involved a biblical interpretation which took literal history (*littera*) as the basis for continuous reference to supra-historical realities figured in terrestrial events. Upon such reference the entire doctrine of the four senses of scripture was postulated.[30] In Christian terms this doctrine was no mere literary technique; the very nature of the Judaeo-Christian revelation posits

---

[27] [Dante *Convivio* IV. xxiv and xxvi (trans. W. W. Jackson [Oxford, 1909] pp. 227, 284–6); cf. T. Silverstein, "Dante and Vergil the Mystic," *Harvard Studies and Notes in Philology and Literature*, XIV (1932), 76–82, and Henri de Lubac, *Exégèse Médiévale*, II, part 2 (Paris, 1964), 237 ff.: "Virgile, philosophe et prophète." For Bernard Sylvester's commentary, see Riedel; cf. John of Salisbury *Policraticus* viii. 24 (Webb, 816–17; Pike, pp. 402–5), and, for another commentary strikingly similar to Bernard's, see E. Franceschini, "Di un commento al VI dell' Eneide attribuito a Nicola Trevet," *Studi e note di filologia latina medievale*, Pubblicazione della Università del Sacro Cuore, serie iv, XXX (1938), 129–40.]

[28] "Integumentum vero est genus demonstrationis sub fabulosa narratione veritatis involvens intellectum, unde et involucrum dicitur" (Riedel, p. 3). [Problems arising from efforts to interpret Bernard's "fabulous demonstration" are exemplified in T. Silverstein, ref. cited above, p. 30, n. 64.]

[29] *Enchiridion militis christiani* (Leyden edition, vol. 5 [1704], p. 7; trans. London, 1905 [reprint of trans. published by Wynkyn de Worde, London, 1533], p. 63: ". . . uti divina scriptura non multum habet fructus, si in littera persistas haereasque, ita non parum utilis est Homerica Virgilianaque poesis, si memineris eam totam esse allegoricam." (As divine scripture has little fruit if you persist in and cling to its literal sense, so Homer's and Vergil's poetry has considerable value if you remember that all of it is allegorical.)

[30] [Most recent and comprehensive review of medieval hermeneutic in Henri de Lubac, *Exégèse médiévale*, 4 vols. (Paris, 1959–64).]

an ongoing interrelationship among things that underlay this hermeneutic approach. No need to dwell upon the principle; it was the extent and the forms taken by the application of the principle that produced a generalized typology and so determined the scriptural symbolism common to the Middle Ages. As a principal consequence of the method, one may note the parallelism between Old and New Testaments which men instinctively and systematically elaborated; illuminators and sculptors gave palpable expression to all that theologians, mystics, moralists, and preachers devised with an assiduity which their writings display.[31] It was not only the great elements of the revealed mystery that entered into a sequence at once historical and prophetic; the least details, individual words themselves, were lifted to the level of a persistent allegory. Peter of Celle classified and interpreted allegorically all the biblical texts that mention bread;[32] and if this author seems to us an eccentric who pushed allegorization too far, we are compelled to recognize that his contemporaries did not regard him as such. John of Salisbury, a man of judgment and a balanced humanist, asked him for a treatise of the same sort on wine, vine, and vineyard. The numerous *Distinctiones*, biblical-theological dictionaries, constituted one of the typical fruits of such labor. The fathers of the church, as is well known, furnished models and sources for this kind of enterprise, but what they practiced spontaneously was now systematized and reduced to rule for teaching purposes.[33]

It would be useless, too, to make detailed inventory of that further

---

[31] See L. Reau, *Iconographie de l'art chrétien, introduction générale* (Paris, 1955), chap. 4: "Le symbolisme typologique, ou la concordance des deux testaments" [cf. E. Panofsky, *Studies in Iconology* (New York, 1962), esp. chap. 1, "Introductory," pp. 3–31].

[32] *Liber de panibus* (*PL*, CCII, 927–1046).

[33] This led to technical formulation of the problem of the relationship between "history," or literal meaning (*littera*), and "signification," or *allegoria*. The literalist position taken by Andrew of Saint-Victor arose in this context, and the solution proposed by Hugh of Saint-Victor found one of its basic motives here, as symbolist theology evolved toward scholastic exegesis. [See Chenu, *TDS*, chap. 7, "La théologie symbolique," pp. 191–209, for discussion of *distinctiones* as a pedagogical exercise and a literary form different from *allegoriae*, with both of them different from *sententiae* and *quaestiones*. Cf. his "Théologie symbolique et exégèse scholastique aux XIIe et XIIIe siècles," *Mélanges de Ghellinck* (Louvain, 1951), pp. 509–26, and "Les deux âges de l'allégorisme scripturaire au moyen âge," *RTAM*, XVIII (1951), 19–28.]

vast domain constituted by symbols not merely spoken or written but performed. Such is the domain of the liturgy, comprising both the sacraments properly so called, the essential structure of which theologians now defined, and lesser rites, the accoutrements and actions of which give symbolic representation to the mystery accomplished once by Christ and preserved effectively in the church. For school use, for meditation, and for public worship, the twelfth century gathered into methodically organized treatises the whole disordered growth of expanded, combined, refined, conceptualized, and allegorized symbol-patterns. The analysis which canonists and theologians gave of the *quadriformis species sacramentorum* (the fourfold form of the sacraments or mysteries) affords a nice example of such ordering of symbolic forms, till then left untouched in their ritual and written profusion.[34]

It is not only the literature that one must examine for evidences of the symbolist mentality; one must also observe the total behavior of Christian society, leaders and common people. Unconstrained by the prescriptions of theoreticians, such behavior had its own force and furnished the religious ground from which the most subtle speculation might spring. Whether in its broadly human or specifically Christian aspects, it can help us most in our efforts to determine the laws underlying symbolism.[35]

Finally, as the last item in this survey of areas in which metaphors are found, let us look into the art that theologians displayed when they took images that would seem fit only to illustrate preformulated concepts and elevated them to the level of thought. To be sure, in *exemplum* literature, as in the rhetoric taught by the *artes praedicandi* (arts of preaching), symbols were readily used as illustrations for Christian values. But in the twelfth century especially, the symbol— that deliberate and systematic "coaptation of visible forms brought forth to demonstrate some invisible matter," as Hugh of Saint-Victor called it—was treated as an instrument capable of penetrating truth, over and beyond any brief and incidental use in mere illustration.

---

[34] See Ghellinck, *Mouvement*, pp. 537–47: "Hugues de Saint-Victor et la 'Species quadriformis sacramentorum' des canonistes et des théologiens."
[35] See below, pp. 202–38, 239–69.

The metaphor of the two trees of the virtues and vices itself prompted and shaped that moral-psychological analysis in which the root of all virtues was found to be love (*caritas*) and the root of all vices cupidity (*cupiditas*), and in which the virtues, like the vices, were intertwined as branches. The nudity of Adam effectively embodied the physical and psychological self-mastery which man had in the state of perfect nature. The "allegorical" chain by means of which Alan of Lille, following existing sources, linked together the temple of Christ's body, the temples in which men worship, the earthly church, and the heavenly city as so many expressions of one metaphoric temple in which Christ offers himself to the Father, afforded a real understanding of many elements, one though diverse, that coalesced in the structured economy of Christian salvation.[36]

In certain cases, metaphor turned into "analogy"—a Greek work which was to take on a technical sense under pseudo-Dionysian influence at the end of the century as men's minds, changing in orientation, sought to find in visible form a foothold from which to mount upwards to the perception of spiritual realities. Taking nature as its basis, such exploration was pursued with marvelous intensity in the area of religious knowledge and still more in that of biblical faith. Symbolism then became at the same time one of the natural techniques of poetry and an avenue toward knowledge of the mystery of things divine and human. In fact, this is why one had to defend the anthropomorphisms constantly employed in scripture. In their different styles, Cîteaux and Saint-Victor were masters in the use of such symbolism. At these two centers, the symbolist mentality showed a special spirit in "the absolute liberty, the freshness and the delight with which faith could make use of metaphoric analogy. All creation and all biblical history were transparent to that faith. It dwelt fondly, it got carried away as it read, discovered, and divined at the heart of the most lowly things and the most simple events those signs and invitations and direct messages which came to it out of the most hidden recesses of love."[37] So with the sermons of St. Ber-

---

[36] *Liber sententiarum* 16 (*PL*, CCX, 236D).
[37] [Source, omitted from French edition, has not been ascertained.]

nard; so with the *Benjamin major* and *Benjamin minor* of Richard of Saint-Victor; so with the numerous commentaries on the Song of Songs. Hugh, as we saw, found in pseudo-Dionysius the definition, the laws, the truth, the beauty of such coaptations, such proportionings between the visible and spiritual worlds: "A symbol is a juxtaposition, that is, a coaptation of visible forms brought forth to demonstrate some invisible matter."[38]

The divine names afforded an outstanding instance of these metaphoric analogies—that is, the biblical names of fire, light, lion, king, which were not transcendental properties expressed in abstract terms. Scientific analysis by theologians would soon define the limitations inherent in the very nature of such metaphors; nonetheless, they concealed, in dialectical suspension between likeness and disparity, the intrinsic bond uniting the material and spiritual realms, here conjoined in a single stroke of thought. The poetic construction of the phrases, biblical or natural, was not allowed to render suspect but rather made to display the innate power and energy of symbols, which abstract knowledge left behind. The "theology" of the twelfth century was saturated with metaphor and symbol; and in these it found, over and beyond its pedagogical and speculative concern for such resources, the means of sustaining the vitality of the sacred texts and the freshness of its own faith, with no detriment to understanding. Both spontaneous and traditional, the use of the metaphoric names would become critically self-conscious; and the entry of pseudo-Dionysian metaphysics would impel that critical self-consciousness to become suddenly analytical in the highest degree.

It is against this background that one must follow the development of the so-called proofs for the existence of God. Treatises devoted to such proofs appeared in the second half of the century, and they tended toward exclusive reliance upon the conceptual analyses of metaphysical reasoning; and yet they still preserved the imaginative and biblical basis involving metaphoric knowledge. Thus, to cite but one case among many, there is the substantial but lyrical discourse upon nature, "book" and "figure" of God, that one reads in

---

[38] See above, n. 5.

the *De tribus diebus* (*On the Three "Days"*) of Hugh of Saint-Victor.[39]

In the proliferation of symbolic forms, both those highly elaborated and those less so, one can readily discern two broad categories —symbolism making use of natural objects and symbolism making use of history. It was possible for the literary, figural, and ideological procedures employed in these two categories to remain identical; but the materials that nature and history afforded imposed a number of profound differences between the two classes of symbol. Nature—physical, vegetal or animal, terrestrial or astral—reflected its creator with a representational power less lofty than that afforded by history, but clear and firm in its determinate structures. Taken all in all, nature displayed harmonies, a total order, or, as certain writers were to say, a dynamic "hierarchy" well suited to give poetic or metaphysical sustenance to an intensely religious and "anagogical" vision of the world. The Greek doctors, as they became better known, would give certain medieval men the material inspiration to experiment with the symbolic cosmos in poems, in speculative writings, or even in figural representations.[40] From another quarter, Augustine

---

[39] Wrongly printed as a supposed seventh book of the *Didascalicon* in *PL*, CLXXVI, 811–38.

[40] See M.-Th. d'Alverny, "Le cosmos symbolique du XIIᵉ siècle," *AHDL*, XX (1953), 31–81. John the Scot, in his *De divisione naturae* v. 3 (*PL*, CXXII, 865–6), had said: ". . . nihil enim visibilium rerum corporaliumque est, ut arbitror, quod non incorporale quid et intelligibile significet" (there is nothing among visible and corporeal things which, as I think, fails to signify something incorporeal and intelligible). This central pseudo-Dionysian principle which, in the twelfth century, transformed the childish imagery of the old lapidaries and bestiaries into a sacred metaphysics, also introduced symbolism into the classification of the sciences as an instrument essential to knowledge of the cosmos. The Cistercian Garnerius of Rochefort (died 1202) ingenuously intruded it into the degrees of abstraction that underlay the Greek division of the sciences into physics, mathematics, and theology; cf. his *Sermo 23* (*PL*, CCV, 730A): "Nam vel *mathematice* speculatur visibiles rerum visibilium causas, vel *physice* invisibles rerum visibilium causas, vel *symbolice* colligit et coaptat formas visibiles ad invisibilium demonstrationem, vel *theologice* contemplatur invisibiles substantias et invisibilium substantiarum invisibiles naturas." (For in *mathematics* one examines the visible forms of visible things; in *physics*, the invisible causes of visible things; in *symbolism* one juxtaposes and adapts visible forms to demonstrate invisible things [one recognizes here the definition of Hugh of Saint-Victor]; in *theology* one contemplates invisible substances and the invisible natures of invisible substances.)

furnished western theologians with the technical verbal distinction between the *vestigia* of God in the physical universe and the *imago* of God in man; the two categories—*vestigia Dei, imago Dei*—became classic. At the same time the term *speculum* came into currency to designate the world and its elements as a "mirror" of God, and Vincent of Beauvais would later compose his *Speculum naturale* (*Mirror of Nature*) and *Speculum historiale* (*Mirror of History*), using titles frequently given to books of the twelfth and thirteenth centuries.[41]

History, in contrast to nature, afforded a loftier matter, for it treated the free destinies of men as subsumed under the free will of God. However, precisely because this was what it treated, its literal content yielded an ulterior significance only on the supposition that temporal events possessed a coherence revealed through prophecy and imposed by the design of God, master of history—unless of course history, like the fables of the gods, were to have been treated as myth, a procedure which faith could not countenance. Statement of the principle was explicit, if not already elaborated, among theologians: tropology operated in history because of the figurative dimension enjoyed by *things*, by persons and events, over and beyond the *words*, the *littera*, of the narrative. The meanings of words and things were connected, to be sure, but they were developed on two different levels, a fact which masters of the twelfth century did not always see clearly. To define the senses of sacred scripture, the "allegorical" levels coexisting with the historical, they gradually worked out the principle that the Bible, having God, master of all events, for its author, differed radically from books composed by men in that it communicated not with words (*voces*) alone as they did, but by the events (*res*) it recounted as well.[42] In such "allegory," history was

---

[41] On the importance of the mirror-image in medieval theology, see H. Leisegang, "La connaissance de Dieu au miroir de l'âme et de la nature," *RHPR*, XVII (1937), 145–71.

[42] See Smalley, p. 199, who cites Stephen Langton's respectful reference to Hugh of Saint-Victor on the point: "Dicit magister Hugo Sancti Victoris: tanta est sublimitas sacre pagine super alias disciplinas quod significata aliarum sunt significantia in theologia; illa enim que sunt res nominum et verborum in aliis facultatibus sunt nomina in theologia." (Master Hugh of Saint-Victor says: Such is the sublimity of the sacred page over other disciplines that the things

the expression of a mind; it had a spiritual sense or meaning. But allegory, with the usage of the fathers for a model, was to by-pass history and, letting itself go, was to abuse incidental literary elements of a narrative by turning them into symbols. Despite some reactions against the practice, systematic allegorization in the twelfth century would universally destroy the literal texture of scripture. The practice sinned against the nature of symbolism, as we shall have to observe; and the error was extremely widespread in all departments of theological endeavor. However, it was still true that knowledge of God and his designs was derived both from nature and from history. These, men said, were the two "books" in which God taught us; for creation, in its metaphorical manner, was a book even as it was a mirror:

> Omnis mundi creatura
> Quasi liber et pictura
> Nobis est et speculum.

"Every creature in the world is, for us, like a book and a picture and a mirror as well." So wrote Alan of Lille,[43] and before him Hugh of Saint-Victor had said: "The entire sense-perceptible world is like a sort of book written by the finger of God.[44] The cosmology of Bernard Sylvester offered a metaphysical projection of the same grand theme: "There, marked down by the finger of the Supreme Scribe, can be read the text of time, the fated march of events, the disposition made of the ages."[45] Analogy, as used by followers of pseudo-Dionysius and under Neoplatonic influence, would operate rather on the level of such cosmic symbolism than through the contingencies of sacred history.

Nature and history—the two sources merged finally in the symbolism of the sacraments, and from their merger one can infer and

---

signified in the others are means of signifying in theology; for the things expressed by names and words in the other faculties are themselves names in theology.)

[43] *Rhythmus alter* (*PL*, CCX, 579A).

[44] "Universus enim mundus iste sensibilis quasi quidam liber est scriptus digito Dei. . . ." *De tribus diebus iii* (*PL*, CLXXVI, 814B). Augustine is the the source; cf. *Enarr. in. ps. 45* 7 (*PL*, XXXVI, 518).

[45] "Illic exarata supremi digito dispunctoris textus temporis, fatalis series, dispositio seculorum" (Barach-Wrobel, p. 13).

understand something of the basic texture of sacramental symbolism. At the same time that each was a ritual representation of the historic mystery and the historic acts of Christ, every sacrament from baptism on, and every smallest sacred gesture, became involved with some element of nature—water, bread, oil, salt, ash, and the like. The constant blending of the historic and the natural sources of symbolism, disparate in their points of origin, their objects, and their operation and structure, would be managed in countless different ways by zealous theologians and liturgists. One cannot understand their occasionally disconcerting lucubrations unless, with them, one is willing to play the game with this double system of signification. The particular allegorization may be disputable, like that of the sacrifice of the mass revived by Amalarius of Metz (d. about 850); still, the key to its understanding will be found in the intermixture of natural and historical symbolism. The sacramentaries of this time make excellent sense, as do the ceremonial activities of the Christian people that they interpret; if this sense so often seems bewildering, it is because the underlying nature symbolism and the sacramentalizing of sacred history remained irreducible to one another even when knotted together in a Christian structure.

The unlimited playing of symbolism across the limits of nature, of sacred history, and of the sacraments and sacramentals—one thinks of the symbolism of water, of fire, of bread, of eating, of the kiss, of love, as these were worked out in all three areas—produced such a verbal and intellectual diffusion that the innate polyvalence of each symbol associated it with various compounds, literary and figural. Such, in their range and complexity, were the fields of operation of what I have called the symbolist mentality of the century.[46] The survey helps define that mentality as practiced by other men as well as by these Christians.[47] In his *Ars versificatoria*, written before

---

[46] Hugh of Saint-Victor checked them off, in his fashion, into the following categories: *res, persona, numerus, factum, tempus, locus* (thing, person, number, event, time, place). See his *De scripturis et scriptoribus sacris* 14–16 (*PL*, CLXXV, 20–24). The basis of his inventory was biblical-historical rather than natural or artistic.

[47] One may at least mention the development of symbolism and myth in medieval Islamic literature: in Avicenna, for example, the allegory of destiny or fate, the myth of the bird, the poem entitled *An Nafs* (The Soul); in Ibn

1175, Matthew of Vendôme exalted the role and the excellence of metaphor, whether simple or protracted: "This trope, by a kind of special prerogative, enjoys a unique preeminence over all other tropes and ought to be used by verse writers especially, for it confers a peculiar charm upon metrical composition."[48] This observation by a teacher of the literary art had validity outside formal aesthetics; it was applicable in every area in which thought sought expression, as Bernard Sylvester and Alan of Lille also testified in the domain of religious philosophy.

Inspiration and Sources

Here, as elsewhere, St. Augustine both inspired and instructed. He did so explicitly by the lessons he gave in his *De doctrina christiana*, an exposition of the principles of his biblical hermeneutic based on a philosophy of signs. All the men of the medieval West knew, if not the text, at least its major propositions. The *Didascalicon* of Hugh of Saint-Victor recast the material completely but faithfully.[49] But Augustine inspired and instructed even more by his practice, in which the symbolic interpretation of the letter of scripture somehow became constitutive of his way of thinking, as much in his popular sermons as in his learned treatises. This is the teaching that all medieval men received, Dante included, for Dante professed the fact explicitly and practiced brilliantly what he had learned.

Everything is a figure. Such was the fundamental law bearing not only upon the ensemble of things but upon each element, one by one; and not only upon the doctrinal and moral substance of revealed

---

Tofail, the myth of Hay-ben-Yaqzan in the philosophical romance bearing his name and treating the concord between religion and philosophy. (Hay represents the active intellect.) Muslim mystics, too, constantly used myth and symbol. The problem of the transmission to the West of Muslim symbolist themes, like that of philosophical doctrines, is well known—particularly the theme of the voyage, ascent or descent, common vehicle of Neoplatonic cosmic imagery.

[48] "Iste siquidem tropus quadam speciali praerogativa inter ceteros tropos singularem obtinet praeeminentiam, et maxime a versificatoribus debet frequentari: praecipuam enim metricae modulationi venustatem accommodat" (Faral, p. 173).

[49] [For summary of structural differences between the *Didascalicon* and the *De doctrina christiana*, see Taylor, "Introduction," pp. 28–32.]

teaching but even more upon things that had no connection with faith and morals: "Anything in the divine word that cannot properly be related to moral uprightness or the truth of faith you can be sure is figurative."[50] Everything was a *sacramentum* in the technical sense of the word, that is, a sign of an inner reality.

Translatio verborum, the transference of words, was thus a normal operation; even more, it was an operation necessary to one's understanding of the sacred text, which included not only *signa propria*, or words, but *signa translata*, transferred words, or as we say today, a figurative sense. The precise object of the *De doctrina christiana* was to furnish the means to clarify the *verborum translatorum ambiguitates*, the double sense of such transferred or figurative words.[51] Behind the biblical scholarship of Augustine the believer, and with no loss to the theology he derived from the spiritual sense, one sees the continuing influence of the method used by Augustine the teacher of rhetoric and by contemporary grammarians in explicating, or "commentating," profane authors. Seen thus, the habit of allegorizing was part of a traditional and accepted method, including the habit of mind it induced. This habit of mind came into play constantly in Augustine's work, not only in his interpretation of Genesis but in the working out of his thought; for he relied upon it to escape from the problems posed by the Manicheans and to achieve his conversion.[52]

His allegorizing entailed two unwieldy practices continued by his medieval disciples: there was the practice of the grammarian-exegete who, commenting line by line, applied his allegorical technique minutely to each separate element; then there was the practice of the Latin rhetorician who, ignorant of the Semitic idiom and style, even of the Hebraic use of parallelism, lumped together imagery that he found obscure—imagery that was figurative but basically literal in sense, like that of the parables—with imagery that actually had spiritual or allegorical meanings. This confusion would operate

---

[50] ". . . quidquid in sermone divino neque ad morum honestatem, neque ad fidei veritatem proprie referri potest, figuratum esse cognoscas." *De doctr. christ.* iii.10 (*PL*, XXXIV, 71).

[51] *De doctr. christ.* iii. 5–37, ii. 11–14 (*PL*, XXXIV, 68–90, 42–46).

[52] *Conf.* vi. 3–4 (*PL*, XXXII, 720–2).

throughout the Middle Ages, even within the systematization of the four senses.

The hidden sense of words and texts was willingly hunted out, as if obscurity were both the pledge of truth and its charm, and as if truth piqued men's curiosity by its very mysteriousness: "No one doubts that things are more readily understood through similitudes and that they are discovered with much more delight when they have been hunted out with difficulty."[53] Glorious luck for Christians if the entire revelation of the New Testament was mysteriously "hidden" in the Old: what this provided was not merely a condition making textual interpretation possible but an occasion for both aesthetic and religious pleasure. No scientific pretension at all, only the free and delightful opportunity afforded by the word of God: "As for those who taunt me with what they call idle and needless exposition, let them know that I did not so much intend to give an exposition of the Gospel as to take from the Gospel the occasion to say what it delighted me to say"—so protested St. Bernard.[54]

Thus, in Augustinian symbolism, it was literary method that dominated—as much the method of the *grammaticus* occupied with the interpretation of his text as that of the believer occupied with his reading of the Bible.[55] The concept of simultaneous multiple meanings to which Augustine was led and which was the law for exegetes in the twelfth century derived from a whole complex of causes. In it we discern the mentality proper to men of letters during the late-Roman decadence; a poetic sensitivity to nature; a direct referring of all reality, even profane reality, to God; an understanding of liturgical rites, both in general and in particular, in terms of Christian sacramentalism; a peculiarly Augustinian theory of illumination

---

[53] ". . . nemo ambigit, et per similitudines libentius quaeque cognosci, et cum aliqua difficultate quaesita multo gra[t]ius inveniri": *De doctr. christ.* ii. 6 (*PL*,XXXIV, 39).

[54] "Noverint tamen qui me tanquam de otiosa et non necessaria explanatione sugillant, non tam intendisse exponere evangelium quam de evangelio sumere occasionem loquendi quod delectebat": *Super "Missus est" homiliae* hom. iv. Excusatio S. Bernardi, quod locum istum Evangelii post alios expositores tractandum sumpserit (*PL*, CLXXXIII, 86).

[55] On Augustine's symbolist hermeneutic, see H.-I. Marrou, *Saint Augustin et la fin de la culture antique* (Paris, 1949), pp. 422–30, 478–98; cf. pp. 646–51 in Marrou's "Retractatio."

with its Neoplatonic context; a philosophy of signs as resources of the human spirit and of language; and all this within the orthodox faith, with its developing and spiritual unity between two distinct but allied strata of the Christian economy. The Middle Ages, era of theologians but era too of poets and of the common people, illustrates to perfection those numerous and endless *praefigurationes* which nourished a symbolism sorted out for us today through many analytical studies.

St. Gregory both extended and placed a special stamp upon this Augustinian heritage, particularly in *moralisatio*, of which he was the uncontested master. His *Moralia in Job*, conceived entirely as a tropological work, inspired an abundance of imitations which suffered increasingly from heavy-handed popularization until at last many exegetes respectfully but expressly discarded such unquestionably overworked moralization in order to return to literal interpretation. It was explicitly against St. Gregory that Richard of Saint-Victor, following the tradition of his school, justified the radical and irreplaceable primacy of the literal sense. It is always necessary, said Richard, to search into the literal sense and not to yield incautiously to such easy principles (Augustine's principles, indeed) as prescribe a symbolic sense for texts literally unintelligible or inconsistent with the faith, or a multiplicity of senses for texts literally obscure. Thus did the Victorines preserve not only the reality of the biblical *historia* but the truth underlying symbolic value.[56]

St. Ambrose swelled the same current, but with an allegorical emphasis traceable to Origen. Fundamentally, Origen's outlook dominated practices and methods in this area. *Lectio divina*, from the monastic "collation" to formal teaching in the schools, was saturated

---

[56] Among other texts in which Richard expresses this sharp reaction, see his *Prologus in visionem Ezechielis* (*PL*, CXCVI, 527–8 and 562) [translations of these passages in Smalley, pp. 108–9, with discussion of Richard's exegesis and his contradiction of St. Gregory's method on pp. 106–11] and his *Expositio difficultatum in expositione tabernaculi foederis* (*PL*, CXCVI, 211): "Qui igitur certitudinis suae testimonium allegoricae expositioni tam fidenter dat, historicae denegat [the reference is to Bede], patenter innuit quod in illa sua expositione nec sibi ipsi satisfecerit." (Therefore, he who so confidently testifies that he gives credence to allegorical exposition and rejects the historical, plainly intimates that when he has produced such exposition of his own, it has failed to satisfy even him.)

with the "spiritualism" of the Alexandrian doctor. Antiochine works involving literal interpretation were cited here and there, but without attention to the tradition they represented. Despite Origen's vicissitudes, and thanks in part to the steadying effect that the practice of the church had upon his reputation, he became, under cover of Augustine's prestige, the inspirer of the symbolist mentality of the Middle Ages.

Another master, however, was to introduce, or at least to reinforce and articulate, the resources of a quite different type of symbolism. In the second half of the twelfth century, the growing diffusion of the great work of pseudo-Dionysius as transmitted by John the Scot provided a theory and practice of the symbol of a wholly different character from those of the Latin tradition. According to this theory, the situation of man in the universe, in the "hierarchy" of the universe, governed the knowledge of which man was capable, especially his knowledge of God. Connatural with matter, a man's intelligence had to work through matter to attain a grasp of transcendent realities, unknowable in themselves. Paradoxically, man's intelligence, in its operation, must heartily accept matter and yet must austerly pass beyond it. The movement between the two aspects of this operation was not a matter of simple psychological transference or of aesthetic interpretation; it derived from the very nature of things, which, given their sacred emanation, comprised graded representations of the inaccessible One, the Godhead. This *anagoge*, this upwards reference of things, was constituted precisely by their natural dynamism as symbols. The image of the transcendent was not some pleasant addition to their natures; rather, rooted in the "dissimilar similitudes" of the hierarchical ladder, it was their very reality and reason for being. The symbol was the means by which one could approach mystery; it was homogeneous with mystery and not a simple epistemological sign more or less conventional in character.

For this very reason, *anagoge* was fundamental to any true understanding of things; for things were true in themselves, in their own being, only because their very being reflected God. One knew things as part of a sacred knowledge, an "initiation"; to stop with things themselves, whether through passion, through self-concern, or even for love of science, was to miss both true science and sanctity at the same time. Symbolism was integral to mystical experience at the same time that it was an excellent instrument of the "negative way," since it required the believer to go beyond it.

These principles proved of eminent worth for scripture, which, by strange paradox, taught divine mysteries in a human language incapable of containing them. One foresaw the enduring necessity for symbolic transposition not only because of the weakness of human understanding but because of the very task scripture was to perform. To read it in its earthly sense, as a human document and without *anagoge*, was literally to profane it, since it was but a primer, a tool of elementary instruction, from which one entered into the silence of God in a state of contemplation completely purified.

The same principles applied even more eminently to the sacraments, concrete acts of the "hierarchy," which, in and through their symbolism, brought about the purification, the illumination, and the perfection of man and so consummated the divine existence in man. Here was a mystical realism which endowed the symbols not only of the seven classic sacraments but of all cultic acts with an efficaciousness that one was compelled to call physical, so close was the correlation between symbol and mystery.

It is important to take stock of the difference between the Augustinian "sign" and the pseudo-Dionysian "symbol." Involved were two distinct philosophies, two distinct theologies, of symbolism, though both were traceable to the same Neoplatonic inspiration. From that common inspiration came a number of common traits: a certain failure to give physical actuality, natural or historical, its due; a viewing of all things in an essentially transcendent light, thus giving all reality a religious character; a preference for *meaning* which expressed the religious character of things, over *explanation* which limited itself to the intrinsic causes of phenomena and ended in science; the technical and psychological irreducibility of such meaning, conveyed in symbols, to explanation, which used reasoning; finally, a certain poetic quality, a lyricism religious in resonance. All these things were the necessary psychological and epistemological consequence of a Neoplatonic vision of the universe.

But as we have seen,[57] Platonic inspiration gave rise to systems

---

[57] See above, pp. 49–98.

and mentalities of markedly disparate character. In the present instance, we meet with the profound differences observable between the Neoplatonism of Augustine and that of pseudo-Dionysius. In the area of symbolism—natural, historical, scriptural, or sacramental—observation of these differences is the more urgent since, in the twelfth century and throughout the whole of the Middle Ages, the two strains were continually crossed and are difficult to distinguish, as one can see even before 1150 in Hugh of Saint-Victor, that master of the sacraments and sacramentalism who was responsive to pseudo-Dionysian modes of thought while remaining basically Augustinian.[58] Augustine's "sign" belonged on the level of his psychology of knowledge and was developed with materials drawn from that psychology. It was conceived as the tool of man's spiritual experience as this experience compassed the whole field of language, including the varieties of figurative expression. It was consequently the knower himself who was the principle and rule of the "sign"; it was he who gave the "sign" its value, over and beyond any objective basis in the nature of things, always extrinsic to the soul. In any Christian conception of "signs," therefore, the interior life of man, and above all faith, were primary. Without faith, understanding of the word of God was finished; without faith, a spiritual sense to sacred history could no longer exist; without faith, efficaciousness disappeared from the sacraments. To this spiritual function and operation of "signs" corresponded a mysticism of the interior life, the methodological principle of which was set forth in Augustine's *De magistro*. Exterior objects or events, even those with greatest authority, were but stimulants and aids. Augustine's illuminationism showed its influence here and, long before *The Imitation of Christ*, a certain individualistic or subjectivist attitude threatened the practice of the sacraments.

In consequence, Augustinian theologians approached "signs" via psychological analysis. The most notable instance of this is found in Augustine's conception of *res et sacramentum*, which became a basic

---

[58] See H. Weisweiler, "Sakrament als Symbol und Teilhabe. Der Einfluss des Ps.-Dionysius auf die allgemeine Sakramentlehre Hugos von St. Viktor," *Schol.*, XXVII (1952), 321–43 [and Roger Baron, *Science et sagesse chez Hugues de Saint-Victor* (Paris, 1957), pp. 171–9].

ingredient of theology in the twelfth and thirteenth centuries.[59] In biblical theology, Hugh of Saint-Victor and his school were to represent the structure of scripture—allegory resting on a historical foundation—as deriving from a psychological technique, namely the double meaning of *verba* and *res* in the Bible.[60] The "sign" conveyed knowledge. It might be secret or mysterious, but its intent was to make something visible; it was the *sacramentum visibile invisibilis formae* (the visible sacrament or mystery of an invisible form). It de*sign*ated; it was like writing. It was partly *ad placitum*, arbitrary and conventional, so that it called necessarily for institutionalized agreement. It had a social value; ultimately, it was a juridical as well as a mystical instrument and appurtenance of membership in visible society. The ecclesiology of the twelfth century was to be a sacramental as well as a political ecclesiology.[61]

For pseudo-Dionysius, it was not the believer who gave signs their meaning; it was objective elements themselves which, before anything else and by their very nature, were so many representations, so many "analogies." The symbol was the true and proper expression of reality; nay more, it was through such symbolization that reality fulfilled itself. By its immediate representation of ultimate mystery, it opened the way for an object-centered culture. For Augustine, no sacrament was possible without the intervention of the human "word" or concept: *Accedit verbum ad elementum, et fit sacramentum* (Man's word, or concept, is conjoined with some element, and a sacrament results). This was the axiom of medieval sacramentalism; and, translated into Aristotelian categories, it would give rise to the scholastic matter-form philosophy universally accepted, even in the pastoral and doctrinal discourse of the church. In pseudo-Dionysian symbolism, wholly taken up with mystagogy, such conceptualization did not come into play. The symbol was the starting point of knowledge, of "initiation," and it was no more reducible

---

[59] See H. M. Féret, "*Sacramentum, Res,* dans la langue théologique de Saint Augustin," *RSPT*, XXII (1940), 218–43.

[60] Cf. Chenu, *TDS*, chap. 8, "La théologie symbolique," pp. 191–209 [and Didascalicon v. 3 (Buttimer, pp. 96–97; Taylor, pp. 121–2)].

[61] See Jean Chatillon, "Une ecclésiologie médiévale: l'idée de l'Église chez les théologiens de Saint-Victor au XIIᵉ siècle," *Irénikon*, XXII (1949), 115–38, 395–411.

to analysis than the mystery it made present. We have here the kind of concern with objects, the kind of objectivism, that gave to liturgical ceremonial, indeed to the institutional church itself, a transcendent dimension into which theurgic action permitted access in a fashion that had nothing in common with scriptural or sacramental allegorizing.

It is at once apparent that the twelfth century's great work on the sacraments was dominated from end to end by the Augustinian conception of "sign" and not by the *symbolon* of pseudo-Dionysius; and even the survival of the ancient and traditional term *mysterium* could not hide a certain desacralization, attested by the very titles of the treatises henceforth called *De sacramentis*. This great theological and ecclesiastical operation of delimiting the seven major sacraments sufficed by itself to manifest the same tendency. Mystagogy did not summon up such an operation any more than it nurtured the Augustinian dialectic between realism and symbolism, particularly in the case of the eucharist. Similarly, the philosophical concept of instrumentality, introduced to explain the operation of the sacraments and to define their peculiar character, was alien to the apophantic outlook; this concept could doubtless account for the potential representationalism of nature, but it denied any mystical content to nature and any native sacredness concealed within it. It was, in any case, the Aristotelians of the thirteenth century who were to elaborate this precious concept of instrumentality.

Finally, the cosmic symbolism of pseudo-Dionysius tended to relegate any reference to history to a place of secondary importance; this was no less true of sacred history, including the deeds of Christ which the sacraments represented. Merely implicit in pseudo-Dionysius was that elaboration, so characteristic of the twelfth and thirteenth centuries, of the three values of liturgical symbols: their reference to the past, which they commemorated; to the present, which they vivified; and to the future, which they foreshadowed. Augustine, on the other hand, supplied medieval men with materials and methods for a symbolism capable of laying hold upon time— Christian time: events, bound up with past and present and future as so many stages of the Old Testament, the New Testament, and the final kingdom, not only prepared for the future but prefigured it in the present. Beyond the mere words (*verba*) of a narrative, the events themselves, the *res*, had significance. The conquest of Canaan was the entry into the promised land; the captivity of Babylon symbolized the hope of liberation; the brightness of dawn was the coming of the Messiah, and then the daybreak of final salvation; manna signified the eucharist to come; the circumcision prefigured baptism in the ongoing formation of God's people "from Abel to the last of the elect" (Anselm of Havelberg chose the phrase as a sub-title in his *Dialogi*[62]); Jerusalem was the figure of the church, while the church in turn prefigured the heavenly Jerusalem; and so on. For both doctrinal and pastoral development, this was the very fabric of sacramental and biblical theology throughout the Middle Ages in the West, even for followers of John the Scot and for Joachim of Floris himself. Augustine and Origen were the doctors of the spiritual sense of history far more than was pseudo-Dionysius, whose attention was fixed upon the ordered emanation of things as created by God.

Still, around this Augustinian theology and to its benefit, the reading of pseudo-Dionysius would stimulate the development of a deep sense of mystery, and this by reason of the leading premise of his theology, namely: Creation was a theophany, a manifestation of God, and symbolism was the means appropriate to that manifestation; even granting a dialectical tension between the power of creation to manifest God and its complete inferiority to God, symbolism revealed nothing less than God's transcendence. The great cosmogonies, moreover, always called symbolism into their service. Later, in university teaching at least, rationalistic allegorization would efface this sense of mystery at the same time that formalism in worship would pervert Christian "initiation" and make it a matter of mere rational instruction.

The Laws of Symbolism

Just as pagan antiquity weighed heavily on the "renaissance" of the twelfth century, so too did Christian antiquity, lively source and

---

[62] *Dialogi* i: "De unitate fidei et multiformitate vivendi ab Abel usque ad novissimum electum" (*PL*, CLXXXVIII, 1141 ff.).

pedagogical basis of medieval theology though it was. In this culture, creativity was often unable to rise above the formalism of mere imitation. This was particularly true of those symbolic values which belonged to men's liturgical, biblical, and natural understanding of the Christian economy of salvation. We shall not minimize this failure. Yet it ought not to obscure for us those powers of expression which, in teaching and reflection, evinced an authentic feeling for mystery. From this point of view, the twelfth century was without doubt, even in the secular domain, preeminent in its feeling for the sacred and in its expression of that sensibility. The myths of "the matter of Greece and Rome" encumbered the imagination of Chrétien of Troyes; but in his *Perceval,* or *Conte du Graal,* that romance of grace, all the freshness of Christian grace breaks forth in endless symbolism, to the point of confusion. Courtly love, new experience that it was, nurtured a cluster of metaphors that the taste for allegory could not deprive of life. Even more, the plastic arts, whether expressing nature or representing sacred history, were inspired by a creative imagination that produced forms unrestricted by ancient models. In these various areas, medieval symbolism testifies to a highly productive sense of the sacred.

We have already noted the sacred meaning men sensed in nature. It is true that rational curiosity about nature eroded, little by little, men's vision of the universe as a symbol; but the scientific explanation of phenomena through discovery of their causes, secularizing though its influence may have been, interfered only incidentally with the meanings men gave to things. For William of Conches, the philosopher of Chartres most interested in nature, the universe, however fully explained it might come to be, remained a sacramental projection of the divine thought; God was always the chief inhabitant of earth. The most trivial and useless realities of nature possessed a symbolic value which made them both beautiful and good.[63]

Turning to things specifically Christian, we must speak of the sacramental value of nature. Liturgical ritual continued to absorb certain images and practices borrowed from a religion of nature to which natural elements and phenomena had given rise, not without

---

[63] Cf. Honorius of Autun *Elucidarium* i. 12, cited above, p. 8, n. 15.

degrading effect. Not for the sake of scholarly speculation but as a result of actual experience did Hugh of Saint-Victor, like the canonists, list among the sacramental forms a series of symbols, "for exercise," he said, among which are found gestures for the hallowing of profane objects. The most stereotyped formulas for blessing cannot hide their modest attention to "meanings" inscribed in created things.

Social life, too, whether among the anonymous crowds or public authorities, prompted symbolic expression of its innate sacral values. It is well known that medieval men, whether simple laymen or theologians, were eloquent about the sacred character of authority; the anointing of princes afforded a sufficient example of this well-spring of symbolism, in which the marvelous was mixed with a genuinely religious conception of power. Guild banquets, too, featured sacred ceremonial.[64]

One would be mistaken to overlook the role of the marvelous in all this proliferation of symbolism. The populace, intellectuals included, were captivated by it; and theologians only slowly defined the distinguishing marks of what was purely a matter of the mystery of grace (*supra naturam*) and the quite different marks of the miraculous, real or imaginary (*praeter naturam*). Whatever the confusion between the two might have been, the taste for the marvelous also inspired metaphorical transfer and the use of symbols, even at the cost of slighting the transcendency of God, who was invoked to lend a sort of bona fide literary and religious quality to these symbols.

Not, then, by a simple lifting of ancient practice, Christian and pagan, did medieval men enunciate and make use of the laws of symbolism. Their own experience, their native and authentic religious sense, revitalized and sometimes rediscovered independently the principles laid down by their forebears in an earlier day. Often, too, their spontaneous practice of symbolism was not sufficiently self-conscious to lead to explicit analysis of the laws underlying their work—except for literature, among the authors of the *Artes*—and we must have recourse, as they did, to pseudo-Dionysius or to Augustine to ascertain the theoretical basis of their figurative writing.

---

[64] See Émile Coornaert, "Les ghildes médiévales, V^e–XIVe siècles," *RH*, CXCIX (1948), 22–55, 208–43.

It was from pseudo-Dionysius that medieval men enunciated the primary law of symbolism. The essential appeal of his dialectic, his "demonstration," seem to have been that it bridged the apparently nontraversible gap that the mind perceived between two realities otherwise akin; to join these two realities within a single symbol was to put the mind into secret contact with transcendent reality, not without a sense of inward exaltation, and certainly with an affective response that inspired poetic creativity. Here was a law that pertained to men's search for understanding, as we have seen; the understanding confronted transcendence and immanence held in simultaneous tension. It was also a law describing the method of symbolic expression; it went beyond mere imagination and touched upon the sources of poetry. Such "demonstration" did not operate like the premises of the dialectician, for there was no logical continuity between the two realities involved; rather, it fixed upon a likeness underlying the contrasting realities and made a leap between them. The result was a double resonance within the single grasp of a "dissimilar similitude," to use the famous phrase of pseudo-Dionysius, and to use it with the same implications.[65]

While theologians of the twelfth century perceived and enunciated the principle of "dissimilar similitude" as governing man's efforts to understand the transcendent, they failed to enunciate the parallel law for symbolic discourse, despite the close relationship between these two expressions of anagogy. The statement of Alan of Lille which was cited at the beginning of this essay is only a very distant reflection of that law. Moreover, poets (think of Bernard Sylvester and his philosophical poem) made only indifferent use of its potential, doubtless because their incessant hardening of metaphor into allegory had weakened their poetic sensitivity or had intellectualized it prematurely. Again, the figural interpretation featured by biblical exegesis drew rather upon Augustine's "signs" than upon the anagogy of pseudo-Dionysius; the latter was the master of symbolic

---

[65] Pseudo-Dionysius *Hier. cael.* ii (*PG*, III, 137, 140, 141). Cf. R. Roques, *L'univers dionysien* (Paris, 1954), pp. 115, 207. The two terms "anagogy" and "symbol" were linked together: "Oportet sursum erigi ad anagogicas et symbolicas formas" [One must be lifted upwards towards the anagogical and symbolic forms].

metaphysics, hardly the master of biblical typology. Let us note, at least, 'that there remained—and still would remain after the advent of scientific theology—an epistemological continuity between the biblical type of symbolic imagery used to name God or describe his mysteries and the purely conceptual type of analogy used as a technical instrument for coming to know transcendent realities and truths. The God of Alan of Lille could be approached by either road, for underneath their different apparatus the two roads were alike and definitive.

In the area of liturgy, privileged province of the symbol in action, the failure was even more evident, for the most realistic elements— water, light, fire, a meal, a table—were handled rather as materials for allegorical instruction than as things having power to represent the mystery to those initiated into it. Thus the mass tended to become a sophisticated and complex figure of the episodes of the passion instead of a sacrificial meal. Pseudo-Dionysius had hardly made a dent on the various treatises *De divinis officiis* that appeared toward the end of the century, nor even on the sacramental theology of the Victorines.

Such reduction of symbolic tension is even more evident in the use to which another pseudo-Dionysian law was put—the law according to which the crudest symbols are seen as those most capable of signifying the mystery. The more gross the material, the more it induced the anagogic leap, as against the peril of anthropomorphism that was nurtured by symbols too closely resembling the thing they symbolized; as against the illusion that "light" could become palpable; and as against an ardent attachment to poetic fictions. Medieval men, of course, took note of the grossness of the language, of the imagery, of the rites both in scripture and in the liturgy; but they took from this a lesson in humility, either exalting the condescension of God or proclaiming the wretchedness of man, enslaved even here to matter. They thus gave a moralizing twist to what is above all a physical necessity for symbolic knowledge. The classic question *de necessitate sacramentorum* (why the sacraments were necessary) was expressly oriented in this direction.

Without always requiring this deliberate grossness, the symbol, in order to effect the transference for which it is the vehicle, calls for matter which does not disappear in the process of signifying, such, for example, as the reality of the natural elements, or the reality of history in biblical typology, or the reality of the material used in a liturgical action. On many counts the masters of the twelfth century responded wholly in favor of this law of symbolic values: these values emerge only in proportion as the *res* retains its integrity while functioning as *signum*. In turning reality into nothing but a figure, tropology weakens itself. Such an insistence underlay the great exegetic and theological undertakings of Hugh of Saint-Victor, who asserted the prior necessity of the *fundamentum* before *allegoria*, of the truth of *historia* before *tropi*. Moralization, even in the masterly commentary of St. Gregory on Job, ended up in attenuated abstraction, for it dissolved the natural or historical materials upon which it operated, even as in former days it dissolved the myths of the pagans.

Simultaneous with such attention to the literal sense of scripture was renewed respect for the value of *things* in various fields employing symbolism. Paradoxical though it may seem, the new interest in nature provided a guarantee for the materials of symbolism; and in itself the concern with explanation by natural causes did not prejudice the imposition of "meaning" upon realities through their ultimate reference to the transcendent. Ultimately, by purging men's minds of the childish ideas found in bestiaries and lapidaries, the increasing knowledge of nature in the twelfth century encouraged men's vision of a symbolic universe of a totally different sort. Changes that occurred in the evolution of plastic representation, as one sees these in the sculptured capitals of medieval churches of different dates, illustrate very well the transformation that took place in religious mentality, even among theologians.

All this sets us pondering over the potentialities of the diverse philosophies that lay behind the symbolist mentality of the century. Augustine, pseudo-Dionysius—theirs were philosophies of the Platonic sort that seems naturally inseparable from symbolism, whether literary, aesthetic, religious, or cultural. Things exist, and exist as true and beautiful, in proportion as they represent the changeless and eternal perfection of ideas in the changing and perishable order; all of physical reality is a revelation of God. "Symbolism is the aesthetic expression of ontological participation."[66] The universe is a system of symbols more than it is a chain of effects. But the potentialities of this system tend readily toward imbalance; symbolic value tends to empty *things* of their earthly reality, their ontological reality, their conceptual reality. It is so with the pseudo-Dionysian symbol of eros, with the *signum tantum* of the Augustinians, with the allegory of love in the Song of Songs, with the moralization of sacred history, with the constant temptation to eschatologism in the Christian economy of salvation. The whole twelfth century can illustrate the peril of such imbalance—an imbalance, moreover, which Hugh of Saint-Victor condemned in his areas of concern and which Peter Comestor condemned in his criticism of St. Gregory's *Libri moralium in Job.*

For Aristotle, ideas were *within* things. The representative value of things, even assuming that the transcendent exists, was to be looked for within things, within their manifest natures. Such "naturalism" was an elementary precondition for symbolism. The pure empiricism of Aristotelian philosophy did away with symbolism as lacking any value for a science of definitions; but if one day Aristotelian noetic were to become opened to the transcendent, then by the reintegration of the ideas, of the *logos*, into the created world, the way of symbolism would be qualified and governed by the internal laws of things. "To the Plotinian view, which tolerated an image only insofar as it constituted an intellectual symbol, which in turn required that all details be elaborated two-dimensionally and that depth, an attribute of matter, be rejected, there succeeded an aesthetics based upon the observation of nature."[67] What Francastel here says of the plastic symbol is no less valid for symbols used in speculation. Just as the artists who covered the capitals with clover, plantain, and fern loved nature for its own sake, so too the theologians of Chartres paid tribute to the Creator in the respect they showed for his creation. Just as Summer ceased to be a pretty goddess and became a peasant farmer sweating at his harvest labors, so too the construction of the world ceased to be looked upon and pictured

[66] E. de Bruyne, *L'esthétique du moyen âge* (Louvain, 1947), p. 93.
[67] P. Francastel, *Peinture et société* (Paris, 1954), p. 57.

as a series of *mirabilia* and was looked upon instead as a genuine and dynamic cooperation of natural forces with the creative act.

Aristotle had not yet been discovered in the twelfth century—not this aspect of his thought, at least. But on the one hand, Boethius, thanks to his eclectic purpose, introduced into this area a large dose of realism; and on the other hand, pseudo-Dionysius himself, thanks to his religious sense, so deflected Platonic idealism toward a keener subjection to sensible realities that, later, he was occasionally bracketed with Aristotle in concordances or "harmonies" of "the authorities" (*concordia auctoritatum*). Besides, as we have observed, the universe was more and more regarded as a collectivity of natures, stable and subject to laws. Occasional remarks made by masters on the pedagogical value of images and figures show that, even without being acquainted with Aristotelian noetic and even while subject to the influences of the reigning Platonism, they were aware that realism was requisite to the operation of symbolism.[68]

With comparable insight, they did not accept without qualification the Augustinian bias that led to considering the sacraments as so many remedies for a fallen world, remedies that would not have existed in a world without the fall where, with matter properly subjected to spirit, man's understanding would not have had to make use of matter in the worship of God. In realist symbolism, on the contrary, including that of pseudo-Dionysius, symbolic action is a normal part of the dynamism of a cosmos reaching upward toward God in hierarchical stages. Sacralization of the seasons, hymns to the day and the night, the multiplication of blessings for profane objects—all were so many effects of an awareness of the profound law of symbolism, of its efficaciousness in human life, and of its proper balancing in doctrinal development and in literature.

---

[68] Twelfth-century authors retained a conception laid down by the texts of Augustine that they read: that metaphoric language, that parables, were intended to surround mysteries with a pedagogically useful obscurity; the veiled forms stimulated curiosity; the secrecy produced an attractiveness that immediate clarity would have spoiled. Cf. H.-I. Marrou, *S. Augustin et la fin de la culture antique* (Paris, 1949), pp. 487–94. Despite their taste for this traditional reverence for the arcane, medieval authors, particularly philosophers and theologians, increasingly asserted the positive and instructive value of imagery that was sensuous alone.

The most constant and not least disconcerting characteristic of the symbol was its polysemousness. So essential a characteristic was this that to constrict its meaning for the sake of conceptual clarity would have been to sterilize it, to kill its vitality. By nature, the symbol was seen as ambiguous. Fire warms, casts light, purifies, burns, regenerates, consumes; it symbolized the Holy Spirit or concupiscence equally well.[69] The bread of the eucharist realized simultaneously the manna of the desert, the Jewish Passover rite, the last supper of Christ, the heavenly banquet, not to speak of natural nourishment. Moreover, each of the things it symbolized was in turn symbolic of yet other elements laden with significations. Jerusalem, historic city of the Jews, was the state of innocence of Adam; it was the church, mystical city; it was the Christian soul, the triumphant church as a whole, and individual beatitude. Herod, whose name means "covered with skin" (*pelliceus*), signified the devil, whose deceits had forced the sinner to put off his robe of immortality and to don those vestments of skin which symbolized his mortality and his fall from grace.[70] The breasts of the spouse in the Song of Songs (*Meliora sunt ubera tua vino*—"Your breasts are better than wine") signified chastity and humility; they were the arms of love with which the Virgin held Christ, God and man; they were flesh and spirit; they were carnal sin and the sophistries of concupiscence.[71] The mystery of the church was illuminated by consideration of a church building (mass celebrating the dedication of a church), of the Temple of Jerusalem (reference to the past), of the heavenly dwelling (reference to the future), of the house of Zacheus (the gospel episode), and of the ample mystical theme of the spouse of Christ. The Woman of the Apocalypse, chapter twelve, was at the same time Eve, the people of Israel, the Virgin, the church; here the polysemous symbol drew upon a profound mystical coherence in the economy of salvation: Israelitic motherhood found its highest expression in Mary, since all parenthood in Israel envisaged the begetting of the Messiah; and

---

[69] Cf. Alan of Lille *Distinctiones dictionum* s.v. "ignis" (*PL*, CCX, 815).

[70] Cf. Richard of Saint-Victor *Sermo super Act. 12* (*PL*, CXLI, 277–306; misplaced among the works of Fulbert of Chartres).

[71] Cf. Alan of Lille *Elucidatio in Cant. cant.* (*PL*, CCX, 54, 62, 79, 98, 100).

Mary in turn was the germinal cell of the church, which as a mother continued to beget Christ upon earth.

Examples of this sort abounded; indeed they resulted from a systematization the laws of which were defined, turned into facile rules of thumb. Masters of the twelfth century practiced these laws to excess, whether observing nature, scrutinizing the sense of sacred history, or interpreting liturgical rites. They delighted in such chains of symbols and in the multiple meanings of any one of them. They were not interested in simple literary, rhetorical, or devotional amplification; they were convinced of the intellectual value, the value for purposes of argument (the *demonstratio* of Hugh of Saint-Victor), of such *coaptationes* (again, Hugh of Saint-Victor's term), so multiplied and so linked.[72] Such a view of meaning for purposes of intellectual construction was as far from Aristotelian logic ("To have more than one sense is to have no sense at all," Aristotle had said) as it was close to biblical literature and to the oriental view of polysemous imagery. One can foresee what epistemological problems it would later pose for a theology organized as a science and possessing logical tools of investigation. In the twelfth century it posed no problem; biblical texts were still the materials with which the theologian immediately worked. When philosophers and theologians of this century occupied themselves with critical analysis, their aim, as we have seen, was to classify and organize meanings, not only the meanings deriving from the scriptural senses that built upon the economy of sacred history, but meanings found in the materials of liturgical worship and ascertained in the observation of natural phenomena.

And so there emerged—if not always explicitly systematized, at least effectively practiced—a logic of the symbol as used in theology,

---

[72] Polysemous interpretations of symbols were often based upon the methods of scriptural exegesis; such were the interpretations of the great scriptural images that lent themselves equally to the spiritual life of the individual, to the church, to the Virgin Mary—expressions of a single Mystery interiorized in the individual soul, institutionalized in the people of God, and consummated one day in glory. But from references to Christ or his sacraments passage was frequently made, even by St. Bernard, to simple psychological or moral applications deriving from literary techniques ingeniously extended beyond the bounds of religious allegory. On this point see H. de Lubac, "La doctrine du 'quadruple sens,' " in *Mélanges F. Cavallera* (Toulouse, 1948), pp. 347–66.

just as elsewhere a logic of propositions was redeveloped. It would be a grave historical and theological error to relegate to the fringes of twelfth-century theological development, or to treat as belonging only to rhetoric or poetic, those works, far more numerous than in the following century, which elaborated in symbolist fashion the deposit of revelation and the traditional capital of the faith. To be sure, their arguments were based upon schemes of meaningful imagery and not upon methods of formal or causal analysis abstractly conducted; but if the coefficient of rational certitude was reduced by this fact, the representational value of such works was enhanced by it and cannot be ignored.

As we have noted, Hugh of Saint-Victor used the word *demonstratio* to designate this procedure; and he saw *demonstratio* as the net result of a *collatio*—a very broad term (it could even mean a simple colloquy) with complex ideological antecedents and indicating mental operations totally different in nature. As its more sharply focused equivalent, he used the term *coaptatio,* which, while it did not belong to a special vocabulary, suggested more precisely the mental operation proper to symbolism; namely, *translatio*, a transference or elevation from the visible sphere to the invisible through the mediating agency of an image borrowed from sense-perceptible reality. This is what we mean by "metaphor," except that here the term had a particular orientation; metaphor was obedient to the necessities imposed by transcendent realities, above all in pseudo-Dionysian theology. Such realities required that in *translatio*, one prescind from the native material content of the images used to symbolize them (*via negativa*—way of negation); this prescinding or negation enabled the *translatio* to deliver a fair representation of the mystery. This happened with all "translation of names" applied to God, including those image-bearing names with which Scripture particularly abounds.

Twelfth-century masters made ready use of the term *translatio*; but its inadequacy led them to transliterate its Greek equivalent into *anagoge,* as Latin versions of pseudo-Dionysius had already done.[73]

---

[73] John of Salisbury witnessed to the inadequacy of the Latin term. He remained curious about the pseudo-Dionysian texts in conjunction with his

Even a spirit as prejudiced against Greek terms as Robert of Melun had recourse to this one, though without much understanding of it; he used it only in his well-known classification of the four senses of Scripture, where he expanded it to apply to *allegoria* in general.[74]

It was not only the exegetical but also the theological handling of symbolism that used fixed procedures. In handling the symbolism of marriage in all the commentaries on the Song of Songs; in handling the symbolism of the dwelling place in allegories woven around the Tabernacle and elaborated into whole treatises;[75] in handling the symbolism of the banquet or of the people of God or of numerous other topics which fill the commentaries, liturgical texts, and homilaries, procedures ranged from simple verbal alliteration to doctrinal analogy properly so-called while pursuing a dialectical argument based on taking a part for the whole. To don a white robe in baptism was a symbolic act to which neither the weave, nor the cut, nor the primary purpose of robe as clothing, but only its whiteness, was relevant. In this instance as in all others, however, it was not by total abstraction that one proceeded; the symbolized reality remained concretely present and visible, for every symbol in a certain way

---

praise of the "new logic" of Aristotle and his summary of the *Topics*, lately "roused as if from death or sleep" (*quasi a morte vel somno excitatus*); subscribing to Aristotle's condemnation of metaphor as radically unsuitable for definitions(*Topics vi*), John directed the force of this point against the term *translatio* (the translation attributed to Boethius [*PL*, LXIV, 909 ff.] used the term *metaphora* instead; John the Scot used the adverbs *translate* and *metaphorice* synonymously); see *Metalogicon* iii. 5; iii. 8 (Webb, pp. 139–43, 147–50; McGarry, pp. 170–5, 181–5). Saint Thomas, also aware of the opposition between Aristotle and pseudo-Dionysius, sustained the position taken by the latter on the function and laws of symbolism in knowledge concerning God; see *De veritate* q. 10, a. 8, obj. and resp. 10 (*Opera omnia*, pp. 167 and 169–70). John of Salisbury, then, located the term *translatio* and its sense within the framework of logic, over and above the literary sense given it by grammarians and rhetoricians and without the sense given it by pseudo-Dionysius and by Alan of Lille, for whom it actually validated analogy, the metaphorical no less than the conceptual, within the framework of anagogy. Finally, the term as applied to scripture followed another course of development stemming from Cassian, far removed from the metaphysics of pseudo-Dionysius, and a systematized expression of Christian eschatology.

[74] *Sententie* i. I.6 (Martin, vol. 1, p. 173).
[75] See Chenu, *TDS*, chap. 8, "La théologie symbolique," pp. 191–209.

contained the reality it expressed.[76] But the relationship between symbol and thing symbolized, between type and antitype, was qualitative; what released and determined the *translatio* of one's mind to the mystery was some quality through which the symbolic relationship was defined, or rather experienced. Participation in the transcendent was not felt to be a matter of *identity* with it ("identity" was a term proper to conceptual logic); rather, such participation was sensed through a dialectic of the similar-dissimilar within a "figure," within the coexistence of the sensible and the spiritual.[77] The same act both fixed and freed the understanding, because the material symbol was preserved in its concrete density. To be sure, rational discourse also could represent the tension between earthly and transcendent reality, but it did so by completely different means. The treatise on the divine names in the *Summa* of Alan of Lille affords a good example.

Though they did not put together a methodological treatise setting forth various formulae for this operation, theologians were nonetheless aware of it over and beyond the simple theory of scriptural tro-

---

[76] Thus in the works of William of Saint-Thierry, susceptible to Greek influences, the psychological imagery of St. Augustine was enlivened by anagogical realism. Cf. J.-M. Déchanet, *Oeuvres choisies de Guillaume de Saint-Thierry* (Paris, 1946), pp. 135, 251–2.

[77] Hugh of Saint-Victor's overly concise definition of "symbol" (see above, n. 5) thus acquires an astonishing significance, for by conjoining metaphoric imagery with a Platonic view of conceptualization, it provided symbology with a unique dialectic. This achievement seems to me to have made the profoundest contribution to twelfth-century thought, as a few references may help suggest. Cf. Richard of Saint-Victor *In Apocal.* i (*PL*, CXCVI, 689): "Omnis figura tanto evidentius veritatem demonstrat, quanto per dissimilem similittudinem figurat se esse et non veritatem probat, atque nostrum animum in hoc magis dissimiles similitudines ad veritatem reducunt, quo ipsum in sola similitudine manere non permittent." (Every figure demonstrates the truth the more clearly in proportion as by dissimilar similitude it figures that it is itself the truth and does not prove the truth; in so doing, dissimilar similitudes lead the mind closer to the truth by not allowing the mind to rest in the similitude alone.) Later than these Victorines and in quite another context, the thought of the Cistercian Garnerius of Rochefort (d. 1202) ultimately evoked the same principle: cf. *Sermo ix* (*PL*, CCV, 630), *Sermo xxxv* (*ibid.*, 794). Pushing the dialectic further, Garnerius distinguished between contemplation that used figures and similitudes (*speculatio aenigmatica; theophania*) and contemplation that was properly anagogical and went beyond all similitude: cf. *Sermo xxiii* (*PL*, CCV, 730B), *Sermo xxxi* (*ibid.*, 765–6), and for the term *fides anagogica, Sermo xxxvii* (*ibid.*, 812D).

pology. One of the signs of this awareness is that they gradually distinguished, even within that theory, between purely literary figures on the one hand and symbolic transfer on the other; this St. Augustine, rhetorician though he was, had not done, despite his views on *significatio*.[78] In this matter, the *Didascalicon* of Hugh of Saint-Victor went beyond the *De doctrina christiana*.[79]

Allegorizing

Frequently in the course of this analysis we have observed the medieval tendency to convert metaphor into allegory; every one of the laws governing the operation of symbols favored, it seems, this propensity. In fact, allegory almost completely took over the various fields we have surveyed—nature, history, liturgical ceremony—just as it invaded every kind of literature—biblical commentary, homily, liturgical texts, formularies of dogma, poetry, and even legal texts, sacred or civil. It was the most widespread literary form. As we look back upon it, it was also decidedly overworked, worn thin, from the personified abstractions of the *De planctu Naturae* to the allegorized explanations of levitical ritual in treatises on the Old Testament.

The complacent satisfaction with which Bernard Sylvester, Alan of Lille, or Chrétien of Troyes personified natural forces, virtues, ideas, or sciences did not derive only from their imitation of antiquity,

---

[78] Cf. St. Augustine's remark on "signs" in the well-known passage about the "lie" of Jacob; *Liber contra mendacium* x 24 (*PL*, XL, 533): "Jacob autem quod matre fecit auctore, ut patrem fallere videretur, si diligenter et fideliter attendatur, non est mendacium, sed mysterium. Quae si mendacia dixerimus, omnes etiam parabolae et figurae significandarum quarumcumque rerum, quae non ad proprietatem accipiendae sunt, sed in eis aliud ex alio est intelligendum, dicentur esse mendacia: quod absit omnino. Nam qui hoc putat, tropicis etiam tam multis locutionibus omnibus potest hanc importare calumniam." (If one attends carefully and with faith, it is not a lie but a mystery that Jacob, at his mother's instigation, seems to have deceived his father. If we call this lying, then we must also call lies all parables and figures upon every kind of matter that has to be shown in a sign; such are not to be taken in their literal features but as promoting the understanding of one thing by means of another. We must refuse to call them lies, for whoever thinks them so can make the same charge against figures of speech and numerous other forms of discourse.)

[79] [Cf. *Didasc.* vi. 10 (Buttimer, pp. 126–8; Taylor, pp. 148–9).]

where allegory was rampant from Prudentius to Boethius; it derived also from their personal taste, even if that taste proved distinctly lacking when it came to adding new values to the ancient stereotypes.

Similarly, it was not from simple fidelity to the doctors of Christian antiquity that they multiplied their pluralistic applications of biblical tropology. For every St. Bernard who animated these with his own grace, there were countless others who systematized, elaborated, heavy-handedly applied, or crudely exaggerated them in contrast to the creative inventiveness of an Origen or an Augustine. The *Allegoriae* of Isidore catalogued them all, ready for the taking.

Finally, in liturgical worship, symbolic actions originally designed to make the mysteries palpable for men were treated as so many "explanations," were finely analyzed and intellectualized, as one sees particularly in the case of the eucharistic meal. The liturgical decay that encouraged such deviation is well enough known.

We are not dealing here with an occasional excess but with a fundamental misunderstanding of the proper character of metaphor as image and consequently of the difference between symbol and allegory. In certain cases, such as the case of the Song of Songs—a major case, it is true—combination of the two genres, or constant modulation from one to the other, was legitimate and was, moreover traditional. But confusion was bound to arise from the institutionalized flaunting of allegory. While metaphor or parable developed an *image* which, by its dissimilar similitude and in its entirety, initiated one to an understanding of the spiritual reality so figured, allegory was the analytical exploration of an *idea* which made use of details dissected and abstracted from an image, with each detail having specific meaning. It was no longer the Ark as a whole which was taken as a type or symbol of the church, but it was each detail of its construction that was explored in a new complex of meanings—its beams, its design, its length, and the like.[80] The panther with its seven colors betokened the priest readying himself for the sacrifice and clothing himself with seven vestments and virtues that served him in combat.[81] St. Peter's liberation from prison, as an event of early church history,

---

[80] [Cf. Hugh of Saint-Victor *De arca Noe morali* and *De arca Noe mystica* (*PL*, CLXXVI, 617–80 and 681–712).]

[81] Honorius of Autun *Sacramentarium, seu de causis et significationibus rituum* xxix (*PL,* CLXXII, 762): "Panthera bestia habet colores septem:

no longer figured man's liberation from sin; instead, we have his four guards representing the four passions, his two chains signifying habit and despair, his sandals signifying perfection, and his tunic signifying justice.[82] The event of the raising of Lazarus became only the occasion for describing three steps attending the sacrament of penance, in which man, first in a state of mortal sin, next repents, lastly is absolved, and is thus brought to life in three "days."[83] So allegory went. "One need attend to the text only to elevate one's mind to the allegory"[84]—here was a program for biblical study that the

---

nigrum, album, griseum, croceum, viridum, aerium, rubeum. Quae panthera varias herbas comedit, constans in petra, languentes ad se venientes flatu suo a morbo sanat. Per pantheram presbyter intelligitur, qui habet septem vestes et septem virtutes. . . . Diversae herbae, diversae sententiae Scripturarum; petra Christus; languidae bestiae homines peccatis aegri. . . . Presbyter dum se praeparat, quasi duellum cum diabolo pro Ecclesia inchoat: humerale ponit in capite, id est spem pro galea; albam, i.e. fidem pro lorica; cingulum, i.e. castitatem pro baltheo; stolam, i.e. obedientiam vel justitiam pro lancea vel funda." (The panther is a beast having seven colors: black, white, gray, yellow, green, bronze, and red. It eats various grasses, stands firm upon rock, with its breath cures from their disease beasts that come to it ailing. By panther one understands a priest, who has seven vestments and seven virtues. . . . The various grasses are the various thoughts of the scripture; the rock is Christ; ailing beasts are men sick with sins. . . . As the priest vests himself, he begins, as it were, a combat with the devil on the part of the church: he places the humeral upon his head, that is, takes hope for his helmet; white, that is, faith for his cuirass; his cincture, that is, chastity for his sword-belt; his stole, that is, obedience or justice for his lance or sling.)

[82] Richard of Saint-Victor *Sermo super Act. 12* (*PL*, CXLI, 277–306; misplaced among the works of Fulbert of Chartres). Comparison of the liberation of Peter with man's liberation from sin was traditional; but Richard allegorized it.

[83] Anselm of Laon among others so developed the notion originating in pseudo-Augustine *De vera et falsa paenitentia* (*PL*, XL, 1122); see "Trente pièces inédites," *RTAM*, II (1930), 70. Such allegorizing obviously lent itself to the demands of polemics, of historical circumstances, of tendentious causes. Scriptural typology turned into millenarism (the schema of the week, the myth of paradise); the comparison of the two swords cloaked the worst ambiguities in theoretical and practical ecclesiology; the theology of the crusader was nurtured on the great allegory of the people of God in the Old Covenant. Thus, allegorizing favored this turning back of the New Testament upon the Old [see below, pp. 146–60], a reflexivity which ran counter to the progressive movement of salvation and which, theologically, depressed the evangelical spirit with the legalism and Leviticalism of the Old Law. The mass was conceived in terms of the Exodus and the Passover lamb when lamb and exodus were merely the figure for the death and redemption of Christ.

[84] See Edmund Martène and Ursin Durand, eds., *Thesaurus novus anecdotorum*, vol. 1 (Paris, 1717), pp. 487–90.

Victorines, for their part, would oppose. Allegorical personifications became allegorized in greater and greater detail: Alan of Lille presented Dame Nature less in terms suggesting cosmic grandeur than in terms that analyzed accessory detail—the embroidery on her garments as representing the variety of created beings.[85] Chrétien of Troyes described Erec's knowledge by sketching on his robe the four arts of the quadrivium.

Symbol—allegory. Symbolism arises out of a persistent habit of our nature. In the course of intellectual experience, we somehow "hide" our clear perception inside images that mediate mystery to us and so acquire their force and value, indeed their aesthetic force and value. As for allegory, it does not start from such aesthetic experience and rise to the purely intellective level; it starts with critical analysis and from it derives abstract thoughts which it ultimately employs in a didactic presentation. In the final stage, explanation submerges signification. "Concerning causes and significations"—so Honorius of Autun entitled his *Sacramentarium,* cited above;[86] and in so doing he lumped together two disparate values. Such was the favorite genre in the Middle Ages. A genre which had retained its vitality as practiced by the fathers, even when they had recourse to hellenistic or other categories, became in the twelfth century a technical procedure—conceptualized, abstract, devoid of that psychological and religious *anagoge* for which pseudo-Dionysius had laid the metaphysical foundation.

And yet, allegory as such and in its place was a form of expression native to a society in which the figurative value of things and events was an essential constituent of its sacred history. The people of God in the Old Testament not only laid the historical groundwork for the church, they prefigured it; the church on earth not only constituted the historical preparation for the heavenly Jerusalem, it prefigured it.

---

[85] Consult R. de Lage, pp. 109–21. Occasionally Alan of Lille observed that allegorizing was not to be everywhere performed; commenting on the vision of Isaiah, he noted that it contained elements that were purely decorative: "Caetera quae aliter haberi dicuntur, non ad prophetiam sed ad picturam referenda sunt." (All other elements, which some say are to be taken differently, should be referred not to prophesy but to visual picturing.) *De sex alis Cherubim* (*PL,* CCX, 171).

[86] See n. 81.

Earthly forms of truth and beauty were not fleeting images of the ineffable beauty and the unique truth but were valid, intelligible, and analyzable analogies of these. Caird has observed: "What modern men, seeking to explain history, look for in the theory of evolution, men of old sought in allegorical method. It expressed for them a prophecy of progress."[87]

Moreover, allegory was a humane literary genre of which the critical art finds the laws. Dante was soon to become its inspired exemplar. "For him, allegory was one of the most natural and satisfying forms of rhetoric, or, if you will, of poetic."[88] He had got from Donatus the seminal idea that every right reader of Vergil would have to look for an allegorical meaning. Every poem has a twofold aim, *delectatio* and *utilitas*, the old grammarian had said, and this is exactly the twofold aim of Dante's allegories—*diletto* and *ammaestramento*.[89] Though lacking Dante's genius, twelfth-century masters, poets, theologians, liturgists, and moralists put that teaching and that method into practice.

---

[87] [The statement, here translated from Père Chenu's French, is cited by him without reference; it is perhaps rather a paraphrase than a direct quotation from Edward Caird, *The Evolution of Theology in the Greek Philosophers* (Glasgow, 1940), vol. 2, lecture 21, "The Philosophy and Theology of Philo," pp. 186–7: ". . . This method of allegorical interpretation . . . served, in fact, the same purpose, which in more modern times has been served by the theory of evolution, enabling men to connect the present with the past without allowing that connexion to become a hindrance to progress." For Caird's further views on the role of symbolism in the development of human thought, see his *The Evolution of Religion* (New York, 1894), esp. vol. 1, lecture 8, "The Objective Form of the Earliest Religion," pp. 199–232; vol. 1, lecture 11, "The Function of Imagination in the Development of Objective Religion," pp. 286–315; cf. his *Essays on Literature and Philosophy* (New York, 1892), vol. 1, 1–53, "Dante in His Relation to the Theology and Ethics of the Middle Ages."]

[88] See A. Pézard, *Dante sous la pluie de feu* (Paris, 1950), pp. 345–7.

[89] *Convivio* I.ii and II.i (W. W. Jackson, tr., [Oxford, 1909], pp. 37 and 73).

4

The Old Testament
in Twelfth-Century Theology

IN A THEOLOGY that remained, not only in its sources but in its aims and methods, a meditation upon the *sacra pagina* (sacred page),[1] the Old Testament held, as one would expect, a position of major importance both as an object of study and as providing a particular doctrinal perspective. Although in the mid-thirteenth century the Bible was still to serve as the textual basis for the teaching of theology, scriptural *lectio* (reading and commentary by the master) had by then become more and more surrounded with *quaestiones*,[2] so that direct apprehension of the Bible became lost in the systematization of theological arguments. In the twelfth century quite the opposite was true. Such tasks were kept subordinate to the *doctrina sacra* (sacred doctrine or teaching) as such, not only within commentaries but in works which went above and beyond the literal text. To be faithful to the spirit of the earlier time, therefore, one must construct its history not around sensational intellectual controversies but around analyses of the methods used in the study of the Bible and in the results these achieved.

Several excellent studies have recently placed research on twelfth-century theology into just such proper perspective.[3] Building upon these studies, I should like to elaborate in some detail upon one of

---

[1] On the term and its history see J. de Ghellinck, "*Pagina* et *sacra pagina:* Histoire d'un mot et transformation de l'objet primitivement désigné," *Mélanges A. Pelzer* (Louvain, 1947), pp. 23–59.

[2] [See below, pp. 270–309, esp. pp. 291–300.]

[3] Principal among these is Smalley.

the essential elements of a sacred teaching that presupposed a single economy of salvation developed across two periods, the Old Covenant and the New, with the former seen as preparing and prefiguring the latter. Depending on how the relationships between the Old Testament and the New were conceived, theology was supplied with different materials and hence was differently constructed.

There are two complementary ways of approaching this project. First, through texts in which masters themselves expressly set forth their own conception and teaching as regards the relationship between the two Testaments. Of such texts Landgraf has made an extensive inventory.[4] A second investigation could both expand and corroborate the first. We might examine the way in which twelfth-century theologians in fact utilized various elements, episodes, instances of behavior, maxims, and laws of the Old Testament to build up a theology, however unsystematic, without stating any explicit theory regarding the relationship between the two Testaments and with their notions about the Bible operating spontaneously. In a way, their spontaneous utilization of the Old Testament is more significant and effective for our purpose, precisely because of its unselfconsciousness, than an abstract theory would be. It shows them working with images, comparisons, and symbols before theorizing about them. Refinements concerning Old Testament-New Testament typology were defined theoretically only after such typology had long been in use.[5]

The investigation to be made here will be limited to one corner of this field of research; namely, to a few representative instances in which theologians of the period did not treat the Old Testament as a bygone and defunct stage in the divine plan but on the contrary resorted to the Old Convenant somehow to illuminate or elaborate elements in the New by recourse to what had gone before. This was legitimate procedure from the point of view of typology, but it raised

---

[4] A. Landgraf, "Die Gnadenökonomie des Alten Bundes nach der Lehre der Frühscholastick," *ZKT*, LVII (1933), 215–53.

[5] Works for use in the schools had primarily to do with Genesis, Job, the Psalms, the Song of Songs, and the Prophetic books; but it is no less important to examine homilies, monastic collations, pastoral documents, and spiritual works, in which scriptural references of every sort are worked into the text.

some problems concerning the principles involved and the results obtained, because the connection assumed to exist between the two Covenants misconstrued their actual development and misinterpreted the course of history. *Novum in veteri latet* (the New lies enveloped in the Old): this axiom was stressed without equal attention to the other half of the diptych—*Vetus in novo patet* (The Old unfolds in the New). The Old Testament was brought to bear upon the New—one might say that the Old exercised a Judaizing influence upon the interpretation of the New. Here we get down to the foundations of a theology which was to be shaken by the evangelical awakening of the last third of the century; we come upon a curious blend of exaggerated allegorizing of the Old Testament and of eschatologism that sometimes undercut the New.[6]

Before analyzing these few particular instances, it is necessary to indicate the quarters from which they appeared and thus to situate them properly. Professional theologians and other writers indulged freely in references to the Old Testament: they made literary allusions to it, drew illustrations imaginatively from it, and used the history of the people of God in a way that was at once vague and perceptive, for they took that history as having a general typological value far broader than the values limited to a few traditionally registered types. Examples relating to different types of work can be found in the vision of the Old Covenant presented by the *Hortus*

---

[6] In limiting consideration to this aspect of the problem, one runs the risk of isolating it from other aspects and of exaggerating its importance. To treat it adequately and in context, one would first of all have to prepare monographs on the theology of the Old Testament held to by various masters— Abelard, Hugh of Saint-Victor, Peter Comestor, and Gratian. Works of secondary importance but still significant would also have to be studied; such as, for example, the *De peregrinante Civitate Dei* (*On the Pilgrim City of God, PL*, CCIV, 251–402) of Henry of Marcy, who died in 1188; its first part considers the "praeparatio materiae Civitatis Dei" (preparation of the material of the City of God). Historians should be considered as well as masters of the schools (see below, pp. 162–201.) Several doctrinal themes and areas would need to be explored: treatises on the termination of the Old Law (*De cessatione legalium*) that belonged to polemic against the Jews, theories on the import of the sacraments or mysteries of the Old Testament, the theology of prophecy, reflections on the letter and the spirit in moral theologians, mystical writers, and writers concerned with eschatology.

deliciarum (Garden of Delights) of Herrad of Landsberg;[7] or in the constant parallelism worked out in "moralizations" of the Bible—Christ blessing the apostles corresponding to Isaac blessing Jacob; or the church coming out from Christ's pierced side as Eve had come from Adam's; or in themes treated by the iconography found on cathedral portals and porches, where scenes from the Old and New Testaments were joined through allegory; or in stereotyped borrowings of biblical imagery found not only in homilies or monastic collations but in the most ordinary exchange of letters, not only in treatments of sacred subjects but in accounts of contemporary affairs, not only in commentaries on the rites of the church but in analyses of human psychology.

At the same time, one must not forget the wholly opposite tendency of Joachim of Floris's *Concordia veteris et novi testamenti (Harmony of the Old and New Testaments)* which, far from searching back into "the age of the Father," declared it finished. And yet this declaration had its ambiguity, thanks to the enigma of allegory. The Old Testament in fact remained actively present in the ever-shifting symbols set forth in Joachim's *Liber figurarum (Book of Figures)*, in which he observed: "The mystery found in the scriptures is a many-sided and involved thing; and it takes first one form, then another, like melted wax."[8]

Such was in general the outlook toward the Old Testament that prevailed in certain genuine disputes, polemical or deliberative, which were conducted in a rationalistic manner somewhat at odds with a basic commitment to typology. By focusing upon a few significant cases, I should like to isolate the principles underlying these disputes.

Let us begin with a case in which recourse to the Old Testament is the more unexpected in that it was used to shed light on the develop-

---

[7] A. Straub and G. Keller, eds. (Strasbourg, 1879–99); cf. *PL*, CXCIV, 1537–42. [See also R. Will, "Le climat religieux de l' *Hortus deliciarum* d'Herrade de Landsberg," *RHPR*, XVII (1937), 522–66.]

[8] "Multiplex est et involutum scripturarum mysterium, et veluti de altera forma in alteram ac si cera liquida commutatur." Cited by M. E. Reeves, "The *Liber figurarum* of Joachim of Fiore," *MRS*, II (1950), 67.

ment of states of life in the church—and this at a time when innovation in these states of life was leading to attacks upon traditional monasticism. The very astute author of the *De diversis ordinibus et professionibus quae sunt in ecclesia* (*On the Various Orders and Professions in the Church*), written between 1125-30, analyzed, defined, and in a certain sense legitimized the new orders by appealing to Old Testament prototypes. Monks, he said, corresponded to the prophets; regular canons had the Kohathites for a model, while regular canons who lived in cities were patterned after the Gershonites; the eremitic life realized the ideal of the pastoral life of Abel as against the urban life of Cain.[9] Was this only a fanciful comparison invented by a long-winded orator? Not at all. One must consider the terms in which he speaks of the comparison: "Now that we have discussed the so-called secular canons as best we could from the standpoint of that shadow of the truth to be found in the Old Law, what shall we say of them from the standpoint of the truth itself, which is Christ?" Again: "When we look for adumbrations of the canons, Levites, and priests of our own age in that shadow of good things to come, the Old Law, and when we consider the truth that fulfilled these adumbrations, our lord Jesus is vividly recalled to our memory. . . ."[10] *Umbra— veritas*; shadow and truth. To be sure, the Old Covenant was only a shadow, as the typologists put it, but a shadow which did not lose its own ideological integrity or substance in the light of the truth that came after it. Moreover, monks found and would continue to find justification and inspiration in the "figure" of the prophets, with whom they identified themselves; they found as much support in it, no doubt, as they did in the cliché that monks were the successors of the primitive apostolic community.

As we move along to the sacred vestments of the clergy and to the objects used in sacred worship, references to the Old Testament multiply in a curious mélange of minuscule rubrics and allegories in-

---

[9] *PL*, CCXIII, 814, 828, 834, 810–11. Cf. below, pp. 202–38.

[10] *Ibid.*, 847, 837: "Ecce de canonicis qui dicuntur saeculares, ut potuimus, secundum umbram veritatis, id est veterem legem, locuti sumus, quid de his etiam secundum ipsam veritatem, quae Christus est, dicemus?" "Ecce dum in umbra futurorum bonorum, id est in veteri lege, canonicos vel Levitas sacerdotesque istius temporis adumbratos fuisse quaerimus, et post illam umbram veritatem sequimur, ille noster Jesus nobis ad memoriam revocatur. . . ."

tended to enhance their importance. Minute interpretations of Hebrew *caeremonialia* (ceremonial matters) found in the treatise on the Ancient Law which every *summa* of the thirteenth century included[11] were normally discussed as prefiguring the rites of the New Covenant; similarly, Christian ceremonies and observances were explained not simply by reference to Christ and his mysteries or by plain reliance upon natural symbolic values but by astonishingly gratuitous attention to the utterly defunct gestures and habits of Levites of the past. The monks had consciously reintroduced into the Christian liturgy numerous rites revived from the Old Testament, especially its sacerdotal code. Ivo of Chartres' sermon, *De significationibus indumentorum sacerdotalium* (*On the Meanings of the Priestly Vestments*), which became classic because of Hugh of Saint-Victor's use of it,[12] carried to disconcerting lengths such symbolism based on the Old Testament. Consecration of the eucharist table was carried out with gestures and formulas from the Old Law, just as if it had been an altar like those of the Aaronic priesthood—a practice not found in the Roman liturgy of the early centuries. Similarly, the dedication of churches was managed as if they had been so many temples of the Law. Although holy oil had originally been intended for the anointing of Christian neophytes, the use of this oil was extended to the consecration of priests and then to that of princes; then, by a sort of scruple, an oil other than the "holy" oil was prepared and the uses of the two distinguished; this was suggested, however, by the reading of the Pentateuch.[13] The theology of baptism became

---

[11] See, *e.g.*, St. Thomas's *Summa theologica* Iª IIᵃᵉ, q. 102 (Aquinas, *Opera omnia*, II, 340–400; Aquinas, *Summa*, VIII, 159–224).

[12] For Ivo's work see *PL*, CLXII, 519–27; cf. Hugh of Saint-Victor *De sacramentis Christianae fidei* II.iv (*PL*, CLXXVI, 434–8; Deferrari, pp. 273–8).

[13] In a charter for the church of Paris in 1143, Louis VII declared: "Both from the authority of the Old Testament and from the practice of the church in our day, we know that only kings and bishops (*sacerdotes*) are consecrated by anointing with the holy chrism. It is fitting that those who, for the ruling of others, are thus linked by their anointing, should busy themselves in providing for them. . . ." Jules Tardif, *Monuments historiques* (Paris, 1866), n. 465. The king of Israel was a figure of Christ; he was consecrated by the pouring of oil over his head, and this was the sign of his legitimacy. This anointing (*sacramentum unctionis*), however, worked two ways to give meaning, as did all typology: it was a sign of the future, but that future also reacted upon the

burdened with long excursions into the ancient rite of circumcision; this parallelism, valid in principle, tended to distort the original balance and sense of the Christian sacrament.

The theology of the eucharistic sacrifice, and especially of its attendant ritual, experienced the effect of such burdens even more. In the Old Dispensation, a good part of the ritualism had been cast into forms intended to compete against those bloody, idolatrous cults toward which the Israelites were constantly attracted. Men of the Middle Ages, instead of seeing these ritual prescriptions as temporary adaptations within a developing structure, treated them as rules having perpetual validity even though they dissolved their elements into a generalized allegory. The detailed extension of this allegory to the eucharist threw out of balance the properly Christian conception of this sacrament as both a meal and a sacrifice and intruded various archaic notions upon it. For example, the entry of the bishop and other officiants of the mass into the assemblage of the people was hailed as the triumphal entry of the king returning to Jerusalem after his victories against the Philistines; the introit represented fanfares for the warriors.[14] To be sure, Ivo of Chartres, in his *De ecclesiasticis sacramentis et officiis* (*On the Sacraments and Offices of the Church*),[15] reacted against the incoherence of the allegories of Amalarius of Metz; but, by his own efforts to unify these he strengthened the principle of sustained allegorizing based on scripture. The mass

---

sign. Innocent III was to introduce a distinction between the anointing of the heads of bishops with the holy chrism and the anointing of the arms of kings with the oil of the catechumens—a significant qualification to current recourse to the Old Testament. "Non judaizat Ecclesia" (the church does not "Judaize"), as was said in *Decretal* I. xv. 1 (Friedberg, II, 134; cf. *PL*, CCXV, 286).

[14] So Honorius of Autun, outdoing Amalarius of Metz; he saw the mass as a battle against the devil; the bishop was a prince, the miter his crown, the processional cross his scepter; mounted on his chariot, he entered the throng of his loyal subjects. Cf. Amalarius of Metz *De ecclesiasticis officiis* iii.5 (*PL*, CI, 1107–13); Honorius of Autun *Gemma animae, sive de divinis officiis et antiquo ritu missarum* i. 72–73 (*PL*, CLXXII, 566–7). The idea was taken up by John Beleth in his *Rationale divinorum officiorum* (*PL*, CCII, 9–166) and Sicard of Cremona in his *Mitrale, seu de officiis ecclesiasticis summa* (*PL*, CCXIII, 13–436).

[15] *PL*, CLXII, 506 ff., esp. *Sermo v, sive opusculum de convenientia veteris et novi sacrificii* (*ibid.*, 535–62).

became a series of antitypes of the sacrifices of the Law; the sacrifice of the New Law was to be explicated, even in the details of its encompassing ritual, by reference to the sacrifices of the Old. Rupert of Deutz extended this operation, and the *De sacro altaris mysterio* (*On the Sacred Mystery of the Altar*) of Innocent III[16] established the reputation of the method and its results.

Given such parallelism with the sacrifices of the Old Testament, the mass presented itself much more as a sacrifice offered by man through giving up some of his own goods than as the unique sacrifice of Christ offering himself once and for all to the Father.[17] The Old Testament was no longer a witness to the Christ who was to come, but Christ became a particular instance of the ritual laws of Leviticus. Even the barbaric rite of the scapegoat took on the wholly spiritual quality of the sacrifice of the cross.

Furthermore, moral and sacramental legislation concerning marriage continued to be weighted down by these references to the Old Testament. The obligation to conjugal abstinence before reception of the eucharist was an explicit application of observances concerning purity under the Old Law. John Beleth referred to the episode recorded in 1 Kings 21 as the basis of a conciliar decree.[18] Similarly, a resurgence of the spirit of Leviticus was responsible for the unanimous teaching that forbade reception of the eucharist after nocturnal pollution. A woman violated without her consent was not culpable and could be consecrated as a virgin, as ascertainable from Deut. 23.[19] Matrimony was considered as serving procreation more than

---

[16] *PL*, CCXVII, 773–916.

[17] The prevailing ideas of the mass were more complex than this. Thus, from the ninth century on, another line of development led to the mass's being considered as a gift of God to the faithful; the gift was highlighted through the elevation of the host at consecration, through concentration upon the activities of the priest rather than upon those of the faithful, through emphasis upon the presence but not upon the participation of the faithful, and the like. But this too showed Levite influence. In neither case was the mass seen as the gift of the whole body of the faithful, the offering of the church in and through Christ, to God. For the details and significance of the whole development, see J. A. Jungmann, *The Mass of the Roman Rite: Its Origins and Development*, vol. 1 (New York, 1950), 92–141, and vol. 2 (New York, 1955), 1–100.

[18] *Rationale div. off.* cxx (*PL*, CCII, 124).

[19] Rupert of Deutz *Liber de laesione virginitatis* xvii (*PL*, CLXX, 560).

conjugal love, and woman was an instrument of procreation more than a personal object of such love. Conceptions borrowed from Old Testament legislation thus had a depressive effect upon the New Testament's exaltation of woman in virginity and marriage alike.

Development of thought concerning trial by ordeal, whether in the popular mind or in canon law, was partly determined by the Old Testament practice of consulting the judgments of God. Behind Gratian's discussion of the subject lay the conflict between two civilizations in the history then unfolding: German civilization favored such trial, Roman civilization opposed it. But also alleged were "authorities" from the Old Testament, and the procedures set for such trial were inspired by episodes that were part of ancient Hebrew experience. For example, if the ordeal vindicated the accused, the accuser was to suffer the fate he had sought to impose, following the pattern set by the episode concerning Daniel and the lions' den. So impressive were the scriptural texts that Gratian doubted the validity of the general prohibition of ordeals by church law.[20]

In the area of social morality, precepts that rested upon Old Testament legislation abounded. The most characteristic case was the forbidding of interest. The people of God, liberated historically (the flight from Egypt) and spiritually (symbolic significance of the flight), were no longer to oppress or exploit their own kind or strangers (Exod. 22:25, Lev. 25:35, Deut. 23:19–21). However, in one whole sector of life the elements of a patriarchal economy, for which the Mosaic legislation had been designed, were disappearing from the twelfth century. In contrast to the preceding centuries, during which men of the West lived in an economy comparable to that reflected in the Bible, the twelfth century experienced a commercial awakening which in fact made Mosaic legislation economically and morally out-of-date. Consequently, men undertook to de-

---

[20] Gratian's reliance upon the Old Testament is the more significant because he was not a teacher of doctrine or a spiritual writer but an expert in institutional law; as such he was equally concerned with the stability of the law and the vitality of the scriptures. Cf. G. Le Bras, "Les Écritures dans le décret de Gratien," *ZRG*, Kanon. Abt., XXVII (1938), 47–80.

termine under what circumstances the taking of interest might be allowed.[21]

In spiritual teaching, the theology of suffering, without making historical distinctions, combined New Testament texts on the God of love and imitation of Christ with Old Testament "authorities." The latter, though undergoing change themselves (think of Job), generally ascribed suffering to personal faults, established as such by punishments that came from God.

This ethics of the will of God, transplanted into quite different conceptions of psychology and moral theology, was to bring about a new synthesis in which "examples" from the Old Testament and a special view of the role of the Law in history gave rise to new criteria of religious fidelity. In the Old Testament, fidelity had been measured against the rigid and meticulous prescriptions of an external Law and judged by God's prophetic interventions; in the Christian dispensation, fidelity was interiorized, and law became the grace of the Holy Spirit. Yet texts commending a pure morality of obedience, commending the will of God as objectified in his commandments, were now adduced from the Old Testament. At the end of the century, this attention to a morality of obedience appeared not only in an evangelical revival inspired by the Holy Spirit but in the systematic inquiries which various philosophies were beginning to make into the nature of moral action.

It was, however, in the evolving social and institutional structures of the kingdom of God that the full weight of ancient Hebraic conceptions was felt. Under the influence of Leviticus, a theology of the priesthood was built up around the *ordo ad cultum* (regulation governing worship) and its validity was of capital importance. But the apostolic character of the bishops, which made them, as successors to the apostles, the very framework of the church, was juxtaposed to the ritual priesthood of the Old Dispensation as described in a series of Old Testament "authorities." In these, the prophets

---

[21] [On medieval ideas on interest and usury, see, e.g., John T. Noonan, Jr., *The Scholastic Analysis of Usury* (Cambridge, Mass., 1957), Pt. 1, "The Scholastic Theory, 1150–1450," pp. 11–195; and LeBras, cited below, p. 226, n. 50.]

exercised a role outside the Levitical priesthood, and it was not till much later that Christ's prayer in John 17 was spoken of as a "priestly" prayer. The characterization of the bishop as a pastor was drawn more from the Old Testament than from the New, and it accordingly stressed his moral governance more than it did his mission as teacher and prophet.

Moreover, from time to time in controversies over the apostolic activities of evangelical groups, preaching by the laity was defended on the ground that in the Old Testament, Levites, that is to say the clergy of the time, were not the only ones to teach the Law; men from other tribes did so too, especially from the tribe of Simeon.[22]

The general conception of the church as the realization of the kingdom of God was profoundly affected by this going back to the Old Testament, for the former dispensation was at one and the same time the first stage towards, the preparation for, and the figure of the new. The synagogue was the figure of the church; the church, therefore, *trans*figured the synagogue. But here too typology was brought into play, for the church searched into its Old Testament "past" to find models for its present conduct. Here we see the tension, the dialectic, that characterizes all typology: intimately connected yet marked by progress, stages unfold within a total historical structure that stretches "from Abel to the consummation of time," to borrow a title from Anselm of Havelberg's dialogues. Twelfth-century ecclesiology was centered about such a typological sense—not only explicit and systematic ecclesiology, but even more the ecclesiology implied by institutions, patterns of behavior, and the play of decision and temperament. A few key indications may be suggested.

---

[22] Even in the thirteenth century Hugh of Saint-Cher was to reply to the objection that laymen might not preach by saying: ". . . laici praedicare possunt, quia non solum Levitae, qui significant clericos, erant doctores in lege, sed etiam alii de aliis tribubus, et maxime de tribu Simeon. Sed illi alii de tribubus aliis gerunt typum laicorum; ergo laici possunt praedicare et docere. . . ." (Laymen may preach, because it was not only the Levites, who signify the clergy, who were doctors of the Law but also men from other tribes, especially that of Simeon; but these other men from other tribes were a type of the laity. Therefore, laymen may preach and teach.) *Quaest. de beneficiis ecclesiasticis* I, obj. 1 (Friedrich Stegmüller, ed., *HJ*, LXXII [1953], 185).

As all levels of political society became Christian, juridically and politically Christian, the kingdom of Christ availed itself of the resources of that political society in a way that the first generations of Christians had never had open to them; and it consequently took on the ways of acting and the rights of the people of God whom one sees organized into a political society in the Old Testament. This was a *christianitas*, a "Christendom," men began to say; and terms like *regnum* (kingdom), *imperium* (empire or rule), *gladius* (sword), or like *plenitudo potestatis* (fullness of power),[23] or even *curia* (court)[24] regained their force within it. The Mosaic idea of separateness thwarted here and there the sense of universalism, of catholicity, which was implicit in the incarnation and which St. Gregory had defined in the gospel's words: "Before it was said: 'You shall not walk in the way of the gentiles'; now, however, it is said: 'Preach the gospel to every creature.' "[25]

Very significant was the use of antitypes which recognized Old Testament kings as ideals for the Christian prince. Charlemagne was Josias; David and Solomon were sacred prototypes; in the concept *rex-sacerdos* (royal priest or priest-king) Saul was the type of the king, Samuel of the priest.[26] The true model of political society was furnished by the Old Testament; its texts and stories filled the "mir-

---

[23] Cf. Gerhardt B. Ladner, "The Concepts of *Ecclesia* and *Christianitas* and Their Relation to the Idea of Papal *Plenitudo Potestatis*, from Gregory VII to Boniface VIII," *MHP*, XVIII, no. 52 (Rome: Pontificia Università Gregoriana, 1954), 49–77.

[24] ". . . quod nunc dicitur curia romana, quae antehac dicebatur ecclesia romana" (now it is called the Roman curia; formerly it was called the Roman church), was Gerhoh of Reichersberg's bitter observation in *De investigatione Antichristi* (written in 1161–2), *MGH: Libelli de lite*, III, 355f., 384; cf. *Comm. in Ps. LXIV, sive de corrupto ecclesiae statu* prol. (*PL*, CXCIV, 9–10). For use of this expression by St. Bernard, see M. J. Congar, "L'ecclésiologie de S. Bernard," *ASOC*, IX (1953), 184; Congar also observes: "The word *curia* was transposed from the imperial to the papal vocabulary during the eleventh century. . . . At first used only rarely and incidentally, it became a technical term regularly employed in the time of Urban II (1089–99) and Paschal II (1099–1118)."

[25] "Ante etenim dictum fuerat: In viam Gentium ne abieritis; nunc autem dicitur: Praedicate omni creaturae"; *Hom. XXIX in Evang.* (*PL*, LXXVI, 1214).

[26] Cf. J. Funkenstein, "Samuel und Saul in der Staatslehre des Mittelalters," *ARSP*, XLVIII (1952), 129–40.

rors of princes." It was only with John of Salisbury that a genuine political analysis based on secular considerations was introduced into moral philosophy.

It was clearly in the Old Testament that the crusade, that distinctive enterprise of all Christendom, found its inspiration, its basis, its rules, and all the ambiguities concerning worldly messianism that form a usual part of the imagery of the prophetic books. The "Lord of hosts" became not only the mystical but the earthly triumphant conqueror in that holy war.[27]

To sum it up, the idea of separateness prevailed as a basic article of this powerful church, which thought of itself rather as a chosen people among the nations than as the mystical body of Christ. It was God's inheritance; and within it one could observe reactions which resembled those characteristic of the Pharisees, the "separated ones," of ancient Judaism. And when this church, through the malice of men, became divided against itself, the definition and circumstances and remedies of schism would be borrowed from the biblical account of the schism of the ten tribes of Israel.

But more significant than the lifting of particular figures and ideas from the Old Testament, which the theology of the great masters balanced with texts from the New, was a whole manner of presenting arguments, a whole turn of style and thought, a whole cast of mind that revealed this envelopment of the New Testament in the Old—*Novum in veteri latet* (the New lies enveloped in the Old). Allegory got heavily involved in this backward look of typology, and here and there it obscured the sense of progress which history was demanding.

However, a sufficient awareness of irreversible progress remained. Men of the Middle Ages recognized and proclaimed the *cessatio legalium* (cessation of the Law). In contrast to the figure of *Ecclesia* with her open and radiant countenance stood the figure of *Synagoga* portrayed as a conquered queen, her crown fallen, her face veiled

---

[27] [For differing interpretations of the development of medieval thought on the crusades, see, e.g., Carl Erdmann, *Die Entstehung des Kreuzzugsgedankens* (Stuttgart, 1935) and Paul Rousset, *Les origines et les caractères de la première croisade* (Neuchâtel, 1945), esp. pp. 13–26 and, on Old Testament parallels, pp. 185–92.]

or her eyes blindfolded.[28] This allegory popularized in art a theme found in polemics against the Jews; namely, that the fulfilment offered by the New Covenant displaced the dead letter of the Law, displaced its barbaric ceremonies and temporarily tolerated practices such as polygamy, divorce, or vengeance, and the like. As Gratian phrased it: "Under the Old Law many things were permitted which today have been abolished by the perfection of grace."[29] Not until the thirteenth century was a just and balanced evaluation of the Old Law proposed within the evangelical freedom of the New. Nonetheless, from the twelfth century on, despite many inconsistencies, the principle of such an evaluation was affirmed; and on a window of Saint-Denis, Suger inscribed the device: *Quod Moyses velat, Christi doctrina revelat* (What Moses conceals, the teaching of Christ reveals).[30]

Let us summarize, then, the theology of the Old Testament in the twelfth century, a period when divine science kept itself close to scripture as a textual continuum.

First, history in the Old Testament was believed to furnish a series of *exempla*. To this term one must give the weighty meaning it had then in both religious and secular thought. "Examples" were not mere illustrations to be used in instructing schoolboys or simple folk; they were normative or "type" actions fitted by their concrete detail to provide an efficacious model for human conduct, which was also governed by general principles. St. Ambrose had already submitted the moral teachings of philosophers to revelation, which fortified that teaching with "examples." Sufficient emphasis has not been placed upon the deliberate use of biblical *exempla*, whether in the practical morality taught by preachers or in the moral theory developed by the doctors, even if, when it came to wicked episodes like David's adultery with Bathsheba, they had to resort to allegory. In

---

[28] [For a full discussion of this theme, see Bernhard Blumenkranz, *Le juif médiéval au miroir de l'art chrétien* (Paris, 1966).]

[29] "In veteri lege multa permittebantur, quae hodie perfectione gratiae abolita sunt": *Decretum*, II[a] pars, c. xv, q. 3 (Friedberg, I, 750).

[30] [For discussion of the window, see Erwin Panofsky, ed. and tr., *Abbot Suger on the Abbey Church of Saint-Denis and Its Art Treasures* (Princeton, 1946), pp. 74–75.]

this practice one meets the conception of history and its uses generally entertained both in Christian tradition and in classical pedagogy. History served men with "examples"; history and moral instruction were joined in education.

But biblical history had its own special law which gave its "examples" a religious import exclusively their own. This history, unfolding according to divine plan, contained stages whose continuity and breaks one had to observe with equal attention. Continuity—"I have not come to destroy the Law . . ."; break—"But I say unto you. . . ." The dialectic between the two was intrinsic to the progress of the economy of salvation, a progress that anticipated its final course through prefigurations of the future. In these matters medieval authors, following the fathers, had a keener sense than we of the typology essential to scripture. Through the force of this dialectic, a twofold tendency came into play: now men were intent upon the absolute individuality, the novelty, of events; now they were intent upon comprehending the "meaning" of these events by harmonizing the new dispensation with the old. Sometimes they "Christianized" the Old Testament; sometimes, in Innocent III's phrase, they "Judaized" the New. Legislation concerning the Sunday was a case in point. Ancient prescriptions for the sabbath determined the basic lines of that legislation, while Christ's proclamation of the freedom of the children of God colored its observance.

Thus did past history remain present—"mystically" present, said twelfth-century theologians after the manner of the fathers. Remembrance of the past was not simply a historical memory. Prescinding from the successive stages of time, it was, as we should say today, an "archetypal" memory; and within it Christian time took shape. In theology, typology was the art of constructing such types. If allegorizing often threw it out of balance, it did not compromise the underlying principle.

I have elsewhere described these religious interpretations of history and the delicate limit of their delineation.[31] Constituting as it did the sixth age of the divine plan,[32] the history of the church stood

---

[31] See Chenu, *TDS*, chap. 8, "La théologie symbolique," pp. 191–209.

[32] On the six ages and their variant sources and senses, see below, pp. 162–201, esp. pp. 179 ff.

in danger of being treated as a simple extension of the first five ages; and the desire to find in scripture some reflection of the church as it presently was, testified to men's troubled awareness of misunderstandings. It was only from the twelfth century on that men, as they pondered the long duration of this sixth age, acquired a keener sense of the uniqueness of what had occurred in the new dispensation, and thereby of the freshness with which the gospel had burst upon the world.

5

Theology and the
New Awareness of History

Truth is the daughter of time.
BERNARD OF CHARTRES

H ISTORIANS OF THEOLOGY, in their sensitivity to doctrinal
polemics and their justifiable attachment to educational institutions and formal pedagogical writings, have given too little attention to a domain outside the program of the schools but essential to the balanced development of Christian thought: that of history as an expression of the temporal order of salvation. Yet it was not the least splendid achievement of Latin Christendom in the twelfth century to awaken in men's minds an active awareness of human history.

To be certain, the front rank in this notable intellectual endeavor was occupied by those disciplines which the discovery of nature encouraged, a discovery in turn nourished by an avid and methodical reading of the *Timaeus* and its imitations, and stimulated even more by what underlay this literary interest: the perception of man's physical environment and of the effective ties between the life of society and the rhythms of nature. From this perception there arose, particularly at Chartres, an anthropology which considered man a "microcosm" whose nature could be rendered comprehensible only by first gaining an understanding of the whole universe. In effect this was a cosmic philosophy which was bound to lead, as it did for example with Alan of Lille, to the positing of Nature, with a capital letter, as a substantive reality. Alan referred to this Nature as the vicar of God, and Jean de Meun would repeat the phrase in the thirteenth

162

century; but this Nature, vicar of God, was insensitive to the passage of time in human history and to the sequence of divine activities. The creation itself was detemporalized and deexistentialized, for it was thought of rather as it exists in the divine "ideas" than as it unfolds in the six days of Genesis.

However, during the same twelfth century, certain men, sometimes the same ones, were following a wholly different line of thought, bringing their curiosity and talent to bear on humanity itself. In their view, the works and deeds of humanity, under the providence of God—the God of the Bible and not of Nature, God as Redeemer and not as the One—comprised a "universe" other than the physical one: the human universe of sacred history. Too often these authors have been treated merely as learned men living on the fringes of the main intellectual activities of their time, whereas in truth they were working out a theology that was firmly tied to the teaching of scripture—scripture whose *historia* was at the basis of clerical education. And it must be added that during the second half of the century, these historians were far closer to the evangelical awakening of the church than the philosophizing masters closed up with their dialectic in the schools.

It remains nonetheless true that, in this century and for a long time afterwards, there was no intention of working into the school curriculum, either for clerical or secular training, *lectiones* on the history of the church as the successor in time to the period before Christ. While a notable deficiency, this lack was not peculiar to the cycle of civilization which we are studying. With peoples as with individuals, contemplation and speculation precede historical curiosity, which is a fruit of reflective ages. The twelfth century was already a reflective age, even in its religious experience; but if the writing of post-biblical history was taken into serious consideraton, it was still only by the private initiative of minds that had grown aware of the life of men in their social collectivity and in the succession of their generations. John of Salisbury cited the ancient historians copiously;[1] and his friend Peter of Blois, taking stock of the sources of

---

[1] *Policraticus* viii. 18 (Webb, II, 363–4; Dickinson, p. 356): "Quae si quis diligentius recenseri uoluerit, legat ea quae Trogus Pompeius, Iosephus,

his culture, listed the historians he claimed to have read frequently, outside the schools, for the benefit of his mind and of his moral life.[2] At the close of the century, Alexander Neckham listed the "historians" in his program of liberal education.[3]

If we look for the milieu that stimulated these minds, we would find it not in the schools but in those places, spiritual after their own fashion, where history was being made more visibly, at least in those times: in the entourages of princes and emperors. These writers were often monks, it is true, and far removed from the urban schools;[4] but by the very strength of a tradition the high culture of which had engendered the "chroniclers," many of these historian-monks worked as spiritual advisers to a powerful secular Christendom, living in the environment of important leaders and in the thick of political battles. Ordericus Vitalis led a calm life in his Abbey of Saint-Evroult, a "seedbed of active scholars" as Ghellinck has called

---

Egesippus, Suetonius, Quintus Curtius, Cornelius Tacitus, Titus Liuius, Serenus et Tranquillus et alii historici, quos enumerare longum est, suis comprehenderunt historiis." (If anyone should wish to look into these things more carefully, let him read what Pompeius Trogus, Josephus, Hegesippus, Suetonius, Curtius Rufus, Tacitus, Livy, Serenus, Tranquillus, and other historians too numerous to mention have included in their accounts.) For an extensive list of John's sources, cf. Webb, *Policraticus*, I, xxi–xlvii.

[2] *Epp.* ci (*PL*, CCVII, 314): "Preter caeteros etiam libros, qui celebres sunt in scholis, profuit mihi frequenter inspicere Trogum Pompeium, Josephum, Suetonium, Hegesippum, Quintum Curcium, Cornelium Tacitum, Titum Livium, qui omnes in historiis quas referunt, multa ad morum aedificationem, et ad profectum scientiae liberalis interserunt." (Apart from those other books which are well known in the schools, I have often had occasion to consult Trogus Pompeius, Josephus, Suetonius, Hegesippus, Curtius Rufus, Tacitus, and Livy—all of whom include in their histories many things which contribute greatly to moral edification and to advancement in liberal knowledge.) It would seem that Peter, in keeping with customary practice, copied the list from the one given by his teacher John of Salisbury. See above, n. 1.

[3] *Sacerdos ad altare* (Haskins, *Studies,* p. 372): "Deinde satiricos et ystoriographos legat. . . ." (Next he should read the satirical writers and the historians.)

[4] Ghellinck, *Essor*, p. 314: "The ironic history of history: eliminated by so cultured a writer as Peter Damian from the list of activities worthy of a monk ('ludicrously useless annals, frivolous telling of frivolous old wives' tales'), it was almost entirely by the efforts of monks that history regained life in the Middle Ages and by their efforts that it flourished brilliantly." This point gains support and importance when we recall that the scholastic masters paid practically no attention to the great historical texts of *The City of God*—texts often pondered, however, by monastic authors.

it; yet his combined Saxon and Norman family background sharpened his interest in the passionate vicissitudes of the Norman adventures in England, in Italy, in Aragon.[5] The Plantagenets found in monastic centers the most brilliant exponents, from William of Malmesbury to Matthew Paris, of their political enterprises and cultural achievements. Otto of Freising, grandson on his mother's side of the Emperor Henry IV and uncle of Frederick Barbarossa, entered the Cistercian Abbey of Morimond but surely did not forget there either the imperial mystique or his Parisian schooling.

It is no part of our program here to redo an already well written chapter—enough to have mentioned Ghellinck—on the historiography of the twelfth century. I intend rather to outline the main features of a mounting curiosity about man's past and the psychological conditions of that curiosity, all within the context of the theological work then in progress.

The Historical Thought of Hugh of Saint-Victor and of Anselm of Havelberg

In consulting the index of words in the *Didascalicon*, where Hugh of Saint-Victor, in line with his dominant approach, had given organic expression to both his method of thought and his classification of the disciplines of the mind, one observes that the term *historia* was employed as often as *logica* and more often than *dialectica*.[6] This quantitative index is significant: we would not find the same results in Abelard or among his contemporaries at Chartres.

This significance becomes defined and focused when we note that, contrary to *logica* and *dialectica*, the use of *historia* was almost exclusively reserved to the second part of the *Didascalicon*, especially books four and five, those devoted to sacred disciplines (*studia divinarum scripturarum*). *Historia* designated the contents and accordingly the manner of thinking of a whole religious structure. The religion of Christ was not based on logic but on a series of facts arranged in a history, a history that one must read—in the technical sense of

---

[5] It suffices to direct attention to the excellent chapter called "L'histoire" in Ghellinck, *Essor*, pp. 313–87, esp. 322–5.

[6] Cf. the *Index verborum notabiliorum* (Buttimer, pp. 148–60).

the medieval *lectio*—according to an appropriate method, not according to the dialectical pattern of some system of thought.

The fact is even more notable that, in the secular disciplines, *historia* also existed as a literary genre, as one of the parts of *grammatica*, along with proses and meters and fables.[7] Presenting these categories without explanation for the sake of brevity, Hugh, via Isidor,[8] took the classification of the ancient grammarians, especially these *fabulae* and *historiae*, which had nothing to do with philosophy, the supreme art, but which were thought capable of assisting the mind to acquire cultivation.[9] But when we pass over to divine history, as he says, we change both object and method, despite the similarity of literary form. *Historia* now designates both the content of this religious economy as it worked itself out through time, and the peculiar method necessary for shaping such an object into a scientific discipline, tied to the literal level of a text, based on the *littera*, on the literal narrative.

The term *historia* thus embraced the same ambiguity which it retains in our modern languages, where it designates at the same time the facts, as the stuff of history (objective sense), and the intellectual discipline which treats these facts (subjective sense). The usage of the word in books four and five of the *Didascalicon* confirms this, where Hugh especially presented, with all the vigorous originality of his own thought, the articulation of theology's two parts: the *lectio historiae* and the construction of *allegoria*. *Historia* was at once the literal contents of the story as opposed to the mystical investigation of allegory, and the method suited to this sacred object, a method entirely different from that of the secular disciplines, whether philosophy properly speaking, or the ensemble of the seven arts preparatory to the study of philosophy.[10]

---

[7] *Didascalicon* ii. 29 (Buttimer, p. 45; Taylor, p. 80).

[8] *Etym.* i. 5. 4 (*PL*, LXXXII, 81–82).

[9] *Didascalicon* iii. 4 (Buttimer, p. 54; Taylor, p. 88).

[10] Hugh of Saint-Victor *De scripturis et scriptoribus sacris* iii (*PL*, CLXXV, 12): "Historia dicitur a verbo graeco ἱστορέω, historeo, quod est video et narro. Propterea quod apud veteres nulli licebat scribere res gestas, nisi a se visas, ne falsitas admisceretur veritati peccato scriptoris, plus aut minus aut aliter dicentis. Secundum hoc proprie et districte dicitur historia; sed solet largius accipi, ut dicatur historia sensus qui primo loco ex significatione verborum

It will come as no surprise that this perception of history developed within a religious framework. One of the well-known constant factors in the history of civilizations is that religious values are favorable to the discovery of realities which are not organized dialectically into a system of thought but rather in time, following a succession of events, expressed in a *series narrationis* (narrative sequence), as Hugh said. Here, at one of the turning points of western history, we have another case of this constant factor. History remained clearly marked by its birth among, and in a climate of, religious things; only bit by bit was secular history to emerge, after a flourishing of "theology" of history.[11]

But for all its religious, that is theological, character, this history was nonetheless history. One can see this clearly in the resistance that Hugh encountered for wanting to maintain the fundamental integrity of history before one attempted theological construc-

---

habetur ad res." ("History" is rendered by the Greek word ἱστορέω which means "I see" and "I recount." For this reason, among the ancients no one was permitted to write about events unless he had seen them himself—so that falsehood would not get mixed in with truth, the fault of a writer who would overstate or understate or differently report things from what they were. Thus is "history" properly and strictly defined. Yet it can be taken in a larger sense, as when "history" is the meaning assigned to things in the first instance by the immediate significance of the words used.) *Ibid. De sacramentis Christianae fidei* prol. 4 (*PL*, CLXXVI, 185; Deferrari, p. 5): "Historia est rerum gestarum narratio, quae in prima significatione litterae continetur." (History is the narration of events which is contained in the first or literal level of meaning.) Cf. *Ibid.* 6 (*PL*, CLXXVI, 185; Deferrari, p. 5) and Robert of Melun *Sententie* i. 1. 6 (Martin, I, 171). In the Middle Ages the standard definition of history was that of Isidore who got it from the Latin grammarians who commented on Virgil; *Etym.* i. 41 (*PL*, LXXXII, 122): "Historia est narratio rei gestae per quam ea quae in praeterito facta sunt, dignoscuntur." (History is the narration of events by which those things which were done in the past are sorted out.)

[11] Karl Löwith, *Meaning in History* (Chicago, 1949), p. 197: "Thus if we venture to say that our modern historical consciousness is derived from Christianity, this can mean only that the eschatological outlook of the New Testament has opened the perspective toward a future fulfillment—originally beyond, and eventually within, historical existence. In consequence of the Christian consciousness we have a historical consciousness which is as Christian by derivation as it is non-Christian by consequence. . . ." On the meaning and validity of the medieval conception of history, cf. Etienne Gilson, *The Spirit of Medieval Philosophy*, tr. A. H. C. Downes (New York, 1936), chap. 9: "Christian Anthropology."

tion,[12] as well as in the encroachment of speculation on theology in the thirteenth century, when the *quaestiones* (and their products, the *summae*) were divorced from the historical *lectio* of sacred texts. Scholasticism detached itself from sacred history. The Victorine's attempt to build an allegorical system on a historical base was doomed to failure; and it was St. Thomas who rejected—as part of the scientific function of theology, one must understand—the dualism of history and allegory, disparate elements despite the tie of biblical typology.

Still, the Victorine pedagogy was helpful for gaining an understanding of Christian revelation as a series of events and thus an appreciation of the human and divine values of history. Indeed, despite the stopping up of certain mental processes and the opposition of dialecticians, Hugh presented a certain number of elements which demonstrated this new sensitivity. For a very long time chroniclers had of course been reporting events, both ancient and modern; and Bede, over four centuries before, had displayed the qualities of a good historian; but now an instinctive awareness was arising, to become a form of knowledge in its own right. Let us note its characteristics, leaving to one side for a deservedly separate study the application of this historical sense to biblical exegesis, where Andrew of Saint-Victor, the "new Jerome," was a master of great stature.[13]

The first significant detail to note is that *series narrationis* was a favorite expression of Hugh of Saint-Victor, an expression which made precise the characteristic trait of history as opposed to the logical connection of theoretical disciplines. It was a *series*, a sequence, and an organized sequence, an articulated continuity, whose themes made sense, which was exactly the object of the intelligible-

---

[12] *Didascalicon* vi. 3 (Buttimer, p. 114; Taylor, p. 136): "Scio quosdam esse qui statim philosophari volunt; fabulas pseudoapostolis relinquendas aiunt. Quorum scientia formae asini similis est. Noli hujusmodi imitari." (I know that there are certain fellows who want to play the philosopher right away. They say that stories should be left to pseudoapostles. The knowledge of these fellows is like that of an ass. Don't imitate persons of this kind.)

[13] Cf. W. A. Schneider, *Geschichte und Geschichtsphilosophie bei Hugo von St. Victor* (Münster, 1933) [Smalley, chap. 4, "Andrew of St. Victor," pp. 112–95].

ness of history—not Platonic ideas, but the initiatives of God within the time of mankind, the events of salvation.[14] Henceforth, time and place became part of history, in events and in the understanding of their significance.[15] Negligible details? So it may seem, but he who scorned them would indeed miss the spiritual pattern.[16]

In its profound—and put simply, mysterious—reality, this *series* resulted from a whole plan, a conscious disposition with a preconceived goal to be realized in the course of time, a plan for which time, as opposed to eternal ideas, was an essential condition. The word *dispensatio* (direction, stewardship, management), by which the western fathers translated οἰχονομία of the Greek fathers,[17] car-

---

[14] *Series narrationis* (narrative sequence), and *series temporum* (sequence of time) were characteristic expressions of Hugh. Cf. *De sacramentis Christianae fidei* i. 1. 29 (*PL*, CLXXVI, 204; Deferrari, p. 27): ". . . et si hoc diligenter in his omnibus secundum seriem temporum et successiones generationum ac dispositionem praeceptorum inquirimus, summam totam divinarum scripturarum fidenter nos attigisse pronuntiamus." (and if we investigate all things carefully according to the sequence of time, the succession of generations, and the arrangement of truths taught, we can claim confidently to have reached all levels of divine scripture.) Cf. *Ibid.* i. 10. 6 (*PL*, CLXXVI, 336; Deferrari, p. 173). Cf. *In Eccles.* praef. (*PL*, CLXXV, 115). Cf. *De arca Noe morali* iv. 9 (*PL*, CLXXVI, 678; CSMV, p. 149): ". . . in serie rerum gestarum ordo temporis invenitur." (The order of time is found in the sequence of events.); *Except. alleg.* (see below, n. 38); etc.

[15] *De arca Noe morali* iv. 9 (*PL*, CLXXVI, 667; CSMV, p. 147): "In operibus restaurationis tribus modis ordo consideratur: secundum locum, secundum tempus, secundum dignitatem. . . . Ordo autem loci et ordo temporis fere per omnia secundum rerum gestarum seriem concurrere videntur. . . ." (Order in the works of restoration is to be considered in three ways: place, time, and dignity. . . . The order of place, however, and the order of time seem to run parallel in almost everything, following the sequence of events.)

[16] *Didascalicon* vi. 3 (Buttimer, p. 114; Taylor, p. 136): "Haec enim quattuor praecipue in historia requirenda sunt: persona, negotium, tempus et locus. . . . Noli contemnere minima haec. Paulatim defluit qui minima contemnit." (For these are the four things which are especially to be sought for in history—the person, the business due, the time, and the place. . . . Do not look down upon these least things. The man who looks down on such smallest things slips little by little.)

[17] St. Augustine *De vera religione* vii. 13 (*CSEL*, LXXVII, 12): "Hujus religionis sectandae caput est historia et prophetia dispensationis temporalis divinae providentiae pro salute generis humani in aeternam vitam reformandi et reparandi." (The key to this religion is the history and prophecy of the temporal dispensation of divine providence for the salvation of the human race, which had to be reformed and restored to eternal life.)

ried all its force in Hugh and similar writers.[18] Time was thus not merely a cosmic duration but a historical succession of events, a *processus saeculi*. The bringing together of the two words *mundus* (world, the earth) and *saeculum* (world, century, age) underscored the human or indeed religious dimension—"by the passage of time until the end of the world" (*decurrentibus temporibus usque ad finem saeculi*)—of this mysterious yet intelligible order that revolved in gear with the physical and geographical order of the cosmos: ". . . from which we might conclude that the end of time is approaching, since the course of events has now reached the end of the world."[19]

---

[18]*De vanitate mundi* iv (*PL*, CLXXVI, 733): ". . . illis (Judaeis) nuntiatus fuit [sic] qui electi erant quasi ministri per quos dispensatio salutis omnium ageretur . . ." (it was announced to them [the Jews] who had been chosen as the agents through whom the dispensation of the salvation of all mankind would be activated.) Cf. *De sacramentis Christianae fidei* i. 12. 9 (*PL*, CLXXVI, 360; Deferrari, p. 201): "Sequitur aliud genus praeceptorum quae mobilia vocantur, quoniam naturalibus mandatis secundum dispensationem ad tempus superaddita sunt. . . ." (There follows another kind of precepts which are called movable since they were added on to the natural commands in the course of time according to the dispensation.) The term also applied to creation: *De vanitate mundi* iii (*PL*, CLXXVI, 721): "Haec autem dispensatio Creatoris magnae fuit machinationis principium. . . ." (However, this dispensation of the Creator was the source of his great act of creation.) The development in stages of this economy of salvation included accommodations and adjustments; thus the word here took on a legal meaning. Cf. Anselm of Havelburg *Dialogi* i. 5 (*PL*, CLXXXVIII, 1147): ". . . ita de gentibus Judaeos, de Judaeis autem Christianos fecit, et paulatim subtrahendo, et transponendo, et dispensando, quasi furtim ad idolorum cultura ad legem, a lege autem, quae quidem ad perfectum non duxit, ad perfectionem Evangelii pedagogice et medicinaliter deduxit, et tandem subtracta omni dispensatione, omnem perfectionem Christianae legis edocuit" (and thus out of the peoples he made Jews, and out of Jews, Christians, and gradually setting some men aside and changing them about, and arranging them, he led men, almost stealthily, by teaching them and curing them, from the worship of images to the regimen of the Law, and then away from the Law, which did not lead one to perfection, to the perfection of the gospel; and once the entire dispensation had been revealed, he taught them the total perfection of the Christian law).

[19] Hugh of Saint-Victor *De arca Noe morali* iv. 9 (*PL*, CLXXVI, 667; CSMV, p. 147): ". . . ut quae in principio temporum gerebantur in Oriente, quasi in principio mundi gerentur, ac deinde ad finem profluente tempore usque ad Occidentem rerum summa descenderet, ut ex ipso agnoscamus appropinquare finem saeculi, quia rerum cursus jam attigit finem mundi" (so that those things which happened at the beginning of time should happen in

Thus there were stages in the realization of this plan. There were constants and laws, such as the curious destiny of human civilization, even of a political empire, to move from East to West. Secular events themselves took on a religious meaning in their material connection with the divine scheme, transcending the intention of the people involved. The professional historians, as we shall see, had the task of recording and explaining all of these details; but the theologian Hugh held to them firmly, whether in his theological construction, as in his treatise *De sacramentis*, or in his spiritual writings, where one would not expect to find them.[20]

It was in this spirit that Hugh respectfully challenged the classic interpretation of the story of creation according to St. Augustine. In his idealism, and to make sense of the nature of things by their *rationes aeternae* in the divine thought, Augustine had seen in the six days of Genesis nothing but a hierarchic classification of the different natures as they were knowable in God, the place where they were really known (*cognitio matutina*, "morning" knowledge), and not in their temporal existence (*cognitio vespertina*, "evening" knowledge). The reality of the "days" faded in this *mane et vespere* ("morning" and "evening"), and so in Augustine's thought temporal succession was done away with. Hugh maintained, along with the Greeks, as against this "mystical distribution," that the conception of a progressive creation in time takes nothing away from the omnipotence of the creator, and in fact conforms more exactly to the behavior of man in whom divine action is reflected.[21]

---

the East, as at the beginning of the world; and that then as time moved on towards the end, the climax of events should pass to the West, from which we might conclude that the end of time is approaching, since the course of events has now reached the end of the world). Cf. *De vanitate mundi* ii (*PL*, CLXXVI, 720; CSMV, p. 182). *Mundus-saeculum:* this combination denotes a very keen perception of the coherence of cosmic time with historical time, and of geography with history. The economy of salvation itself embraces this double dimension. See *De arca Noe morali* iv. 9 (cited above, n. 15). Hugh not only composed a chronicle but also designed a world map.

[20] His most important observations on history occur in the so-called "spiritual" works: *De arca Noe morali* iv. 9 (*PL*, CLXXVI, 677–80; CSMV, pp. 146–53) and *De vanitate mundi* iv (*PL*, CLXXVI, 732–4).

[21] *De sacramentis Christianae fidei* i. 1. 3 (*PL*, CLXXVI, 188; Deferrari, pp. 8–9): "Nobis autem videtur (excepto eo quod nihil in hac re temere diffinire volumus) omnipotentiae Creatoris in nullo derogari, si per intervalla

We find the same temporal realism in Hugh's lively opposition to the thesis of Abelard requiring even of the just people of the Old Testament an explicit knowledge of the incarnation of Christ; the unity of the faith required that its contents remain unchanged through all ages. Augustine had once said: "The times may change, but not the faith."[22] "Christ will come," "Christ comes," "Christ has come." It was always the same truth; the coefficient time modified it only externally, as a mere circumstance. Peter Lombard and many others, using here the theory of the nominalists on the logical identity of propositions that in fact deal with chronologically separated phenomena, deexistentialized in some sense the principal facts of the *dispensatio*, under the guise of assuring the unity of faith and salvation through time. Hugh of Saint-Victor denounced the senseless con-

---

temporis opus suum ad consummationem perduxisse dicitur. . . . Omnipotens etenim Deus . . . in eis omnibus faciendis illum praecipue modum servare debuit, qui ipsius rationalis creaturae commoditati ac causae magis congruus fuit." (We do not wish to make any rash assertions about this matter, yet it seems to us that it is in no way derogatory to the omnipotence of the Creator to say that His work has been brought to completion over periods of time. . . . For the omnipotent God . . . in making all these things must especially have observed that mode of operation better suited to the benefit and interest of the rational creature himself.) St. Thomas was to say later, at a time when theology constructed disparate truths out of exemplarism and the existence of things, *De veritate* q. 8, a. 16 (*Quaestiones disputatae*, ed. P. Mandonnet, 3 vols. [Paris, 1925], I, 234; *Truth*, tr. R. W. Mulligan, 3 vols. [Chicago, 1952], I, 399): "Respondeo dicendum, quod hoc quod dicitur de matutina et vespertina Angelorum cognitione, introductum est ab Augustino hac necessitate, ut posset ponere, et quae in sex primis diebus facta leguntur, sine successione temporum esse completa; unde per dies illos non temporum distinctiones vult intelligi, sed Angelorum cognitionem." (Reply: The expression "morning and evening knowledge" was introduced by Augustine so that he could hold that the things we read about as having been made in the first six days were really completed without any succession of time. Consequently, he wanted those days to be understood as referring, not to distinct times, but to angelic cognition.) It was another form of Platonic idealism—the genuine form, that of the *Timaeus* —to which Hugh objected; for in his interpretation of the Genesis account he insisted upon the historicity of the works of God and on a progressive evolution of the universe, in opposition to the Chartres-style Platonism of William of Conches. See Hugh's *Adnotationes in Pentateuchon* iii-iv (*PL*, CLXXV, 33–34). [Cf. Taylor, pp. 227–8, n. 3.]

[22] *Tract. in Joan.* xlv. 9 (*PL*, XXXV, 1722). For the thesis of Abelard, see *Introductio ad theologiam* ii. 6 (*PL*, CLXXVIII, 1056) and *Theologia Christiana* iv (*PL*, CLXXVIII, 1285).

sequences of this abdication from history, from its progress, from its stages, from its successive renewals.[23]

In brief it was in the basic design of their theological efforts that the difference between Abelard the dialectician and Hugh was reflected: whereas the theoretical analysis of the former led him to divide up the matter of sacred doctrine into categories pedagogically valid, to be sure, but established entirely outside the course of history, namely, *fides, caritas, sacramentum* (dogma, moral theology, sacraments we would say, and do say, today), Hugh molded his plan according to *historia dispensationis temporalis divinae providentiae* (the history of the temporal dispensation of divine providence).[24] Abelard, it is true, invoked the elements of historical criticism in his treatment of contradictory authorities; but this was but one means among many to arrive at a speculative coherence by the *concordia discordantium* (concordance of discordances).

Although Hugh of Saint-Victor attached the movement of sacred history to terrestrial happenings in the period through the life of Christ, he did not interest himself at all in the historical development

---

[23] *De sacramentis Christianae fidei* i. 10. 6 (*PL*, CLXXVI, 335; Deferrari, p. 173): "An secundum mutationes temporum mutata sit fides" (Whether faith was changed according to changes of the times). On this controversy, cf. M.-D. Chenu, "Contribution à l'histoire du traité de la foi," *Mélanges thomistes* (Paris, 1923), pp. 123–40. From the start, scholasticism experienced a dual temptation to detemporalization: Platonic idealism and the attraction of logic. This is already seen in Abelard and the *Nominales* (Bernard of Chartres) with their theory of the timeless truth of propositions. See, for example, the *Sententiae Parisienses*, a work which shows the influence of Abelard (Landgraf, p. 22): "Eventus perpetui sunt: quia Petrum modo sedere, hoc verum fuit a principio mundi, et verum etiam post diem judicii me sedisse hic." (Events are perpetual, for that Peter now sits has been true from the beginning of the world, and that I have sat here will be true also after the day of judgment.)

[24] The phrase comes from St. Augustine; cf. note 17 above. Peter Comestor's *Historia scholastica* belongs in the same line of historical emphasis and, in twelfth-century teaching, is accorded no less esteem than Peter Lombard's *Sententiae*. Comestor sought to understand the Bible as history, hoping to rediscover—as against the outlines which doctrinal glosses had imposed on the text—the truth of history (*veritas historiae*) and, in order to reach that truth, going back to the histories even of the pagans. Cf. Comestor's own prologue and Smalley, pp. 196–263, chap. 5: "Masters of the Sacred Page: the Comestor, the Chanter, Stephen Langton."

of the church or of dogma. On the other hand, his contemporary and fellow regular canon, Anselm of Havelberg, a Premonstratensian, gave vigorous expression in famous texts to the mobility and variations of the kingdom of God, even within the church. Wholly different from Abelard, who was preaching an abstract unity of the faith in logically identical propositions, Anselm observed facts, within which the unity of the faith was ultimately defined across the successive shifts of different periods in a "church" which was to extend from Abel to the very last of the blessed. What were the facts? In the first place there were the great "mutations" within the ancient and new covenants, and then within the final consummation. Moreover, within these larger periods and determined by them, there were institutions, social forms, ritual symbolisms, moral and disciplinary rules that from generation to generation were modified or adapted, now giving in to increasing decadence, now overcoming traditional conformities, advancing bit by bit, as if furtively, according to the pedagogical and curative precautions of a God who knew and respected the mentality of human beings.[25] Sacred history did not stop with the coming of Christ; it continued in the church, carried on by the presence of the Spirit.

The cause of this astonishing sensitivity to history in Anselm undoubtedly stemmed from the needs of his controversy with the Greeks, whose doctrinal and institutional immobility he could overcome only by arguing from an unfolding evolution within the transcendent unity of faith; but even more, these views stemmed from his

---

[25] Anselm of Havelberg *Dialogi* i (*PL*, CLXXXVIII, 1141–60), entitled "De unitate fidei et multiformitate vivendi ab Abel justo usque ad novissimum electum" (On the unity of the faith and the multiple manners of life from Abel the just to the last of the elect). See the passage from *Dialogi* i.5 quoted above, n. 18; also *Dialogi* i.6 (*PL*, CLXXXVIII, 1148): "Neque etiam facilis erat transpositio eorum, quae longa consuetudine, et prolixo tempore in venerationem devenerant; ideoque tanquam ab infirmis evangelica et salubris pharmacia paulatim suscepta est, arte divina benignioribus medicinaliter commista." (Nor was it easy to alter things which had come into veneration through long custom and over a great stretch of time; hence, the health-giving remedies of the gospel were received bit by bit, as if by sick men, and mixed as medicines by the divine art for men growing better.) Cf. M. van Lee, "Les idées d'Anselme de Havelberg sur le développement des dogmes," *Analecta praemonstratensia*, XIV (1938), 5–35; also G. Schreiber, "Anselm von Havelberg und die Ostkirche," *ZKG*, LX (1941), 354–411.

personal and competitive participation, outside the monastic tradition, in a highly animated transformation of the various states of life in the western church.[26] The tension between a traditionalist moral reformism and a creative, if disordered, enthusiasm must have provoked this awareness of change brought about by time and by the advance of God's kingdom.

In stressing these characteristics of the thought of two professional theologians, we do not wish to pretend that this constitutes a theology of history, even less a philosophy; but it is noteworthy that, next to the work of actual historians and in another line from that of St. Bernard's meditation, for whom the entire *historia verbi* came down to the progress of love, there was now growing up a conscious awareness of the historicity of the Bible, and thus of religious man, a historicity whose principle was the supremacy of God, not only over all the cosmos, but over all earthly events. These events were no longer merely the stuff of quickly allegorized symbols in which their reality was dissolved. They existed with all the necessary and irreducible solidarity which time brings to all human reality, even more and in quite another way than to cosmic realities.

However, it was not merely by religious meditation on biblical history that, in the course of the twelfth century, theologians and historians became sensitive to the march of time. The general progress of intellectual awareness and of its intellectual laws supported this awakening in a rising civilization. The evolution of literary forms showed this progress. Of course feudal people had always been interested in the past and enjoyed hearing about it; but they sang of the great deeds of their ancestors, and their imagination transformed the exaltation of these memories into epics. Men of the second half of the twelfth century remained sensitive to the dramatic and lyrical seduction of the *chansons de geste*, which they overloaded with episodes. But the "epic fermentation," as Gaston Paris called it, did not deal with contemporary material, that of the crusades for example, which would have lent itself to the same treatment. They began to distinguish the description of the real from pure escape literature. Apart from the literature of fables and dreams, and even if contami-

---

[26] See below, pp. 202–38.

nated by legend, "true history, bit by bit, took the place of the epic in the collective memory."[27] This was a new awareness that went beyond the isolated individual to embrace all of society, a society for which human affairs became a legitimate matter of concern.

There had long been narrators of events, and in the religious domain some writers can for their times be properly treated as masters. But, however capable they were, they hardly ever went beyond the genre of annals (*annales*) or of the deeds (*gesta*) of kings, except for individual biographies (*vitae*). These names show that we are still far from history, far even from the "chronicle" whose results hitherto had generally remained mediocre. It was the same with painters who, even in their historical scenes, were incapable of feeling with equal acuteness the reality of the past and its distance. But now there were some who analyzed feelings, who observed logical sequences and causes, who tied together entities that belonged together. From Sigebert of Gembloux (died 1102) to John of Salisbury (died 1180), from Otto of Freising (died 1157) to Matthew Paris (died 1259), we can follow the development of this historical awareness in a Christian society anxious to become acquainted, even more by the events of its existence than by abstract definitions, with the conduct of God towards itself, and with the internal laws of its life on earth—a Christian society occasionally disturbed by signs of a termination which it felt had to be imminent, given the aging of the world. All this cannot be considered gratuitous curiosity. Rather it represented a desire to find, with the aid of an active knowledge of the substance of faith, lessons furnished by the past (*exempla*);[28]

---

[27] Bloch, I, 105; also I, 88–102, chap. 6: "The Folk Memory."

[28] Antiquity left a conception of history as a practical art for the improvement of morals as well as an account susceptible of embellishment for the instruction of men. Alexander Neckham *Sacerdos ad altare* prol. (Haskins, *Studies*, p. 372) recommends the reading of historians to his student ". . . ut vicia etiam in minori etate addiscat esse fugienda et nobilia gesta eorum desideret imitari" (so that he learn at a young age to flee from vice, and desire to imitate their more noble deeds). St. Thomas said in the *Summa theologica* Ia Pars, q. 1, a. 2, ad 2 (Aquinas, *Opera omnia*, I, 2; Aquinas, *Summa*, I, 3–4) that the story of Abraham, Isaac, and Jacob does not enter into sacred doctrine as a principal element but rather "as an example of behavior, as in the moral sciences" (in exemplum vitae, sicut in scientiis moralibus). This conception outlived the Renaissance: Michelet's title at the Collège de France was "professor of ethics and history," and he took the title to heart.

and at a time when the symbol of the primitive church was about to nourish the evangelical awakenings, it represented a desire to find the major demands on the life of the church inscribed in its early history.

The Dimensions of Time

The first indication of the coming of history in a given cultural cycle is the awareness, in a universal or quasi-universal view, of human activity considered as a whole. In the first place there is a noteworthy quantitative enlargement; but this in turn leads, beyond a description of the facts, beyond a recitation—*vitae, gesta, annales*—to still unsophisticated but very intelligent consideration of the ties between facts. Historical causality becomes perceptible with social awareness.

The chronicle of Ordericus Vitalis (died 1143) demonstrates this passage to the universal. His *Historia ecclesiastica*, first conceived as a history of his abbey, developed little by little and at the cost of a balanced outline into a general history. As for English historians, one trait of their work was the expansion of their horizon beyond frontiers to include even the Orient. "So eager was the desire to reveal the impetuous flow of the great river of time beyond the present moment that many authors, even among those concerned primarily with recent local events, nevertheless considered it useful to provide by way of preamble, a sort of rapid survey of universal history."[29] Thus we see them going right back to the incarnation, and their style accordingly displayed evident contrasts as they passed from ancient periods described in bits taken from their reading to the contemporary period provided by first-hand testimony.[30] But as soon as "the writer left the safe shelter of literature and found himself obliged to make his own investigations, the diversity of society overtaxed his competence, so that frequently, by a singular contrast, as narration developed, it became both richer in detail and narrower in geographi-

---

[29] Bloch, I, 88–9.

[30] Thus Henry of Huntington (died about 1155) could distinguish those things "which we find out from reading in the books of the ancients" (quae in libris veterum legendo reperimus) from those "which we know from having seen them" (quae videndo scimus); cited in Ghellinck, *Essor*, p. 378.

cal scope. Thus the great history of the French, compiled by Adhémar of Chabannes in a monastery near Angoulême, gradually came
to be scarcely more than a history of Aquitaine."[31]

In this perspective one can see that the great undertakings of
Christendom such as were developing in the crusades would be not
only fit for adventure stories but also favorable to an historical awareness of the workings of destiny. Indeed historians of the crusades,
William of Tyre in the lead (*Historia hierosolymitana*,[32] 1169-84),
furnished the most useful contributions to reflective theology as well
as to the literary genre of history. But it took the impact of the
missionary enterprises of the mendicants in the thirteenth century to attain a total universalism, including even a secular
universalism.

A sensitivity to the universalism of humanity was of course one of
the original strengths of the Christian church. What writers of history now added to this was an awareness of this universalism in time:
a sense of continuity; the definition of constant causes this side of
transcendent providence, either in the determinism of natural phenomena—for example, geographic causes—or in the play of free
human agencies—for example, the failure of human efforts in the
face of nature or in human society; stages in the development of
civilization; identification of certain groups and peoples as leading
the course of civilization—the Jewish people, the Greek intellectuals,
the Roman Empire, etc.

Since there was seen in history a sequence which permitted no
return, contrary to the ancient cyclic view of history,[33] this unfolding
took place by stages. Twelfth-century writers of history found in early
Christian authors categories long in use, beginning with the biblical
framework of periodization. They exploited these categories and
demonstrated, in determining the epochs or ages (*aetates*), one of

---

[31] Bloch, I, 89.

[32] [*Recueil des historiens des croisades, Historiens occidentaux*, I (Paris,
1844); *A History of Deeds Done Beyond the Sea*, tr. E. A. Babcock and A. C.
Krey, 2 vols. (New York, 1943).]

[33] This view was well known to medieval authors. Cf., for the twelfth
century, Hugh of Saint-Victor *In Eccles. hom.* xix (*PL*, CLXXV, 144).

the major resources for the interpretation of history; namely, so many ways of outlining the progress of time.[34]

Naturally enough, secular chronology was brought into agreement with the sacred epochs of scripture, which furnishes divisions and points of reference by a symbolic utilization of some of its texts. Thus the four empires of the emblematic and extrahistorical vision of Daniel (Dan. 7)—the Babylonian, the Medo-Persian, the Macedonian, and the Roman—were projected into the succession of time, following Eusebius, Jerome, Augustine, Orosius, and the *Glossa ordinaria*, in such a way that the last of these empires, the Roman, coming at the end of this succession, served as the immediate preparation for the coming of Christ. It is well known that Otto of Freising based on this the imperial ideology of which, for a Christendom defined as the Holy Roman Empire, he was the most prolific of theologian-historians.

The most common division, though, was one suggested by a symbolic utilization of the days of the week; this dated back to the fathers and remained valid until the Renaissance.[35] The symbol was here borrowed from nature: if the week was a figure for the working out of time, if the septenary of Genesis signified the totality of time, it was because man spontaneously matched the rhythm of history to

---

[34] St. Augustine *De civitate Dei* x. 14 (*Corpus Christianorum, Series Latina* [Turnhout, 1955], XLVII, 288; *The City of God*, tr. M. Dods [New York, 1950], p. 319) :"Sicut autem unius hominis, ita humani generis, quod ad Dei populum pertinet, recta eruditio per quosdam articulos temporum tamquam aetatum profecit accessibus, ut a temporalibus ad aeterna capienda et a visibilibus ad invisibilia surgeretur." (The education of the human race, represented by the people of God, has advanced, like that of an individual, through certain epochs, or, as it were, ages, so that it might gradually rise from earthly to heavenly things, and from the visible to the invisible.)

[35] This division passed from Augustine to Isidor's *Chronica* (*PL*, LXXXIII, 1018–58), and to Bede; it provoked some very elementary reflection among historians and theologians. It embraced variations and subdivisions of all sorts, most often inspired by number mysticism. Cf. H. de Lubac, *Catholicism*, tr. L. C. Sheppard (New York, 1950), pp. 73–76, where the principal specimens of it are gathered. Here as elsewhere, the temptation to indulge in typology bore down heavily; e.g., the temptation to transform the symbol of the week into millenarism, thereby ruining its historical quality. On the Jewish origins of these six ages, cf. W. M. Green, *Augustine on the Teaching of History* (Berkeley, 1944), p. 322.

the rhythm of the cosmos, even where the occurrence of events in the plan of revelation escaped the determinism of natural cycles. Hugh of Saint-Victor noted explicitly the correspondence between the succession of the days of creation and the stages in the redemptive restoration in biblical chronology: *sex dies* equaled *sex aetates*. There were as many major divine interventions in the one case as in the other. The seventh day was to be the day of rest in the final beatitude of eternity. "The work of creation was done in six days. . . . The work of the restoration of man can be completed in six ages. The six of the one repeat the six of the other so that he who was creator may be recognized as redeemer."[36]

The six major interventions of God were seen in the creation of Adam, the law of Noah, the call to Abraham, the reign of David, the Babylonian exile, and the coming of Christ.[37] This repartition was put to use and redefined by other arrangements of the historical material, such as that of Richard of Saint-Victor who introduced in these ages four "successions" which are still used today: the era of the patriarchs, the era of the judges, the era of the kings, and the era of the priests.[38]

---

[36] Richard of Saint-Victor *Exceptiones allegoricae* ii. 1 (*PL*, CLXXVII, 203). Likewise Hugh of Saint-Victor *De sacramentis Christianae fidei* i. 1. 28 (*PL*, CLXXVI, 204; Deferrari, p. 26): "Opera conditionis sunt quae in principio mundi sex diebus facta sunt; opera vero restaurationis quae a principio mundi propter reparationem hominis sex aetatibus fiunt." (Thus the works of creation are those which were made at the beginning of the world in six days; but the works of restoration are those which from the beginning of the world are made in six ages for the renewal of man.) The cosmological idea of creation never enjoyed, beginning right with the Old Testament, an existence independent of its soteriological idea.

[37] Among the innumerable statements of these "periods," one of the most doctrinally oriented is that by Garnier of Rochefort *Sermo* xix (*PL*, CCV, 695–9).

[38] *Exceptiones allegoricae* iv. 1 (*PL*, CLXXVII, 215): "Item quinque praecedentes aetates ab Adam usque ad Christum per quattuor successiones dividuntur: prima successio patriarcharum fuit ab Adam ad Moysen, secunda Judicum, a Moyse usque ad David, tertia Regum, a David usque ad transmigrationem Babylonis, quarta Sacerdotum, a transmigratione Babylonis ad Christum." (The five preceding ages, from Adam to Christ, are divided into four successions: the first succession was of the patriarchs, from Adam to Moses; the second of the judges, from Moses to David; the third of the kings, from David to the Babylonian exile; and the fourth of the priests, from the Babylonian exile to Christ).

More notable than these variants was the frequent slipping of this notion of an age from the cosmic sense to the human life-span. The ages were made to correspond no longer with the six days of Genesis, but with the ages of a man from earliest infancy to old age. Augustine had already suggested this transfer, which some people, from Honorius of Autun to Thomas Aquinas,[39] had again taken up and which the illuminators of the *Liber Floridus* (1120) illustrated in their parallelism between the universe and the human microcosm.[40] It was of course not the numerical computations that mattered, glossed St. Thomas, but the sense of progress—a reflection which is still valid for those who count by centuries as if they were historical entities.

This reference to the growth of man, which evidently broke the ancient symbolic parallelism between the time of nature and the time of history, favored the pedagogical conception of an order in which God began by treating humanity like an infant. The theologians continued to exploit the instructive potential of this parallelism; but historians drew from it, even for Christianity, an evolutionary perspective on institutions and events.[41] The insufficiency of this

---

[39] For St. Augustine, see above, n. 34. Honorius of Autun *De imagine mundi* ii. 75 (*PL*, CLXXII, 156): "Sunt sex aetates hominis: prima, infantia ad septem annos; secunda, pueritia ad quattuordecim annos; tertia, adolescentia ad viginti et unum annos; quarta, juventus ad quinquagesimum annum; quinta, senectus ad septuagesimum annum; sexta, decrepita ad centum annos vel usque ad mortem. Sunt nihilominus sex aetates mundi: prima ab Adam ad Noe. . . ." (There are six ages of man: the first goes from infancy to age seven; the second, childhood to age fourteen; the third, adolescence to twenty-one; the fourth, young manhood to age fifty; the fifth, old age to age seventy; the sixth, extreme old age to age one hundred or right until death. It is the same with the six ages of the world: the first goes from Adam to Noah.) St. Thomas *In Epist. ad Heb.* ix. lect. 5 (Aquinas, *Opera omnia*, XIII, 744): "Aetates enim mundi accipiuntur secundum aetates hominis, quae principaliter distinguuntur secundum statum proficiendi, non secundum numerum annorum." (The ages of the world are understood by analogy to the ages of man, which are mainly distinguished by a stage of his progress and not by a number of years.)

[40] In the Chantilly and Leyde MSS of the *Liber Floridus* of Lambert of Saint-Omer are drawn the macrocosm (mundus major et etates seculorum) and the microcosm (mundus minor, idest homo et etates eius). Cf. M.-Th. d'Alverny, "Le cosmos symbolique du XIIe siècle," *AHDL*, XX (1953), 78.

[41] Cf. Humbert of Romans *Opusc. tripartitum de tractandis in concilio Lugdunensi* i. 11 (E. Brown, ed., *Fasciculus rerum expetendarum et fugiendarum* . . . [London, 1690], II, 192): ". . . secundum successiones temporum

computation of the six ages became apparent where historians dealt with the history of the church. What of this *aetas sexta* in which they were living? Was it to be the age of old age and decay? How were they to integrate into it the modern developments which did not seem very near to ending?

Another traditional division of time in religious history had deeper meaning: the time before the Law (of Moses), the time of the Law, and the time of Grace (*ante legem, sub lege, sub gratia*).[42] Freed from all symbolic trappings, situated apart from all cosmic references, this division had a direct value for the theology of history since it expressed the very disposition of the order of salvation, but the historical facts threatened to disappear below the surface of these spiritual categories. This division left intact without any further distinction the entire period following the fullness of time of the incarnation (I Cor. 10:11)—the entire period of the church, its past, its present condition, and its duration.

Time continued to roll out; despite the *plenitudo temporis* of the incarnation, there was taking place an increment of time (*incrementum temporis*).[43] How were men able to conceive of its contents,

---

et varietates causarum, Christianitas varios status habet, sicut et puer crescendo antequam veniat ad senium habet varios status." (According to the successions of periods and the shifts of causes, Christendom has various stages just as a growing boy who, before he becomes aged, goes through a number of stages.) On revelation conceived as a system of pedagogy, cf. St. Thomas *Summa theologica*, IIa, IIae, q. 1, a. 7, ad 2 (Aquinas, *Opera omnia*, III, 7–8; Aquinas, *Summa*, IX, 16–18).

[42] Augustine remained the perennial source for such consideration; cf. *Enchiridion* cxviii (*PL*, XL, 287; *The Enchiridion*, tr. J. F. Shaw [Chicago, 1961], pp. 136–8). For a discussion of such grand historico-doctrinal categories as *Natura, Lex, Gratia*, and finally, *Patria*, cf. Hugh of Saint-Victor *De sacr. legis natur. et scriptae* (*PL*, CLXXVI, 32) and *De sacramentis Christianae fidei* i. 8. 11 (*PL*, CLXXVI, 312–3; Deferrari, pp. 148–50). Discussion of these ideas is often accompanied by the theme of the six ages of man; cf. Hugh of Saint-Victor *De scripturis et scriptoribus sacris* xvii (*PL*, CLXXV, 24) and Robert of Melun *Sententie* i. 1. 14, 17 (Martin, I, 197–9, 202–5).

[43] Cf. St. Thomas *In Epist. ad Heb.* i. lect. 1 (Aquinas, *Opera omnia*, XIII, 668): "Tangit tempus traditionis hujus doctrinae, quod est tempus praeteritum, quia olim, idest non subito: quia tam magna erant quae de Christo dicebantur, quod non poterant credi, nisi cum incremento temporum prius didicissent." (He [Paul] refers to the time taken for this handing down of doctrine, which is time gone by, because he uses the phrase "a long time ago,"

which were expanding before their eyes, without the coming of the seventh day of the end of the world? Once they got beyond a simple chronicle of events, our historian-theologians began to reflect about this mysterious duration. The cliché of the ages of man led them to envisage this present era as an old age, a pessimistic interpretation which brought them back to the view of the nearness of the end of the world. It is true, St. Thomas said, that the old age of man could last for a long time, from age sixty to one hundred and twenty years.[44] But on this point Otto of Freising confirmed his pessimistic philosophy of a continual decadence: ". . . we see the world . . . already on the decline and exhaling the final breath, so to speak, of advanced old age."[45] The grandeur and the accountability of the great and mighty showed clearly the ambiguity of history. Biblical themes and Augustinian inspiration together made up the grandeur of Otto's dramatic vision of history.

Anselm of Havelberg on the contrary, like all minds sensitive to the movement of history, presented a triumphant optimism, even in the midst of fights, persecutions, and failures of the church; and he framed his description of the seven successive stages of the modern

---

i.e., not "suddenly just now"; for so lofty were the things said about Christ that they could not have been believed unless they had first been learned through an accumulation of ages.)

[44] *Ibid.* ix. lect. 5 (Aquinas, *Opera omnia*, XIII, 744): "Ista prima aetas fuit ante diluvium, in qua nec lex scripta nec punitio, sicut infantia. Alia a Noe usque ad Abraham: et sic de aliis, ita quod ultima aetas est status praesens, post quem non est alius status salutis, sicut nec post senium. Sicut autem in aliis aetatibus hominis est numerus annorum determinatus, non autem in senio, quia senium incipit a sexagesimo anno, et aliqui vivunt per centum et viginti annos; ita non est determinatum quantum iste status mundi debeat durare; tamen est consummatio saeculorum, quia non restat alius ad salutem." (The first age was before the flood, an age which knew neither written law nor punishment, as in infancy. The next went from Noah to Abraham, and so it is with the other ages. Thus the final age is the present period, after which there is no other stage of salvation, just as there is no age after old age. However, as in the various ages of man there is a fixed number of years, except with old age, for old age begins with sixty, and some people go right on living to age one hundred and twenty; so there is no way of telling how long the present stage of the world is going to last; nevertheless, it is the consummation of the ages, for no other stage of salvation remains.)

[45] *Chronica* v. prol. (Lammers-Schmidt, pp. 374–5; Mierow, p. 323): ". . . mundum . . . nos jam deficientem et tanquam ultimi senii extremum spiritum trahentem cernimus."

era in a double, solemn declaration of the "youth of the church," renewed from one age to the next by the growth of truth: "The holy church, passing through various stages which in turn gradually succeed themselves up to this present day, is renewed just as the eagle's youth is renewed; and it always will be renewed."[46] In more summary fashion, Adam of Dryburgh and John Beleth were witnesses to a confidence in the flourishing peace of the church in a third age which succeeded the age of the creative rise and then the age of the fight for life,[47] whereas Hugh of Rouen was more sensitive to the critical dangers of his own times (*angustia temporis*).[48]

The interest of the successive historical stages of Anselm of Havelberg lies in his awareness of an *aetas moderna* within the time of grace and of the church, an awareness for which Otto of Freising and others furnished much of the raw material. In the same way, at Saint-Victor where Hugh tried to analyze historical materials before invoking any allegorical construction, this awareness led to a division of historical evolution into coherent periods, despite discontinuity in the history of the empire. After sacred history (from Adam to Christ) and ancient secular history (from the first empires to the Roman Empire), the era of the incarnation was thus divided: the first Roman emperors; from Trajan to Constantine; from Constantine to Zeno; from Zeno to Charlemagne; then, connecting with the Franks, from the origins of the Franks to Charles the Simple, and to the Normans.[49] One recognizes here the current theory about the

---

[46] *Dialogi* i. 6 (*PL*, CLXXXVIII, 1149): "Sancta Ecclesia pertransiens per diversos status sibi invicem paulatim succedentes, usque in hodiernum diem, sicut juventus aquilae renovatur et semper renovabitur."

[47] Adam of Dryburgh *De triplici sanctae Ecclesiae statu*, Sermo 8 in adventu Domini (*PL*, CXCVIII, 144); cf. below, p. 268, n. 50. This terrestrial security of an established church—as against the sensitivities of Anselm of Havelberg—is a common theme which will be spread by John Beleth *Rationale divinorum officiorum* xxii (*PL*, CCII, 33, 60). Cf. texts cited by H. de Lubac, *The Splendor of the Church*, tr. M. Mason (New York, 1956), pp. 135–6.

[48] *De fide catholica* (*PL*, CXCII, 1345).

[49] Richard of Saint-Victor *Exceptiones allegoricae;* note the plan of chapters 6 through 10, with the final chapter devoted to the Normans (*PL*, CLXXVII, 239–84).

continuation of the empire in the person of Charlemagne, king of the Franks, now styled emperor of the Romans. The historical myth carried forward the myth of ancient Rome and Christian Rome locked together.

Among the medieval writers we are discussing, this *translatio imperii* (transference of the empire) was in fact the prime element in the theology of history, which was based on the ancient ideas of various western Christian writers going back at least to Augustine. The one essential part adhered to by this theology was the destiny—the predestination—of the Roman Empire. The substance of this destiny, masterfully worked out by Otto of Freising, is well known. At the very same time, the birth of nationalities led other historians, such as Ordericus Vitalis, to dissociate Christian history from this political monolith.

It remains that all agreed on placing the Roman Empire at the end of a succession of ancient empires as a providential preparation for the age of Christ, in the course of history as well as in the geography of salvation. One knows well enough how heavily this theological interpretation of history still weighs on Christian ideology. The crucial role of this destiny was the role which the empire played in unifying mankind, rendering all men open to the workings of grace. One of the most significant pages of this theology was the exploration of the earthly transfer undergone by the economy of salvation, passing from the predestined kingdom of Judea to the land of Rome, victorious over the Jews themselves. In reply to a student intrigued by these "concussions and fluctuations," Hugh of Saint-Victor explained professorially the historico-moral reasons for this succession:

If, however, we look carefully into the state of the world at the time, plainly we find that the coming of the Lord can be understood in relation to political rule among the gentiles no less than among the Jews. For since he came not only to claim the kingdom of the Jews as his own but to conquer the kingdom of the gentiles and subject it as well, he wished to find a foreigner ruling in Judea and a stable and strong kingdom among the gentiles, with all their scattered power unified. . . . Consequently, he waited until the whole world had brought its forces together under one empire and until victorious Rome had reared its head with proud disdain over all kingdoms. Then, when pride ruled all, he came in lowliness that he might bring down the loftiness of the world by his own humility.[50]

The unity of the empire, in realizing the unity of the world, thereby realized the condition of the universal kingdom of Christ. The earthly agents of the unity of mankind were the providential promoters—even if they were pagans and persecutors—of the Christian world order.[51]

As for the distant agglomeration of barbarians who had formerly been a problem for the theologians faced with the collapse of the empire, the theory of the transference of the empire to the Germans resolved this problem peacefully for twelfth-century writers, though at the same time it plunged them into the myth of an empire reborn as the Holy Empire.[52] Byzantium bore the cost of this operation.

This *translatio* led theologians to observe and formulate another law of history: the movement of civilization from East to West. Place, according to Hugh of Saint-Victor, entered along with time into the composition of history: *loca simul et tempora*.[53] The meeting of place

---

[50] Hugh of Saint-Victor *De vanitate mundi* iv (*PL*, CLXXVI, 732–3): "Tamen si diligenter statum universitatis attendimus, non minus adventum illius (Domini) ex regno gentium quam Judaeorum intelligi posse manifesta ratione invenimus. Quia enim ille et Judaeorum regnum quasi suum vindicare, et gentium regnum quasi contrarium expugnare et sibi subjicere venit, idcirco et in Judaea alienigenam regnantem, et in gentibus (collectis quasi in unum viribus) regnum stabile ac robustum invenire voluit. . . . Idcirco expectavit donec mundus totus in unum vires suas conflasset imperium, et Roma victrix super regna omnia superbo fastu caput extullisset. Tunc ergo dominante superbia humilis venit, ut in sua humilitate celesitudinem mundi sterneret. . . ."

[51] This "theology" of the Roman Empire is maintained—and perverted—by many authors through a belief in its eschatological role. Cf. J. Adamek, *Vom römischen Endreich der mittelalterlichen Bibelerklärung* (Würzburg, 1938). [See also W. Goez, *Translatio Imperii. Ein Beitrag zur Geschichte des Geschichtsdenkens und der politischen Theorien im Mittelalter und in der frühen Neuzeit* (Tübingen, 1958)].

[52] This theory was recorded in the official acts of the Roman pontiffs. Thus Innocent III in his famous *Deliberatio super facto imperii*, 1200/1201 (*Regestum Innocentii III papae super negotio Romani Imperii*, ed. Friedrich Kempf, *MHP*, XII [Rome, 1947], 74–91), and in the decretal *Venerabilem*, 1202 (*ibid.*, pp. 166–75), turned the theory to his own advantage: the pope is necessarily involved in the selection of an emperor because it was by and for the pope that the empire was transferred from Greece to Germany.

[53] *De arca Noe morali* iv. 9 (*PL*, CLXXVI, 667; CSMV, p. 147): ". . . loca simul et tempora, ubi et quando gestae sunt, considerare oportet" (it behooves us to consider both times and places, where and when things happened).

and time, of geography and history, was expressed by this westward advance. "It seems to have been arranged by divine providence, so that those things which happened at the beginning of time should happen in the East, as at the beginning of the world; and that then as time moved on towards the end, the climax of events should pass to the West, from which we might conclude that the end of time is approaching, since the course of events has now reached the end of the world."[54] The Roman Empire, at the end of the world (*mundus*), was the decisive episode at the end of the march of history (*saeculum*). When man went beyond the ocean frontier, history as well as geography changed; the medieval period was over.

Otto of Freising found a way to perpetuate the theme of Orosius, based on the description of the succession of empires in Daniel. He showed authority passing providentially from Rome to Byzantium to the Franks to the Lombards and finally to the Germans, along the same route taken by civilization.[55]

---

[54] *Ibid.*, See above, note 19. Cf. *De vanitate mundi* ii (*PL*, CLXXVI, 720).

[55] *Chronica* i prol. (Lammers-Schmidt, pp. 12–13; Mierow, p. 94): ". . . regnum Romanorum, quod in Daniele propter tocius orbis bello domiti singularem principatum, quam Greci monarchiam vocant, ferro comparatur, ex tot alternationibus, maxime diebus nostris, ex nobilissimo factum est pene novissimum, ut iuxta poetam vix 'magni stet nominis umbra.' Ab Urbe quippe ad Grecos, a Grecis ad Francos, a Francis ad Lombardos, a Lombardis rursum ad Teutonicos Francos derivatum non solum antiquitate senuit, sed etiam ipsa mobilitate sui veluti levis glarea hac illaque aquis circumiecta sordes multiplices ac defectus varios contraxit." (the Roman Empire, which in Daniel is compared to iron on account of its sole lordship—monarchy, the Greeks call it—over the whole world, a world subdued by war, has in consequence of so many fluctuations and changes, particularly in our day, become, instead of the noblest and the foremost, almost the last, so that, in the words of the poet, scarcely "a shadow of its mighty name remains" [Lucan of Pompey, *Pharsalia* i. 135]. For being transferred from the City to the Greeks, from the Greeks to the Franks, from the Franks to the Lombards, from the Lombards again to the German Franks, that empire not only became decrepit and senile through lapse of time, but also, like a once smooth pebble that has been rolled this way and that by the waters, contracted many a stain and developed many a defect.) Cf. *ibid.* v. prol. (Lammers-Schmidt, pp. 372–3; Mierow, p. 322): "Et sicut supra dixi, omnis humana potentia vel sapientia ab oriente ordiens in occidente terminari cepit. Et de potentia quidem humana, qualiter a Baboniis ad Medos et Persas ac inde ad Macedones et post ad Romanos rursumque sub Romano nomine ad Grecos derivatum sit, sat dictum arbitror." (As I have said above, all human power or wisdom, originating in the East, began to reach its limits in the West. Regarding human power—

The role of these secular events and of their laws, and at the same time a more extensive knowledge of non-Christian civilizations, posed for theologians the problem of these pagan times and spaces, which, it seems, had remained, at least for a while, outside the Christian consciousness (however unique its broad historical appreciation). How was the time of the world, pagan time, to enter into their religious categories? Was it not independent of Christian events?

The missionary drive of the thirteenth century, with its discovery of the nonbiblical civilizations of the Far East, posed another problem for Christendom, which until that time was thought to coincide with the surface of the earth, excepting the area under Islamic occupation. In the twelfth century, the integrity of Christendom remained intact. Only in regard to the past was the question asked, and

---

how it passed from the Babylonians to the Medes and the Persians and from them to the Macedonians, and after that to the Romans and then again to the Greeks under the Roman name—I think that enough has been said.) Cf. Roland of Cremona *Expos. in Job* prol. (MS Paris, BN lat. 405, fol. lv): "Prius enim magi Pharaonis, et ante philosophos Egipti Caldei, et ante Caldeos Indi, quia de Oriente ad Caldeos, de Caldeis ad Egiptios, et de Egiptis ad Grecos, et de Grecis ad Latinos amor processit sapientie. . . ." (Before the wise pharaohs and before the philosophers of Egypt, there were the Chaldeans, and before the Chaldeans the Indians, for out of the Orient the love of wisdom passed to the Chaldeans, from the Chaldeans to the Egyptians, from the Egyptians to the Greeks, and from the Greeks to the Latins.) The classic theme of this *translatio* was not yet exhausted. In the fourteenth century, Richard of Bury traced it beyond the German Empire and the French Kingdom to "Britain, the most noble of islands," in his *Philobiblon* ix (ed. A. Altamura [Naples, 1954], p. 108; tr. A. Taylor [Berkeley, 1948], p. 61): "Minerva mirabilis nationes hominum circuire videtur, et a fine usque ad finem attingit fortiter, ut se ipsam communicet universis. Indos, Babylonios, Egyptios atque Grecos, Arabes et Latinos eam pertransisse iam cernimus. Iam Athenas deseruit, iam a Roma recessit, iam Parisius preterivit, iam ad Britanniam, insularum insignissimam, quin potius microcosmum, accessit feliciter, ut se Grecis et barbaris debitricem ostendat. Quo miraculo profecto conicitur a plerisque quod, sicut Gallie iam sophia tepescit, sic eiusdem militia penitus evirata languescit." (Admirable Minerva seems to traverse the nations of men, and mightily she reaches from one end of the earth to the other that she may reveal herself to all. We see that she has already visited the Indians, the Babylonians, the Egyptians and Greeks, the Arabians and the Latins. Already has she forsaken Athens, departed from Rome, passed by Paris, and is now happily come to Britain, the most noble of islands, nay, the very microcosm, that she may show herself debtor both to the Greeks and to the Barbarians. From this wonder it is plainly conjectured by many that, even as the learning of France is now become lukewarm, so her soldiery is greatly weakened and unmanly.)

more enthusiastically as a renaissance of antiquity developed. The Bible itself suggested the reply by placing in its history so many oriental empires as well as the Roman Empire. Just as all of ancient learning, catalogued in the encyclopedia of the seven arts, was considered a preparation for sacred doctrine, so ancient history in its various forms was a preparation for the *aetas sexta,* for the sixth age, the era of the incarnation.[56] In the mind of Frederick II, the same proposition was to be set forth in two parallel forms: secular culture had its own value in the mind of a believer; likewise the political order of the empire was independent of the unitary pretensions of the sacerdotal order. Regarding this point Otto of Freising had already insisted on the unity of history, whose triumph was marked by the advent of Constantine. The dualism of the two cities was resolved; the earthly city was henceforth within the church. "From that time (Theodosius the Great) on, given that not only all men but all the emperors, with few exceptions, were Catholics, it seems to me that I have written the history not of two cities but—so to speak— of just one, which I call the church. Because the elect and the reprobate still live together, I cannot therefore any longer call these cities two, as I have done above (the title of his work being of course *Historia de duabus civitatibus*); I must say that they are properly regarded as just one, for the wheat is all mixed in with the tares."[57]

---

[56] Otto of Freising *Chronica* iii. prol. (Lammers-Schmidt, pp. 208–11; Mierow, p. 220): "Deinde paulatim crescente ac proficiente tam ex societate hominum simul commanentium quam ex collatione eorundem ad leges condendas sapientia philosophorumque mediante doctrina, cum, ut dixi, iam totus mundus tam virtute Romanorum inclinatus quam sapientia philosophorum informatus fuisset, essentque hominum ingenia ad altiora vitae precepta habilia capessenda, salvatorem omnium in carne apparere novasque mundo leges condere decuit." (Then as this age gradually grew and made progress— partly through the association of men dwelling together, partly through the putting together of their wisdom for the purpose of establishing laws, and partly through the agency of the wisdom and of the teachings of the philosophers—it was fitting that the Saviour of all should appear in the flesh and establish new laws for the world at the time when, as I have said, the whole world had now bowed before the power of the Romans and had been moulded by the wisdom of the philosophers, and the minds of men were suited to grasp more lofty precepts about right living.)

[57] *Ibid.* v. prol. (Lammers-Schmidt, pp. 374–5; Mierow, pp. 323–4): "At deinceps, quia omnis non solum populus, sed et pricipes, exceptis paucis, katholici fuere, videor mihi non de daubus civitatibus, sed pene de una tantum,

This was political Augustinianism—unfaithful to Augustine! It was the political counterpart to cultural Augustinianism, for which the sciences and humanities were but the tools of Christendom.

In any case, this revival of antiquity and the new conceptions which the revival inspired led historians to sense more vividly the "modernity" of their epoch. Ralph of Diceto (1148-1202), in the prologue to his *Abbreviationes chronicum*, classified events into three periods: *vetustissima* (oldest times, pagan antiquity), *vetera* (old times, the Christian era), and *moderna* (modern times, his own time, since 1148). Walter Map on the other hand, with an ever-advancing present, designated the last one hundred years as *modernitas*.[58] In fact, most historians implicitly considered modern the period for which they had been able to learn the history by evidence, direct or indirect, instead of having to resort to books, as for earlier periods. "We have come thus far," said Otto of Freising early in the seventh book of his world history, "based on what we have read in books; what follows, since it is of recent memory, consists in what I have heard from trustworthy men plus what I myself have seen or heard."[59]

We have intentionally left aside a final division and qualification of the stages of history, corresponding to the persons of the Trinity: the age of the Father, corresponding to the Old Testament; the age of the Son, initiated by the incarnation; the age of the Spirit, working out the promise of Christ. This structure, built on solidly traditional elements and already articulated by the most perspicacious of the fathers of the church, had deep theological meaning. But it takes one decidedly far away from historical categories. It is enough to mention some of those who expressed it in the twelfth century, men of high quality and of sharply opposed views: Rupert of Deutz,

---

quam ecclesiam dico, hystoriam texuisse. Non enim, quamvis electi et reprobi in una sint domo, has civitates, ut supra, duas dixerim, sed proprie unam, sed permixtam tanquam grana cum paleis." Cf. A. P. d'Entrèves, "Ottone di Frisinga e la storiografia del medio evo," *RIFD*, XX (1940), 360–7.

[58] See below, p. 320, n. 24.

[59] *Chronica* vii. 11 (Lammers-Schmidt, pp. 518–9; Mierow, p. 417): "Hucusque tam ex . . . libris lecta posuimus. Ceterum secuntur, quia recentis memoriae sunt, a probabilibus viris tradita vel a nobis ipsis visa et audita ponemus."

from the conservative monastic milieu, and Anselm of Havelberg, from the emerging canonical milieu.[60] But in the final quarter of the century, by a liberal extrapolation effected by Joachim of Floris, this theological vision of the economy of salvation suddenly took on a considerable historical value by transposing to chronological space some basic biblical ideas. The seductive and dizzying turns of thought that led Joachim and his disciples to consider the age of the Spirit upon them, about to replace the age of the Son, now definitely dead and closed, are well known. This view entailed the breaking up of the unity of the era following the incarnation and the bankrupting of the period of the church. The evangelism of the years around 1200 found there, amidst authentic values, a corrupting ferment which was to be at work for more than a century among the "Spirituals." We have found it necessary at least to mention, among the various theologies of history, this literally revolutionary conception.[61]

This eschatology brings us to the recognition of a final characteristic of these twelfth-century historians: they turned to symbolism to explain the advance of history. In order to present the work of Constantine as definitive, to consider the church as established in a triumphant peace, to identify the kingdom of God with the church, Otto of Freising tended to run together without distinction the messianic and eschatological conceptions of that kingdom. But it is noteworthy that whenever a new awareness of time, of time in the collective conscience, arises, apocalypses discover a new popularity and thus hold open the future with its perpetually new possibilities. Joachim's excess was but an exaggeration of this sensitivity to history which found expression in the work of historians most attached to the facts. The facts were worked into this pattern, to the extent that they were treated as events of the sacred order. To express their

---

[60] Rupert of Deutz *De Trinitate et operibus ejus* prol. (*PL*, CLXVII, 199–200); the three ages, which relate to the Father, the Son, and the Holy Spirit, all under the sole control of God, form the basic outline of this work. Anselm of Havelberg *Dialogi* i. 6 (*PL*, CLXXXVIII, 1147–8).

[61] Cf. the important work of W. Kamlah, *Apokalypse und Geschichtstheologie: Die mittelalterliche Auslegung der Apokalypse vor Joachim von Fiore* (Berlin, 1935). [Cf. M. W. Bloomfield, "Joachim of Flora: A Critical Survey of His Canon, Teachings, Sources, Bibliography, and Influence," *Trad.* XIII (1957), 249–311.]

kinship to the eternal plan, historians discerned in these facts a signifi-
cànce which the current practices of symbolism translated, just as
the naturalists accorded to phenomena of the universe a certain
symbolic value which would define their profound nature. In each
case the operation was risky. The historian, however taken up with
the concrete reality of his story, was yet inclined to dabble in symbolism, tempted to transfer analogically to the era of the church the
typology which was the law of the Old Testament and which did not
easily defer to any allegorical interpretation of biblical history. Spörl
has quite correctly shown the importance of this perspective and
symbolic method in the historians of the twelfth century.[62] He was
wrong to restrict it to those among them who were endowed, in contrast to rational scholasticism, with a Germanic temperament—
Honorius of Autun, Hugh of Saint-Victor, Hildegard of Bingen. This
was a common outlook in history as well as in cosmogony.

Of course neither Ordericus Vitalis nor John of Salisbury would
have tolerated a futurist systematization; and the eschatological view,
while hovering high above, did not weaken the fabric of their history.
But they made good use of it to explain the religious purpose of this
history, and symbolism was the literary method suited to this extra-
temporal dimension of Christian time. One must therefore not treat
as mere literary trimmings or as childish imagery or as obsolete theology the use they made of the theme of anti-Christ, or of the parable
of the workers of the eleventh hour, or of the catastrophic signs of
nature, or the persecutions, or even of the allegory of the two cities.
With the visions of Caesarius of Heisterbach,[63] the dreams of popular

---

[62] J. Spörl, *Grundformen hochmittelalterlicher Geschichtsanschauung,
Studien zum Weltbild der Geschichtsschreiber des 12. Jahrhunderts* (Munich,
1935).

[63] These visions gave a messianic role to the Capetian princes in the period
prior to the reign of the final days. *Dialogus miraculorum* v. 22 (ed. J.
Strange, 2 vols. [Cologne, 1851], I, 305–6; *The Dialogue of Miracles,* tr. H.
Scott and C. C. S. Bland, 2 vols. [London, 1929], I, 349): "Regi Francorum
subiicientur omnia regna et filio ejus, qui erit in tempore Spiritus sancti, et
non morietur; et dabuntur duodecim panes Regi Francorum, id est, scientia
scripturarum et potestas." (All the kingdoms of the earth will be subject to
the king of the Franks and to his son, who will live under the dispensation of
the Holy Spirit and will never die; and there will be given to the king of the
Franks twelve loaves, i.e., the knowledge and power of the scriptures.)

millenarianism, or the invectives of preachers, one must not group the modes of interpretation employed by twelfth-century historians. But neither should one exaggerate the rational progress of their historical consciousness, which expressed itself precisely by seeing the connection of events within a messianic and eschatological perspective. Moreover, Otto of Freising finished his *Historia* with a discussion of final goals—with anti-Christ, the final consummation, the resurrection, and the end of history.[64]

In all this one observes a feature typical of Christian thought: an involvement with the very texts of scripture when composing historical narrative, and a close attention, in consequence, to the unfolding of the divine plan; but also the risk, in this very fidelity to the Bible, of getting closed up in past history and being cut off from the present. Drawing a lesson from the Jewish experience, Bultmann sounds a warning to the Christian thinker: "By binding herself to her past history, Israel loosened her ties with the present, and her responsibility for it. Loyalty to the past became loyalty to a book which was all about the past. God was no longer really the God of history, and therefore always the God who was about to come. He was no longer a vital factor in the present: his revelations lay in the past. History was likewise brought to a standstill. The nation lived outside history. God no longer raised up prophets and kings as he had done in the past; he no longer poured forth his Spirit. He would not do so until the last times."[65] In these terms men would have recourse to a desired salvation only on the day when, beyond the historically temporal future, sacred history will become complete. For the history of the world, eschatology can only introduce ambiguity; and allegorical interpretation is the literary effect of this ambiguity.

Theses and Biases

As we are mainly interested in the history of theology, it is not our present task to analyze the contents of these works of history, or even the evolution of historiography. What is important, by way of con-

---

[64] *Chronica* viii (Lammers-Schmidt, pp. 582–681; Mierow, pp. 453–514).
[65] R. Bultmann, *Primitive Christianity*, tr. R. H. Fuller (New York, 1956), p. 60.

clusion, is to isolate the forces which stimulated the growth of this historical consciousness in a period when the events of the world raised doubts about the events of sacred history, or at least the conception one had had of them in the West since the time of Augustine and Orosius. Here again we see a rather disturbing achievement of the twelfth century, when theology not only encountered a renaissance of ancient thought, but with results just as striking ran up against a rapidly evolving political society. The solutions found in these two cases proved to be widely different; here is a brief critique of them.[66]

We have noted several times that the pivotal point on which historical reflection turned was the existence and role of the Roman Empire. By the vision of Daniel, scripture in some sense authenticated this view beforehand. History was supposed to give justification to the substance of a tie between the economy of salvation and the power of the empire. The persecutions, once they had been subjected to moralizing, became the leading case of the triumph of humility over pride; and the conversion of Constantine became the basis for a definitive consecration of the church peacefully established on earth. The thesis of the *translatio imperii* to the Germans saved the doctrine while adjusting it to the course of events—the empire turned over to the barbarians!—not, however, without some doctrinal and institutional loss for the already existing break between East and West. Through all this, the crowning of Charlemagne maintained the glitter of the myth of Rome. Think of that poem from the ninth or tenth century which begins: *O Roma nobilis/orbis et domina* (O noble Rome, mistress of the earth).[67] Frederick Barbarossa had Charlemagne canonized in 1168, though by an anti-pope. The empire remained the instrument of Christendom. Secular history entered into sacred history: Otto of Freising said so clearly. The notion of empire belongs clearly to that category of deceptively clear myths which

---

[66] Spörl, cited above, n. 62.

[67] L. Traube, *O Roma nobilis. Philologische Untersuchungen aus dem Mittelalter* [Abhandlungen der philosophisch-philologischen Klasse der Königlich Bayerischen Akademie der Wissenschaften, XIX (Munich, 1892), 297–395]. Cf. the narrative of the pilgrim in the twelfth-century *Mirabilia urbis Romae* [refs. in M. Manitius, *Geschichte der lateinischen Literatur des Mittelalters*, III (Munich, 1931; reprint, 1964), 245–8].

exercise strange powers of fascination on the evolving human community.[68]

This sacred role was based on two elements: first, the empire maintained order so that the gospel could be spread about unhindered; second, the empire by its universalism prepared the ground for a universal church which Jewish ethnocentrism had blocked. This was a grandiose theology of history, but one not lacking a serious relativism. The illusion of a "political" peace extended to these theologians,[69] and catholic universalism was long held in check by the myth of the unity of the Holy Empire. In the sixteenth century, Bodin was to denounce this myth, as against Melanchthon who was entirely immersed in an Augustinianism turned to the profit of Germanism.

That the empire had until then been the means of gathering the destiny of all mankind into a single, significant historical framework was proven by the very disagreement of twelfth-century historians on this point. A survey of their positions and choices on this point will show that something more than politics was involved.

Otto of Freising was the propagandist of the Holy Empire. Terrestrial form of the city of God, it resolved by itself, despite quarrels with the papacy, a dualism of powers that would have torn Christendom apart. More than the professional theologians, this historian, perspicacious by virtue of his obsession with a universal empire and his taste for inordinately huge enterprises, professed a political Augustinianism in which, without Augustine's subtlety, the political

---

[68] Cf. R. Folz *L'idée d'empire en occident du V° au XIV° siècle* (Paris 1953). Thus all political theology was for a long time to be focused—despite the reaction of the new evangelical groups of the thirteenth century—on the destiny of Rome: emulation of ancient Rome; interest in the *Pax Romana;* exaltation of Augustus, reincarnate in Constantine; then the Constantinian theology of the God-king, etc. Ernest Lavisse has suggested that the empire seemed like a necessary condition of the world's existence, an entity superior to the accidents of history [see his *General View of the Political History of Europe,* tr. Charles Gross (New York, 1910)].

[69] Cf. Haymo of Halberstadt *In Cant.* (*PL,* CXVII, 320): "Subjectis principibus catholicae fidei, Ecclesia, quae antea premebatur, coronatur et gloriatur in Christo, sicut factum est tempore Constantini, quando illo converso mirabiliter glorifica est Ecclesia." (When princes became subject to the catholic faith, the Church, which previously was suppressed, was crowned and glorified in Christ; this was done in the time of Constantine, when by that conversion the Church was marvelously glorified.)

order was nothing more than a tool of the kingdom of God and of the principate of the church. His peculiar way of linking this together extended to this Christian empire's feudal forms—and thus it implied a feudal Christendom—insensitive to the economic and democratic transformations already realized in the evolution of the Italian cities. Were it only because of that, time would have quickly rendered obsolete the theology of Otto. It was no accident that Lombardy was soon to become one of the centers of the evangelical reaction against this Christendom.

Ordericus Vitalis was not born in the empire, either geographically or intellectually. An Anglo-Norman, he willingly left Charlemagne to his glorious past and observed the successive emergence of new peoples running the affairs of the world, with the Normans in the lead, their epic ranging over land and sea, supporting the crusades, proliferating the monastic life. He wrote of great events in the history of civilization and, at the same time, of the church, giving the impression that he had lived through them, though he wrote in the accessible and cultured solitude of Saint-Evroult, all without having to invoke any sort of imperial mystique. He gave witness to another Europe that was emerging and of another philosophy of history.

John of Salisbury can be taken as typical of a third attitude. He also lived outside the empire. He was even opposed to a supranational empire whose task was to maintain the unity and peace of the world. Born in England, educated in French schools (like Otto of Freising in this, however), known to all the leaders of the scholarly world before being known to all the princes, bishop of Chartres, where he had first studied, John was more a philosopher than historian. His *Policraticus* makes us better acquainted than does his *Historia pontificalis* with his conception of the state, of which he assessed the strictly secular values. It is not that he favored reducing the powers of the church, as his tenacious loyalty to Thomas Becket testifies, but, as a worthy disciple of Chartres, in his philosophy of nature and in his general intellectual discipline, he portended the development which, with the entry of Aristotle in the thirteenth century, proclaimed the autonomy of the forms of nature, of the methods of the mind, and of the laws of society. He was surely the "modern" one in the twelfth century, among the historians as among the humanists. Endowed with the political maturity of the Angevin princes, he went beyond the moralism of the "mirrors of princes" literature to launch a science of power in a state conceived as an objective body, in an administration based on functions rather than on feudal oaths, in a procedure freed from the "judgments of God" still current among the Germans. By its political development, the Anglo-Norman kingdom had furnished good material, better material than had imperial feudalism, for the theological reflection of John of Salisbury who, as a good historian, was sensitive to the value of secondary causes.

Just as, above, when classifying the general resources of historiography, we noted the play of Christian eschatological values in the perspectives and writings of historians, so here, in surveying the spectrum of ways of thinking, one must at least point out the views which, among Christians of the time, encroached to some degree on their construction of history and are more or less oriented toward temporal messianism. It was collective conscience which maintained both the permanence of the past and the determining influences of the future in order to interpret the present, for it was as much based on the future which it anticipated as on the heritage it assumed. Was not man on the move, a *viator* (wayfarer)? Was not the church, itself, also on the move in an open-ended messianic perspective? This gets us away from history, properly speaking, for this prophetical writing was highly ambiguous. In addition, the people who engaged in this were not exactly the masters and theologians of whom we have been speaking, but quite ordinary, sometimes simple, Christian people, most often members of seriously disoriented movements. Crowd instincts, including Christian instincts, also made up an awareness of history. Thus we can expect to find summary views, intellectual incoherencies, imaginative myths, a disconcerting literary genre, doctrinal heresies. But these are not sufficient reasons for treating these collective efforts as foreign to Christian thought or the church. This messianic hope could be tested and proven in the experience of any perverse dislocation of the Christian order. It remained founded in truth; it entered into Christian awareness of the course of time, the historicity of the church, the end of the world—an awareness which the corruption of the world developed and sometimes overextended.

Two types of mind participated in this universal excitement. On the one hand there were those reformers who, lined up against the sociological failures of the church, appealed to its eschatological destiny to liberate it from its worldly ties. From Gerhoh of Reichersberg (died 1169) to Gerald of Wales (died 1223), they found their argument in apocalypses. Even Ordericus Vitalis said, *Antichristi tempus appropinquat* ("the age of anti-Christ approaches"), lamenting the corruption of his times. On the other hand there were those would-be imitators of the apostles who, under the influence of some of the worst revolutionary or doctrinal childishness, tried implicitly to exclude the church from history on the pretext of purifying it by dispossessing it of its temporal institutions, even the most sacred of them. It should also be pointed òut, though, that the professional theologians of the schools, in their justifiable critique of these popular errors, did not always know how to keep alive the messianic hope which would have given their speculations the total dimension of the kingdom of God in the style of scripture and of the fathers.

If we had to trace the trajectory of the rise of an historical awareness, it would now be necessary to acknowledge those who wrote in the vernacular languages. Towards the end of the twelfth century, in both France and England, and in the field of history especially, their advent carried a decisive significance that went beyond literature and language. It implied, to use the expression of Charles Homer Haskins, a secularization and popularization of history.[70]

---

[70] Haskins, *Renaissance*, p. 275: "By 1200 vernacular history had come to stay, and this fact is one of more than linguistic or literary significance, since it involved ultimately the secularization and popularization of history." One example is that of Godfrey of Viterbo who wrote the *Memoria saeculorum* in 1185 and dedicated it to Henry II of England. Godfrey traveled widely, having been sent on mission twice to Sicily, three times to Provence, once to Spain, often to France, and forty times from Germany to Italy as an imperial chaplain. This well traveled author was content to present his observations in a popular manner in order to attract a considerable lay reading public. One major example is the twelve thousand-verse poem *L'estoire de la guerre sainte* (ed. G. Paris [Paris, 1897]; *Three Old French Chronicles of the Crusades*, tr. E. N. Stone [Seattle, 1939]), composed before 1195 by a certain Ambrose,

Clerics, writing in Latin, immersed in very strong intellectual traditions, could neither feel nor express, in their immediacy or totality, the events and causes of the earthly progress of humanity. The princely courts furnished the structures and the men, and the cities the popular awareness, of this new trend in history.

Limiting ourselves to the role played by theology in this awakening, we can, right within this new trend of human destiny, find evidences of its influence.

We see right off, in the beginnings of a theology turned henceforth into an organized discipline, the scientific worth, so to say, of a vision of the world conceived as an economy developing through time, surrounding events and determining their contents and meaning. These events constitute the *dispensatio salutis* (the economy of salvation) which God realizes freely, but which transformed the very ground on which the generations advance. At just the very time when the influence and attraction of a philosophy of the world was being exerted, especially of the various platonizing philosophies which tended to eliminate time and history, we have here a prime example of the ineradicable view of Christianity as an itinerary of man's journey toward the divine, a view which could not be reduced to a cyclical conception of the cosmos with neither commencement nor consummation. In the twelfth century, Hugh of Saint-Victor was the master of this traditional perception, from which the awareness of history was born, while the Christian commentators of the *Timaeus* at Chartres implicitly surrendered to the absorption of nature and the destiny of man within the macrocosm. The masters of the thirteenth century were to have a task in reconciling Greek idealism with a providentialism controlled by the free wishes of God, or, within this framework, in synthesizing the naturalism of essences with the liberty of the individual and collective graces of the Lord.

Our theologian-historians observed in this "divine government" not only the designs revealed in sacred history, but their active realization in the successive stages of humanity. This humanity, conceived once more in terms of the cliché of the "ages" from infancy to senil-

---

doubtless a jongleur from around Evreux, in any case an eye-witness of the retinue of King Richard in the Holy Land.

ity, was, as St. Augustine had said, like one man advancing towards his perfection in a collective and regular progress, directed by the definitive interventions of God.[71] The violent reaction against Joachim of Floris, after the astonishing appeal of his spiritual evolutionism, marked the critical point of this vision, at the same time that this reaction defined the orthodoxy of the vision. The Fourth Lateran Council, which condemned this evolutionism even long before it raged among the Spirituals, was at the same time a witness to this sensitivity to the church's progress through its earthly stages, just as Anselm of Havelberg understood and expressed it.

Conclusion

Since this divine society of humanity was terrestrial, it included in its total and unique finality, and for its full understanding, the reality of human events themselves other than as a neutral and amorphous matter. In the twelfth century there was not yet a "secular" history; but in various theological views, secondary causes, as one would soon come to call them, were being taken into consideration, as was already evident in John of Salisbury's dualism. The Roman Empire was the chief of all secondary causes but its future was henceforth contested under pressure of new developments which raised questions about the Holy Empire. Charlemagne could no longer fill the role of Constantine.

Theologians were thus led, more or less consciously, to place themselves and their era in the "sixth age," an age decidedly longer than had been foreseen. At the end of it was to come the parousia, the prospect of which had terrified simple people towards the year 1000 but which did not trouble the serene construction of theology in the schools. They thus found themselves at a moment whose coordinates they had the curiosity to study, in relation both to the

---

[71] *De vera religione* xxvii. 50 (*CSEL*, LXXVII, 36): ". . . sic proportione universum genus humanum, cuius tamquam unius hominis vita est ab Adam usque ad finem huis saeculi, ita sub divinae providentiae legibus administratur, ut in duo genera distributum appareat" (thus by analogy the entire human race, whose life is so to speak that of a single man from Adam to the end of the world, is so governed by the laws of divine providence, that it appears divided into two kinds).

ancients and to the movement of civilization towards the West.[72]

The causes and effects of these transfers from East to West, of which the University of Paris was going to be the enlightened conscience, gained credit and by the same fact lent themselves to different interpretations. Germans, Normans, French—all built for themselves a world increasingly removed from the remaining eastern half of the ancient empire, whose memory Charlemagne had focused on himself, to form a new Roman prestige, while Islam still in this twelfth century blocked the spiritual and geographical frontiers of Christendom. The "West" existed in their very terminology. While detecting a renaissance therein, theologians enthusiastically accepted the fresh newness of their times, which perhaps the ambiguous phrase "Middle Ages" still conceals from us.

Thus Christendom became aware of its historical evolution in the twelfth century. That was a major development which, if it stood alone, would have made of this a great century, if it be true that collective awakenings can bring about not only the internal transformation of behavior, but also the development of minds.[73] That this awakening did not take place in the schools should not be surprising, for such awareness is periodically provoked in the church by contacts with the world—the world of nature or the world of thought. And these occasions of growth make good material for a theology of the "City of God"—*De peregrinante civitate Dei* (*The Pilgrim City of God*)[74]—which Augustine had already shown goes far beyond the earthly institutions of the church.

---

[72] Cf. E. Gilson, *The Spirit of Medieval Philosophy*, tr. A. H. C. Downes (New York, 1936), chap. 19: "The Middle Ages and History."

[73] Cf. W. Kamlah, *Christentum und Geschichtlichkeit, Untersuchungen zur Entstehung des Christentums und zu Augustins 'Bürgerschaft Gottes'* (Stuttgart, 1951).

[74] The title of a work by Henry of Marcy, abbot of Clairvaux, 1176–9 (*PL*, CCIV, 251–402).

6

Monks, Canons, and Laymen
in Search of the Apostolic Life

THE SCHOLAR WHO will someday write the history of the theology of grace in the church of the twentieth century will certainly not find the real and interesting substance of that theology in some neo-scholastic controversy, in polemics between some paleo-Thomist and a neo-Molinist. He will have to find it in problems concerning nature and grace newly raised by young Christian thinkers aware of changes taking place in the fundamental structure of society, aware of economic developments, and of new conceptions of the world and of history that are in process of formulation.

The same is true with any history of the theology of grace in the church of the twelfth century; it cannot rest content to draw up an inventory of opinions and controversies between celebrated masters. If it limited itself to these, such a history would note in Abelard a tendency to establish a semi-Pelagianist connection between nature and grace; in Peter Lombard, on the other hand, a bogging down of the Augustinian tradition into a rather simplistic pessimism; then, on a profounder level, Hugh of Saint-Victor drawn by the implications of Platonism to conceive of nature and grace as participations in the divine life rather than as distinct forms. These would all be significant observations, but too detached from the actual behavior of Christians and from their collective consciousness in a church undergoing profound transformation. The economy of salvation is not defined exclusively in the reflective and cautiously reasoned understanding of a few licensed thinkers, but also in the concrete decisions, in the states of life embraced, in the ideals of sanctity, in the evangelical work which the church, in its head and members, approves, sets up, promotes—in short, defines.

This sociological approach to ideas is illuminating for any period. But it seems especially appropriate for the twelfth century when Christians found themselves having to make various clear-cut religious choices even before they had had a chance to orient themselves intellectually. In using these options they consciously faced up to the perennial problems of nature and grace, of the world and the gospel; and for them this problem was not so much an object of theological debate as it was the shifting, controverted, or bold expression of their encounter with a new society which they were having to penetrate as apostles. Admittedly, their recourse to a philosophy of nature came from reading ancient pagan literature and was of capital importance, at Chartres for example, where the *Timaeus* was to nourish several generations of students, or at Paris towards the close of the twelfth century, where Avicenna was to give a curious shape to the Augustinian outlook. But this erudite and bookish recourse was itself born of and nourished by a whole view of the universe and of the evolution of society. And so in the following century, when St. Thomas Aquinas crowned this lofty doctrinal effort to resolve the problem of nature and grace by introducing the Aristotelian notion of nature into theology, his work was not solely the result of admirable speculation but the fruit of a new Christian awareness of nature and of man.

One must be careful not to assign these beneficial doctrinal labors to the realm of philosophy, the "philosophy of the world" as they said at Chartres, or the "knowledge of man" as they said at Saint-Victor and even at Cîteaux. These labors really belonged to theology, to the science of God, and to the science of salvation implicit within it; for an evangelical revival, fertile in its vicissitudes as in its forms, engaged minds as well as wills in its task. Throughout this century, the return to the primitive life of the church, to the life of the apostles, the *vita apostolica,* by inspiring new states of life, inspired as well a new awareness of the ways that grace could take root in nature.

Monastic Evangelicalism

It would obviously be impossible to reduce all of Christian history in the West during the early middle ages to a single prototype of spirituality. The figure of St. Benedict, it is true, dominated both institutions and ways of thought in this early period. Apart from John the Scot, whose important role was played out posthumously in the twelfth century and not in the ninth, the line of doctrinal development showed slight variation, even in the actual controversies that arose (such as those over predestination or the eucharist), for these were almost all concerned with positions and formulas enunciated by St. Augustine. But in this church which had passed from the Roman Empire to the barbarian kingdoms, much time and great distances had encouraged the development of a wide variety of institutions, ideas, and cultural orientations.

Still, the inner drive of this church stemmed almost entirely from the ideals and inspirations of the monastic life, from which of course its leading intellectuals as well as its great administrators and missionaries were recruited. The stages and variations, the corruptions, even the divisions of this monastic life served only to underscore its essential unity not only of form and spirit, but of doctrine as well. The term "monastic theology" has been justly employed to describe its peculiar manner and method of defining the essential components of the Christian economy of salvation.

At the start of the twelfth century, at the time when, as we shall see, certain elements of this monastic life were brought into question by the evolution of society and of the church in that society, there took place an extremely severe examination of the resources and goals of this sector of the church. And so one finds within the unbroken tradition of monastic literature two important themes being systematically and simultaneously developed, the more so as a result of competition from the regular canons, who were then very much on the rise: one such theme was the return to evangelical and historical sources as a guarantee of authenticity, and the other was the permanent value of the monastic state of life face to face with the new society.

For the first decades of the twelfth century, Rupert, a monk of

Saint-Laurent of Liège and then abbot of Deutz from 1119 until his death in 1130, can be selected as an especially self-conscious, trustworthy, and voluble exponent of these themes.[1] His commentary on the *Rule* of St. Benedict, his correspondence, his essays on the relation of the monastic life to the world and to the contemporary church constitute impressive documentation for this judgment. To them can be added, despite some grave doubts about its authenticity, a tract with the significant title, *De vita vere apostolica* (*On the Truly Apostolic Life*).[2] The traditionalist tone of this tract does nothing to diminish its close touch with reality. The context of this reality was lucidly analyzed in the remarkable *Liber de diversis ordinibus et professionibus quae sunt in ecclesia* (*Book Concerning the Various Orders and Professions in the Church*), composed at the same time, between 1125 and 1130, probably by a canon of Liège, Raimbaud, provost of the collegiate church of Saint-Jean.[3]

De vita vere apostolica—it was a traditional and fundamental theme, this claim that monastic life was the realization of the apostolic life; i.e., an imitation of the life led by the apostles themselves. The adverb *vere* denotes the apologetic and critical accent which the author adopted to oppose the hypothesis of an inevitable evolution of institutions as well as the arguments of his contemporaries. We should be careful not to attribute modern meanings to his use of the term "apostolic." There is nothing here of the apostolate, of the preaching of the word of God which characterized the role of the apostles in the primitive church where they were commissioned to

---

[1] His adversary Anselm of Havelberg, the theoretician of the states of life in the church, said of him: "In ordine Cluniacensium, Rupertus abbas Tuitiensis, totius pene veteris ac novi testamenti expositor illustris, ordinem illum aureum tanquam topazius perornat." (In the Cluniac Order, Rupert the abbot of Deutz, noted expert on nearly the whole of the Old and the New Testaments, adorns that golden order like a topaz.) *Liber de ordine canonicorum* xxix (*PL*, CLXXXVIII, 1111).

[2] (*PL*, CLXX, 609–64). To be dated after 1121. G. Morin, *The Ideal of the Monastic Life Found in the Apostolic Age*, tr. C. Gunning (Westminster, Md., 1950), pp. 68–69, maintains the attribution to Rupert. Others believe it to be by a Victorine, a defender of the views of the regular canons. See the suggestions of C. Dereine, "L'élaboration du statut canonique des chanoines réguliers spécialement sous Urbain II," *RHE*, XLVI (1951), 550.

[3] (*PL*, CCXIII, 807–50). Cf. C. Dereine, "Les origines de Prémontré," *RHE*, XLII (1947), 359–60.

teach and to baptize. The term applied instead to the internal life of the first Christian communities which with their fraternal regimen prefigured and in a sense constituted the first monasteries. It referred therefore not to a function, *officium*, however exalted, but to a mode of life, *vita*. The church, according to Rupert, had been instituted in the monastic life. "If you wish to consult the relevant passages of scripture, you will find that they all seem to say plainly that the church originated in the monastic life."[4] Later monastic legislators, such as St. Benedict, had merely formulated some regulations for an institution long since established by the apostles, its true "authors." The monastic *regula* was in fact the *regula apostolica*.[5] The apostles had been monks,[6] and thus monks were the authentic successors to the apostles. "This is the authority that leads me to assert that the life and rule of monks are equal to the dignity and gospel of the apostles."[7] The gospel, the perfection and dignity of the apostles (*apostolica perfectio, apostolica dignitas*), had become the characteristic platform, the exclusive preserve of the monks, because they alone achieved its full reality: abandonment of all private goods in favor of the common life. The text which inspired this mode of life was the classic description of the first Christian community at Jerusalem in Acts 4:32, a text expressing the evangelical ideal for all time. Wherever churches had been built or were yet to be built, this prototype would be reproduced. Monastic expansion kept pace with expansion of the church. Such was the claim.

Vita apostolica equals *vita communis*—the equation was not simply a banal formula applying to the traditional cenobitic life. It was

---

[4] *De vita vere apostolica* iv. 4 (*PL*, CLXX, 644): "Si vis omnia scripturarum consulere testimonia, nihil aliud videntur dicere quam ecclesiam inchoasse a vita monastica." The author cites Philo on the origins of the Egyptian monasteries.

[5] *Ibid*. iii.15 (*PL*, CLXX, 641–2).

[6] *Ibid*. iv.11 (*PL*, CLXX, 648): "Quod omnes apostoli vere fuerunt monachi." Cf. Peter of Celle, a Cluniac (died 1183), in his *Disciplina claustralis* ii, "De apostolica disciplina" (*PL*, CCII, 1102): "Quid dicam de monachis istis, videlicet apostolis" (What shall I say of those monks, namely, the apostles)?

[7] *De vita vere apostolica* prol. (*PL*, CLXX, 612): "Vitam et regulam monachorum tanta auctoritate evangelio et dignitati aequiparavi apostolorum."

also the platform for the reform undertaken at the start of the eleventh century—that to which Peter Damian and Hildebrand devoted so much effort. For clerical decadence too, the great remedy was the *vita communis*. The term had become charged with a new relevance which the monks were claiming for themselves in lively competition with the secular clergy and the regular canons, as against whom they asserted their title to primacy in age and experience of the world. All the elements of traditional asceticism—simplicity of food, clothing, and shelter; modest manners; fraternal correction; and penitential manual labor—reappeared in this inspired movement against established customs and the general relaxation of standards. This renewal was a call to return to the primitive church. At the council of Rome in 1059, Hildebrand urged the common life, following the example of the primitive church (*vita communis, exemplo primitivae ecclesiae.*)[8]

But this return to the primitive church brought with it an intense awareness of the problems posed for the monastic life by its need to confront modern times. The common life would have to be more than the sum of several saintly lives, of several individual poverties. It had to be an institution, and the monastic life, though a seedbed of saints and paupers of Christ, had assumed an institutional form in a temporal regime which just could not model itself after the little fraternal community at Jerusalem. Times had changed, and the *ordo monasticus* had become a power in twelfth-century Christendom—a spiritual power to be sure, but a temporal power also, at once a product and a mainstay of the feudal system. One should see it—and it is a wonderful thing to see—shaken by the call of the gospel, there in the midst of feudal society, where bit by bit through the centuries it had become comfortably and conveniently established. Rupert of Deutz experienced both excitement and annoyance at that call; his claiming an evangelical character for monasticism raised serious questions about the forms which the monastic regimen had assumed, from the most general principles to the most minute details.

Poverty, the economic and spiritual basis of the *vita communis*,

---

[8] Text in J. Mabillon, *Annales ordinum Sancti Benedicti*, IV (Paris, 1707), 686.

was the first such form to present problems. The monastic economy was inextricably bound up with a wide range of temporal services, a normal, visible, triumphant effect of the implantation of the church in secular society. The civilizing potential of monasticism did not stem solely from its moral prestige and continuing example. It made itself felt in institutions—tithes, hospital services, distribution of food, aid for travellers—services that were all carried out by monks. Even more, juridical and administrative structures, autonomous courts and the carrying out of their decisions, tax systems and their administration all became monastic responsibilities. How could one have not reacted sharply to the incongruity of all this in the face of the new evangelical appeal and the comparisons with the primitive apostolic community it implied? The author of the *De diversis ordinibus in ecclesia* was a witness to this problem, though he handled it very discreetly. But it became more and more acute with the progressive breakup of the old system in which the monastic order's secular responsibilities had been given a religious coloring. The *De diversis ordinibus* noted specifically the emancipation of serfs who, to escape prosecution by their erstwhile masters, sought refuge and legal status in the temporal and juridical domain of churches.[9] The social role of the monastic order inevitably compromised any attempt on its part to regain the apostolic life. Rupert testified to this conflict, the spiritual by-product of which was an uneasiness of soul which his fervor tended only to exacerbate. A solid barrier against the corruption of a secular clergy too much wrapped up in private life, the monastery was at the same time the heart of an earthly community whose economic organization was determined by spiritual ends.

Assured of regular sources of income by this economic system, the secure monastic community was no longer obliged to live from day to day by the work of its hands, as provided in the venerable *Rule* where St. Benedict envisaged a concrete form of apostolic perfection. Rupert weighed the consequences of the transformation that had taken place and that touched the spiritual comportment of the monks as well as their daily occupations. He devoted the third book of his commentary on the *Rule* to an apology for this transformation:

---

[9] *Liber de diversis ordinibus* xxvi (*PL*, CCXIII, 821–2).

"Which activity is more legitimate, to do manual labor as ordered by St. Benedict and thus live the life of apostolic perfection, or to live by the altar in the service of the Lord's worship?"[10] According to Rupert, Benedict did not intend to lay down a basic precept of the monastic life, but simply to sanction an occupation which, beyond helping to meet material needs, would fend off laziness. Far more worthy was the holy and exalted service of the altar where one is fixed in meditation on the mystery of Christ. This was not of course to suggest contempt for voluntary poverty, but to praise emphatically the grandeur of the liturgical life. And was not that, after all, the life of the apostles, of whom it was never said that they worked with their hands all of the time, but who, on the contrary, shifted their material burdens onto deacons and devoted themselves to the word of God (Acts 6:1-6)?

This new allocation of monastic occupations had a great many profound implications for the equilibrium, the mentality of the monks as well as in the external organization of their lives. Economic responsibilities were depreciated as a result of the absolute precedence given to sacred functions, more precisely to liturgical ceremonies whose aristocratic glamor gave to this earthly community the allure of a heavenly court resplendent with the music of angelic choirs, as if in foretaste of paradise. But this glamor had the unintended effect of so reducing the stature of wretched earthly life that humility and penitence were all that was left to any extra-clerical evangelism. Certain monastic reforms that antedated the lay movements of the later twelfth century rejected this disjuncture between a high liturgical religion and a new evangelicalism that was closer to secular realities and liberated from the splendors of feudalism. The protracted controversy about the manual labor of monks, already

---

[10] *Super quaedam capitula regulae divi Benedicti abbatis* iii.4 (*PL*, CLXX, 513): ". . . utra pars firmius fundamentum rationis habeat: illa, quae praefert opus manuum secundum ordinationem regulae beati Benedicti, et de labore manuum vivere perfectionem apostolicam esse contendit, an ista, quae servire altari, et de altari vivere melius esse asserit." [For the evolution of the *Rule* of St. Benedict and an appreciation of the Cluniac style of life, see Joan Evans, *Monastic Life at Cluny, 910–1157* (London, 1931), esp. chap. 5, "Daily Life," pp. 78–97. Cf. David Knowles, *The Monastic Order in England*, 2nd ed. (Cambridge, 1963), pp. 148–50.]

under way in the time of Rupert, found in this disjuncture a source of disagreement that ran deeper than petty squabbles about individuals and institutions. From this time forward, the expression *vita apostolica* underwent a significant shift in meaning.

Meanwhile, a parallel development reinforced these changes: more and more monks were being ordained priests, which made it only more normal that they should spend their time at the altar.[11] Again, Rupert is a good source for the problems which this posed. St. Benedict, he said, had made almost no mention of the celebration of mass, but these manual labor fanatics "who place nearly all their hope in manual labor" (*qui in opere manuum fere totam spem suam ponunt*),[12] had better appreciate the eminent dignity of the sacrifice of the altar where the delights of the heavenly meal are prefigured. Times had changed; the present condition of the church demanded an increased number of priests now that, Christianity having triumphed, princes and kings were everywhere heaping riches upon the churches and monasteries.[13] Paul and Anthony, the founders of monasticism, had not been priests. But to proceed to the priesthood was the way to apostolic perfection;[14] and the priest, by his function if not by his own merit, was thereby closer to the apostle than was the simple monk. Thus in yet another, not altogether unambiguous, way did the meaning of the terms *apostolus*, and *vita apostolica* undergo change.[15]

But if we now extend the "apostolic" activity of the monks to include not only their liturgical functions but their preaching and sanctifying functions vis-à-vis the laity—preaching, baptism, in brief all the activities promoting conversion which are understood in the modern term "apostolate"—the ambiguity of the term *vita apostolica*

---

[11] *Super quaedam capitula regulae divi Benedicti abbatis* iii.11 (*PL*, CLXX, 518).

[12] *Ibid.*, 10 (*PL*, CLXX, 517).

[13] *Ibid.*, 11 (*PL*, CLXX, 519–20).

[14] *Ibid.*, 9(*PL*, CLXX, 517).

[15] Rupert is all the more qualified as a source, for he himself long refused ordination. Cf. his *De gloria et honore Filii hominis* xii (*PL*, CLXVIII, 1601–2). As the Cistercian says in the *Dialogus inter cluniacensem et cisterciensem monachum* ii.58 (E. Martène and U. Durand, *Thesaurus novus anecdotorum* [Paris, 1717], V, 1626): "Monachus qui dignus est ordinari non fiat sacerdos nisi coactus." (A monk who is worthy of ordination will not be made a priest unless he must.)

becomes yet more involved and imposes the task of coordinating the broad range of meanings which it can express. Rupert's tract, the *De vita vere apostolica*, takes a sudden, sharp turn in announcing that the life of apostles does not consist entirely in preaching and in administering the sacraments, for what makes an apostle is not preaching or baptising but being virtuous and, in particular, living more humbly than anyone else.[16]

This final definition, so insensitive to the task of proselytizing— also apostolic and evangelical, after all—leads us to attempt a reconstruction of the monastic understanding of the phrase *vita apostolica*. The understanding derived not only from the model (a sociologist today would say the "myth") of the first community at Jerusalem but from the doctrines and principles of that community as well. These were vigorously restated, and the peculiar accent which the contingent circumstances surrounding the Gregorian reform gave them did not diminish the force of their appeal. Now and then, to be sure, the return to the gospel was diluted in the minutiae of some paltry or infantile reforming stir. But for the most part it was carried on at a lofty spiritual level, at the level, say, of Hildebrand, who advocated a conversion based on an austere penitential code that would lead the way to the kingdom of God. The laws of this conversion were the beatitudes, so internalized that they seemed more ascribable to the liberty of love than to some set of teachings. They took care to follow the evangelical values to the letter, especially those of poverty and fraternity, soul and structure of the *vita communis;* these, despite the exaltation of elaborate liturgy, were presented as the basic laws of the monastic life. Five or six centuries of experience supported the wisdom and fertility of this ideal.[17]

---

[16] *De vita vere apostolica* ii.16 (*PL*, CLXX, 631–2): "Nam non facit apostolum praedicare, baptizare et miracula facere, sed virtutes habere, et sicut illis injunctum est, prae caeteris seipsum humiliare." (For it is not preaching, baptizing, and performing miracles that makes the apostle, but being virtuous, and, as it was taught to them, to make themselves humble before others.)

[17] Cf. J. Leclercq, *La vie parfaite. Points de vue sur l'essence de l'état religieux* (Turnhout-Paris, 1948), especially his remarks on traditional elements of the religious life in chap. 3, "La vie apostolique," pp. 82–105; also the earlier statement, first published in 1912, expressed with great finesse, by G. Morin, *The Ideal of the Monastic Life Found in the Apostolic Age*, tr. C. Gunning (Westminster, Maryland, 1950).

However, the very success of this monastic claim to evangelical inspiration encouraged an explicit identification of the concept of a Christian community with the monastery to the latter's benefit. The result was that a Christian community could hardly be conceived or at least pictured any longer without a sacralization embracing all of its elements, even its secular elements such as its public services. The mirage of the primitive Jerusalem community confirmed but also constricted the great Augustinian theme of the city of God. The monastery became the realization of this city, but with grave losses to the historical, cosmological, and eschatological dimensions of Augustine's vision.

In fact the opposition of the two cities, so essential in Augustine, disappeared in the context where the church had absorbed the world,[18] where the triumphant splendor of monasticism (*splendor monachici ordinis*)[19] reigned over humanity. The ideal Christian, or more simply the Christian, was the monk, a Christian dead to the world. The Christian vocation was nothing but the germ of the monastic vocation. The gospel was its "rule." Yet at the same time, the monks had taken charge of the principal needs and services of mankind, not without some scrupling, but yielding to the temptation of a theocratic ambition. They wished to make mankind over into a veritable monastery, joyous and active, living in expectation of the heavenly reward.

The end result of this sacralized universe, of this perfected terrestrial city of God, would be to make proselytizing, the *ministerium verbi inter gentes*, pointless and unnecessary. Yet how deceptive this dream was, for at the start of the twelfth century the monastic world was shaken by a call to the apostolate and, with glorious references to such great forebears as St. Augustine of Canterbury and St. Boniface, monks did claim the right to preach.[20] But the channels of communication through which this call and this legitimate claim might have been implemented remained blocked, within this paramonastic

---

[18] In this connection the reflections of that great monastic lord, Otto of Freising, are very revealing, even if his work was called *History of the Two Cities;* see above, p. 189, n. 57.

[19] Rupert of Deutz *Altercatio monachi et clerici* (*PL*, CLXX, 540).

[20] *Ibid.* (*PL*, CLXX, 537–42); *Epistola ad Everardum* (*PL*, CLXX, 541–4); *Epistola ad Liezelinum canonicum* (*PL*, CLXX, 663–8).

world, by the lack of an encounter with the secular realities which
condition any apostolic conquest. The monastic claims to the right
to the apostolate remained abrupt and somewhat resentful in tone.[21]
And when the occasion to proclaim this kingdom beyond their bor-
ders actually did arrive, the monks were surprised, even disconcerted,
as for example the Cistercians whom Rome called into action against
the Albigensians. One cannot fail to see the connection between
Rupert's reduction of the apostolic act to personal holiness and the
vain appeals of late twelfth-century pontiffs for a missionary cam-
paign to evangelize a restive populace and a dechristianized world.[22]
"Most dreadful silence" (*pessima taciturnitas*) Peter the Chanter
would say.[23] Of course certain individuals maintained brilliantly the
traditions of the Bonifaces and the Augustines; the name of Bernard
alone reverberated throughout Christendom. Yet the institution
seemed, because of its very triumph, to rest comfortably on the Christianity it had built; and the people of God had only to enjoy this
triumph. In its final realization, this *vita apostolica* left out of its
consideration that confrontation of the world which the gospel demanded.

Evangelicalism in the Canonical Reform

This outburst of the *vita apostolica* impressed itself on contemporary events and even language. Yet within thirty years the meaning of *vita apostolica* changed markedly.[24] Or rather, those aspects
of the primitive church to which it referred received a new orientation. Whereas Rupert and his like had built their world about the

---

[21] After maintaining the identity of the apostolic life of the first Christians
with the monastic life and its dying to the world, Rupert reverses the argument
to say to the priest-apostle that this death to the world is not the exclusive
preserve of the monk, henceforth cast off from the world, but of all baptized
persons, even in the midst of the world. He quotes Jerome: "Monachus non
habet docentis officium, sed lugentis." (The monk's duty is not to teach but
to mourn.), *Altercatio monachi et clerici* (*PL*,CLXX, 538–9).

[22] Cf. Mandonnet, II, 41–42; Larkin, pp. 147–9.

[23] *Verbum abbreviatum* lxii (*PL*, CCV, 189).

[24] This is not the place to trace the entire earlier history of the term. E.
Delaruelle has written of the meaning it had for Jonas of Orléans in the ninth
century when it expressed the ideal of the pastor in the *ordo episcoporum:*
"En relisant le *De institutione regia* de Jonas d'Orléans," *Mélanges Halphen*
(Paris, 1950), pp. 185–92. For the general problem, see L. M. Dewailly,
"Notes sur l'histoire de l'adjectif 'apostolique'," *MSR,* V (1948). 141–52.

vita communis,[25] a wholly different group of evangelicals, expressing a hope that more and more people were coming to share, was formulating a definition that stressed the proselytizing activities of the apostles. Preaching, itinerant preaching—as opposed to monastic stability and as distinguished from episcopal preaching—was central to this new *vita apostolica*. After all, it was the apostolate which made the apostle: *vita vere apostolica* (the truly apostolic life). This reversal of vocabulary, with all the fluctuations and permutations that go with such a reversal, has been clearly pointed out. Here we can only confirm the point.[26]

The same basic texts, Acts 4:32 and Luke 10:1-12, were taken up again; but of these two, Luke was to be the more important, for there the regimen of poverty was expressly commanded by Christ as part of the apostolic mission.[27] While the common life based on the total abnegation of private property continued to be the economic and spiritual basis of the *vita apostolica*, that life was swept up and trans-

---

[25] The equation *vita apostolica* equals *vita communis* had been a cliché from the days of Hildebrand. It appears in a letter of Nicholas II (Mansi, XIX, 873): "Rogantes monemus ut ad apostolicam, scilicet communem, vitam summopere pervenire studeant." (We admonish them asking that they strive with the greatest care to reach the apostolic, i.e., the common, life.) Cf. A. Mouraux, "La 'vie apostolique' à propos de Rupert de Deutz," *RLM*, XXI (1931), 71–78, 125–41.

[26] Cf. Mandonnet, II, 167–92; Larkin, pp. 258–90. Also C. Dereine, "Vie commune, règle de S. Augustin et chanoines réguliers au XIᵉ siècle," *RHE*, XLI (1946), 365–406.

[27] This is the great text (Luke 10:1–12) of the apostolic mission: "After this, the Lord appointed seventy-two others, and sent them on ahead, two by two, into all the cities and villages he himself was to visit. The harvest, he told them, is plentiful enough, but the laborers are few; you must ask the Lord to whom the harvest belongs to send laborers out for the harvesting. Go then, and remember, I am sending you out to be like lambs among wolves. You are not to carry purse, or wallet, or sandals; you are to greet no one on the way. When you enter a house, say first of all, 'Peace be to this house'; and if those who dwell there are men of good will, your good wishes shall come down upon it; if not, they will come back to you the way they went. Remain in the same house, eating and drinking what they provide, for the laborer deserves his wages; do not go from house to house. When you enter a city, and they make you welcome, be content to eat the fare they offer you: and heal those who are sick there; and tell them, 'The kingdom of God is close upon you.' But if you enter a city where they will not make you welcome, go out into their streets and say, 'We brush off in your faces the very dust from your city that has clung to our feet; and be sure of this, the kingdom of God is close at hand.' I tell you, it shall go less hard with Sodom at the day of judgment, than with that city."

formed by a new dynamism. In mid-eleventh century, Peter Damian heralded the apostolic reform: "The only men fit for the office of preaching (*officium praedicationis*) are those who lack the support of earthly riches and who, because they possess nothing whatever of their own, hold everything in common."[28] Such was the impact of this idea that for a time it seemed as if the *officium praedicationis* would have to be taken away from the clergy altogether so as to allow for faithful imitation of the apostles. Whatever may be said of this constitutional error, it delivered a psychological and sociological blow to traditional institutions and led to loss of esteem for the monastic order of the feudal type described above. Rupert was highly sensitive to these changes and fought valiantly against the evolutionary hypothesis that certain men built upon them. He said, in effect, to one of his acquaintances:

I recall certain remarks you made and I don't think I like their implications. You told me that the Babylonian kingdom was established, then reached its height, and then collapsed. And that it was supplanted by the Persian kingdom which in its turn collapsed. Then came the Macedonian kingdom. And so it goes, by a similar pattern, you added, with the grandeur of the monastic orders, especially Cluny (about which I have never heard a friendly word fall from your lips). They will collapse in their turn, since new, still modest institutions will rise up to take over. What an altogether wrong and insulting comparison between the monasteries of the kingdom of God and those monstrous kingdoms destined to the fires of hell.[29]

---

[28] *Contra clericos regulares proprietarios* vi (*PL*, CXLV, 490): ". . . illi duntaxat idonei sunt ad praedicationis officium, qui nullum terrenae facultatis possident lucrum, et dum aliquid singulare non habent, communiter omnia possident."

[29] For Rupert's exact words, see *Super quaedam capitula regulae divi Benedicti abbatis* iv.13 (*PL*, CLXX, 535–6): "Recordor cujusdam dicti quod ex te audivi, de quo et judicare dubito quale sit, vel quali a spiritu processerit. Dixisti enim: Postquam regnum Babylonium crevit in immensum, crescere desiit et succrevit aliud, scilicet regnum Persarum atque Medorum, et deinde super hoc aliud, videlicet regnum Macedonum. Ista, quasi similitudine praemissa, subjunxisti sic futurum esse, jamque fieri debere, ut magnitudo sive altitudo illorum, qui hactenus in conversatione monachica vignerunt, maximeque Cluniacensium, de quibus nescio utrum aliquod unquam dixeris amabile verbum, deprimeretur, atque minueretur admodum, atque humilibus suborientibus fieret aliud principium. Qualis est ista similitudo sive comparatio? Quattuor namque illa regna bestialia sine Deo fuerunt, monachica vero conversatio, sive omnis ecclesiastica religio, nequaquam similis, imo contraria est bestiis illis, utpote pertinens ad ministerium quo ministratur Antiquo dierum, et Filio hominis, cui ille tradidit potestatem, et regnum suum, qui judicavit de bestiis illis et sublata potestate corpora eorum igni tradidit."

Even apart from the radicalism of the new view, the evolution Rupert feared could nonetheless be seen taking place in fact: the Cistercian reform dealt with constitutional problems (among others, emancipation from feudal ties) over and beyond moral problems. The revival of the eremitic life penetrated the new monastic constitutions (Grandmont, the Vallombrosians, the Carthusians, etc.)—to say nothing of the unhealthy extremes which evangelical simplicity reached. This evolution was also registered in texts. A bull of Pope Urban II, addressed to the church of Raitenbach in Bavaria in 1092, took account of it and thereby became the charter of an institutional dualism henceforth accepted in the church: both monastic and canonical life were forms of the apostolic life, the life "instituted by apostolic practice and originating in the first days of the holy church" (*apostolicae instituta disciplinae, in primordiis ecclesiae sanctae exorta*). Augustine was the legislator and Jerome the teacher of the canonical life. "It should not seem any less praiseworthy," said Urban, "to revive this earliest life of the church with the inspiration and help of the Spirit of the Lord than to maintain the prosperous religion of the monks through continuing steadfastly in the same Spirit."[30] However varied the forms the regular canons gave to their revival of the ancient way of life and despite constant cross-borrowing, with monks assuming pastoral charges and communities of canons assuming monastic observances,[31] a line emerged which

---

[30] *Epp. et privilegia* lviii (*PL*, CLI, 338–9): "Nam minoris aestimandum est meriti, hanc vitam ecclesiae primitivam, aspirante et prosequente Domini spiritu suscitare, quam florentem monachorum religionem ejusdem spiritu perseverantia custodire." The article by Dereine (cf. above, note 26) includes, along with a partial text of this bull, several later documents which repeat its salient points. M. H. Vicaire observes (Mandonnet, II, 178; Larkin, p. 267): "It is remarkable that this historical view, in which one can see the influence of Peter Damian even, recognizes the *vita primitivae ecclesiae* only in the canonical life and not in the monastic life. And what is more, this document had an astounding success. It may be found separate from the original privilege, which is in *Epp. et privilegia* cclxxix (*PL*, CLI, 535). It constituted an official decree in the view of the canons and it appears as such in the bull establishing Prémontré. It was often invoked in polemics. . . ."

[31] On the diversity and similarity one encounters and on the caution one must henceforth observe in making general remarks on this subject, see Charles Dereine, "Chanoines réguliers," *DHGE*, XII, 353–405; and J. C. Dickinson, *The Origins of the Austin Canons and Their Introduction into England* (London, 1950).

clearly differentiated the canonical forms of the evangelical ideal. Urban's choice of words was significant: "not less praiseworthy to *revive* than to *maintain*"; not that the monk Urban II was slighting his monastic profession—he simply asserted that the canons who revived the lost fervor and those monks who maintained the fervor they had never lost were equally faithful to the Holy Spirit.

Anselm of Havelberg, the defender of the new forms against the conservatism of Rupert, was fully aware of this revival prompted by the Spirit.[32] The declaration of principles which opens his *Dialogi* (1145), under the significant title *De unitate fidei et multiformitate vivendi ab Abel usque ad novissimum electum* (On the Unity of the Faith and the Variety of Ways of Life from Abel to the Last of the Elect), is a manifesto in behalf of the evolution of the various states of life within the church. "Many people are amazed and create problems for themselves and others. As slanderous inquisitors they ask: Why all these novelties in the church of God? Why these new orders? Who can keep up with so many orders of clerics? Who is not amazed at so many types of monks? . . . More than that, who would not scorn a Christian religion subjected to so many variations, altered by so many innovations, upset by so many new laws and by

---

[32] Anselm of Havelberg is for the new *vita apostolica* as capable a spokesman as Rupert was for the old. This is surely why they were lined up against one another. Before praising Rupert (see above, n. 1), Anselm had said of him in his *Epistola apologetica pro ordine canonicorum regularium* (*PL,* CLXXXVIII, 1120): "Postremo vero nescio cujusdam Roberti doctrinam adnectis, cujus auctoritas quia in ecclesia ignoratur, ea facilitate contemnitur, qua probatur; fortasse tamen apud vos magnus habetur, non ob id, quod aliqua magna scripserit, sed ob hoc, quod monachorum abbas exstitit; ego sane quaedam scripta illius, fateor, curiosa novitate legi, ipsum etiam novi et vidi, sed pulchre dictum (apud) Graecos proverbium in illo verum reperi: Pinguis venter non gignit tenuem sensum." (Finally, you added the teachings of someone or other named Rupert, whose authority, because he is unknown in the church, can be dismissed as easily as it can be tested critically. Yet he is probably considered a great man among you people not because he has written some great works but because he ranks high as an abbot among monks. I confess, of course, that I have read some of his writings out of curiosity for new things; indeed I have seen the man and met him, but have found that the proverb well phrased by the Greeks proves true of him: 'A fat belly does not produce a fine perception.') For Anselm's use of the term *vita apostolica*, see *ibid.* (*PL,* CLXXXVIII, 1119, 1123); also his *Dialogi* i (*PL,* CLXXXVIII, 1142); for his upsetting the balance of the equation *vita monastica = vita ecclesiae primitivae*, see *PL,* CLXXXVIII, 1119.

customs changed nearly every year. . . . All these people, because they have nothing else to do, pose such questions and disturb simple souls, saying that a religion is contemptible if it changes like this. For, they say, how could a wise man imitate anything so mobile, so variable, so instable? Its very instability shows there is nothing there which one can really grasp."[33] Many controversies developed between monks and canons on precisely the authenticity of the *vita apostolica*. It is not episodes and passionate outbursts[34] that are of interest here but the spiritual implications of this debate for the sociology of the church, implications which Anselm perceived so clearly.

The *De diversis ordinibus* contains a very lucid appreciation of this proliferation of new forms, so disconcerting for conservatives and so frankly accepted by our author. He had some difficulty in distinguishing enduring features from transient ones, essential elements in the new forms from incidental local variations; but it is noteworthy that in order to classify them in some way, he took for his criterion their relative penetration of worldly society, or, to put it the other way, their relative distance from centers of population.[35] In using

---

[33] *Ibid.* (*PL*,CLXXXVIII, 1141): "Solent plerique mirari, et in quaestionem ponere, et interrogando non solum sibi, verum etiam aliis scandalum generare: dicunt enim, et tanquam calumniosi inquisitores interrogant: Quare tot novitates in ecclesia Dei fiunt? Quare tot ordines in ea surgunt? Quis numerare queat tot ordines clericorum? Quis non admiretur tot genera monachorum? . . . Quinimo quis non contemnat Christianam religionem tot varietatibus subjectam, tot adinventionibus immutatam, tot novis legibus et consuetudinibus agitatem, tot regulis et moribus fere annuatim innovatis fluctuantem? . . . Tales, cum otiosi sunt, inducunt quaestiones, et corda simplicium pervertunt, dicentes omnem religionem tanto esse contemptibiliorem, quanto mobiliorem. Quod enim, inquiunt, est tam mobile, tam variable, tam instabile, quomodo alicui sapientum digne potest esse imitabile? Propria quippe sui varietate probat se respuendum esse."

[34] Let us point out, since we have been discussing Rupert of Deutz, his lively opposition to Norbert of Xanten as put forth in the article on Rupert in *Hist. litt.*, XI, 422–587; reprinted in *PL*, CLXX, see col. 791.

[35] *Liber de diversis ordinibus* ii (*PL*, CCXIII, 814): ". . . quorum alii a turbis omnino segregati . . . alii juxta homines in civitatibus et castellis et villis positi . . ." (some of them are separated from the tumult of society altogether . . . whereas others are placed near men in towns and castles and villages). *Ibid.* v (*PL*, CCXIII, 827): ". . . alii a turbis omnino . . . segregentur; alii juxta homines positi sint, alii inter homines habitent" (some are separated from the tumult of society altogether, some are placed near men, and still others live among men). As proof of the astonishment provoked by the new form of religious life, consider the attitude of many people toward the conversion of

this criterion he touched the very heart of the crisis that arose in this hour of new encounter between the gospel and society.

Evangelicalism Among the Laity

The *De diversis ordinibus* did not introduce the old lay-clerical distinction for classifying the new forms of life in the church. In fact, laymen everywhere took part in this upsurge. The historian who looks back today can trace amidst the tangle of enthusiasms the laity's role as one which in practice was of far greater significance than on paper. It represented a full-fledged vocation, quite distinct from that of "lay" monks (non-ordained monks) of the old monastic order. These laymen were among the most effective promoters of the *vita apostolica*, the ideals and needs of which were far from being exhausted by the reform of the regular canons.[36]

The new role of the laity was a logical and necessary outcome of the revolution in progress. Since the evangelical awakening took place not by a revision of existing institutions but by a return to the gospel that by-passed these institutions, one could predict what its dynamics had to be: witness to the faith, fraternal love, poverty, the beatitudes—all these were to operate more spontaneously and sooner among laymen than among clerics, who were bound within an institutional framework. The risk could be great—and in this case it was great—that laymen would grossly abuse their evangelical liberty, for, once on the way to imitating the apostles, they would claim that the right to teach derived from that liberty. It was difficult to distinguish public witness by the faithful from the function of teaching. At the end of the twelfth century, Innocent III established a basic statute embodying this critical and extremely useful distinction.[37]

William of Champeaux who became a regular canon of Saint-Victor, by the gates of Paris: Abelard *Historia calamitatum* (*PL*, CLXXVIII, 120; Muckle, p. 18): ". . . fere omnes discipulos discretos de religione ejus plurimum haesitare, et de conversione ipsius vehementer susurrare, quod videlicet a civitate minime recessisset . . ." (nearly all men of sense have grave doubts about his piety and were loudly whispering about the sincerity of his conversion because he had not left the city).

[36] Cf. Grundmann, *passim* and Mandonnet, II, 183–92; Larkin, pp. 272–81.

[37] For Innocent III, see below, p. 260. The distinction was made as early as 1170 in the *Dialogus inter cluniacensem et cisterciensem monachum* ii.49

Yet even while this ambiguity remained, beginning well before the time of Peter Waldo and up through the success of St. Francis, laymen were among the most active agents of the apostolic life. It is consistently true that when the church, in circumstances like these, seeks to find again its proper theater of activity in the world, it has recourse to laymen, who are familiar with and inhabit this world, and not first to clerics, who have more or less abandoned it.

The same Urban II who had articulated and stressed his belief that the Holy Spirit was inspiring the reform of the regular canons, also observed, and in striking terms, that the "communal life" of these laymen was modeled upon the "distinguished pattern of the primitive church." Bernold of Constance reported this bull and described the spiritual movement which it ratified as comprising an innumerable multitude of men and women (*innumerabilis multitudo virorum et feminarum*), a multitude that spread out even into rural districts and included married as well as unmarried people.[38]

(E. Martène and U. Durand, *Thesaurus novus anecdotorum* [Paris, 1717], V, 1621–2), where the Cistercian says: "Omnis homo habens intellectum, illum scilicet talentum quod nequam servus fodit in terram, si non est solitarius, si habitat cum hominibus, officium habet docentis, quia debet fratrem suum quem videt errare a veritatis vel morum via, ad rectam viam docendo reducere. . . . Sed officium praedicandi, id est publice docendi, non habent nisi missi, id est episcopi et presbyteri in ecclesiis suis, et abbates in monasteriis suis, quibus commissa est cura animarum." (Every man who has intellectual understanding, namely, that which the wicked servant buried in the earth, if he is not a hermit, if he lives among men, has a duty to teach, because he owes it to his brother whom he sees stray from the path of truth and moral behavior to lead him back to the right way by teaching. . . . But the duty to preach, that is to teach publicly, is reserved to those specifically sent: bishops and priests in their churches, and abbots in their monasteries, to whom the care of souls is entrusted.)

[38] Bull of Urban II (*PL*, CLI, 336): "Quosdam accepimus morem vestrorum coenobiorum corrodentes, quod laicos saeculo renuntiantes et se suaque ad communem vitam transferentes, regendos in obedientia suscipitis. Nos autem eamdem conversationem et consuetudinem, sicut oculis nostris inspeximus, laudabilem, et eo perpetua conversatione dignissimam quo in primitivae ecclesiae formam impressa est judicantes, approbamus, sanctam et catholicam nominamus, et per praesentes litteras apostolica auctoritate confirmamus." (We have learned about those who are agitating against the custom of your communities, in which you receive under obedience laymen who renounce the world and devote themselves and their belongings to the common life. However, we approve of this way of life and of this custom, having inspected them as if with our own eyes and found them praiseworthy

Another common though variable trait of this expansion beyond inherited institutions was the rejection of "rules" and traditional conformity in favor of a singular reliance upon the gospel. And since it was the true rule (*regula*) of Christians, the gospel was enough to make *regulares* out of believers. James of Vitry (died 1240), an astute observer of contemporary movements and himself a popular preacher, declared in his history: "In my judgment, it is not only those who renounce the world and go into religion who are *regulares*,

and all the more worthy of being perpetuated for their being cast in the form of the primitive church. We consider them holy and catholic, and by virtue of our apostolic authority we confirm them with this letter.)

Here is the context furnished by Bernold of Constance *Chronicon* (*PL*, CXLVIII, 1407–8; *MGH*, *Scriptores*, V, 453): "His temporibus in regno teutonicorum communis vita multis in locis floruit, non solum in clericis et monachis religiossissime commanentibus, verum etiam in laicis, se et sua ad eandam communem vitam devotissime offerentibus; qui etsi habitu nec clerici nec monachi viderentur, nequaquam tamen eis dispares in meritis fuisse creduntur. . . . Quapropter invidia diaboli contra eorundem fratrum probatissimam conversationem quosdam emulos incitavit, qui eorum vitam malevolo dente corroderent, quamvis ipsos ad formam primitivae ecclesiae communiter vivere viderent. . . . Non solum autem vivorum sed et feminarum innumerabilis multitudo his temporibus se ad hujusmodi vitam contulerunt, ut sub obedientia clericorum sive monachorum communiter viverent, eisque ancillarum quotidiani servicii pensum devotissime persolverent. In ipsis quoque villis filiae rusticorum innumerae, conjugio et seculo abrenunciare et sub alicujus sacerdotis obedientia vivere studuerunt; sed et ipsi conjugati nichilominus religiose vivere et religiosis cum summa devotione non cessaverunt obedire. Hujusmodi autem studium in Alemannia potissimum usquequaque decenter effloruit." (In these times [around 1091], there flourished in many places in the German kingdom the common life, not only among priests and monks committed to religious stability, but indeed among laymen, who offered themselves and their belongings very devotedly to this common life, who although not seen to be dressed as either priests or monks, were by no means to be thought unequal to those in merit. . . . Wherefore the envy of the devil incited certain men to jealousy against the most upright way of life of these brethren and got them to snap at it with the sharp tooth of malice, even though they could see that these brethren were living communally in the pattern of the primitive church. . . . [Bernold here quotes the bull of Urban II, then continues.] An innumerable multitude of women as well as of men took up this kind of life in these times, so that they might live together in obedience to priests or to monks and most faithfully discharge for them the weight of the daily service of auxiliaries. And there were also in these villages countless peasants' daughters who renounced marriage and society to live in obedience to priests. But married people themselves strove to live no less religiously and to obey religious men with great devotion. Moreover, this pursuit, strongest in Germany, flourished impressively everywhere there.) Cf. Mandonnet, II, 186; Larkin, p. 275.

but all the faithful of Christ who serve the Lord under the gospel's rule and live by the orders of the single greatest Abbot or Father of all."[39]

It followed that the definition of the Christian life, far from being shaped about the monastic life as in Rupert of Deutz, on the contrary came to be formulated in its own terms, independent of the peculiarities of this or that state. The monastery could no longer be considered the "city of God" to which one would lead society. Society existed and Christians lived in it; to do so was their calling. Secular callings or states of life were matter for grace and salvation. Quite apart from monastic profession or the clerical state, baptism already constituted a renunciation of the devil and of the "world." "Whoever has renounced at baptism the devil and all his trappings and suggestions, even if that person never becomes a cleric or a monk, has nonetheless definitely renounced the world. . . . Whether rich or poor, noble or serf, merchant or peasant, all who are committed to the Christian faith reject everything inimical to this name and embrace everything conformable to it. Every order and absolutely every profession, in the catholic faith and according to apostolic teaching, has a rule adapted to its character; and under this rule it is possible by striving properly to achieve the crown of glory."[40]

It was not just by chance that this claim for the Christian value—

---

[39] *Libri duo quorum prior orientalis . . . alter occidentalis historiae* (Douai, 1597), p. 357: "Non solum eos qui seculo renunciant et transeunt ad religionem, regulares judicamus, sed et omnes Christi fideles sub evangelica regula Domino famulantes, et ordinate sub uno summo Abbate viventes, possumus dicere regulares."

[40] Gerhoh of Reichersberg *Liber de aedificio Dei* xliii, "Quomodo praefecti vectigalium, judices, milites, aliique, qui propriis renuntiare nolunt, apostolicam regulam sequantur" (How tax administrators, judges, knights, and others not wishing to renounce what is proper to them, should observe the apostolic rule; *PL*, CXCIV, 1302): "Qui in baptismo abrenuntiavit diabolo et omnibus pompis ac suggestionibus ejus, etiamsi nunquam fiat clericus vel monachus, mundo tamen renuntiasse convincitur . . . ut, sive divites sive miseri, nobiles ac servi, mercatores et rustici et omnino cuncti qui christiana professione censentur, illa respuant quae huic inimica sunt nomini, et ea quae sunt apta sectentur. Habet enim omnis ordo, et omnino omnis professio in fide catholica et doctrina apostolica suae qualitati aptam regulam, sub qua legitime certando poterit pervenire ad coronam."

the apostolic value—of all walks of life was presented by a representative of one of the less radical among the new apostolic groups, namely by Gerhoh of Reichersberg (died 1169). "Judges, knights, tax collectors, merchants, and peasants follow the apostolic rule," he said. Gerhoh was the author of the *Liber de aedificio Dei* (*On God's House*) in which he described what was requisite for the construction of the church. Two types of materials were involved in this contruction: the material, properly speaking, consisted of men, those destined for the heavenly city; but there also entered into this edifice, as serviceable for its construction, the entire universe (*tota universitatis structura*), of which no element, however modest, was purposeless. Therefore in the economy of salvation one had to distinguish the final and definitive city of God, which was in course of preparation here below, from the terrestrial institution, embracing all creatures and bound to space and time (what we understand by the historical existence of the church).[41] This distinction, to which theologians in similar circumstances have often turned, is easy to make; but it was very significant in 1130.

Once again in the twelfth century we are at one of the great turning points in the history of western Christian spirituality, at the beginning of what Dom Wilmart called the "religion of modern times." A long road lay ahead of this new consciousness of what it meant to be a Christian. It was soon explicitly propounded from the pulpit, where the idea of vocation was extended by virtue of God's provi-

---

[41] This is the theme of the first chapter of the *Liber de aedificio Dei* i (*PL*, CXCIV, 1193): "Haec est illa magna totius mundi fabrica et quaedam universalis officina, in qua, Deo mirabiliter operante, quoddam aedificium fabricatur, quo peracto, et malleus confringetur et ipsa fabrica secundum statum, quem nunc habere videtur, omnino destruetur. Civitas autem Dei, quae est in electa rationabili creatura, neque nunc neque tunc destruetur, sed nunc aedificatur irrevocabili profectu, et tunc stabit sine defectu. Verum quia constat de futura et permansura istius civitatis stabilitate, nos de temporali statu ejus agamus. . . ." (This is that great workshop of the world, that cosmic factory in which, by the wondrous workings of God, a certain kind of edifice is assembled, and when it has been completed, the tools will be smashed and the factory itself, as we now know it, will be entirely destroyed. Yet the city of God, which exists in the chosen rational creature, shall be destroyed neither now nor later; but irrevocable progress in construction is being made now, and later it shall stand without defect. Indeed since the future and permanent stability of that city is beyond doubt, let us discuss its condition in time.)

dence to the secular states of life without distinction.[42] It was soon propounded by pastors, who worked out a certain evangelical morality for each secular trade and profession. Honorius of Autun included in his *Speculum ecclesiae* (*Mirror of the Church*, before 1121) a sermon *ad milites* (for soldiers), one *ad mercatores* (for merchants), and one *ad agricolas* (for farmers);[43] and, in the thirteenth century, Humbert of Romans, master-general of the Dominican Order, produced a collection of model sermons for these various states.[44] Even the merchants were not omitted, for now they were considered the mainspring of the new commercial economy. Back in the time of the landed stability, the social and economic immobility, of the feudal regime, merchants had been considered as having a base profession (*ignobilis mercatura*)[45] because they neither lived off the land nor fit into a class structure bound by oaths and the rules of vassalage. "You are the servants of all peoples" (*Omnium nationum ministri estis*), said Honorius of Autun, in pointing out the grave risks run by merchants.

---

[42] Cf. N. Paulus, "Die Wertung der weltlichen Berufe im Mittelalter," *HJ*, XXXII (1911), 725–55; also the same author's "Der Berufsgedanke bei Thomas von Aquin," *ZKT*, L (1926), 445–54.

[43] *Speculum ecclesiae*, "Sermo generalis" (*PL*, CLXXII, 865–6).

[44] *De eruditione praedicatorum* ii, "De modo prompte cudendi sermones circa omne hominum et negotiorum genus disseritur" (in P. Despont, ed. *Maxima bibliotheca veterum patrum et antiquorum scriptorum ecclesiasticorum* [Lyon, 1677], XXV, 424–567).

[45] The phrase appears in the anonymous eleventh-century *Vita sancti Guidonis* (*Acta sanctorum*, September, IV, 42). Cf. *Decretum*, I[a] pars, dist. 88, c. 11 (Friedberg, I, 308): "Mercator vix aut nunquam potest Deo placere." (A merchant is rarely or never able to please God.) Honorius of Autun expressed the traditional opinion in his earliest work, *Elucidarium* ii.18, "De variis laicorum statibus" (*PL*, CLXXII, 1148–9; Lefèvre, pp. 428–9): "Quam spem habent mercatores? Parvam, nam fraudibus, perjuriis, lucris omne pene quod habent acquirunt. . . . Quid de agricolis dicis? Ex magna parte salvantur, quia simpliciter vivunt, et populum Dei suo sudore pascunt." (What hope have merchants got? Not much, for they acquire almost all they have by fraud, lying, and greed. . . . What do you say about farmers? For the most part they shall be saved, for they live simply and they nourish God's people by their own hard work.) But seventy-five years later, around 1185, Godfrey of Saint-Victor said, while praising the various trades and crafts in his *Microcosmus* lvii (Delhaye, p. 216): "Ex commerciis mercatorum merces suas de terris in terras transportantium adjuvatur inopia terrarum." (The deficiencies of some areas are made up for from the trade of merchants transporting their goods from one place to another.)

Undoubtedly it was the men who rejected all worldly goods, who devoted themselves to lives of total fraternal dedication, or who embraced an apostolic vocation, that gave sparkle and brilliance to the grace of God. But quite as important were the ordinary people who, observing the basic precepts of Christ without heroism, did no harm to their fellow men, helped the unfortunate, and accomplished their daily tasks. Not only did they thus strive for salvation but by their lives they adorned the church. It was Godfrey of Saint-Victor who expressed such high esteem for the secular life.[46]

Eventually the old image of the church and society became outmoded. A twelfth-century monastic manuscript[47] of the *Moralia in Job* represents this image as a crenellated tower on which there are three figures. In the center stands a priest, dressed, in a magnificent purple cloak, holding a sword in his right hand. To his left stands a knight armed with a sword. And to his right stands a weeping monk. These three of course represent the three orders of the church: the sacerdotal order, carrying the spiritual sword; knighthood, also an order, carrying the temporal sword; and the monastic order, whose only weapon was prayer.

There now took place a curious evolution in the meanings of the terms *ordo* and *status*, a rearrangement in which religious and secular values met. *Ordo*, a term inherited from antiquity, never suggested sacred orders in its early usage; an *ordo* was a division of society, temporal as well as ecclesiastical, but a regular division, in accordance with the divine plan.[48] However, in that Christian society the contents of ideas and institutions tended to become sacralized. The principal case was that of knighthood, a secular profession which in

---

[46] *Ibid.*, cxcvi (Delhaye, p. 216).

[47] MS Troyes 43.

[48] St. Thomas *Summa theologica* Ia pars, q. 108, a. 2 (Aquinas, *Opera omnia*, I, 414; Aquinas, *Summa*, III, 429): "Quae quidem diversitas ordinum secundum diversa officia et actus consideratur, sicut patet quod in una civitate sunt diversi ordines secundum diversos actus, nam alius est ordo judicantium, et alius pugnantium, et alius laborantium in agris, et sic de aliis." (This diversity of orders arises from the diversity of offices and actions, as appears in one city where there are different orders according to the different actions; for there is one order of those who judge, and another of those who fight, and another of those who labor in the fields, and so forth.) [On the meanings of *ordo*, see above, p. 81, n. 60.]

its rites and ideals came more and more under the sacralizing influence of the church. By around 1100 one no longer "made" a knight, instead one "ordained" him.[49] This was at the height of feudal society and the word *ordo* came to be applied in this religious sense to several other occupations as well. But the occupation of merchant, free from personal ties, free from the services imposed by fief-holding, manipulating money without working, was suspect to the regime and thus suspect in the Christendom run by this regime. Merchants did not constitute an *ordo;* they upset the conformist system of ethics which was insensitive to the new market economy. Thus the lending of money for interest, usury, raised serious problems, which were to fill pages of the literature on casuistry.[50] The evangelical groups, who in their poverty fiercely condemned money as a source of corruption, were the very ones who undertook to bring the gospels home to merchants; they were the born chaplains of the guilds.[51] From Peter Waldo to Francis of Assisi, were they not after all in large part recruited from the new, powerful, open, and cultivated milieux of commerce?

Married people, on the other hand, were worthy of classification as an *ordo,* a natural enough religious promotion once the sacramental value of conjugal love was recognized; and this was exactly the time when such full sacramental recognition was to be given to this secular state, if such it is. James of Vitry in his *Historia occidentalis* and Robert of Sorbon in his sermons argued that married people constitute an order. The Dominican William of Perraud in his *Summa virtutum et vitiorum,* which was widely read, listed twelve reasons for attributing this dignity to marriage. The Franciscan Berthold of Ratisbonne went so far as to say: "God has sanctified marriage more than any other order in the world, more than the bare-footed friars, the preaching friars, or the gray monks, who upon one point cannot match holy matrimony; namely, society could

---

[49] Bloch, II, 314–6.

[50] G. LeBras, article "Usure," *DTC*, XV, 2336–72 [cf. Noonan, cited above, p. 155, n. 21].

[51] For the Christian merchant, see the precise discussion and balanced treatment by Jacques LeGoff, *Marchands et banquiers au moyen-âge* (Paris, 1956). The new orders provided the theologians of the market economy (LeGoff, p. 95) as well as of marriage, next discussed.

not do without the latter. God therefore commanded it, whereas the others he merely counseled."[52]

The word *status*, on the other hand, while often a synonym for *ordo*, remained a secular category. Its use increased under the new regime, thanks to the growth of groups and social conditions which obtained juridical definition of their liberties and prerogatives, of their *status* or estate. Not until the fifteenth century did the modern abstract political notion of estate emerge; it still meant condition, situation, position, perhaps even job. These worldly occupations were no longer suited to sacralization, even when they involved oaths. They were answerable, however, to ethics and, before ethics, to the Christian gospel. St. Thomas sought to define them by combining ancient juridical notions with conceptions drawn from contemporary conditions of freedom and servitude; and it was in this sociological framework that he worked out his social ethics, insofar as he systematized one.[53]

The displacement of the boundary between sacred and secular did not strip the kingdom of God on earth of its all-encompassing character, which remained a constant premise of the faith despite these variations in sociological conditioning. On the contrary, this displacement restored to earthly occupations their proper integrity and their peculiar functions within the universal compass of the church; henceforth a clear sense of their objects and their laws of operation was retained. Without detracting from the special vocation of those who devoted themselves exclusively, like the ancient Levites, to the service of the Lord, the lay Christian was a complete Christian; and, even if he had divided interests (I Cor. 7:33), he was an active agent for the construction of the kingdom of God in the world. The famous text of Gratian on the "two kinds of Christians," clerical

---

[52] Cf. G. LeBras, article "Mariage," *DTC,* IX, 2123–224; also N. Paulus, "Mittelalterliche Stimmen über den Eheorden," *Historisch-politische Blätter für das katholische Deutschland,* CXLI (1908), 1008–24.

[53] *Summa theologica* IIa, IIae, q. 183, "De officiis et variis statibus hominum in generali" (Aquinas, *Opera omnia,* III, 612–5; Aquinas, *Summa,* XIV, 145–53). Cf. A. O. Meyer, "Zur Geschichte des Wortes Staat," *Welt und Geschichte,* X (1950), 229–39; G. de Lagarde, *Ockham et son temps* (Paris, 1942), chap. 2, "Structure de la société civile," pp. 67–131; A. Robilliard, "Sur la notion de condition (*status*) en S. Thomas," *RSPT,* XXV (1936), 104–7.

and lay, had given canonical definition to the organizing principle and outlook of an older Christendom which did not fully appreciate the worth, the functions, and the initiatives of the simple believer.[54] Whereas the monastic view of God tended to reduce the truth and the causality inherent in things to little more than symbols or occasions of grace, and hence to reduce the use and enjoyment of things to a concession, the evangelical outlook allowed, and more than that encouraged, the discovery of the laws of nature, an awareness of the demands of reason, and the value of social structures—all within the realm of grace. The evangelical outlook regarded grace as having a unique dominion, but a dominion in which nature, reason, and society as always served faith and grace all the better for not being under some infantile tutelage but autonomous in their methods of operation.[55]

The consequences of this development worked their way into doctrines and institutions slowly. Dante would still envision a static hierarchy where worldly occupations remained the mere substructure supporting a sacralized society. Yet these consequences had immediate repercussions on Christian behavior. The system of monastic worship was evidently ill-suited to the condition of the new Christian in society, to the majority of people, to their culture. Under

---

[54] C. 7, q. 1, c. 12 (Friedberg, I, 678): "Duo sunt genera christianorum. Est autem genus unum, quod mancipatum divino officio, et deditum contemplatione et orationi, ab omni strepitu temporalium, cessare convenit, ut sunt clerici, et Deo devoti, videlicet conversi. Κλῆρος enim graece, latine sors. Inde hujusmodi homines vocantur clerici, id est sorte electi. . . . Aliud vero est genus christianorum ut sunt laici. Λαός enim est populus. His licet temporalia possidere, sed non nisi ad usum. His concessum est uxorem ducere, terram colere, inter virum et virum judicare, causa agere. . . ." (There are two kinds of Christians. One of these, having charge of the divine office and being given to contemplation and prayer, is accustomed to remain away from all the din of secular society. Such are the clerics and those wholly devoted to God, that is the religious. The Greek word κλῆρος [casting of lots, a lot, clergy] means *sors* [casting of lots, a lot] in Latin. And so these men are called clerics, a class of men chosen by lot so to speak. . . . But there is the other kind of Christian; these are laymen. Λαός means people. These are permitted to possess worldly goods, but for use alone. To these it is permitted to marry, to till the soil, to adjudicate among men, to pursue their affairs.)

[55] For a historico-theological perspective on this development, see M.-J. Congar, *Jalons pour une théologie du laïcat* (Paris, 1953), chap. 1, "Moines, clercs et laïcs," pp. 19–45.

pressure from the mass of the faithful, the uniformity of liturgical practice gave way; the monastic or canonical office became something for religious who specialized in worship. There took place an extensive proliferation of popular forms of prayer: chaplets, rosaries, celebration of the joyful mysteries of Mary's life, etc., as well as some contemplative observances. The penitential system was transformed: a new psychological orientation was institutionalized in sacramental confession. The ethical analysis found in the *summae confessorum* (compendiums for confessors), a literary genre which expanded greatly after the Fourth Lateran Council of 1215 and which found its masters among the mendicants, replaced the crude schedules of misdeeds and penances found in the penitential handbooks of earlier centuries. Traditionally the monastic life had been primarily thought of for its penitential value, as providing vicarious penance for all the faithful. Henceforth the religious life was no longer considered primarily as a turning to a state of penance. The distinction between the counsels and precepts of Christ, subtle despite the firmness of its evangelical foundation, stimulated theologians and pastors to engage in lengthy discussions which found their way into the *quaestiones disputatae* and *summae* of the thirteenth century. Developments in ethics absorbed a great deal of attention, particularly the elaboration of a body of secular or lay morality within a religious framework.[56] Extremely suggestive in themselves are the doctrinal analyses and pastoral applications called forth by the objective and subjective adjustment attempted between the "Christian" virtues (e.g., the evangelical virtues of poverty, meekness, compunction, purity, mercy, etc.) and the cardinal virtues of justice, prudence, fortitude, and temperance which were secular in origin and character.

---

[56] The research of P. Delhaye shows the importance and difficulty of this undertaking that went on throughout the twelfth century. Cf. among his works "La place de l'éthique parmi les disciplines scientifiques du XIIᵉ siècle," *Miscellanea moralia A. J. Janssen* (Louvain, 1948), I, 29–44; also his "L'enseignement de la philosophie morale au XIIᵉ siècle," *MS*, XI (1949), 77–99. By itself, the success of the *Moralium dogma philosophorum* (*PL*, CLXXI, 1003–55), both in Latin and in vernacular translations, is significant. [For a review of the vexed question of the authorship and dedication of the *Moralium dogma philosophorum*, see John R. Williams, "The Quest for the Author of the *Moralium Dogma Philosophorum*, 1931–1956," *Spec.* XXXII (1957), 736–47.]

Thus paradoxically those famous apostles, so set against the "world," took charge of men's growing awareness of human values; they introduced and exalted secular values ranging all the way from the demands of conjugal and commercial life to a philosophy of nature and reason.[57] They were the pioneers of a new equilibrium between nature and grace, first in their apostolic experience and then in theology.

The New Equilibrium between
Nature and Grace

One cannot adequately define the potentialities of this new Christian equilibrium in terms simply of the opposition raised against the excesses and errors that here and there compromised it. To be sure, the drives toward naturalism and laicism which were making their appearance from widely different sources in the course of the twelfth century—and beyond that, in the thirteenth century, which saw the indiscriminate condemnations in the famous syllabus of 1277[58]— provoked doctrinal, pastoral, and institutional reactions on the part of the church. Nonetheless it was also within the church, within the limits of its orthodoxy as well as of its established rule, that this equilibrium proved itself adaptable and responsive to the changing conditions of human life. The institutional and spiritual innovations that we have been discussing give striking proof of this. To appreciate their quality and depth, we must turn attention to the sociological causes prompting them from below, under the inspiration and guidance of grace.

The most obvious and general of these circumstances was the calling into question of the feudal forms and customs held to by certain sectors of the church. Among those institutions which concern us here, among those which claimed to lead the *vita apostolica* and to strive for Christian perfection, the monastic order, whose

---

[57] On this merging of an evangelical reform with a renaissance of rationalism, see G. B. Ladner, "Die mittelalterliche Reform-Idee und ihr Verhältnis zur Idee der Renaissance," *MIOG*, LX (1952), 31–59.

[58] *CUP*, I, 543–58 (n. 473, giving a list of the 219 condemned propositions).

temporal success was rooted in that feudal structure, began to lose even its spiritual effectiveness when that structure began to crumble. All the same, the monasteries even more than the episcopal hierarchies had shaped their administrative forms as well as their ideals of holiness by the economic, political, and social life of the feudal domain: predominance of land and cultivation, stability of places and persons, fidelity to oaths, granting of benefices, serfdom, etc. As late as the twelfth century, the granges newly established by monasteries for raising and collecting revenues were themselves transformed into the seigneurial type of exploitation. Cîteaux, which refused tithes and the ownership of churches, was able to de-feudalize neither institutions nor modes of thinking. And now, as the vital centers of civilization shifted, as towns assumed political and economic importance, as markets gave rise to a class of merchants and the perpetual circulation of money and men, as an ever greater number of men escaped feudal ties, as culture developed away from the old monastic schools, as the taste for liberty was aroused along with the fraternal solidarity of guilds and leagues, the approaches and methods of the monasteries no longer suited the needs of the age. Meanwhile prelates and abbots were for the most part insensitive to the immense changes which were taking place, whether peacefully or violently, right before their eyes.

Yet it was precisely in these social contexts that the new apostolic evangelism usually found its leaders, its support, and its tasks. One should certainly not yield, as some have done, to the temptation to transform these movements of highest religious quality into mere secondary effects of a social crisis;[59] this would be to misunderstand the real causes of the apostolic movement, under the pretext of emphasizing the circumstances surrounding it. It was unmistakably the discovery of the gospel which lay behind this development of Christianity, and each of the leaders of this reform movement said so most candidly. But neither were the circumstances wholly incidental phenomena upon which this reform landed, as somebody's private inspiration from heaven; they were an essential ingredient of this new Christianity. As the new groups were formed, they asserted their

---

[59] Cf. Grundmann, pp. 34–35, 157–68.

solidarity with the new elements in society; they did so both by their internal organization and by their pastoral activities. The natural infiltration of Franciscans as well as others into the university corporations suffices to illustrate this crucial fact in the history of civilization and, if one may say so, in the history of grace. It was to insure its own existence and its truth that the church planted itself in the world.

Another occurrence, more profound than these socio-economic ruptures—this time in men's minds—enlarged the context we are studying. During the twelfth century, there appeared an increasingly acute sensitivity to natural phenomena: to the harmony of the cosmos; to the place of man in this universe where his liberty asserted itself amidst certain determinisms of which he was aware; where he was himself a nature; where he tried to exercise his mastery in full consciousness of his own reason for being; where man's autonomy of action was experienced as the condition of his moral perfection, indeed of his religious value.[60]

"The world is an ordered aggregation of creatures," said Master William of Conches.[61] And indeed the world was no longer an incoherent series of phenomena and events, which the pious soul ascribed out of hand to the mysterious and implacable will of a demiurge; it was an organic, homogenous ensemble, the observation of which was not only possible but worthwhile and satisfying. For the mind it was an exciting and precise exercise. Even before philosophy benefited from it, the imagination was astounded by it. Whereas in the preceding century men's imaginations delighted in the epic terms and monstrous visions of romanesque iconography, they were now reproducing elementary and familiar natural images in the gothic cathedrals, images of nature's flora and fauna, of its seasons and its everyday events. They showed real men as well: the carpenter; the wheelwright; the cloth-dyer of Amiens; the laborer especially; in brief, man at his trade taking possession of matter and of the world. "The iconography of the thirteenth century rejected at

---

[60] See above, pp. 1–48.
[61] *Glossa in Timaeum* (Parent, p. 146; Jeauneau, p. 103, cf. p. 125): "Et est mundus ordinata collectio creaturarum."

once visions, the epic, the East, and monsters. It was evangelical, human, western, and natural. It brought Christ down practically to the level of men. . . . of course he remained enthroned on high in the tympanum, presiding over the resurrection of the dead and over eternal punishment; yet even there he remained the Christ of the gospels and retained his human gentleness."[62]

It was not simply by chance that in the portals of Chartres the themes of the creation and the origins of man were so boldly treated; for it was in the schools at Chartres that a philosophy of the world[63] was being worked out, that among the seven arts the study of the quadrivium with its mathematical resources was being pursued with increasing intensity. This interest in physical reality extended as well to man, the "microcosm" in whom the laws and motions of the great universe were mirrored. In treatises on the soul, whether by the mystical Cistercian William of Saint-Thierry or the Chartres naturalist William of Conches, anatomy and physiology took the place of moralizing pseudospiritualism. Even ethics came to be based on nature, whose laws are the rules of well-being and the guarantee of happiness. All of this in their view did not detract from the absolute power of God; for this nature, mistress of the universe, was the expression and "vicar" of the Almighty, in the words of Alan of Lille.[64]

St. Bernard's contempt for the world did not deny the Christian value of these attitudes; it was doubtless even balanced by them, at a time when Christendom tended towards extremes. The various representations at Chartres show the religious depth of this discovery of nature. Of course it would become necessary to condemn the semirationalist ethics of the followers of Gilbert of La Porrée, the exaggerated laicism of the emancipated communes, the perversions of the *Ars amandi* of Ovid that were found in every library, the usurious avarice of the great merchants and bourgeois—excesses, disorders, and errors that were all of a kind in the evolution then

---

[62] H. Focillon, *The Art of the West*, tr. Jean Bony, 2 vols. (London, 1963), vol. 2, "Gothic Art," p. 72.

[63] William of Conches *De philosophia mundi* (*PL*, CLXXII, 39–102); Bernard Sylvester *De universitate mundi* (Barach and Wrobel).

[64] Cf. Paré, chap. 5, "La confession de Nature et l'allégorie de Nature," pp. 327–46.

taking place. The ecclesiastical establishment denounced these disorders and excesses, but those who confronted them directly were the *pauperes Christi,* who, by being present in the world, discovered its needs, assessed its worth, shared its aspirations, and at the same time, by unyielding loyalty to the gospel, testified against its errors. But these errors and excesses were merely perversions of the new spirit whose less respectable partisans were at work even within the most profoundly Christian institutions and precisely within the evangelical revival with all its creative fervor.

In the controversy which for nearly three decades has turned about the ambiguous concept "Christian philosophy," historians of the Middle Ages have brought into sharp focus the effectiveness of Christian revelation—apart from its religious potential—in arousing men's minds to problems which were themselves rational and secular. Revelation provided more than an external corrective to mistakes in philosophical speculation; it inspired men of faith to produce a frame of reference which served them in their rational constructions no less than in their art or culture. Neither the essential disparity between philosophy and religion nor the transcendence theology assigned to faith limited the possibilities of a Christian exercise of reason, without faith in any way supplanting reason or perverting the workings of the rational process.

The influence of Christian revelation upon the development of thought was by no means limited to theoretical knowledge. Art and letters and culture manifested the same solidarity with faith while preserving the same autonomy in their methods. All secular values experienced the same thing at the moment when, like philosophy, they were acquiring an independence which raised more problems than it solved. One will see this vital interaction between traditional faith and new secular values whenever men collectively discover, in and about themselves, values which have long lain dormant. It is not simply a question of a type of moral control exercised from without by a susceptible faith upon the wicked progress of civilization; it is instead a matter of positive inspiration motivated only by the sensitivity of faith—and, let us add, in the language of the gospel, of hope and of love—to the realities of a developing world.

This evangelical sensitivity was at work in the twelfth-century church at every encounter between the church and the world, and to the benefit of both. This encounter was accomplished as always by a pure and simple testimony more than by the apparatus of a Christianity made powerful but compromised by its establishments. The gospel was the leaven in the dough; but the leaven, through too much kneading, seemed to have lost its effect. Now it regained its original force. Poverty made the necessary break, for it represented both a rejection of the avarice and vanity of the new world and a liberation from the temporal security of the old regime. Here was the fullest manifestation of the Holy Spirit's presence, expressed in a sensitive awareness of human affairs whose very structures dictate the forms grace will take in the world. Thus it involved more than moral purification inspired by the good will of reformers; the twelfth century already had enough of that. It involved the shaping of an evangelical truth to a determined socio-economic form. The fervent fidelity of Rupert of Deutz was not, of itself, of less quality than the itinerant enthusiasm of Norbert of Xanten, nor was the rude life of the Cistercians any less self-denying than that of the Poor Men of Lyon or of the Humiliati of Lombardy; but the latter in each case simply settled down in a different world, with which it was necessary to be in communication in order to address to it the word of God. The invectives of Stephen of Tournai, the great abbot of Sainte-Geneviève of Paris (1177-92) and bishop of Tournai (1192-1203), against the communes and the new theologians,[65] and the strained reserve of the monastic historian Matthew Paris (1195-1259) towards the mendicant orders gave indirect and further proof of the necessity for such communication.

The paradox begins to clear up when we see that the apostolic

---

[65] *Epp.* cxcv (*PL*, CCXI, 478): "Tria sunt murmurantia super terram, et quartum quod facile non quiescit: communia rusticorum dominantium, cetus feminarum litigantium, grex porcorum ad unius clamorem grunnientium, capitulum diversa vota sectantium. Cum primo pugnamus, secundum irridemus, tercium contempnimus, quartum sustinemus; a primo et quarto, libera nos, Domine." (There are three sources of grumbling on earth, and a fourth which is not easily silenced: communes under the control of peasants, a pack of quarreling women, a herd of pigs all grunting at once, and a chapter torn by conflict. With the first we fight, with the second we get a good laugh, the third we ignore, and the fourth we endure. Deliver us, O Lord, from the first and fourth.) See below, p. 299, n. 64, and also p. 311, n. 4.

reformers became the theologians of this new Christianity: the Franciscan St. Bonaventure and the Dominican St. Thomas Aquinas became, though in very different styles, its leading intellectual spokesmen. Of all these secular values, no less recognized or admired for having been appropriated by the gospel, the first and most captivating was certainly reason—mistress of nature and rule of thought. Through reason, the dialectic between the gospel and the world penetrated beyond apostolic action to the innermost reaches of the faith, where it kindled a constructive new vigor. No longer did men simply comment on sacred texts, or explain them in homilies, catechisms, or glosses, or arrange them in a coherent order so as to elucidate sacred history—not even, as at Saint-Victor, to construct on the basis of this history an allegorical edifice by clothing the events of the sacred past with a typological interpretation. Henceforth men wished, in the light of faith and by using the heritage of revelation, to intellectualize and systematize their beliefs and to explain the word of God in a human way. As the incarnation of divine truth in the human mind, faith was not some extraordinary charisma whose transcendence would keep it above human modes of thought. Faith put to work the various resources of reason, thus introducing them into the mystery of God. By engendering a theology, faith was achieving its logical perfection.

Theology thus became equipped with a scientific discipline, and the more rational and searching minds of the age exercised their powers in the light of faith. At the same time the social enterprises of the communes and corporations became the spiritual charge of the new religious orders. Thus in the temporal order grace achieved a signal success, and nowhere more than in the universities, where theology was the queen of the sciences. Theology, the theological science, was conceivable and attainable only by and in a faith that was content to yield a total obedience to the word of God and its authorized spokesmen; but it could reach its fullest development only if this faith, supplied with technically developed rational means, were to use these means to promote that development. There was a wondrous effusion of the Spirit in these men whose theology gave reason full citizenship in the religious life. Theology was a science. The gospel had engendered scholasticism. Later imperfections could compromise neither its Christian value nor its scientific truth. And if it was to be justifiably condemned later on for insensitivity to new developments, that is because it was being untrue to its origins.

This did not mean that "monastic theology" had to be abandoned or that one had to grant everything to that opponent of Rupert whose radical evolutionism had so displeased the *ordo monasticus*. The values of the old theology were lasting, and a scholasticism that would slight them—as happened sometimes—would cut its own roots. Still valid, however traditionally expressed, were the questions to which Rupert demanded answers as he went to encounter the masters of the new schools, William of Champeaux and Anselm,[66] and to espouse, in discussing the problem of evil against their subtle presentations, the permanence of mystery and the open, unpretentious confession of faith in the goodness of the Father in heaven.[67] Still valid, despite their passionate rhetoric, were the diatribes of St. Bernard against the pretentious and too clever dialectic of Abelard who neglected the mysterious *via negativa* of all theology. Still valid was the appeal of the conservatives at the Fourth Lateran Council—those who had challenged the evangelical enterprises and the new religious orders—who declared, "There is less of a similarity between creatures and the Creator than of a dissimilarity,"[68] and that consequently the mystery of God was impermeable to reason. Theology was thus a kind of wisdom more truly than it was a science, and the theologian could never be more than a professor, i.e., one who professes. Herein lay both the triumph and the defeat of theology. A scientific approach must be used to build the spiritual and temporal framework of Christendom in any age—and such an approach triumphed in the thirteenth century. But it could continue triumphant only if it continued evangelical, always carrying the word of God as a message, returning always to the ancient testimonies, resisting the subjection of mystery to an irresponsible scientism, preserving a free

---

[66] See below, p. 270, the quotation which introduces "The Masters of the Theological 'Science.'"

[67] *De voluntate Dei* ii (*PL*, CLXX, 438); *De omnipotentia Dei* xxiii–xxiv (*PL*, CLXX, 473–4).

[68] Cap. ii (Mansi, XXII, 986): "Inter creatorem et creaturam, non potest tanta similitudo notari, quin inter eos major sit dissimilitudo notanda."

and close relationship with faith even while pursuing the most rigorous investigations.

Conclusion

The evolution of three states of life—monks, canons, and laymen —in the church of the twelfth and thirteenth centuries has led us to stake out the lines of an evangelical revival which, within a single century and amidst the most delicate tensions, achieved its state of perfection, including even a mature theology. To see clearly the connection between start and finish in this revival, we have had to isolate the elements out of which the framework of life and thought were constructed in the church of the twelfth century. Despite the identity between the church's mission and its government, neither the life nor the thought of the kingdom of God developed according to an abstract, uniform design. The diversity of the church's manifestations was essential to that kingdom, yet did not diminish its transcendence.

The heart of this paradoxical situation can be seen in the dialectic between the gospel and world. This dialectic evoked a dual response from the individual Christian as he both returned to the gospel and remained in the world. A dual response and not two responses, for history shows that it was the Christian's return to the gospel which guaranteed his presence in the world and that it was this presence in the world which secured the efficacy of the gospel. Each time there has been an important new discovery of nature or a new historical era, the church of Christ has accommodated to that discovery or that new era—as it first did in the apostolic age—thanks to its evangelical purity and liberty.

When St. Thomas Aquinas defined the transcendence of grace by invoking the Aristotelian idea of nature, he was not merely making a reasoned option in favor of the Philosopher. Rather he was giving supreme expression to that Christianity in which a return to the gospel had secured for the believer a presence in the world, for the theologian a mature awareness of nature, and for the apostle an effective appreciation of man.

7

The Evangelical Awakening

"IF ANYONE SHOULD ask you to what religious order you belong, tell him the order of the gospel, which is the basis of all rules. And let this always be your answer to any inquirers. As for me, I would not allow myself to be called a monk, or a canon, or a hermit; these titles are so exalted and holy that it would be presumptuous to apply any of them to myself."[1] This was the firm resolution of Stephen of Muret, leader of the self-styled *pauperes Christi*, a group which became the order of Grandmont. Stephen died in 1124, but countless episodes and nearly a century had passed before his resolution assumed institutional form. At that time, though Innocent III was bound by the canons of the Fourth Lateran Council to admit no new orders, Francis of Assisi came before him to plead: "I do not come here with a new rule; my only rule is the gospel." Thus did the gospel confirm its inalienable vitality and relevance, in galvanizing both human understanding and even ecclesiastical foundations. It is the common inspiration of all Christians of all times and all milieux, but its abrupt recrudescence periodically provokes a spiritual and institutional crisis, against which it is clearly preferable to measure the pace and standards of the life of the church.

This particular opening of a new evangelical period was marked by an acute sensitivity to the appearance and to the forms of the primitive church. With its poverty and humility, the religious life of the primitive church became an ideal, indeed a sort of mystique

---

[1] Stephen of Muret *Sermo de unitate diversarum regularum*, cited in E. Martène *De antiquis ecclesiae ritibus* (Antwerp, 1738), IV, 877.

that engaged the productive energies of men.[2] Often it served a violent reform movement, and occasionally a lunatic fringe. In the midst of the twelfth century, when there flourished a politically involved and propertied church, ever ready to engage in diplomatic or even military ventures, Otto of Freising asked which was preferable for the church: the humility and poverty of the primitive period or the grandeur of the present. The earlier condition, he replied with melancholy, was better, but the second was more agreeable.[3] That Otto, member and chief apologist of the imperial family, should have taken that position is no surprise; but a generation was about to appear which would not consent to an "agreeable" church, which instead aspired to restore it to its primitive state. This aspiration not only provoked a drive to moral reform, but also nourished a deep inquiry into the Christian faith that brought significant advances in theology.

The Social Context of Apostolic Poverty

For a century already, from the original impetus given it by Gregory VII, this evangelical revival had tended increasingly to take institutional form, carrying its demands beyond moral reform to reform of the political and economic structure of society. Liturgical reform was brought about as well, both by a return to early Christian practices and by a loosening of the hitherto rigid clerical caste sys-

---

[2] From many available facts and accounts it suffices to cite a particularly qualified text of James of Vitry, witness and historian of the period (his *Historia occidentalis* contains a celebrated description of the apostolic movements), who declared in a model sermon designed for regular canons: ". . . tempore scilicet primitivae Ecclesiae et Apostolorum. In eis [ordinibus] enim ad statum priorem Ecclesia reformatur, quando omnia temporalia tanquam stercora reputabant. . . ." (the time of the primitive church and of the apostles. In these orders, the church is restored to its original condition, when all worldly things were regarded as dung.) Text cited in Mandonnet, I, 236; II, 197–8; Larkin, pp. 286–7.

[3] *Chronica* iv prol. (Lammers-Schmidt, p. 294; Mierow, p. 274): "Ego enim, ut de meo sensu loquar, utrum Deo magis placeat haec ecclesiae suae, quae nunc cernitur, exaltatio quam prior humiliatio, prorsus ignorare me profiteor. Videtur quidem status ille fuisse melior, iste felicior." (Speaking frankly, I do not really know whether the current prosperous condition of the church is more pleasing to God than its earlier humility. That earlier condition was perhaps better but the present one is more agreeable.)

tem. The canonical movement in the twelfth century launched this program into a social and ecclesiastical sphere, thereby assuring its success and expanding its intellectual and institutional dimensions well beyond those conceived by the Gregorian reformers. The *vita apostolica* (apostolic life), a juridical as well as a spiritual concept, became the principal theme of the new movement. Thus fortified, the movement deprived the monastic order of its traditional primacy, precisely on the ground of its own derivation from the early church, and also because it was so much better received by a new society which cried out for baptism. By proselytising in the cities, the new reformers transubstantiated the Gregorian ideal; and the remarkably long list of their foundations covering a half-century demonstrates the extent and variety of the renewal they achieved.

The movement itself was in turn expanded and greatly strengthened by the proliferation of groups of laymen who, though part of the new society, had sufficiently broken with the world to proclaim the absolute and literal value of the gospel—and to proclaim it even at the risk of causing institutions fundamental to the church to be questioned. The story of these groups is well known. To the great benefit of the word of God, they led to the formation of numerous orders of "poor men" on the eve of the Lateran Council, and shortly thereafter to the foundation of the mendicant orders, which not only brought evangelism and the church into happy equilibrium but, in the field of *doctrina sacra* (sacred teaching), blended study of the Bible with theological construction.

If I call attention to this conjunction of evangelism and the church, of Bible study and theological construction, it is because there was latent within it great potential for doctrinal development. This potential stemmed from the vital sources of the faith itself, and not so much from the appropriation by this faith of rational methods that could equip it to cope with the developing renaissance of secular culture and thought. Aristotle was not the prime mover in the evolution of sacred doctrine any more than, in the case of St. Francis, it was sociopolitical aspiration which determined the lay, apostolic movement, even where he took over that aspiration and evangelized it.

It would be well to review the principal traits of this conjunction, traits which gave institutional shape to this heralding of the word of

God. The point of impact was obviously poverty, considered now not merely as moral asceticism among members of a fraternity that held their goods in common, but as the proper institutional condition of the kingdom of God in this world. Such an outlook was not unambiguous, as the facts show; but at least it went well beyond the political provisions of the Concordat of Worms (1122). In distinguishing between temporal and spiritual investiture, the Concordat preserved by law the essential ecclesiastical institutions, to the benefit of their liberty, and accommodated the Gregorian demands to the feudal regime, which was, after all, accepted by the church itself. The "poor men," however, sought the liberty of the church, not any longer in terms of delicate feudal arrangements, but in the disengagement of the church from a situation wherein supposedly apostolic institutions had assumed the forms and in turn the mentality of temporal society. That great feudal prince, Innocent III himself, lent these "poor men" his support and, after administering appropriate correction, gave them status in a church where episcopal princes had once fought against the reforms of Gregory VII. Innocent reconciled the Humiliati, communities consisting mainly of artisans, but having a few priests; he authorized the Poor Catholics of Durand of Huesca; and at Milan he protected Bernard Prim against the local clergy, placing him "under the protection of St. Peter."

Moreover this conjunction of poverty and Christian liberty found its theatre and effectiveness among that clientele of the church which was susceptible to the apostolic message, among the poor who became the privileged object of its ministry. All of the new apostles, from Robert of Arbrisselles (died 1117) to Francis of Assisi, addressed their wonderful message to the little people of the shops and the cellars—"in the winecellars, in weavers' shops, and in other such subterranean hovels" (*in cellariis et textrinis et hujusmodi subterraneis domibus*)—to the unfortunate ones with neither fire nor shelter, to the serfs bound to the soil. "Robert preached the gospel to the poor, he called the poor, he gathered the poor together."[4]

---

[4] "Iste [Robertus] revere pauperibus evangelizavit, pauperes vocavit, pauperes collegit" (*PL*, CLXII, 1055).

It was not, however, only economic poverty which was in question here but, more than that, the social poverty of those who for one reason or another were living on the fringes of society—feudal society based on territorial stability—and who were consequently outlaws. Such, to begin with, were the merchants who had abandoned all feudal ties. They were ready customers for itinerant preachers who, in similar fashion, had broken with the system of ecclesiastical benefices, including the possession of churches. It was precisely this break that led to the practice of mendicant poverty by such preachers. Going out to beg for food became for them merely a way to get a footing among those groups who were sympathetic with their new style of life. The lay apostolic movement developed in this new urban class, tied to the economy of the market and of trade, not without resentment against feudal society. Cadet sons without land, progeny who in the overpopulation of the twelfth century could find neither status nor property and who thus organized their lives on the margins of society, wage earners living on commerce, dusty-footed (piepowder) merchants—all these constituted a homogeneous milieu for the "poor men" of Christ. Peter Waldo was the son of a merchant from Lyon, and Francis the son of a cloth-maker from Assisi, one among those cloth-makers who, as a group, were noted above others for a critical spirit that included a sharp anticlericalism directed against feudal prelates and rich monasteries.

A few nobles and rich men entered into the movement, however, as against the great majority of feudal lords, lay and clerical, who sought to rid their Christendom of these dangerous reformers. Some entered into it by a sudden and total conversion; others supported it in local struggles against their adversaries, not without political advantage to themselves; in both cases they attacked what they had long held dear. Intellectual circles became especially involved, in particular the clientele of the rapidly growing urban schools of which the University of Paris would become, early in the thirteenth century, the prototypical fulfillment. As always, students were at the center of a most active ferment in which intellectual culture and fresh spirituality collaborated and even produced new institutions. In 1201 the Order of the Valley of Students was founded by William Langlois and three other doctors of Paris, with thirty-seven students, all committed to the total rejection of property and of temporal lordship.

Thus poverty, beyond its ascetic purport, emerged as a disruptive force in this social agglomeration known as feudal Christendom, so that in fact the church had to use interdicts to protect the feudal regime from which it benefited. It is not as if the "poor men" of Christ attacked social problems directly. It was their evangelical purity that set their objective; and the temporal effects of their striving toward that objective, however powerful these were in the civilization then emerging, were not at all the determining factor in their inspiration. All this, as it turned out, did not keep their poverty from being formidable and double-edged—so effective a dissolvent was their rejection of earthly goods. Seen in this light, papal policy, in the course of several apparently incoherent steps, demonstrated an admirable faculty for selecting the pure and well-balanced parts of an evangelical reformism whose socially disruptive elements menaced the church as much as they did civil society.

The most telling and most characteristic trait of this poverty was sensitivity to the distress of sinners, the poor among the poor before the Lord, for such sensitivity, too, was an integral part of the evangelical life. Vitalis of Mortain, a hermit-preacher of the early twelfth century, specialized in bringing women of ill-repute back to a virtuous life. Henry of Lausanne, to whose career St. Bernard called attention, exhorted his listeners to marry prostitutes in order to save them. Fulks of Neuilly also, in the late twelfth century, dedicated much of his preaching effort to the saving of prostitutes.

The preaching of the word of God was central to this evangelical revival and determined the spiritual and social shape it took; and the *vita apostolica*, in the new sense of the term, governed the whole of this preaching, its inspiration as well as its formal structures. This portion of the program succeeded, for after the papacy had been insisting emphatically on the importance and necessity of preaching for a half-century, the Christian people were finally going to hear the gospel. Peter the Chanter had denounced the "most dreadful silence" (*pessima taciturnitas*) of the clergy, and both Peter and Innocent III had invoked a phrase from Isaiah (56:10) to repudiate "these muted dogs who don't have it in them to bark" (*canes muti*

244

non valentes latrare).[5] But in fact, neither the episcopacy nor the monastic orders, not even Cîteaux, had the desire or the means to take on this mission. The story is well known, indeed its import has been overinflated, of how Dominic relieved the Cistercian mission to Narbonne and established in its place, instead of the machinery of the prelates with their political procedures, a program based on Luke 9:1-6 and 10:1-16: "acting and preaching as had the master, going on foot, without gold and without silver, imitating in everything the way of the apostles." As for the prelates and monks, they were not only, or always, ignorant or even lacking in zeal; rather, they were somehow unable to speak the same language as these Christian people. With their feudal orientation, these prelates and monks felt completely turned about in urban society as if they were in a strange land, whereas the new apostles bore their testimony among men with whom they had established close human relationships and of whom they had intimate knowledge.

No less important for this social context were the institutional forms into which the apostolic movement more or less rapidly crystalized. Their variety and their maneuverability in encounter render classification difficult; but, looking over the movement as a whole and despite crossbreeding in it, one can discern two basic patterns of foundation on the level of action in the church. One was a special adaptation of the christianized feudal institution of knighthood; the Knights Templar and Knights of the Holy Sepulchre served, both within Christendom and on its frontiers, as a militia of Christ, with the approval and active support of St. Bernard. The other was the fraternity, the penitential order, based on institutional poverty, lacking a hierarchy of authority, owning no material possessions, disaffected from the trappings of ecclesiastical life—even from the traditional liturgy—in brief, little inclined to conform to any classical patterns.

The final trait, of yet more dubious value, in this social disestablishment of the church was one which sometimes seriously compromised the very truth of the unbreakable tie between the Holy Spirit and the

---

[5] Peter the Chanter *Verbum abbreviatum* lxii (*PL*, CCV, 189); Innocent III *Reg.* iii.24 (*PL*, CCXIV, 904). Cf. above, pp. 202–38.

visible church. The evangelical revival represented for some the work of the Holy Spirit operating through earthly agencies in a church henceforth purged of all worldly defect and headed towards the end of time. As formerly in the Old Testament, so now again the poor were the born prophets of the messianic kingdom; and in the New Testament, it was the Book of the Apocalypse which nourished hopes and odd desires, not all of them healthy. This it did not so much by its predictions, which fostered temptations to millenarism, as by the promise of an eternal judgment upon the contingencies of time. In the divine plan, the best means were not to be confused with ends, nor were external forms to be observed for their own sake. From Peter Damian and the Gregorian reform to Francis of Assisi and the mendicant orders, a continuous prophetic tradition held many people firm in their resolve not to compromise, for example, in their resistance to formalism. The first generations of Franciscans and Dominicans exploited to their advantage the views of Joachim of Floris. But the very mention of the name of this Calabrian monk recalls the spurious value of the prophetic bent of the "poor men" of Christ. It also recalls the discernment of the Roman Church which, while respectful of personal sanctity, was determined to protect the authentic institutional guardians of the biblical and sacramental heritage against extravagant spiritualist movements.[6]

The Evangelical Theology

It is desirable to abstract the doctrinal implications of these apostolic impulses and activities; for the new apostles, whether in groups or as individuals, elaborated their faith in a self-conscious, organic system of theology. Indeed it was the faith itself which was in question in the evangelical message and the tensions it stirred up. Though seemingly little inclined to intellectualism, these "poor men" of Christ

---

[6] For a bibliography of numerous works on "apostolic" heresies, see L. Sommariva, "Studi recenti sulle eresie medievali (1939–52)," *Rivista storica italiana*, LXIV (1952), pp. 237–68. [Cf. J. B. Russell, "Interpretations of the Origins of Medieval Heresy," *MS*, XXV (1963), 26–53; J. B. Russell, *Dissent and Reform in the Early Middle Ages* (Berkeley and Los Angeles, 1965); and Raffaello Morghen, "Problèmes sur l'origine de l'hérésie au moyen âge, *RH*, CCXXXVI (1966), 1–16.]

were to revitalize the resources of theology, even in the schools. They were the ones who would become tomorrow's masters in the new universities, leaving monastic traditionalism to its fate, while creating within the church a new theological method as well as a new exemplar of sanctity.

If the *vita apostolica*, in the literal sense of the term, was the decisive force and model of these new groups, it was because the word of God took priority in their thought as in their zeal. Alan of Lille, in his brief tract on the art of preaching, undoubtedly based on his missionary experience among the Cathari (after 1185), placed preaching at the top of his ladder of perfection, as the seventh degree, over the investigation of doubts (fifth degree), and the exposition of sacred scripture (sixth degree), a marked change for those familiar with the usual categories of the classical ladder.[7]

This awakening to preaching towards the close of the twelfth century, an awakening which led to the founding of an Order of Preachers, is all the more striking when compared with the deadly silence that prevailed in the church during the previous decades despite pathetic appeals from Rome. The awakening to preaching was not simply the result of zeal—the Cistercians had surely had enough of that—but the concomitant effect of Christian witness as such, for the letter of the gospel insured a radical dynamism of spirit. For St. Francis, the gospel was, in absolute terms, the rule of his religious fraternity; and one had to read it and practice it *sine glossa*; that is, without any of those explanations which dilute the meaning in order to accommodate it to passing conditions.[8] Personal witness was the

---

[7] *Summa de arte praedicatoria* praef. (*PL*, CCX, 111). [The ladders, for example, of St. Benedict, St. Bernard, and Hugh of Saint-Victor, though not identical, have in common their goal of personal perfection, whereas the ladder of Alan has a social orientation. For Benedict, see *Regula monachorum* vii (J. McCann, ed. [London, 1952], pp. 36–49); for Bernard see G. B. Burch, tr., *The Steps of Humility* (Cambridge, Mass., 1940); for Hugh, see the *Didascalicon* v.9, 10 (Buttimer, pp. 109–12; Taylor, pp. 132–4).]

[8] Cf. the *Testamentum* of St. Francis (D. Vorreux, ed. *Les opuscules de Saint François d'Assise* [Paris, 1955], pp. 152–4): "ut non mittant glossas in regula neque in istis verbis dicendo 'Ita volunt intelligi'; sed, sicut dedit mihi Dominus simpliciter et pure dicere et scribere regulam et ista verba, ita simpliciter et sine glossa intelligatis et cum sancta operatione observetis usque in finem" (let them not add glosses to the rule or to my words here, saying: 'This

only suitable medium for this communication; it existed only by and in an exchange where the sociological situation rendered human dialogue possible. The evolution of preaching during this century, leaving aside those geniuses who would excel in any period, expressed this law singularly well. It would be misleading to pay attention only to little episodes, after the fashion of chroniclers and hagiographers, without appreciating the broad significance of preaching for both institutional life and theology. Moreover, in official documents as well as in solemn pronouncements by the leaders of the movement, the very phrases of the gospel regained their original sharpness and their compelling force. The apostolic letters of Innocent III contain, beneath their legal language, some flashes that are as striking and forceful as the appeals of St. Bernard or the prophecies of Joachim of Floris.

The needs arising from preaching the word in true apostolic fashion led not only to a broad diffusion of biblical texts but to translations of at least parts of the Bible into the vernacular languages. The history of these versions has been studied at great length.[9] The fact of such translations, exemplified by the translation made by Peter Waldo and presented to the pope in 1179, is recalled here only for the spiritual, apostolic, and doctrinal principle it implied, and implied far more forcefully than would a legal pronouncement on Bible reading. Innocent III made official note of this fact and these implications as well as of the conditions governing the use of scriptural translations in the church, as against all the procedures followed in conventicles. He took such a stance in his famous letter to the faithful at Metz in 1199, and this in turn became general church policy by its insertion in the Decretals.[10] The University of Paris was soon to undertake a translation of the entire Bible after completing a revision of the Latin text in 1226.

---

is what they mean'; rather, just as God gave it to me to speak simply and purely, and to write the rule and these words, so should you understand them simply and without glosses, and so should you keep them to the very end in holy conduct.) [For the pejorative meaning of *glossa*, already signifying "glossing over," see Smalley, p. 271.]

[9] See, for example, H. Rost, *Die Bibel im Mittelalter. Beiträge zur Geschichte und Bibliographie der Bibel* (Augsburg, 1939).

[10] Innocent III *Reg.* ii.141 (*PL*, CCXIV, 695); *Decretal.* lib. 5, tit. 7, c. 12 (Friedberg, II, 784–7). "The very terms of this juridical text," comments M.-J.

To keep these principles in balanced perspective, one should note that since the diffusion of the gospel was a pastoral task, it was tied to the conditions of pastoral enterprise, i.e., it tended, in the twelfth century, to be spread as much by the spoken word, by visual representations, and by liturgical drama and spectacle, as by the written and read text, or perhaps more. Thus, between 1168 and 1175, the bishop of Paris, Maurice of Sully, published a series of homilies which he had given each Sunday, first summarizing and then commenting upon the gospel; these soon gained wide distribution in French and other languages.[11]

The pontiffs' insistence on the urgency of sacred teaching is not to be seen strictly as an insistence upon the founding of schools, but, as was everywhere evident, and typically in the affair of the Humiliati,[12] as an insistence upon the preaching of the gospel, a task which various preparatory agencies came to subserve. In this way theology came into the service of preaching the word of Christ to the Christian people; and this reinforced the *vita apostolica*, which met its responsibilities more and more as the Christian people became increasingly aware of their needs by their access to the scriptures.

Congar, *Jalons pour une théologie du laïcat* (Paris, 1953), p. 437, "and all that we know, furthermore, of the open attitude of Innocent III (cf. Grundmann, pp. 70–72; 87; 100, n. 55; 114, n. 89; 129) show that L. Hardick is correct in ascribing to Innocent a sort of inner joy and receptiveness." Cf. L. Hardick, "Franziscus, die Wende der mittelalterlichen Frömmigkeit," *Wissenschaft und Weisheit*, XIII (1950), 135. It would be easy to document with contemporary testimonies the judgment of Innocent III on the danger represented by these conventicles, in which an ignorant man would set himself up as a learned authority. See, for example, the *Débat d'Yzarn et de Sicart*, ed. P. Meyer (Nogent-le-Rotrou, 1880), cited by P. Alphandéry, *Les idées morales chez les hétérodoxes latins au début du XIIIᵉ siècle* (Paris, 1903), p. 91. The Waldensians, who prescribed learning scripture by heart, urged their faithful to preach, claiming to follow the message of James 4:17. Cf. G. de Lagarde, *La naissance de l'esprit laïque au déclin du moyen âge*, I (Paris, 1956), 82–90.

[11] C. A. Robson, *Maurice de Sully and the Medieval Vernacular Homily, with the Text of Maurice's French Homilies* (Oxford, 1952).

[12] Excommunicated by Lucius III in 1184, the Humiliati, who represented in northern Italy a phenomenon similar to that of the Waldensians in southern France, were reconciled in 1201 by Innocent III who gave them—even laymen —the power to preach; i.e., to give witness to faith (*verbum exhortationis*) but not to teach doctrine (*articuli fidei*). The Humiliati then organized schools to offer training in this giving of witness.

Another indication of the same concerns and needs, but in another sector, is seen in the widespread popularity of the *Historia scholastica* of Peter Comestor (died c. 1179), both in its Latin form, which circulated in various redactions, and in several translations as well. This history sanctioned and extended the current usage, in the schools and in preaching, of the historical-literal method of Saint-Victor; it was to become, along with the *Sentences* (but without provoking controversy as Peter Lombard's work had done), one of the basic books of the century. The *magister historiarum* should not be separated from the *magister sententiarum*. Its importance can be seen, for example, in Anthony of Padua (died 1231), who in his sermons, despite occasional contaminations of allegory, frequently cited the *Historia* of Comestor and in fact relied upon it extensively. The biblical reform of the Victorines thus lent a scientific support to the evangelical movement. It furnished the elements for a transition from the monastic interpretation of the Bible (in the *collatio*, collection and comparison of texts) to the scriptural theology of the mendicants (in the *lectio*, systematic explication by their masters).

For the *magister in sacra pagina* (master who taught scripture) was not, as an expositor of scripture, in every respect a direct descendent of the *abbas* (abbot), of whom St. Gregory remained the venerated prototype. To be sure, as between abbot and master, a continuity of aim and of scriptural faith remained, but not without a certain evolution in method that paralleled the transition from monastic to scholastic theology. When Philip of Harvengt (died c. 1182), abbot of the Premonstratensian monastery of Bonne Espérance near Cambrai, addressed students in Paris, he did not seem to perceive this evolution, for he gave them an exhortation that would have been suitable for monks: "Schola claustrum alterum dici debet" (The school ought to be considered another cloister).[13] But the Parisian

---

[13] *Epp.* xviii (*PL*, CCIII, 158–9). Cf. *ibid.* iii (*PL*, CCIII, 31): ". . . volo te non tam litteraliter quam spiritualiter erudiri, sic scripturas capere, ut internam illarum dulcedinem diligas experiri." (I want you to become not so much textually educated as spiritually formed, to study scripture in such a way that you will love tasting its inner sweetness;) also *ibid.* xx (*PL*, CCIII, 165): ". . . habes quod ad refocillandum animam expedire perhibetur, divinae series lectionis." (You have the means for rekindling your soul—repeated reading of scripture.)

master Robert of Courçon, who prepared his *Summa* between 1204 and 1207, declared that "whoever reads out the sacred scripture in public chooses for himself a path of greater perfection than does any monk from Clairvaux."[14] In the generation between these two men, the influence of the evangelical awakening of the *vita apostolica* intervened, following upon the work of the regular canons and the doctrinal enterprises of the three great masters Peter Comestor, Peter the Chanter, and Stephen Langton. In the same interval, the ministry of the word of God regained, in various forms and before various audiences popular and scholarly, the dynamism of its dialogue with the world. Its regained dynamism took the form of proclaiming the gospel, controversy with heretics,[15] and the absorption of reason into theology. The persistence of old literary genres and intellectual traditions, themselves good and useful, partially concealed this new dynamism; yet it was not to be without effect on the treatment of the word of God, which was at work like a leaven in the minds of the faithful.

We have elsewhere remarked on the close bond existing between the evangelical movement and the flowering of the *quaestiones* in the biblical *lectio* and culminating in scholastic theology, principal instance of the tie between grace and nature among these theologian-apostles. It is no accident that these mendicants turned out to be both the harbingers of the new Christianity and the masters of the new universities.[16] The transformation that was accomplished at the same time in scriptural understanding (biblical theology, we would call it today) was more subtle, but not less significant. The pivotal point of this transformation was the essential relationship between the fundamental literal sense and the construed spiritual sense as it had been

---

[14] MS Paris BN lat. 14524, fol. 74, cited by C. Dickson, "Le cardinal Robert de Courçon, sa vie," *AHDL*, IX (1934), p. 73: "Qui legit publice sacram scripturam iter maioris perfectionis arripuit quam aliquis clarevallensis."

[15] It would be worthwhile to analyze the ways and means, the spirit, the techniques, and the contexts of the encounters between St. Dominic and the heretics in southern France. The accounts by chroniclers have greater theological significance than the *Contra haereticos* of Alan of Lille, who was in the same region at about the same time.

[16] See above, pp. 202–38.

worked out by the Victorines against the allegorical idealism that so delighted the monastic mind.[17] Further and more precisely, the new relationship involved definition of the proper nature, use, and limits of the spiritual sense. All plainly considered the spiritual sense to be coterminous with a valid understanding of scripture, both in its history and in its doctrine. But whereas in the monastic *collatio* allegory was more or less a way for secret and aristocratic initiation into the mystical meaning in the style of the Alexandrians, now the primacy of the letter was respected and upheld through the techniques developed bit by bit by the new generations of *scholares*.

The master—a common name among the new evangelists for a teacher in the schools or for the leader of an apostolic group[18]—had to accomplish three operations in order to bring the word of God into full exercise: *legere, disputare, praedicare* (to explicate, to dispute in the sense of resolving *quaestiones*, and to preach). Thus did Peter the Chanter (died 1197), whose *Verbum abbreviatum* was the *summa* of pastoral and institutional theology for the late twelfth century, formulate a master's three-fold function in a division that would

---

[17] While the reputation of Gregory the Great as the leading monastic exegete remained high, as with Guibert of Nogent, *De vita sua* i.17 (*PL*, CLVI, 874; *The Autobiography of Guibert, Abbot of Nogent-sous-Coucy*, tr. C. C. S. Bland [London, 1926], p. 70) and Hugh of Saint-Victor, *Didascalicon* v.7 (Buttimer, p. 105; Taylor, p. 128), Richard of Saint-Victor did not hesitate to point out the weaknesses in Gregory's method: *In visionem Ezechielis* prol. (*PL*, CXCVI, 527) and *Expositio difficultatum* prol. (*PL*, CXCVI, 211). See below pp. 310–30.

[18] *Magister* was the common twelfth-century term for the leader of a group of itinerant preachers. It was used, for example, in reference to Robert of Arbrisselles, Norbert of Xanten, and Bernard of Thiron. Cernai called Diego d'Osma and his companion Dominic "praedicationis principes et magistri" (leaders and masters of preaching.) Of St. Francis himself, James of Vitry, a contemporary, wrote in his *Historia occidentalis* xxxii (Douai, 1597), p. 352: "Vidimus primum hujus ordinis fundatorem magistrum, cui tanquam summo priori suo omnes alii obediunt." (We saw the order's founder and first master whom all the others obey as the highest and first among them.) This term "master" had over others such as "lord" or "abbot" the advantage of being free from implications of power or temporal responsibilities. In the *Vita* of Robert of Arbrisselles (*PL*, CLXII, 1052), Baudry of Dol wrote: "Praelatum suum magistrum tantummodo vocabant, nam neque dominus, neque abbas vocitari solebat." (They called their prelate master only; they did not call him either lord or abbot.) Cf. Mandonnet, I, 53, 130; Larkin, pp. 38, 141.

long remain a classic.[19] One must not think of this, however, as an inviolable division. In fact, in the works of the masters of that time, it is difficult to distinguish explication from the two other exercises; the line separating explication from preaching was seldom drawn clearly.[20]

What we need to sense in this instructional formula, as much as the specification of functions, which showed up noticeably in the new statute of teaching and in the diversity of its methods, is the necessity that a full coordination of these functions be achieved in order to promote a total and active understanding of God's word. True mastery *in sacra pagina* called for preaching. The theology of the word of God could be accomplished only in the transmission of its message. Exegesis, dogmatics, and preaching could not be separated for one who would master the gospels, because they could be fully comprehended only by participation in the immediate action of the word. Did not Alan of Lille consider the preaching of the word of God the highest act of the Christian advanced in perfection? We have come far from the monastic program, not only by the steady

---

[19] *Verbum abbreviatum* i (*PL*, CCV, 25): "In tribus igitur consistit exercitium sacrae scripturae: circa lectionem, disputationem et praedicationem. . . . Lectio autem est quasi fundamentum et substratorium sequentium, quia per eam ceterae utilitates comparantur. Disputatio quasi paries est in hoc exercitio et aedificio, quia nihil plene intelligitur, fideliterve praedicatur nisi prius dente disputationis frangatur. Praedicatio vero, cui subserviunt priora, quasi tectum est tegens fideles ab aestu et a turbine vitiorum." (The study of sacred scripture consists in three operations: in explication, disputation, and preaching. . . . Explication is a sort of foundation or base for what follows, because upon it other uses of the text rest. Disputation is a sort of wall in this exercise, this building, because nothing is fully understood or faithfully preached unless first analyzed by disputation. Preaching, however, which the previous ones support, is a sort of roof protecting the faithful from the raging storms of vice.) [Cf. Smalley, p. 208.]

[20] Smalley, p. 209, analyzes the literary genre of the *Summa super Psalterium* of Prepositinus of Cremona, a work that was undoubtedly "preached," and of the *Distinctiones super Psalterium* by Peter the Chanter and Peter of Poitiers. In the face of this apostolically oriented combination of the master's three functions, one ought to reexamine the history of preaching in this period. One can presume that such an effort would bring into relief, alongside popular preaching, a literary genre almost entirely perverted by dialectic to the detriment of sacred rhetoric. Cf. T. M. Charlier, *Artes praedicandi, contribution à l'histoire de la rhétorique au moyen âge* (Paris-Ottawa, 1936).

introduction of *quaestiones*, but by the treatment of a divine word which now appeared as a word directed to men.

A new equilibrium was thus about to be established, one which the Victorine reform had not been able to accomplish. That it had not been able to accomplish this in practice is shown by the typical case of Stephen Langton's work. Its reputation was assured only by his development of *quaestiones* and his proliferation of *moralitates*—but not by his sense of religious history. His biblical scholarship was not sound; and men were led astray by its errors, even in their preaching. Neither had the Victorines achieved this equilibrium in principle, and their ultimate failure was written into their position on allegory. One could not base a scientific understanding of scripture, St. Thomas was later to say, on the symbolism of the spiritual senses.

It was the mendicants who were finally to establish this equilibrium. Its establishment was signaled and accomplished in two facts: first, St. Francis proclaimed in thought and action the literal appreciation of the mystery of Christ; and second, the earliest generation of Dominicans at the Convent of Saint-Jacques in Paris surprised "moralists" and "questionists" alike by organizing the direct study of scripture in its textual simplicity.[21] "The old allegories and moralities were fading before an intense realization of the literal meaning."[22] By a

---

[21] Hugh of Saint-Cher, the leader in this vast undertaking, told of the double opposition encountered by the friars (*Postillae in Bibliam* [Paris, 1530–45], VI, fol. 86): "Hi sunt reprehensores fratrum studentium qui nimis sunt intenti circa studium scripturarum. Dicunt morales: non est bonum in theologia tot questiones implicare. Dicunt questioniste: non est bonum tot moralitates fingere. Et quilibet reprehendit quod nescit." (These are the critics of the friar-scholars who are wholly intent upon the study of scripture. The moralists say, "It is not good to concoct so many questions in theology." The questionists say, "It is not good to contrive so many moral interpretations." And each side criticizes what it does not understand.) [Cf. Smalley, p. 269.]

[22] Smalley, p. 284. See esp. chap. 5, "Masters of the Sacred Page: The Comestor, the Chanter, Stephen Langton" and chap. 6, "The Friars" for a full discussion of the development which is being discussed briefly here.

It is at this critical juncture that one can see the connection between the evangelical reformers with their literalism and the exegetes who were faithful to the historical letter, as against the old-style Gregorian allegorizers who considered this "history" superficial. St. Gregory had written in his *Hom. XXII in evang.* (*PL*, LXXVI, 1174–5): "Lectio sancti evangelii, quam modo, fratres, audistis valde in superficie historica est aperta, sed ejus nobis sunt mysteria sub brevitate requirenda. *Maria Magdalena, cum adhuc tenebrae essent, venit ad monumentum* (John 20:1): juxta historiam notatur hora; juxta intellectum

kind of scriptural monophysitism, decadent symbolism would still too often swamp the *lectio* of the schools with allegory and public preaching with tropology; but this double deadweight could not stifle the power of the gospel to move, a power rediscovered both in the apostolic life of the church and in its theological reflection.[23] The theological and apostolic programs, each defined by the other, overlapped in their subservience to the primacy of the word of God. By this meeting, both the vital center of pastoral theology and even the superficial aspects of the pastoral ministry were modified. Despite his basically impeccable reputation, Gregory the Great, author of the hitherto supremely influential *Regula pastoralis* and inspirer of the monastic *collatio*, found his authority eclipsed by such an approach as that taken in Peter the Chanter's *Verbum abbreviatum*, and even more by the spiritual style of the new apostles.

Faith meant assent to the word of God; and according to that word, faith was the prime and characteristic act of the Christian. It was certainly not by chance that, in keeping with their custom of reviving evangelical terms, these men of faith called themselves properly and, so to speak, technically, *credentes* (believers), imitating the expression *multitudo credentium* of the first Christian community (Acts 4:32).[24] By itself alone the term "believer" properly expressed the ideal of the apostolic life in contrast to the ideal that inspired the reform of the canons: the crucial point in the activity,

---

vero mysticum requirentis signatur intelligentia." (The reading of the holy gospel which you have just heard, my brothers, is sufficiently clear on the historical level, but its mystical meaning has to be searched for by us for a while. "Mary Magdalen, while it was still dark, went to the tomb": according to a historical reading, this tells us the hour; but by a mystical understanding, this tells us the state of mind of one seeking the Lord.)

[23] Maurice of Sully, bishop of Paris (died 1196), took up the *Allegoriae* of Richard of Saint-Victor in his French homilies. See above, n. 11. But soon Francis of Assisi was to speak a clear, evangelical language.

[24] Cf. Mandonnet, II, 187, n. 58; Larkin, p. 276, n. 54: "One attributes perhaps too readily the giving of the name *credentes* to the Cathari faithful to the fact that their apostles preached a new faith, distinct from the catholic faith; and one rejects on the same account the usage of the chroniclers who nearly all apply the term *credentes* to the Waldensians, who were *not* heretics." The crucial text of Acts 4:32 reads: "Now the company of those who believed were of one heart and soul, and no one said that any of the things which he possessed was his own, but they had everything in common."

the itinerant poverty, of the new apostles was the force of a believing witness which ignored any distinction between clergy and laity, whereas the other reforms had involved clerics searching for virtue and effectiveness within settled and observant communities. And the difference between their two approaches to poverty—between subjecting clerical avarice to moral control and rejecting out of hand an entire economic system[25]—emphasized the differences underlying their inspiration and their proselytism.[26]

On this theological plane the old moral reformism was discredited, at least relatively, and its methods were easily criticized. In an astonishingly strong chapter, "Contra traditionum onerositatem et multitudinem" (Against the Burdensome Host of Traditions"), Peter the Chanter, citing a phrase from Acts 15:10 about the "unbearable burden which neither we nor our fathers have been able to carry," proclaimed the primacy of the gospel and of its spiritual liberty as against the proliferation of precepts, however useful they might have been. To this he added a long list of stultifying burdens, especially those found in monastic life. He recalled that St. Anthony, when his disciples asked him for a rule and observances, was content to hand them the gospels.

There are other traditions that are allowable, even inoffensive in any least way to God's commandments. And yet when they are numerous they

---

[25] St. Bernard's morally severe criticism of avarice did not go to the heart of the new monetary and commercial economy, which it simply condemned as perverse; this criticism could have been just and effective only in the feudal agrarian society to which the monk belonged. The new poverty expressed the break between evangelical principles and the old regime and thus put itself in a good position from which to denounce the disorders wrought by the new regime.

[26] Cf. Mandonnet, II, 190; Larkin, p. 279: "Whereas among reformed priests, entry into the Augustinian Order, with the life of poverty which that entailed, was considered the proper means of achieving the life of apostolic perfection, it signified nothing of the kind for the masses of people involved in the various apostolic movements. For these people, the practice of the common life and of poverty dated from much further back than the foundation of the Augustinian regular life. The establishment of a juridical organism added nothing to their imitation of the primitive church. The regular life represented for them not so much religious progress as social stabilization and, for the church, a recuperation, insofar as this stabilization saved wandering masses from anarchy or even heresy. The tremendous success of the apostolic movement, its immense Christian vigor maintained in spite of its stormy history, gave this recuperation its great value."

weigh heavily upon those who uphold them and upon those who transgress them; unless such traditions are kept brief and few and have been instituted for the most obvious and useful reasons, they become an obstacle to obeying divine precepts. They restrict the liberty of the gospel. . . .

Note that the Apostle had no traditions except a few venerable and mystical ones. Also when certain religious came to the hermit Anthony seeking a rule and a model for the religious life, he gave them a copy of the gospels. At the Lateran Council [the Third Lateran, 1179], John of Salisbury said to the assembled fathers who were discussing some decrees: "God forbid that any new ones be set up or a lot of old ones resurrected and renewed!"

We are oppressively burdened with a multitude of contrived practices, although authority speaks, because even some useful things have to be tossed aside or we get borne down by them. We ought rather to teach and work to get the gospel observed, since so few now observe it. . . .

[Next, after citing the words of Christ against the legalism of the Jews and texts from St. Paul against judaizing Christians, he continues:] Do not abandon the vital spirit of the letter in favor of anybody's tradition or refinement or obscure explanation.[27]

As it happened, the new apostolic movements shunned the classical forms of the religious life. The Humiliati refrained from drawing up complex regulations. Francis of Assisi would not agree "to be diverted into the monastic or eremetic life."[28] It was Innocent III who guided

---

[27] *Verbum abbreviatum* lxxix (*PL*, CCV, 233–9; punctuation altered): "Sunt et aliae (traditiones) licitae, nullumque offendiculum mandatis divinis parientes, et tamen prae multitudine sua gravant constituentes, et inobedientes illis transgressores[;] nisi in parcitate et paucitate, et nonnisi pro manifestissima causa et utili instituendae essent[,] obicem videntur praebere divinis praeceptis. Hae evacuant evangelicam libertatem. . . .

"Vide Apostolum nonnisi paucas traditiones honestas et mysticas instituisse. . . . Antonius etiam eremita quibusdam religiosis quaerentibus ab eo regulam et formam religiose vivendi, tradidit eis codicem Evangelii. In Lateranensi etiam concilio, sedentibus patribus ad condenda nova decreta, ait Joannes Carnotensis: Absit, inquit, nova condi, vel plurima veterum reintigi et innovari!

"Multitudine etiam inventorum praegravamur, cum dicat auctoritas, quia etiam de utilibus aliqua post ponenda sunt, ne multitudine utilium gravemur. Imo ideo potius praecipiendum et laborandum esset, ut Evangelium observaretur, cui nunc pauci obediunt. . . .

"Non reliquas spiritum litterae vivificantem, propter traditionem, determinationem, vel remotam alicujus expositionem."

[28] Thomas of Celano *Vita prima S. Francisci* xiii (*Analecta Franciscana* [Florence, 1926–41], X, 26): ". . . ut ad vitam monasticam seu heremeticam diverteret. . . ." One recalls here the famous scene in which St. Francis, under pressure from Cardinal Ugolino to go back to the legislation of St. Benedict or of St. Augustine, led Ugolino silently before his brothers and then, from the depths of his soul, cried out: "Fratres mei, fratres mei, Deus vocavit me per viam simplicitatis et humilitatis, et hanc viam ostendit mihi in veritate

these movements firmly but gently to a more organized mode of life. In any case, the rule of St. Francis was far different from that of St. Benedict. The *Expositio quattuor magistrorum super regulam fratrum minorum* (*Explanation of the Rule of the Friars Minor by Four Masters*)[29] displayed a mentality utterly foreign to monastic paternalism. Without any prejudice against the classic term *regula*, the elaboration of what the Preachers chose to call their *Consuetudines* or *Institutiones* did not present itself as a commentary upon an already established rule.

In the interpretation of texts and, even more, in the application of these texts to daily life, the new apostles experienced a balancing off of letter and spirit of the kind which, once the church became engaged upon its apostolate, solved for it the problem of relating mystery and institution without violating the unity of the Spirit. The seemingly simplistic literalism of their reading of the gospels (think, for example, of their custom of traveling two-by-two, of their eating whatever was given them, of their obsession with the number twelve, of their rigorous application of evangelical poverty, pardon, and fraternity) paradoxically guaranteed their most absolute apprehension of the spiritual sense, if it is true that that sense is contained within the letter. Thus always has understanding of scripture proceeded to coordinate letter and spirit in passages susceptible of both literal and spiritual interpretation but often restricted to the latter by allegorization of details. The literature of the' new apostles of the twelfth and thirteenth centuries gave a new example of this law. As

---

pro me et pro illis qui volunt mihi credere et me imitari. Et ideo nolo quod nominetis mihi aliquam regulam, neque sancti Benedicti, neque sancti Augustini, neque sancti Bernardi, nec aliquam viam et forman vivendi, praeter illam quae mihi a Domino est ostensa misericorditer et donata." (My brothers, my brothers, God has called me by the way of simplicity and of humility, and He has pointed out this way as being the true way, both for me and for those who wish to believe me and imitate me. So don't talk to me about some rule or other, neither that of St. Benedict, nor of St. Augustine, nor of St. Bernard, nor about any life or way of living other than that which the Lord has mercifully shown and given to me.) *Speculum perfectionis* lxviii (ed. P. Sabatier, vol. 1 [Manchester, 1928], p. 196). Cf. Thomas of Celano *Legenda secunda* cxli (*Analecta Franciscana*, X, 237–8).

[29] L. Oliger, ed. (Rome, 1950). In the midst of a very significant crisis, four masters of theology were officially summoned for consultation.

concerns institutions, the labored development of the Franciscan Order, in particular the affair of the Spirituals (how significant the very name of these men who objectified the letter in the service of a shaky Spiritualism!) ought to illustrate not only the risks involved in this coordination of letter and spirit, but also its pervasive vitality, which derives from the very heart of the law of grace.

A whole theology of law, of its role and its subservience to grace, grew out of this interaction of thought and behavior. For example, whereas for St. Benedict any transgression of the rule constituted a fault, the laws of the Dominicans and later on of other groups did not as such oblige in conscience—*non obligant ad culpam sed ad poenam* (they do not entail a fault but only a correction).[30] At the time that the rules of the order were taking shape, in 1220, Dominic declared that if anyone thought otherwise he would himself go ceaselessly about the Preachers' convents erasing the regulations with his own knife.[31] The Gregorian reformers could not have imagined such a violation of the binding force of law, just as they could not have aroused such an evangelical enthusiasm for obedience as the new friars showed. When St. Bernard was asked by the Carthusians of Saint Peter in 1140 whether all monastic regulations obliged in conscience, he had replied that some obliged gravely, others lightly, but never once suggested that there could be any whose violation involved no sin.[32]

It was no accident that the apostolic movements, unlike the Gregorian reform and the canonical movement, thrived as well if not better among laymen than among the clergy. The evangelical shock reverberated throughout the Christian body of the church wherever it encountered the world, especially at those points where laymen bore witness in secular society. Peter Waldo and Francis of Assisi were laymen. The Humiliati formed mixed lay and clerical communities.

---

[30] *Constitutiones Ordinis Praedicatorum* prol., in H. Denifle, "Die Constitutionen des Predigerordens in der Redaction Raimunds von Peñafort," *ALKG*, V (1889), 534. Humbert of Romans said that St. Dominic enunciated this principle at the chapter of 1220; see Humbert of Romans *De vita regulari* (ed. J. J. Berthier [Rome, 1889], II, 45).

[31] *Ibid.*, p. 46; ". . . si hoc crederetur, ipse (Dominicus) vellet ire semper per claustra, et omnes regulas cum cultellino suo delere."

[32] *De praecepto et dispensatione* i (*PL*, CLXXXII, 861–2).

The Poor Catholics set up religious houses (1212) to accommodate members of both the clergy and the laity, women as well as men. The clericalization of Franciscan brotherhoods (1210), which incorporated their members into the ecclesiastical hierarchy, did not go unchallenged, nor was it accomplished without qualms of conscience for Brother Francis. The penitential orders spread sporadically in the thirteenth century as third, or lay, orders.

The principle and the laws of this apostolic shock in fact transcended the clerical-lay distinction. The pontiffs through express legislation sought to build them into the structure of a church in which apostolic initiatives would not be limited to the sacramental and priestly apparatus, to which, from a conventional point of view, they belonged. Here we have the church's long struggle to give juridical and sacramental authenticity to the apostolic drive, which in dissident groups tended to corrupt rapidly. This was especially the history of the first Franciscan brotherhood, as foreshadowed by the case of the Lombard "poor men." And the key to these developments lay in the legislation and executive directives gradually worked out for the preaching of the word, which, arising from the evangelical force of the faith, could be exercised only within the apostolic magisterium. The "poor men" of Lombardy, the Humiliati, like the Waldensians, refused all control, to the point where they found themselves excommunicated by decree of Lucius III in 1184. But by 1201 a good many of them had been reconciled, and Innocent III gave them permission to preach. He made explicit the distinction between the preaching of doctrine (*articuli fidei et sacramenta*), which was reserved, and giving witness to faith and morals (*verbum exhortationis*).[33] In 1207 some Waldensians led by

---

[33] G. Tiraboschi, ed., *Vetera Humiliatorum Monumenta* (Milan, 1776), II, 133–4: ". . . singulis diebus dominicis ad audiendum Dei verbum in loco idoneo convenire, ubi aliquis vel aliqui fratrum probate fidei et expertae religionis, qui potentes sint in opere ac sermone, licentia diocesani episcopi verbum exhortationis proponent iis qui convenerint ad audiendum verbum Dei, monentes et inducentes eos ad mores honestos et opera pietatis, ita quod de articulis fidei et sacramentis ecclesiae non loquantur. Prohibemus autem ne quis episcopus contra praescriptam formam impediat hujusmodi fratres verbum exhortationis proponere, cum secundum Apostolum, non sit Spiritus extinguendus." (Every Sunday they assembled in a suitable place to hear the

Durand of Huesca and persuaded by Dominic that they could keep to their former way of existence within the church were reconciled and granted permission to engage in this same limited form of preaching (*licentia exhortandi*); the same happened in 1210 with a group of priests and laymen led by Bernard Prim.[34] And in fact these various people did exercise the *verbum exhortationis* each Sunday.[35] In the same year the companions of St. Francis received the same privilege, to be administered at the discretion of Francis himself, free of all episcopal control. "The pope gave Francis and his brothers permission to preach penance everywhere, provided that whoever was going to preach got approval from the blessed Francis. And to any of the brethren, layman or cleric, that had the spirit of God, he gave permission to preach."[36] Thus under these formulations a consistent policy was developed; it was not merely a casuistical solution but a substantive discrimination in the laws and titles governing the apostolic transmission of the faith within the institutional magisterium.

Apart from these lay groups with their authorized witness within the apostolic movement,[37] certain confraternities and brotherhoods became a vehicle for the religious and social expression of the new Christianity. Themselves ancient institutions, they now became

---

word of God, and there, one or more of the brethren of approved faith and experience in religion and powerful in deed and word, with permission of the bishop of the diocese, exhorted those who had gathered to hear the word of God, admonishing them and leading them toward upright conduct and pious works—but not speaking of the articles of the faith or of the sacraments of the church. We forbid any bishop to violate the prescribed rule and interfere with the exhortations given by such brethren, for, as the Apostle says: "The Spirit is not to be extinguished.")

[34] Innocent III *Reg.* xiii.94 (*PL*, CCXVI, 293).

[35] Grundmann, p. 112.

[36] *Legenda trium sociorum* (*Acta Sanctorum*, October, II, 737–8): "Dedit eidem licentiam praedicandi ubique paenitentiam ac fratribus suis, ita tamen quod, qui praedicaturi erant, licentiam a beato Francisco obtinerent. . . . Quicumque ex ipsis spiritum Dei habebat, sive clericus, sive laicus, dabat ei licentiam praedicandi." Cf. H. Felder, *Geschichte der wissenschaftlichen Studien im Franziskanerorden bis um die Mitte des 13. Jahrhunderts* (Freiburg-im-Br., 1904), pp. 33–57.

[37] One would here have to take into account the works written in defense of the faith by laymen, right in the thick of the apostolic movement with all its variations and ambiguities—works such as the *Disputatio inter catholicum et paterinum* by a certain George, the *Liber supra stella* by Salvo Burci, etc.

caught up in the general forward movement of the temporal and spiritual economy. They had always been established on a ground where sacred and secular met. From this recrudescence of the religious confraternity, craft and trade and professional guilds now drew a religious inspiration that related meaningfully to their temporal involvements and their most material preoccupations. Here, wholly outside the framework of canon law, the church encountered concrete realities and, to its satisfaction, societies based on occupation and devoted to mutual aid and entertainment. Confraternities, guilds, charitable enterprises, festivals—all sponsored and organized independent meetings and ceremonies which, as ecclesiastical authorities complained, upset the traditional order of things in the churches and cluttered every church with one altar after another.[38]

It is in this context that one must appreciate the new and consistent expression given to Christian prayer, penitence, fraternal charity, and morality whether by active participants in the confessional societies organized by occupation or by the little people whom Chrétien of Troyes celebrates in his lament of the weavers.[39] It is in this context especially, rather than in light of occasional scepticism concerning doctrine, that one ought to see the sometimes rather violent outbreaks of anticlericalism that continued on the rise into the thirteenth century. At times this anticlericalism was reformist in tendency and could thus be used openly by the church. At other times, in its critique of the social sluggishness of the church, it directly and firmly opposed the church itself. This major theme of a return to the primitive Christian community, to its poverty and humility, nourished more than the reforms of the regular canons and the several manifestations of apostolic movements. Its ambiguity was exploited by Arnold of Brescia and by the Patarini. In the midst of one of his disputes with the papacy, Frederic II (emperor from 1212 to 1250) proposed that all clerics of whatever rank or order, but especially the higher clerics,

---

[38] G. LeBras, "Les confréries chrétiennes," in *Etudes de sociologie religieuse* (Paris, 1956), II, 423–62. See also E. Coornaert, "Les ghildes médiévales, V[e]–XIVe siècles," *RH,* CXCIX (1948), 22–55, 208–43. For complaints at the Council of Rouen, 1189, see Mansi, XXII, 585–6.

[39] See above, pp. 228–29.

be reduced to the status they held and the functions they performed in the primitive church. The same proposition was expressed by the French barons in 1246, with the approval of King Louis IX (reigned 1226-1270).

These polemics, which fed diplomatic quarrels and military engagements with a mixture of partisan ideology and sincere faith, tended to relocate the border between the sacred and the secular, not without endangering orthodoxy. The development of new political entities (the new national kingdoms against the Holy Empire, for example) and a naturalistic philosophy of man, including man-in-society, bolstered one another more or less consciously; together they took on the character of secondary causes autonomously at work in the kingdom of God on earth. No one formulated this into an explicit principle, either as a philosophy of society or as a theology of the church. Yet the popes, especially Alexander III and Innocent III, in the very midst of their struggles against the princes, developed in their official writings, as close analysis of these will reveal, a delicate but decisive recognition of the elements comprising Christendom. The term *Christianitas* was henceforth charged with a concrete meaning that embodied these elements—cosmic, ethnic, cultural, political.[40]

The evangelical fraternities were sensitive to such secular elements, to the point of being susceptible to their influence. Instinctively, on the other hand, and in virtue of the spiritual mission to society of these fraternities, the Roman pontiff, in addressing directives to them, avoided the term *Christianitas*; for that Christendom was no proper part of their apostolic business.[41] Once again, a new border between sacred and secular: the fraternities invalidated after a fashion the traditional and more or less sacred tripartite division of society into

---

[40] Cf. J. Rupp, *L'idée de Chrétienté dans la pensée pontificale, des origines à Innocent III* (Paris, 1939). Also, G. B. Ladner, "The Concepts of *Ecclesia* and *Christianitas*, and Their Relation to the Idea of Papal *plenitudo potestatis*, from Gregory VII to Boniface VIII," *MHP*, XVIII (Rome, 1954), 49–77.

[41] In making a systematic survey of the use of *Christianitas* and its related forms, J. Rupp found no mention of such terms in pontifical texts addressed to the fraternities and new orders. Neither St. Francis nor St. Dominic belonged to this "Christendom."

clerics, knights, and peasants.[42] That division offered no sociological or religious identity to their clientele, who included merchants and urban artisans. They were not averse to a certain desacralizing of authority, however divine it was thought to be in ultimate principle. In their electoral system there was never any thought of consecrating their priors in the way that abbots were consecrated. On another plane and reflecting the same tendency, while the anointing of kings continued to be an awe-inspiring religious rite which brought great political prestige to the monarchy, the popes made every effort to strip monarchy of its sacramental character. Innocent III, at the end of a long evolution to which canonists and liturgist-theologians had contributed, went against popular beliefs[43] and against the weight of Old Testament texts to make official a distinction between two kinds of anointing. Kings were to receive princely power (*potestas principis*) by being anointed on the arm with the oil of catechumens; prelates were to receive pontifical authority (*auctoritas pontificis*) by being anointed on the head with the holy chrism.[44]

The dubbing of a knight, a "sacrament" of feudal society, acquired the formalism of liturgical pomp as the social function of the knight became increasingly a matter of privilege; it became the initiation

---

[42] Adalbero of Laon *Carmen ad Robertum regem francorum* ccxcvii–ccxcviii (*PL*, CXLI, 771–86): "Triplex Dei ergo domus est, quae creditur una;/ Nunc orant alii, pugnant, aliique laborant." (Thus the Lord's house, which is thought to be one, is really three-fold: while some pray, others fight, and still others work.)

[43] Cf. M. Bloch, *Les rois thaumaturges* (Paris, 1924). The Gregorians had failed in their attacks on the popular belief in the supernatural powers of kingship. Otto of Freising *Gesta Frederici* ii.3 (Simson, pp. 103–4; Mierow-Emery, pp. 116–17) still spoke, on the occasion of the coronation of Frederick I in 1152, of the *sacramentum unctionis* (sacrament of anointing) and of the emperor as *Christus Domini* (the anointed of the Lord).

[44] Innocent III *Reg.* vii.3 (*PL*, CCXV, 284); *Decretal.* lib. 1, tit. 15, c. 1 (Friedberg, II, 131–4). Even if one insists upon the synonymous connection between *potestas* (power) and *auctoritas* (authority), which this text would seem to split apart, the distinction did already appear in the letter of Pope Gelasius I (494) to the Emperor Anastasius: *Epp.* viii (*PL*, LIX, 42): "Duo quippe sunt, imperator Auguste, quibus principaliter mundus hic regitur: auctoritas sacrata pontificum, et regalis potestas." (There are two means, august emperor, by which this world is mainly ruled: the sacred authority of the priesthood, and the royal power.)

rite of a caste ("O, God, you have constituted in nature three degrees among men . . . ," declared the eleventh-century pontifical of Besançon) and no longer the sanctifying of a social value. This anointing of out-dated privilege was the sin of a Christendom whose ceremony, bereft of religious value, survived as a symbol devoid of human relevance. At the same time, merchants—despised, held suspect in moral and religious thought—remained profane by birth in the new society.

The oath (*sacramentum*) of vassalage—the institutional keystone of feudal society, of social morality (*fides*, the virtue of fidelity), and of a sacral society—was bit by bit stripped of its three-fold relevance. Its decline was regarded by traditionalist theologians as scandalous both because emancipation from it necessitated infidelity to the oath and because society was now being built upon non-sacralized agreements. The new formations—guilds, communes, fraternities—substituted a horizontal and fraternal agreement for vertical and paternalistic fidelity, and this agreement was affirmed not in a religious rite but in the solidarity of the "brothers" and in democratic deliberation. And the new evangelists stupefied the feudal ecclesiastics with their bold claim that the new regime no less than the old was in accord with the faith, with the good news of the gospel, and with the love of charity.

This process of desacralization extended to the political order itself. The scaling down of the imperial anointment was a liturgical indication of the scaling down of the idea of a *sacrum imperium*. At a time when the papacy under Innocent III reached the height of its power, realizing to some extent Gregory VII's program for papal aggrandizement; at a time when the papacy was able to manipulate feudal forms to its own advantage vis-à-vis the princes; at a time when the papacy seemed to be turning into a giant theocratic monolith engrossing both the sacred and the secular spheres—the most consistently reliable expressions of its power implied the conception of an empire completely stripped of its "sanctity," functional and political, while at the same time of course the imperial jurists claimed a sacred role for their sovereign. The polemical texts of this most tangled debate are highly revealing. The efforts to desacralize the empire and those to force the papacy out of politics had in common a recognition of the autonomy of the temporal, and this recognition ran throughout the debate as a leitmotif.[45] The exclusive dedication to the apostolate on the part of the mendicant orders took into account this new type of relationship even before it had been defined, a relationship in which the Gregorian principles concerning *libertas ecclesiae* found a workable sociological base as well as a proper theology.[46]

All this would have consequences. One important political yet implicitly religious consequence was that the new monarchies would be emancipated not only from the pretensions of the empire, but from the pseudoreligious myth of a political oneness of the world deriving necessarily from the catholic oneness of Christians. The *Ludus de Antichristo*, wherein the king of France finally submits to the emperor in the church triumphant, had been convincing back in the 1160's. But when Frederick II tried to revive the theme, the mystical pretensions of the Hohenstaufen seemed anachronistic in a church now animated by the mendicants and no longer by monastic feudalism. The universalism of the church was opportunely shaken free from its political matrix at the very moment when it seemed to have realized that universalism in a new empire of its own conceived as the *respublica christianitatis*. The relations between Innocent III and the emancipated monarchies could now take into account passing circumstances or personal political options; the relations so determined would soon find expression in theological writings, to the great advantage of the liberty of the kingdom of God. The remains of the holy empire would continue to drag along with a few jurists, and even some poets, to say nothing of genuine partisans. But the theolo-

---

[45] Among other sources one could cite are R. Folz, *L'idée d'empire en occident du Ve au XIVe siècle* (Paris, 1953); A. Dempf, *Sacrum Imperium* (Munich, 1929); and P. E. Schramm, "Sacerdotium und Regnum im Austausch ihrer Vorrechte," *Studi Gregoriani*, II (Rome, 1947), 403–57.

[46] [For *libertas ecclesiae*, see Gerd Tellenbach, *Church, State, and Christian Society at the Time of the Investiture Contest*, tr. R. F. Bennett (Oxford, 1959), chap. 5. The notion was conceived wholly within the feudal age and so did not extend to a disengagement of the church from the holding of property. Only after certain important sectors of the church had left the land and become disenchanted with the money economy, which served in place of land, did the notion *libertas ecclesiae* include freedom from all entanglements in property. (Added with author's concurrence.)]

gians would here and there retain only an occasional verbal or fossi-
lized trace of it.

Of the several indications of this shift in frontiers, to the advantage of the apostolic faith, not the least significant was the rejection
of the myth of Constantine. It was replaced, especially in Germany,
by the myth of Charlemagne, the loyal protector of Christianity in
the guise of the ideal knight. Constantine had been first the author
and next the symbol of the confusion—ideological, mystical, and
political—of two traditions: the papacy as heir of the Roman Empire, and the empire as consecrated by a religious mission. The liturgy
had incorporated this symbol by having the pope receive, in token
of investiture on the day of his election, the purple mantle given by
Constantine to Sylvester; and the official imperial theology had embroidered it with allegory.[47] All the reformers, St. Bernard included
("In these things you have succeeded not Peter but Constantine,"
he said in reproaching Eugenius III[48]), denounced this confusion.
The new apostles treated it with contempt. Joachim of Floris wove
his anathema of the first corrupter of the spiritual church into his
prophetic scheme of history. Thus the apostolic movement came to
inject its evangelical views into the dialogue of the two swords.[49]

The final trait of this theology, let us say of this politics of grace
and nature, was that the evangelical revival brought a sharpened
sensitivity to eschatology. This was an expected reaction, since the
success of monastic Christianity had led many souls into the subtle
temptation of surrendering themselves complacently to heavenly contemplation, as if to get a foretaste of glory. The church, they said,

---

[47] Cf. Honorius of Autun *Gemma animae* iv.58, 60 (*PL*, CLXXII, 710–11),
where the parallelism Solomon-Constantine is presented in the most fantastic
symbolism amidst the texts on the seventh Sunday after Pentecost. Or, in
Adam of Dryburgh *De tripartito tabernaculo* ii.13 (*PL*, CXCVIII, 713), for
an exaltation of the conversion of Constantine and its extraordinary results.

[48] *De consideratione* iv.3 (*PL*, CLXXXII, 776): "In his successisti non
Petro sed Constantino"; Eugenius III was trying to maneuver between the
senate and the emperor. The force of Bernard's outburst stemmed from moral,
not institutional, concern.

[49] On the contexts of this development—on the one hand economic, social,
political, and on the other hand doctrinal—see Georges de Lagarde, *La
naissance de l'esprit laïque au déclin du moyen âge*, vol. 1: *Bilan du XIIIe
siècle* (3rd ed.; Paris, 1956).

had sanctified the world. Evoking the three stages of church history, called Zion, Jacob, and Jerusalem, Adam of Dryburgh had said: "What now remains except that the church, endowed with the tranquility of peace, should turn from the name 'Jacob,' which expressed its toilsome struggle, to that name which heralds peace, namely 'Jerusalem.' "[50] According to the Cistercian Otto of Freising, Constantine had inaugurated an era of sacred peace, extending to secular princes;[51] it was now reaching fulfillment in a radiant church.

As it settled down in the world, this monastic eschatological ideal withdrew into its secure fantasies, inattentive to the drama of life, to the desperate call of the church in a state of rapid expansion and in peril. It was the apostolic movement which renewed the messianic hope, seeking to detect the advance signs of the time, signs at least of the urgency imposed by that consummation. Here again we see an instance of that troubled ferment wherein the worst is mixed with the most pure in the critical rebuke given to institutions conspicuously too well established. *Peregrinamur a Domino* ("We are straying from the Lord"). Here come the laborers of the eleventh hour, who are going to relieve the faltering first teams. Here are the true people of Israel, decidedly liberated from terrestrial servitude. Here is the new Jerusalem, triumphing over the antichrists foretold by the apocalypses. And here, near at hand, is the coming of the Spirit. In manifestoes, in programs, in pontifical approbations, in sermons, in polemical tracts, in chronicles, these scriptural themes of the messianic era were exploited to convey with unction the message of hope about to be realized. The allegorization of history, however customary, was not simply a literary device; it was a means of explaining the working out in time of the kingdom of God by successive stages.[52] The way was perhaps open to interpretations by a delirious messianism;[53]

---

[50] Adam of Dryburgh *De triplici sanctae Ecclesiae statu*, sermo 8 in adventu Domini (*PL*, CXCVIII, 144): "Quid jam superest, nisi ut dum ei [ecclesiae] pacis tranquillitas indulta est, a nomine quod est Jacob, in quo laboriosa ejus expressa est lucta, ad nomen illud pacis insigne prae se ferens conscendat, quod est Jerusalem."

[51] Otto of Freising *Chronica* v. prol., vii prol. (Lammers-Schmidt, pp. 374, 496; Mierow, pp. 323, 404).

[52] See above, pp. 162–201.

[53] For examples see P. Alphandéry, "Notes sur le messianisme médiéval

at least it was an entirely different eschatology which called for reflection upon the course of history and which drew understanding and drive for the present from the future.[54]

Like St. Peter speaking to the community at Jerusalem (Acts 2:14-21), the leaders of the apostolic movements took up the text of Joel on the day of the Lord: "I will pour out my spirit upon all of mankind, and your sons and daughters will be prophets. Your young men shall see visions, and your old men shall dream dreams." This prophetic attribution, common enough in tradition and liturgical anointing, had a special vigor for these generations. Teaching, the ministry of the word under ecclesiastical mandate, took among them the form of testimony, which gave it a prophetic accent. Honorius III's use of the word "prophets" to describe the Dominicans was not merely pious verbiage. This was not a matter of making predictions about the future, even if a taste for the exotic turned it into that in some Franciscan and Dominican chronicles. Instead it was an understanding of faith which gave to the teacher an aptitude for presenting in all its urgency the present working out of God's plan, especially since that urgency was experienced while awaiting the Lord's return. From such a perspective, the interpretation of events left itself open, as always, to all sorts of infantile or shameful fantasies; but even with fantastic elaborations it remained the manifestation of an inner charisma within the ordinary magisterium of the church (as in the case of a Francis or a Dominic). One should analyze all the chronicles or legends here, for they are all in their own way, both in content and as a literary genre, good witnesses to theological and apostolic activity in the midst of contemporary social stagnation.

Thus, one can define the evangelical reawakening as an active presence of the gospel, not only because men took up the text and read it directly in its literal fullness, but also because, at the same time, the word of God was announced as real and present by action of the Holy Spirit in a vibrant church and a revitalized theology.

---

latin (XIe–XIIe siècles)," *Rapport de l'Ecole pratique des hautes études* (Paris, 1912), pp. 1–29.

[54] This eschatological accent of the mendicants is lacking in John of Garland *De triumphis ecclesiae* (first half of the thirteenth century; ed. T. Wright [London, 1856]).

8

The Masters of the Theological "Science"

I went into France particularly to engage in a fighting dispute with those masters whose authority stood so much above and against me that whenever I recall those times I have also to recall that true passage from Ecclesiasticus (13:28-9): "The rich man spoke and all were hushed; they praise his speech to the skies. The poor man spoke and they say, 'Who's that?' " One of these men, you see, was a bishop as well as a master; the other one was more famous than any bishop, though he himself was not one. I marvel now at that picture I have in my memory—how I set out virtually alone on a wretched donkey, a younger man than I am now, attended only by a boy, heading for far-off cities to struggle against men who, as I know, had tongue as well as talent, ecclesiastical and professorial dignity equally high; and how I didn't expect what would happen, namely that a throng of masters as well as students, a not very small army of them, collected to hear me, to overwhelm me. But I find it even more marvelous that just as I was coming into the city, one of the men just mentioned, the particularly eminent master, was drawing his last breath and immediately after I entered, died. As for the other one, with whom I tangled sharply, I don't know whether he lived another full year.[1]

T HUS DID RUPERT, now old and abbot of Deutz, reminisce with a satisfaction still full of animosity as he told of the trip he had made in 1117, while yet a monk at Saint-Laurent of Liège, to engage the two celebrities of the school of Laon in public debate on

---

[1] *Super quaedam capitula regulae divi Benedicti abbatis* i (*PL*, CLXX, 482-3): "Ivi in Franciam, ut potissimum contra magistros illos praelium disputationis committerem, quorum tanta super me et contra me auctoritas erat, ut quoties illius temporis recordor, simul et recordari debeam dicti illius verissimi, quod Sapientia dixit: 'Dives locutus est, et omnes tacuerunt, et verbum illius usque ad nubes perducent; pauper locutus est, et dicunt: Quis est hic?' (Eccl. 13: 28–9). Nam alter eorum magister simul et episcopus[;] alter, quovis episcopo famosior, quamvis ipse non esset episcopus. Mirum mihimet nunc est illud recordationis meae spectaculum, quomodo solus ego vili asello resi-

their home ground. These celebrities were William of Champeaux, bishop of Châlons-sur-Marne, and Anselm of Laon, even more famous than William and at this very moment near death.

The controversy had been going on for some time already, and Rupert had been sparing neither his energy nor his pen: How was one to reconcile the existence of evil under the all-powerful providence of God; or rather, what ways and means did one have at hand for resolving this troubling problem?[2] The two masters had formulated a distinction between two wills in God—a permissive will (*voluntas permittens*) that tolerates evil, and an approving will (*voluntas approbans*). This distinction was to gain authoritative currency and was based, apart from the dialectic involved, on their observation of the different ways man's will in fact works. However unsophisticated, this definition of a permissive or tolerant will, deriving from the philosophical categories to act (*agere*) and to bear (*pati*), engaged the mind in a wholly different manner of thinking from that of scripture. The book of Job, for example, is not concerned with such overly clever human concepts. Rupert, a great biblical commentator but at the same time an ardent contemplative whose faith delighted in mystery, could not bear this denigration of the scriptural outlook. Such a distinction, made up by masters of arts (meaning that it involved use of worldly science), was nothing short of scandalous, even in the terms invented by reason. Such a meaningless, sterile distinction (*tam inertem divisionem*)[3] could only lead to the blasphemous notion that God wills evil. One ought not to speak of the permission of God, but rather, as in scripture, of the patience of

---

dens, juvenculus, uno tantum puero comitatus, ad exteras tam longe civitates ad conflictum contra tales profectus sum, quibus adesse et os et ingenium, et magnam tam officii quam magisterii dignitatem noveram, nec defuturum quod et factum est, ut magistrorum pariter ac discipulorum coetus quasi non parvus conveniret exercitus ad me audiendum, ad me convincendum. Illud autem magis mirum videtur quod me ingrediente civitatem, jam dictorum alter et praecipuus magistrorum ultimum trahens spiritum, statim post ingressum meum vitam finivit, alter cum quo acerbum habui conflictum, nescio an integrum annum supervixerit."

[2] The historical episodes and doctrinal positions taken were reported by Rupert in two treatises written between 1115 and 1117: *De voluntate Dei* (*PL*, CLXX, 437–54) and *De omnipotentia Dei* (*PL*, CLXX, 454–78).

[3] *De voluntate Dei* i (*PL*, CLXX, 437).

God; a patience which is not a "specific" way of willing evil, but merely goodness and forbearance and benevolence, synonymous terms charged with biblical vitality. Rupert continued by saying that he had not followed the schools of dialectic but that even if he had mastered all their knowledge he would not use it, for it would only lead to the worst incongruities while adding nothing to the holiness and simplicity of the divine truth. The simple words of the shepherds and fishermen who were Christ's companions were worth far more than all the discussions of philosophers.[4] With stinging irony Rupert made sport of his adversaries who with their supposed dilemma tried to trap him in a denial of God's omnipotence. Armed with all of scripture from Genesis to Revelation, Rupert proclaimed that the hand of God extends everywhere: "Whatever can be thought up apart from sacred scripture or fabricated out of argumentation is unreasonable and therefore pertains in no way to the praise or acknowledgment of the omnipotence of God."[5] Such was Rupert's scriptural absolutism, the result of a faith that would allow only its own understanding of its object. Theology is nourished by faith, he felt, and not by "reasoning" in the manner of the schoolmasters, the *scholares*.

The Advent of the Masters

Rupert was criticized precisely for not having attended the schools. Far from giving in to this criticism, though, the elderly abbot gloried in the fact that he had never wandered from city to city in quest of knowledge and culture, and that from the time of adolescence he had stayed home; i.e., in the monastery, where "the living springs of Christ give better nourishment than the fountains of men."[6]

---

[4] *De omnipotentia Dei* xxiii (*PL*, CLXX, 473): "Valentiora quippe esse censeo verba simplicia pastorum et piscatorum, cum quibus locutus est Deus, quam argumenta philosophorum vel sapientium quos in reprobum sensum tradidit Deus." (Of far greater value are the simple words of the shepherds and fishermen with whom the Lord spoke than the arguments put forth by the philosophers or the wise whom God delivered over to a corrupted perception.)

[5] *Ibid.* xxvii (*PL*, CLXX, 478): "Caeterum quidquid extra hanc scripturam sanctam cogitari, vel argumentando potest confingi, sicut expers rationis est, ita nullatenus pertinet ad laudem vel confessionem omnipotentiae Dei."

[6] *Super quaedam capitula regulae divi Benedicti abbatis* i (*PL*, CLXX, 481): ". . . quia balneis sive cisternis hominum viva fontis Christi fluenter

Rupert was thus not of this new generation in which the young elite, like Abelard, traveled about to hear one popular master after another. Masters—*magistri*—a new social category was in fact appearing outside the structures of old secular and ecclesiastical feudalism, far removed from the bellicose and privileged knights, in nearly every case without ties to the monasteries which until that time had been the chief promoters of culture and education. The masters lived in cities where their allies, the bourgeois, were emancipating themselves by forming communes—and not without violence, as for example had been the case at Laon itself. The masters were detached from the countryside and thus free to take an interest in business and commerce. Their new mobility enriched them, exalted them, and at the same time left them with no place in the old society. Occasionally they were advisers to princes, great and small, and were alert to all kinds of novelties and adventures and impatient for every kind of liberty, of the body as well as of the mind. Rainald of Dassel, chancellor under Frederick Barbarossa, had been a student in the schools of Paris; so had Stephen Langton, archbishop of Canterbury, one of the leaders of the baronial revolt against King John. Arnold of Brescia referred to himself as a student of Abelard. From the old monastic schools we pass with these people to the new city schools where the clerical teachers, under episcopal control, were fulfilling the needs and aspirations of students of their own kind, a clientele that could not have been assimilated intellectually any more than socially into the monasteries. These were no longer men of the cloister (*claustrales*) but scholastics, scholars (*scholastici, scholares*).[7]

Schola—in developing his conception of the monastic life, St. Benedict had long ago appropriated the term "school," and associated terms, for the service of God. Christ was henceforth the "mas-

---

ju/iter manantia meliora sunt." *Ibid.* (*PL*, CLXX, 480): ". . . non circuivi mare et aridam, sicut divites negotiatores illi quorum apud cogitationes pauper sum. . . . Ierunt enim in longinquum, et apud magistros inclytos peregrinati sunt. . . . Hinc ego apud cogitationes illorum pauper et contemptibilis et dixerunt: 'Quis est hic?' " (I have not traveled all over land and sea like those rich dealers who think of me as a pauper. . . . For they have traveled far and wandered among famous masters. . . . Hence in their view I am poor and contemptible, and they ask: "Who is this?")

[7] For the meanings and evolution of these terms, see G. Paré, A. Brunet, and P. Tremblay, *La renaissance du XIIe siècle* (Paris-Ottawa, 1933), pp. 50–60 (*scolaris*), pp. 69–72 (*scholasticus*).

ter," and the monastery was the "school of the Lord's service" (*dominici schola servitii*).[8] The Cistercians were to take up the word again and insist on the active implementation of this old Benedictine tradition. In lively competition with the new schools and their secular masters, the Cistercians pressed for an exclusive definition of "school," a definition which rejected any variant conception as intolerable. The "school" of the primitive church (*schola primitivae ecclesiae*),[9] ideal of the Cistercian reform, was plainly not a school but a certain mode of evangelical life. The monk (*monachus*) was not a scholastic (*scholasticus*). When Rupert was praising one Siegfried of Laon, he slipped by saying that Siegfried was a great scholastic even though a monk.[10] Rupert's revealing distinction helps us define two types of Christian high culture, each with its own theology: the monastic and the scholastic.

The first of the masters in the new style, the founder of the line, at least the one acknowledged *magister magistrorum* at the time, seems to have been Manegold of Lautenbach who died in the early years of the twelfth century. "Manegold the priest, master of the modern masters" (*Manegoldus presbyter, modernorum magister magistrorum*), said the anonymous author of Melk.[11] In any case, by the first few decades of the century, the word designated an officially recognized position and status: Master Ivo of Chartres, Master Anselm of Laon, Master Bernard of Chartres, Master Abelard, Master Gilbert, Master Hugh of Saint-Victor, Master Peter Lombard (who would come to be known as the "Master of the Sentences"), and so on.

Beyond accrediting individuals, the title certified the value of their teachings and pronouncements. The "masters" were called upon along with the fathers to give authoritative interpretations of revelation. The *Liber Pancrisis*, which originated in the school of Laon towards the middle of the twelfth century, is an example of the compendia in which *magistralia* (opinions of the masters) were added

---

[8] *Regula monachorum* prol. (ed. J. McCann [London, 1952]), pp. 12–13.

[9] Anon. *Exordium magnum ordinis cisterciensis* i.2 (*PL*, CLXXXV, 998).

[10] *Super quaedam capitula regulae divi Benedicti abbatis* i (*PL*, CLXX, 496).

[11] *De script. eccl.* cv (*PL*, CCXIII, 981).

to *auctoritates, sententiae* (judgments of the fathers). Already included in it were William of Champeaux, Ivo of Chartres, Anselm of Laon and his brother Ralph. Honorius of Autun proposed explicitly to construct his *Elucidarium,* c. 1110, on four columns: the prophets, the apostles, the biblical commentators, and the masters.[12] After praising the ancients, Peter of Celle, abbot of Saint-Rémy from 1162 to 1180, recommended: "If new things please you, then look into the writings of Master Hugh or [Master] Bernard or Master Gilbert or Master Peter Comestor where you will find no lack of roses and lilies."[13] John of Cornwall in his *Eulogium* of 1177, a collection of texts concerning various theories on the incarnation, cited concurrently the two types of sources, fathers and masters, ". . . so that the light armament of the learned men of our time may supplement the heavy armor of the saints," and accordingly furnished the authoritative texts of the masters (*auctoritates magistrorum*) after those of the saints (*auctoritates sanctorum*).[14] In his description of the *translatio studiorum*, the gradual migration of culture from east to west, Otto of Freising referred to the masters as the protagonists of the final stage: ". . . and following that, learning appeared most recently in the far West, i.e., in Gaul and Spain, in the age of the great teachers Berengar, Manegold, and Anselm."[15] Thus the masters gained official recognition, although their writings could not have

---

[12] *Elucidarium* prol. (*PL*, CLXXII, 1110; Lefèvre, p. 359): "Fundamentum igitur opusculi supra petram, id est Christum, jaciatur, et tota machina quattuor firmis columnis fulciatur. Primam columnam erigat prophetica auctoritas, secundum stabiliat apostolica dignitas, tertiam roboret expositorum sagacitas, quartam figat magistrorum solers sublimitas." (Let the foundation of this work be rested upon a rock, that is, Christ, and the whole structure be supported by four firm columns. Let the authority of the prophets raise the first column; the apostolic dignity steady the second one; the sagacity of the commentators make strong the third one; and the sublimity of the masters fix the fourth in place.)

[13] *Epp.* clxvii (*PL*, CCII, 610): "Si nova placent, ecce magistri Hugonis, ecce s.[*sic*] Bernardi, ecce magistri Gilleberti, et magistri Petri scripta, in quibus nec rosae, nec lilia desunt."

[14] *Eulogium* iii (Haring, p. 265): ". . . ut fortissimis sanctorum cuneis etiam doctorum hujus temporis levior armatura preludat."

[15] *Chronica* v. prol. (Lammers-Schmidt, pp. 374–5; Mierow, p. 323): ". . . ac post ad ultimum occidentem, id est ad Gallias et Hispanias, nuperrime a diebus illustrium doctorum Berengarii, Managaldi, et Anshelmi translatam apparet."

been said to carry the definitive authority accorded to those of the fathers.[16]

As the schools became organized and their regulations established, the *licentia docendi* (license to teach) became the prerequisite for this now official title of master.[17] The *licentia* certified one not only as a teacher but as a theologian; it designated an asset hitherto unknown, displaying an epistemological stock-in-trade, all quite beyond the bishop as teacher of the faith. The place of the masters in the church became increasingly difficult to determine as they organized theology into a science with its own rules, constructed within the faith and its premises to be sure, but according to criteria stemming from the intelligible nature of the subjects they were examining, and not according to the needs and opportunities of pastoral responsibility or of subjective, pious intentions. There would now necessarily be "theological" errors, wheras hitherto the term heresy simply denoted any lapses from orthodox faith.[18] In the second half of the twelfth century there was a long list of masters who came under suspicion of heresy, rightly or not, privately or publicly. At the council of Reims in 1148, Gilbert of La Porrée was thus incriminated, rather by his fellow theologians, as it happened, than by the bishops who were teachers of the faith. The fundamentally traditional theory of appropriations in trinitarian theology, of identifying *potentia* (power), *sapientia* (wisdom), and *bonitas* (goodness) respectively with the three persons of the Trinity, was denounced by William of Saint-Thierry, while at the same time Robert of Melun justified Abelard's use of it.[19] The question "whether Christ is a 'something' " (*utrum Christus sit aliquid*) provoked a lively controversy in which anathemas were exchanged during some thirty years, all concerning

---

[16] Cf. M.-D. Chenu, "Authentica et Magistralia," *Divus Thomas*, XXVIII (1925), 257–85; reprinted in Chenu, *TDS*, pp. 351–65.

[17] Cf. G. Post, "Alexander III, the *licentia docendi*, and the Rise of Universities," *Anniversary Essays in Medieval History by Students of Charles Homer Haskins*, ed. C. H. Taylor (Boston, 1929), pp. 255–78.

[18] The word "heresy" was to continue to designate all kinds of errors, even an error unconsciously involved in some activity (*simoniaca haeresis*), and did not come to have its more specific modern meaning until much later, in the course of the methodological controversies of the sixteenth century.

[19] Cf. R. M. Martin, "*Pro Petro Abelardo:* un plaidoyer de Robert de Melun contre saint Bernard," *RSPT*, XII (1923), pp. 308–33.

a matter which, even in its terminology, belongs clearly to the working out of technicalities and to the freedom of viewpoints found within an orthodox faith.[20] These rather abstruse controversies testify in their way to the weightiness and credibility henceforth attributed to the activities of the masters. The case of Peter Lombard illustrates this point exactly, as much by the condemnations of his work as by its subsequent influence, as much in his theological "opinions" as in his expressions of orthodox faith. No theologian was so widely discussed, as can be seen in the expanding list of "positions in which the Master is not agreed with" (*positiones in quibus Magister non tenetur*), and none was so widely followed, for his *Sententiae* was to remain the basic book of theological studies on into the sixteenth century and even beyond.[21]

Even more in their schools did the masters emancipate themselves from the pure and simple administrative control of the bishop. In an episcopal chapter, the *scholasticus* or master was an official who was named and who could be recalled at any time by the bishop. If a master's teaching led to the growth of a school, the school came automatically under the administrative supervision of the diocesan chancellor. But as the number of masters and of their schools increased, which happened gradually in the larger towns, they began to organize themselves, not only to distribute their increasingly specialized responsibilities (for example, among the seven arts, law, biblical study, etc.), but to gain independence in their activity. Thus at Paris, where until the final years of the century the schools of the cloister of Notre Dame remained under the bishop's control, already before 1212 the arts faculty had emigrated to the left bank of the Seine. The battle was joined; corporate rights with their administrative privileges, like those of the craft guilds, were at stake. Theologians and jurists, in order to escape the demands of the chancellor and to guarantee the rights accorded them by the Holy See, soon joined the teachers of the arts in their new location, thus shattering the conservatism of the school of Notre Dame. History was to reveal

---

[20] Cf. R. F. Studeny, *John of Cornwall: An Opponent of Nihilianism. A Study of the Christological Controversies of the Twelfth Century* (Diss., Vienna, 1939); also Haring.

[21] Cf. J. de Ghellinck, article on "Pierre Lombard," *DTC*, XII, 1941–2019.

the significance of this episode: it marked the intellectual and institutional birth of what we have come to call the "university."[22]

Such is the context within which the interventions of the masters, alongside the authoritative writings of the fathers, came to play an increasingly decisive role in the intellectual affairs of Christendom. The masters were consulted in matters both public and private; for example, by Thomas Becket in his conflict with Henry II; or, when consulted on a difficult question, Peter of Blois referred his correspondent to the schools at Paris.[23] The masters made pedagogical, literary, scientific strides. They established definitions and formulae, even rudimentary etymologies; e.g., "The Parisian masters say that *cassidile* (small bag or wallet) is derived from *casse* (hunting net)," against other masters who interpret it as coming from *capsa-sedile*.[24] Through official resolutions, they took stands in current debates, as seen for example in the list of ten errors censured by the chancellor and masters of Paris in 1241.[25] Finally—and this came to happen more and more in the thirteenth century—they formed common opinions (*communis opinio magistrorum*) after a period of free debate that eliminated some superficial but wholly inadequate explanation of a tenet of faith. Not, however, that this common opinion could not be questioned. Thus Prepositinus, speaking of the relationship between nature and grace, was able to say, "The masters commonly agree that. . . . However, it seems to me. . . ."[26]

The high reputation of the masters was symbolized in the legend of the three brothers; that is, of Peter Lombard, Gratian, and Peter

---

[22] Cf. G. Post, "Parisian Masters as a Corporation, 1200–1246," chap. 1 of *Studies in Medieval Legal Thought* (Princeton, 1964), pp. 27–60; also C. Thouzellier, "L'enseignement et les universités," chap. 4 of *La Chrétienté romaine, 1198–1274* (Paris, 1950), pp. 349–55 (*Histoire de l'Eglise*, ed. A. Fliche and V. Martin, vol. 10).

[23] *CUP*, I, 21 (#21) and 35 (#29): "Qui interrogant interrogent Parisius, ubi difficilium questionum nodi intricatissimi resolvuntur." (Let whoever have questions ask them in Paris where the most intricate knots of difficult questions are untied.)

[24] Alexander Neckham *Sacerdos ad altare* (MS, Cambridge, Gonville and Caius College 385, fol. 15; cited by Haskins, *Studies,* p. 364).

[25] *CUP*, I, 170 (#128).

[26] *Summa* (MS Todi 71, fol. 89; cited by J. B. Kors, *La justice primitive et le péché original d'après saint Thomas, les sources, la doctrine* [Lille, 1922], p. 61): "Via magistrorum communis est. . . . Nobis autem videtur. . . ."

Comestor.[27] These authors of the three great masterworks which from the late twelfth century became the basic texts for instruction in theology, law, and biblical history respectively were believed to be brothers. However naive this conception, later accounts could accept it wholesale. Especially in theology, the influence of the Lombard became increasingly strong, less because his opinions were accepted than because his writings were institutionalized. His *Sentences* became the basic textbook of instruction, not without curtailing the fundamental importance of scriptural study in theology. Already before 1250, Albert the Great made a revealing admission in the course of debates concerning original sin: "What I do not actually believe myself I am nonetheless allowed to maintain because it was the Master's opinion."[28]

From Sacred Text to Sacred Doctrine

In every branch of learning, the *magister* predictably introduced methods and tools into each pursuit which, in its special function and competence, was hereafter considered a profession. Theology—the science of God—did not have to avoid this progress; in fact faith was not averse to borrowing, even for matters of belief, the new techniques employed by the human mind. "Theology," Jacques Maritain reminds us, "is the primary and great technology of the Christian world."[29] The key developments in the professionalization of theology took place in the twelfth century; its techniques reached perfection during the following century and just beyond in the works of Albert the Great, Bonaventure, Thomas Aquinas, and Duns Scotus. *Ars fidei* (art of the faith), Alan of Lille's phrase in the title to a tract dedicated to Pope Clement III (reigned 1187–91), could well serve to characterize the whole effort of the twelfth century.[30] Faith

---

[27] Cf. Ghellinck, *Mouvement*, pp. 214 and esp. 285.

[28] *In II Sent.* d. 24, a. 1, sol. (*Opera omnia*, ed. A. Borgnet, 38 vols. [Paris, 1890–9], XXVII, 397): "Quod tamen ego non credo, licet sustineam propter Magistrum."

[29] *Distinguish to Unite; or, the Degrees of Knowledge*, tr. G. B. Phelan (New York, 1959), p. 294.

[30] Alan of Lille *De arte seu articulis catholicae fidei* (*PL*, CCX, 597): "Nempe editionem hanc *Artem catholicae fidei* merito appello. In modum

was being fashioned into a science. In the pre-Aristotelian language still in use, as reflected in the terminology of the seven "encyclopedic" arts, *ars* and *scientia* remained very close, so long as *ars* was further qualified as a *disciplina*.[31]

Of course, the techniques of grammar and rhetoric and of dialectic had long been employed in the service of understanding the sacred text and of shaping doctrinal concepts. *Tropi* and *schemata* had been in use since the Carolingian renaissance; the tools of dialectic, since the times of Berengar and of Abelard. But in the second half of the twelfth century, reason and its various disciplines no longer furnished simply the tools for studying the sacred text (*sacra pagina*). Reason, by introducing "well ordered arrangement" (*artificioso successu*), somehow entered into the structuring of the faith itself, as Alan of Lille suggested in his *Ars fidei*. This is what so upset Rupert of Deutz, even though he consented to all the artifices of rhetoric, including even fables.[32] The discovery of the *Analytics* and of the *Topics*, so

---

enim artis composita diffinitiones, distinctiones continet, et propositiones artificioso successu propositum comprobantes." (I call this work *The Art of the Catholic Faith* for a reason. Put together as any art is, it contains definitions and distinctions, and propositions which demonstrate a point through their well ordered arrangement.) [The authorship of this work has long been debated. While Père Chenu names Nicholas of Amiens as author, the translators have substituted Alan of Lille in accordance with the recent work of M.-Th. d'Alverny, *Alain de Lille* (Paris, 1965), pp. 68–9.]

[31] The classic expression of these notions is a statement of Isidore quoted by Hugh of Saint-Victor *Didascalicon* ii.1 (Buttimer, p. 23; Taylor, p. 61): "Ars dici potest scientia, quae artis praeceptis regulisque consistit." (Knowledge can be called an art "when it comprises the rules and precepts of an art.")

[32] *De Trinitate et operibus ejus*, "De operibus Spiritus Sancti" vii.11 (*PL*, CLXVII, 1765): ". . . schemata, tropos, prosam, metra, fabulas, historiam descibere ac distinguere praesentis negotii non est; verumtamen haec in illa contineri vel observari usque adeo verum est, ut fabulam quoque non praetereat." (It is not our present business to describe and distinguish . . . figures, tropes, prose, meter, fables, history; so true is it, however, that these are contained and can be seen in [scripture] that even fables are not excluded.) See also Rupert's *De victoria verbi Dei* xi.2 (*PL*, CLXIX, 1444): "Omnes modi vel tropi sive schemata, omnes omnino ornatus locutionis, de quibus quasi auctores gloriati sunt saeculares magistri, sparsim in divinis inveniuntur scripturis, et prius erat quam hi qui horum putantur adinventores, fuissent nati." (All styles, tropes or figures, indeed all the refinements of speech, in which the secular masters glory as if they were themselves great authors, can be found scattered throughout divine scripture; and these refinements were there long before those who are supposed to have invented them were born.)

appreciated by John of Salisbury, as also the practice of the Neo-platonic *resolutio*, undoubtedly furnished the necessary and fertile apparatus for a deep penetration into the faith. But it was deep reflection upon the faith itself, whether for defense as in Alan of Lille's *De fide catholica contra haereticos* ("On the Catholic Faith, against the Heretics"), or whether for theological construction as in Alan's *Regulae* ("The Rules") or in the summas written by Prepositinus, William of Auxerre, and so many others, that brought the faith to a reasoned fulness, or better, gave it a kind of reasoned fruitfulness that the dialectic of Abelard did not achieve alone. St. Anselm, it is true, had attempted to establish the *rationes necessariae* (necessary ideas) through which the *intellectus fidei* (understanding of the faith) could be secured. But this brilliant purpose, as it was yet intransmissible, had certainly not hit upon the needed methodology, which only the techniques of forming propositions, definitions, probable arguments, and demonstrations could supply.

In commenting on a scriptural text, or on any text for that matter, a master quickly showed what he was after: to give a literal account of its structure, before extracting its ideological content. In defining his purpose at the beginning of his commentary on the *Timaeus*, William of Conches declared: "Although no doubt there are many commentaries and glosses on Plato, nevertheless because these have not carefully followed and explained the literal text but have only attended to the ideas of the work, we have undertaken at the urging of our colleagues. . . ."[33] One can see here an application of the method of reading which Master Bernard of Chartres (after 1115) had pioneered for teaching the texts of the ancient pagan authors. In the opinion of John of Salisbury, Bernard had been sensationally successful in this method—that of a schoolmaster, in the original sense of *scholasticus*.[34]

When applied to scripture, this system of commentary had the

---

[33] Jeauneau, p. 57: "Etsi multos super Platonem commentatos esse, multos glosasse non dubitemus, tamen quia commentatores, litteram nec continuantes nec exponentes, soli sententie serviunt . . . rogatu sociorum . . . proposuimus. . . ."

[34] Cf. John's sympathetic description of Bernard's *usus legendi* (method of teaching), *Metalogicon* i.24 (Webb, pp. 53–58; McGarry, pp. 65–71).

effect of distinguishing exegesis with its historico-literal techniques not only from systematic theological construction but even from the establishment of the doctrinal content of scripture: study of the *littera* (literal or historical level of scripture) was prior to study of its *sensus* (the sense) and to the *sententia* (the deeper meaning) in the three levels of the text distinguished by Hugh of Saint-Victor.[35] The method and spirit of the masters of Saint-Victor rested on recognition of this order of study; and it was Peter Comestor, the *magister historiarum*, who combined all three levels in a method of biblical analysis wholly different from that of the monastic *collatio*.

The second major innovation of the *magistri* was to import into sacred doctrine categories taken from the rational analysis of secular phenomena. The process was not without some risk, but when done correctly (its rules were searched out minutely), it brought considerable profit to the religious dimension of faith and to the knowledge and understanding of God. Historians of theology, following the lead of historians of dogma, have studied the importation of such concepts as *substantia, essentia, persona, natura,* etc., into speculative theology. In reading their studies, one becomes aware of these innovations and the subtle controversies over theological method (not over dogma) that they provoked; for, in the science of theology, these rational concepts implied a whole method which could only lead—it is clear enough with the *magistri*—to differences of opinion within the defined dogmas of the faith. In any case, the consideration of *De translatione nominum de naturali facultate ad theologicam* ("On Transferring Terms from the Study of Nature to Theology"), whether it treated natural denominations for the divinity or scriptural expressions, formed a standard and critically important chapter in the theological treatises of twelfth-century *magistri*. I have had occasion elsewhere to analyze some elements of this theology, especially those contributed by the Neoplatonic metaphysics of participation.[36]

Moreover, let us also note that such importation extended well beyond the limits of specialists' debates, going right to the heart of

---

[35] *Didascalicon* vi.8–11 (Buttimer, pp. 125–9; Taylor, pp. 147–50).
[36] See above, pp. 49–98, esp. pp. 79–88.

common ways of thinking, of feeling, of reflecting in the whole realm of faith and morals. St. Bernard, in describing the dispositions (*affectiones*) of the soul toward God in his sermons on the *Song of Songs*, specified the relationship to God which each of these dispositions imposed on the soul; and to do this he relied solely on categories taken from biblical language and from experience: fear (*timor*) imposed the relationship of a servant or slave (*servus*); hope (*spes*), of a paid employee (*mercenarius*); obedience (*obedientia*), of a disciple (*discipulus*); respect (*honor*), of a son (*filius*); and love (*amor*), of a spouse (*sponsa*).[37] The masters, however, were to reduce these subjective descriptions to categories worked out by philosophers in their objective analyses of the passions *timor, spes, amor*, etc. Thus at the end of the twelfth century, Raoul Ardent endeavored to establish a rational and coherent classification of the virtues comprised in fortitude.[38] The term *affectus, affectio* (disposition, affection) would be rejected, not out of ignorance of its meaning but out of preference for *passio* (passion, or undergoing) which the philosophers had used. In the same way the degrees of charity and the ladder of humility would no longer be conceived in scriptural terms combined more or less arbitrarily but would be established according to the properties of the objects concerned. Such operations obviously could not take place without a bit of semantic juggling where the two types of analysis crossed, each valid in its own domain and each, at least in principle, capable of suitable accommodation. When Guerric of Igny spoke of justice as one of the elements needed in forming a taste for eternal truth,[39] he was clearly talking of the biblical virtue of justice, and not of the specific virtue which the masters had defined in relation to the laws of earthly society. Not the least important result of all this was a sorting out of

---

[37] *Sermones in Cantica canticorum* vii.2 (*PL*, CLXXXIII, 807).

[38] *Speculum universale* x (MS Paris BN lat. 3240, fol. 54ᵛ), cited by R. A. Gauthier, *Magnanimité* (Paris, 1951), pp. 273, 286.

[39] *Sermones in epiphania Domini* iii.7 (*PL*, CLXXXV, 53): ". . . per haec tria fidem, justitiam atque scientiam, proficiat ad sapientiam, idest saporem et gustum aeternorum." (By these three things, faith, justice, and knowledge, may one arrive at wisdom, i.e., a taste and desire for the eternal.)

virtues and dispositions which evangelical fervor had presented in a tumble of religious contexts and criteria and which now were differentiated and classified according to the inner faculties of the human subject. There now appeared, for example, psychologically and ethically based classifications of virtues, a bit pedantic sometimes but revealing precious sources of understanding being put to the service of an intellectuality increasingly enlightened in thought and aim. These classifications reached maturity in the moral sections of the thirteenth-century *summae*.

Seen thus, the twelfth century shows advances in theology that have not been sufficiently appreciated. The masters elaborated a psychological science which would carry on and organize the spiritual experience accumulated by tradition and recorded first by the fathers and later by monastic authors. The instigator of this theological anthropology was Master Abelard who, in close connection with his theory of knowledge, showed the importance of subjective factors in human behavior, including its supernatural phases. His conclusions were sometimes not beyond dispute, but their venturesomeness underscored the novelty of his method. Thus, he proclaimed the primacy of intention as determining a good act as well as a sin, and thereby the primacy of the judgment of man's conscience without which his act would not exist. From this in turn followed the importance of contrition in the sacrament of penance, with absolution downgraded to a mere parting word; from this his notion of original sin, in which the absence of personal will eliminates guilt strictly speaking; from this his anti-Augustinian stand on the naturalness of sexual pleasure, which intention alone could contaminate; from this his theory, condemned in 1140 at the Council of Sens, on the clear conscience of the executioners of Christ; from this his analysis of the act of faith, in which, as in moral consent (*consensus*), interior assent (*assensus*) had supreme value; from this the general deepening of his teaching on the nature of virtue. Here was a fine example of theological work, where the rational options were perfectly coherent, even when their implications were imperfectly explored in the conclusions—thus giving a foothold to critics of his orthodoxy. But even his critics, from Peter Lombard to William of Auxerre, perpetuated his central principle.[40] This theology of human action—which scriptural study by itself could not have produced in this fashion—was, moreover, supported by an awakening of conscience in the Christian people, who were being trained slowly and steadily through a general rise in their level of culture and the refining of their hitherto gross personal manners, to engage in personal prayer, examine their conduct, and practice moral criticism. The material penances of the old penitential books, so vigorously denounced by Abelard, gave way to the considered judgment advocated in the *summae* of confession. Use of the sacrament of penance as a means of pastoral care found ready sponsors at the Fourth Lateran Council in a significant combination of new apostolic reformers and students of the masters.[41]

If it is true that definition is the goal of intellectual investigation, then the masters were properly successful if they got their definitions widely accepted as valid. In fact several definitions of the masters (*definitiones magistrales*) gained currency toward the end of the twelfth century and afterwards, and they became part of the standard curriculum even though they sometimes stirred up controversy in the schools. Such was the case with their definition of truth: "The 'true' lies in the bond between being and the subject possessing being" (*Verum est indivisio esse et ejus quod est*), based on a text of Avicenna; or of sacramental character: "This character is a distinction which the 'eternal character'[42] imprints upon the rational soul" (*Character est distinctio a charactere aeterno impressa animae ra-*

---

[40] Cf. O. Lottin, "L'intention morale de Pierre Abélard à Saint Thomas," chap. 22 of *Psychologie et morale aux XIIᵉ et XIIIᵉ siècles*, 6 vols. (Louvain, 1942–54), IV, 307–466. In the same period and on the same professional level, other masters were active on the institutional and spiritual planes. These were the masters of canon law, who were working out the distinction between the inner conscience and the outer conscience, a distinction which benefited the rights of the conscience and the individuality of one's relationship to God.

[41] The new *summae de paenitentia* were to be composed by members of the new mendicant orders, using the resources of their university schools. One of the first of these was the school of the Dominicans at the Convent of Saint-Jacques in Paris. [Cf. *DTC*, XII, 734–8.]

[42] [Cf. Hebrews 1:3, where Christ is called the "character" of the divine "hypostasis" (Χαρακτὴρ τῆς ὑποστάσεως).]

tionali); or of person: "A hypostasis distinguished by its property" (*Ypostasis proprietate distincta*).

Perhaps we can best see the strictly theological work of the masters in the way they brought into question certain accepted propositions that had the strongest possible patristic backing but that suddenly became problems in the face of new demands being made by the "science of faith" (*scientia fidei*). The long quarrel over the *assumptus homo* was the most notable case. Of the three opinions to which Peter Lombard, in a schematization that immediately became classic, reduced current thought on the hypostatic union in Christ, the first, careful to maintain the integrity of Christ's humanity, the absolute perfection of his human individuality and liberty, defined this humanity as a *homo assumptus* (man elevated); and in support of this were cited qualified authorities all the way from St. Athanasius, who wrote of a *homo dominicus* (man-lord) right through to the recent theologians. Yet, as theological reflection progressed, this position was debated; it became suspect; and soon it was explicitly rejected as false, indeed as heretical, by the masters of the thirteenth century. From the level of patristic tradition, where different expressions were employed and more often complemented than opposed one another because they generally involved spontaneous instead of philosophical notions, men passed to the mature level of reasoned theology where traditional expressions took on an intellectualized character, a particular metaphysical significance, newly precise and defined, and varying with the systems which scrutinized and made use of them. At this level of maturity, the three opinions revealed implicit differences which forced individuals to opt for one or another, yet with no peril for these different orientations within an orthodoxy that had become far more exacting in its formulations. Involved here was not only the problem of how to handle authorities critically—for example, how to resolve the difficulties raised by the Latin translation of the acts of the Council of Ephesus—but also a difficult task of sensitive theological discernment.[43]

---

[43] Peter Lombard *Libri IV Sententiarum* iii, d. 6 (2 vols. [Quaracchi, 1916], II, 573–82). Cf. A. Gaudel, "La théologie de l'*Assumptus homo:* histoire et valeur doctrinale," *RSR*, XVII (1937), 64–90, 214–34; XVIII (1938), 45–71, 201–17; reviewed by H. Dondaine, *Bulletin thomiste*, VI (1939–40), 674–9.

The same kind of thing happened in the controversy over the beatific vision which, like the former controversy, achieved a balanced though hardly uniform resolution among the masters of the thirteenth century: Did this vision, the object of man's hope, involve an immediate, direct knowledge of the divine essence? In this case, patristic opinion seemed torn between two contradictory assertions found in scripture itself: God is invisible; yet the saints are to see him as he is. The Greek fathers had favored the transcendence of the invisible God and were reluctant to infringe this cardinal tenet even when speaking of man's ultimate "face-to-face" encounter with God. The Latin fathers had postulated from the start that man's vocation was to see God, and it was in those terms that they approached the question of God's invisibility. But new access to the Greek sources had shocked western masters into admiration and reserve. The shock reverberated across the entire surface of theological study, and the controversy over the beatific vision was one of its most critical episodes. Here too, as differing conclusions accumulated, faith acquired increasing mastery of its object; orthodoxy was illuminated as diverse theological systems freely explored the legitimate implications of their particular spiritual or philosophical bias. The intervention of the masters of Paris in 1241, even if in the service of orthodoxy, remained under the influence of a Latinism little open to the insights of the most authoritative Greek doctors and to the problems they raised.

A certain number of these theological problems took root in the interpretation even of scriptural texts. Once one sought to make their contents intelligible, not only in their *littera*, not only in their *sententia*, but in their structure as stories and in the bearing of their historical and doctrinal contexts, problems quite unknown to earlier interpreters appeared. The masters of the twelfth century became qualified artisans in biblical theology (the term should be taken as naming a searching and constructive endeavor), and it would be very profitable to describe the methods and results of this lofty labor of which one of the determining influences was the reaction of Master Hugh of Saint-Victor. Here, too, it was not a matter of establishing or even discussing an orthodoxy, but of theological inquiry where options and conclusions were unfixed and debatable. It is well known that Hugh's symbolist theory, admirable as an attempt to construct an allegorical edifice upon a solidly worked out literal foundation, fastened certain unquestioned traditional values onto the spiritual sense. A century later, however, this procedure was expressly banished from sacred doctrine by Master Thomas Aquinas.

In this biblical theology there were many different elements and various methods. To cite an example from the highest level of speculative work, take the considerations concerning the primitive state of man in the earthly paradise. In tracing the investigations and controversies of the masters, one can see how, in place of varying textual interpretations, they used certain presuppositions on the nature of man, on the laws of the mind, on the necessity for grace. The criteria of truth were no longer based solely upon the rule of faith as operative in the revealed texts but also upon the rational coherence of propositions taken from a philosophy of man and here used as the minor premises of syllogisms. One could undoubtedly define twelfth-century humanism by the portraits it produced of Adam. While Prepositinus advanced the view that man was created in a state of grace from the very start to assure the goodness of his nature and the personal value of freely given love, William of Auxerre became the leader of those who worked out the notion of original justice as a gift of nature, transmissible with nature.[44] These views certainly had great bearing upon the understanding of one's faith; but the constructions on which they were based, even where the analysis proceeded by demonstration, lacked the direct support of either scripture or its official interpreters.

Without getting into such involved constructions, and yet to give an introductory understanding of the text, the master would introduce into his commentary notions by which the biblical passage became intellectualized even to its verbal particulars. Peter Comester the historian, commenting on the grammatical variations of God's word *fiat* (let there be) in the creation account, glossed the verses of *Genesis* in this way: "When *fiat* is said, it refers to the foreknowledge of God; *fecit* (he made) refers to the material product of his work; and *factum est* (it was done) to the work in its es-

---

[44] Cf. J. B. Kors (cited above, n. 26), pp. 61–66.

sence."[45] When the masters encountered the word *oblatio* (offering), they analyzed the four required conditions for making an offering; when they encountered the word *timor* (fear), they analyzed the different types of fear. The preposition *per* (through, by, across, because of) designated an indirect causality; the conjunction *ut* (in order that), the relationship of the means to its end, etc. The result was a form of theological literature altogether different from the patristic and monastic commentaries; this was the university *lectio* (explication). It was certainly not exegesis in the sense in which we understand it today, but instead a peculiar theological exposition based upon the thread of the text and employing a persistent conceptual scheme. This was therefore still the reading of the sacred text, but greatly expanded into what was truly a scholastic exegesis. It is according to the rules of this new literary form, including the law of typological and allegorizing symbolism, that one must read, understand, and appreciate the commentaries of the masters, including those of Master Thomas Aquinas in the thirteenth century.[46]

We have suggested several times how this theological approach could and often did lead, quite consciously, to a wide variety of opinions.[47] But still more interesting were the observable differences in the very methods of this *intellectus fidei*. The theology that grew out of the twelfth-century schools was and remained abundantly rich in methodological variation until post-Tridentine scholasticism regrettably imposed a system of methodical conformity.

St. Anselm, who combined a superior dialectical virtuosity with perfect contemplative control, undertook to discover the depths of the faith (*profunda fidei*); that is, the necessary ideas (*rationes necessariae*) through which one's faith progresses towards the beatifying

---

[45] *Historia libri Genesis* iv (*PL*, CXCVIII, 1058): "Cum dicitur fiat, ad praescientiam Dei refertur; fecit, ad opus in materia; factum est, ad opus in essentia."

[46] Cf. Chenu, *St. Thomas*, chap. 7, "The Commentaries on the Bible."

[47] Cf. the case of Peter Lombard in his Christological positions, according to John of Cornwall *Eulogium* iii (Haring, p. 265): ". . . michi et omnibus auditoribus suis qui tunc aderant, protestatus est, quod hoc non esset assertio sua, sed opinio sola, quam a magistris acceperat" (to me and all his listeners who were there, he protested that these did not really represent his beliefs but only an opinion picked up from the masters).

vision. Such a vision was the eminent gift of a theology that was not some diversified luxury for the mind, but the organic law of the believing intelligence, a law which it could not ignore without gross negligence: "It seems to me a case of negligence if, after becoming firm in our faith, we not strive to understand what we believe."[48]

For Abelard, the word "dialectic" referred to a wholly different process: it was a matter of scientifically arranging the texts of tradition, grouped in opposites, *sic et non*—texts which Anselm had kept, like scripture itself, subordinate to his personal contemplative thought. And then, after that task of positive and critical investigation, Abelard set out to apply "the analogies of human reason to the fundamentals of the faith"[49] with an audaciously rational clarity which threatened to weaken all taste for mystery.

Hugh of Saint-Victor, contrary to Anselm and Abelard, laid hold upon Christian mystery within its sacred historical context—a context that furnished an intellectually and religiously indispensible foundation on which to build allegorical constructions that yielded a sort of transcendent understanding, beyond time though based on symbols.

Richard of Saint-Victor, like Anselm, was not especially concerned with scriptural citation, and the fathers were far from satisfying to him. Intellectually intoxicated by his faith, he gave himself over to speculation which, even in its conceptual framework, its *sobria ebrietas* (sober intoxication), strikes one as deriving from the pressures of his mystical life.

The *Regulae* of Alan of Lille represents a nearly unique attempt in the West to weave the free wills of God and the disparate moments of man's salvation into a deductive and axiomatic system—a system which related the creative extension of the divine Unity into the multiplicities of created realities and the causal reintegration of all these realities in Christ and the sacraments.

---

[48] [*Cur Deus homo* i.2 (*PL*, CLVIII, 362; *Basic Writings: Proslogium; Monologium; Gaunilon's On Behalf of the Fool; Cur Deus homo*, tr. S. N. Deane, 2nd ed. [LaSalle, Illinois, 1962], p. 179).]

[49] *Historia calamitatum* ix (*PL*, CLXXVIII, 140–1; Muckle, p. 39): ". . . ad ipsum fidei nostrae fundamentum humanae rationis similitudinibus disserendum."

From William of Auxerre, at the time of the Fourth Lateran Council, we have a prototype of the classic *summa* of the thirteenth century where every element in the legacy of revelation was brought into question and dealt with by various rational methods in order to extract certain internal connections and convincing subtleties of the objects of the faith. Thus conceived, theology would more and more assume the forms and procedures of the Aristotelian science (*scientia*).

New Forms of Theological Literature

In a sacred doctrine equally venturesome under its many forms, the rational curiosity of faith began to employ a technique that henceforth found its strength not merely in the simple dialectic of the arts faculty, but in an Aristotelian method. This method was brought into lively activity by the new kind of biblical *lectio*, in which interpretation opened with a "statement of the question" concerning elements of the text under study. The question (*quaestio*) was the characteristic act as well as the literary form assumed by scholastic theology.

The commentary (*lectio, expositio*) remained the basic literary form in theology just as in the other disciplines, such as literature (think of the *auctores*), the sciences, philosophy, etc., plus of course the central Biblical text, received and read in faith, decisive in its influence upon any subsequent intellectual construction. The course given by the masters continued well into the thirteenth century to consist in the reading and exposition of scripture. The Bible was still the basic text of learning; the *summae* were personal works of scholarship and not part of the general curriculum.

Without doing harm to this institutional and scientific practice, in fact from the very progress of this textual exposition, was born the question. It grew spontaneously on the surface of the text, the natural result of the literal and doctrinal difficulties presented by the text. It had existed for a long time, even among the fathers, who had developed a literature of questions and answers (*quaestiones et responsiones*). But, in the twelfth century, this spontaneous development became systematic; i.e., because the curiosity of faith became so widespread and the use of dialectic gave such useful implements, the *lector* (reader-commentator) began to pose questions technically, artificially on each proposition, or at least on the important points of his text. This was the crucial step in the making of scholasticism, as much for its basic mode of thought as for its method of arranging arguments. One can see a youth awakening to the life of the mind when, still in mental puberty, he begins to subject to question (in the sense in which we have been using the term) what he had hitherto accepted passively. Western reason, even in theology, had achieved maturity. Henceforth the professor, as *lector*, would not be only an exegete, but a master who, according to the usage which developed, "determined" the questions. To do this, he no longer marshaled old authorities who left one's understanding empty —even if obedient and confident—but he searched out and displayed "reasons" that got to the root of things.[50]

John of Salisbury gave an excellent description of this important episode in the history of teaching and of theology; he attributed the first important step, at least in dialectic, to his master Alberic:

> The first of these (Alberic), meticulous about everything, found something to question everywhere, so that even a polished surface was not devoid of some imperfection and, as they used to say, to him a bulrush would not be free of nodes, for even there he would show you what needed to be smoothed out.[51]

This reference to Master Alberic of Reims takes us as far back as the schools of Paris around the year 1136. But the reference, however exact, ought to be broadened and carried back over the previous decades. The masters of Chartres, readers of the *auctores*, of the *Timaeus*, of Boethius, of the Bible, were surely the ones who got the

---

[50] It is thus, word for word, that at the height of this method Thomas Aquinas defined the functions of the theologian in the *disputatio magistralis* in *Quodl.* iv, art. 18 (*Quaestiones quodlibetales*, ed. P. Mandonnet [Paris, 1926], p. 155): ". . . alioquin si nudis auctoritatibus magister quaestionem determinet, certificabitur quidem auditor quod ita est, sed nihil scientiae vel intellectus acquiret, et vacuus abscedet." (Otherwise if the master determines the question by appeal to authorities only, the student will be convinced that the thing is so, but he will have acquired no knowledge or understanding and he will go away with an empty mind.)

[51] *Metalogicon* ii.10 (Webb, p. 79; McGarry, p. 96): ". . . quorum alter, ad omnia scrupulosus, locum questionis inveniebat ubique, ut quamvis polita planities offendiculo non careret et, ut aiunt, ei cirpus non esset enodis. Nam et ibi monstrabat quid oporteat enodari."

new method going. Gilbert of La Porrée first formulated the method thus:

One must remember that a question is established by an assertion and its contradictory negation. But not every contradiction makes a question. For when one of the parts of a contradiction seems to be true while the other seems to have no direct evidence of truth . . . or when neither part is able to show proofs of truth or falsity . . . then the contradiction does not constitute a question. But where both parts appear to have valid arguments, there you have a question.[52]

Clarenbaldus of Arras, also at Chartres but coming towards the close of this evolution, defined its result in this way:

It is apparent that one must bear in mind what a question is. . . . When he (Aristotle) said, "the wise and the many each have the same opinion among themselves," he had in mind the kind of questions formed from undisputed propositions, such as the following: "Is a pearl a stone or not?" Consequently in the same book of the *Topics* but in another chapter (*Topics* i. 4. 101b28-34) he notes that a problem can be made from any proposition. But those questions which are constructed out of undisputed propositions have nothing but the form of a question.[53]

---

[52] *Commentarium in librum Boetii de Trinitate* (*PL*, LXIV, 1258): "Hic commemorandum est quod ex affirmatione et ejus contradictoria negatione questio constat. Non tamen omnis contradictio questio est. Cum enim altera contradictionis pars esse vera, altera vero nulla prorsus habere argumenta veritatis videtur. . . . aut cum neutra pars veritatis et falsitatis argumenta potest habere. . . . tunc contradictio non est questio. Cujus vero utraque pars argumenta veritatis habere videtur, quaestio est."

[53] *Commentarium in Boetium de Trinitate* (ed. W. Jansen, *Der Kommentar des Clarenbaldus von Arras zu Boethius De Trinitate* [Breslau, 1926], pp. 33*–34*): ". . . quid questio sit, videtur esse commemorandum. . . . In eo autem quod dixit [Aritoteles]: 'utrosque idem utrisque opinari,' illud genus questionum voluit intelligi, quod de certis propositionibus constituitur, ut est hoc: utrum margarita sit lapis necne. Quare in eodem Topicorum tractatu, sed alio in loco (i.4), de omni propositione problema posse fieri commemorat. Sed illae quidem questiones, quae de certis propositionibus constituuntur, nil habent quaestionis praeter formam." [Boethius cited Aristotle, *Topics* i.11.107b 1–5, to differentiate three kinds of doubt expressed by a question: (1) a doubt concerning which men can have no opinion either way, (2) one concerning which the wise and the many disagree, and (3) one concerning which the wise and the many achieve an identical opinion among themselves. It is the third form of doubt that Clarenbaldus cites here and to which he denies the status of a true question, even if it be expressed in the form of a question. Note that the modern text of Aristotle differs from the medieval text or Latin translation on this kind of doubt.]

Boethius always furnished, quite rightly, an occasion for defining this form of the question. Cf. Adhémar of Saint-Ruf *Commentarium in Boethium de*

Nil habent quaestionis praeter formam ("they have nothing but the form of a question"): no longer was the question a spontaneous inquiry raised by an obscure point met in the text or in some teaching; it had become a deliberately and methodically applied technique —even where no difficulty to speak of had been met. It was a scholarly formality that risked taking technique as an end to itself, while losing sight of the real goals in studying the texts. In fact—and Roger Bacon complained about this bitterly—the taste for *quaestiones* gradually diminished the appetite for reading the texts themselves, the sacred texts included. Resistance took shape already in the twelfth century, and not only in the work of William of Saint-Thierry, who kept those "annoyances of questions" (*quaestionum molestiae*) out of his commentary on the *Epistle to the Romans*.[54] The same resistance, sometimes very intelligent, sometimes less so, was seen in the schools even where certain ones, religiously dreading the effect of reason on faith, refused in their teaching to engage in a disrespectful manipulation of sources. Stephen of Tournai denounced this scandalous indiscretion in his letter to the pope: "They violate all sacred constitutions by holding public disputation about the incomprehensible deity. Even on public streets the indivisible Trinity is taken apart and wrangled over."[55] It is worth noting that in the entire pedagogical method described by Hugh of Saint-Victor in his *Didascalicon*, there is barely an allusion to the *disputatio*.[56]

Trinitate prol., in F. Pelster, *Studia mediaevalia in honorem admodum reverendi Patris Raymundi Josephi Martin* (Bruges, 1948), p. 145: "Hanc autem questionem Boethius, sicut ipse in hujus operis prologo dicit, rationibus formavit et mandavit litteris. Dedit enim praedicte questioni formam, utramque partem ejus per ordinem disponens et utrique parti rationem, qua posse probari videbatur, subiungens, deinde vero huius questionis nodum dissolvens, eam partem, quam Catholici defendunt, theologicis rationibus confirmando et Arrianorum partem improbando." (Moreover Boethius, as he himself says in the preface to his work, formulated the question by reason and expressed it in writing. For he gave the said question its form, placing each part of it in order, applying reason to each part in a way that seemed capable of rendering proof, but then effectively resolved the problem underlying the question; he thereby confirmed the arguments that the Catholics were defending with theological reasons and he disproved the case of the Arians.)

[54] *PL*, CLXXX, 547.

[55] *Epp.* ccli (*PL*, CCXI, 516): "Disputatur publice contra sacras constitutiones de incomprehensibili deitate. . . . Individua Trinitas et in triviis secatur et discrepitur. . . ."

[56] For Hugh, as for Boethius, the word had only an elementary meaning,

But the die was cast. In the normal course of events the "question" grew further and further away from the text which had produced it in the first place, eventually to become a form unto itself, independent of the *lectio*. Among the first works showing this development were Robert of Melun's *Quaestiones de divina pagina* (c. 1145), Odo of Soissons' *Quaestiones* (c. 1164), and Simon of Tournai's *Disputationes* (c. 1201), which dealt with problems arising from scripture. More notably, as works like Peter Lombard's *Sentences*, which dealt with problems arising from the Fathers rather than from scripture, became standard teaching devices, the headings *Hic quaeritur* ("Here it is asked . . .") made it possible to foresee already how the questions would eventually become more important than the texts being commented upon. This independence from texts was an external sign of the independence of a new doctrinal style and scientific curiosity. Problems and their solutions were no longer immediately associated with some text. The age of the *summa* had arrived.

This is not the place to describe the competence and varied application of this method, which had different values for theology from those it had for other disciplines, such as canon law and Roman law; nor is it the place to go on into the thirteenth century to treat the further stage of its development in the disputed question (*quaestio disputata*), whose name obviously suggests a debate for and against, carried on in public between masters. In the thirteenth century this was the characteristic and singularly effective activity of the university masters: the *disputatio magistralis*.[57] But we must insist on its great intellectual force, especially in the speculative disciplines where it furnishes an instrument superbly suited to the mental processes, at least to certain processes and to certain modes of thought. The scholastic "question" is different from the Socratic interrogation, Platonic

---

which he only slightly extended to define dialectic. *Didascalicon* ii.30 (Buttimer, p. 47; Taylor, p. 82): "Dialectica disputatio acuta verum a falso distinguens." (Dialectic is keen-edged disputation which separates the true from the false.)

[57] With Simon of Tournai (died c. 1201), we already have the disputation. The statute of Robert of Courçon for the University of Paris, promulgated in 1215 (*CUP*, I, 78 [#20]), gave detailed regulations for this practice of the masters, implying thereby that the disputation had already been known and in use for several years. On this point of the evolution of the question, cf. *Les Disputationes de Simon de Tournai*, ed. J. Warichez (Louvain, 1932), introduction.

reduction, Cartesian doubt, and Hegelian dialectic. Even in the Middle Ages there continued to exist other methods, inductive and deductive. Yet the *quaestio* was preponderant: as the principal act of the *intellectus fidei,* it determined the outline of the *articulus* (article), which provided the basic unit for the *summa,* the *summa quaestionum.*

It should also be noted right away that the unit in this case did not imply uniformity. The pressure exerted by certain Aristotelians would one day lead a few scholastics to construct the medieval *quaestio* in the form of a syllogism. But this was to restrict seriously the manifold flexibility of its forms, for it was not incapable of either the circular movement of pseudo-Dionysius or the *resolutio* with which the Platonic movement, in analyzing transcendent ideas, could not have slipped into the univocal syllogism. The twelfth-century masters did not consciously survey the whole range of syllogistic techniques. Even when they used the syllogistic form, they used it sometimes for an ostensive rather than a demonstrative purpose, to extend one's awareness of a reality that did not reveal and assert itself progressively but which was evident from the outset.

The leading example of this flexibility is that of the arguments later known as arguments of convenience. John of Salisbury measured the efficacy of the dialectic of probability and perceived the value of such demonstration as found in the *Analytics*; Alan of Lille made a pertinent distinction between a demonstration *ad quid* (for what purpose?) and a demonstration *quoniam* (since)—*quando per effectum probatur causa* (when a cause is established by its effect), which did not lead to complete knowledge, as in our knowledge of God.[58] But in theology, neither Alan of Lille, in the axiomatic rigor of his *Regulae,* nor Richard of Saint-Victor, in the ecstasy of his trinitarian speculation, reflected on the quality and epistemological limits of the *demonstrationes* they presented, any more than St. Anselm had calculated the formulation of his "necessary reasons" (*rationes necessariae*). At best, these masters, Victorines or followers of Gilbert of La Porrée, took occasion to discuss the different degrees of certitude when they commented on the golden rule of Boethius at the head of their

---

[58] *Summa* (Glorieux, pp. 136, 282).

commentaries on the *De Trinitate*: ". . . a learned man ought to try to form his belief about everything according to exactly what it is."[59]

Suspending their Aristotelian technique, the masters made fundamental use of symbolic procedure when called for in handling a subject which scripture puts together in typological sequence. Superficially, this sequence often assumes a rational guise, but in truth its profound value arises from a movement quite other than that of science; and one would distort it if one tried to find "proof" in it. That is surely what was involved when men fastened onto only those elements in Hugh of Saint-Victor that have a scholastic touch about them, to the detriment of that scholasticism; and that is why Richard of Saint-Victor and many others disappoint us by what we incorrectly consider a lack of discipline. Even if one disagrees with their theological science, as St. Thomas did, one must see in them the means of approaching mystery through exploration of its time-bound analogies. The spread of the procedures of the masters was not accomplished, it is true, without an annoying confusion of logical and allegorical types of research or reasoning. This at least has the advantage of making us aware of the variety and mobility, in this creative period, of the ways and means of the *intellectus fidei*.

It was in these contexts that the use of the *quaestio* expanded to gain a greater understanding of its divine object: from the simple *problema dialecticum*,[60] where it merely put into use the tools of the arts of the trivium reinforced by the new logic of Aristotle, it moved on to the investigation of causes where, in the very fabric of theological science in the thirteenth century, it served as the instrument of a new metaphysics, of a new psychology, of a new ethics.[61]

It was not only in and by questions that the masters gained their intellectualization of the faith: the questions having become autonomous, the masters gathered them and built them into *summae*.

---

[59] Boethius *De Trinitate* ii (*PL*, LXIV, 1250): ". . . eruditi est hominis unumquodque, ut ipsum est, ita de eo fidem capere tentare." This is a principle that bears at once on the diversity of knowledge, on the autonomy of methods, and on the different levels of assent. The masters proudly implemented this principle in the theological disciplines.

[60] John of Salisbury *Metalogicon* ii.15 (Webb, p. 88; McGarry, p. 107).

[61] This is referred to as the "third entry" of Aristotle. Cf. M.-J. Congar, "Théologie," *DTC*, XV, 375–8.

The rational ordering of revelation was to be, in the thirteenth century, the great work of the masters.

At the start, the *summa* was only a collection. Separated from their underlying text, the questions were gathered in no other order than the thread, later to be ignored, of the text which had evoked them. Very soon, however, the questions began to be arranged on the basis of the very subjects with which they dealt and of the logical interconnections among them. The clear goal of the *summa* of the masters was to embrace the totality of sacred knowledge. "For what is a *summa*," asked Robert of Melun, "if not a concise unifying of individual items? . . . Indeed, a *summa* is a comprehensive collection of these."[62] But much more, the *summa* proposed to give to this knowledge an internal order which would generate its highest intelligibility. The *Summa sententiarum* (beginning of the middle third of the twelfth century) was no longer simply a compilation of the sayings of the fathers but an organic and rounded out collection, however close it remained to the texts it coordinated. This is a good point on which to observe that advantage which the masters of theology held over the masters of canon law: among the latter, the sense that there was a harmony in the laws did not lead up to the learned architectonic structures of theology. One would look in vain for a doctrinal order (that of the seven sacraments) in Gratian's *Concordance*, the sequence of which stems perhaps only from the sources that lay at hand to exploit. The internal arrangement of the canonical *summae* remained singularly awkward.[63]

More and more the term *summa* designated a new responsibility in which the systematizing process paralleled in depth the work of conceptualizing. In its broadest range, it came to signify the synthesis in which the initial investigation was completed, with the pedagogical advantage of an *ordo disciplinae*, in a system of thought. In his violent opposition, Stephen of Tournai was fully aware of the range of this new form of theological literature, in which conceptual-

---

[62] *Sententie* praef. (Martin, I, 3): "Quid enim summa est, nonnisi singulorum brevis comprehensio. . . . Siquidem summa est singulorum compendiosa collectio."

[63] Cf. G. LeBras, *Histoire du droit et des institutions de l'église en occident*, vol. 1: *Prolégomènes* (Paris, 1955), pp. 81, 89, 95.

ization and systematization went together to make up the *summa*: he denounced these masters who, in their youthful impetuousness, were usurping the title, the teaching, and the methods that belonged to the "authentic" doctors.[64]

It follows that the masters would also construct, within the bounds of orthodoxy, different *summae*, different not only because of the subject matter with which they dealt (for example, a *summa* of penitence, whose title and purpose are self-explanatory), but different also because of the principal options which directed the organization of their work. Abelard constructed his theology of three elements which seemed to him to embrace all the essentials of salvation: "There are three things as I see it, in which the *summa* of human salvation consists; that is, faith, charity, and sacrament."[65] When, according to the Platonic scheme of pseudo-Dionysius, one envisages the incarnation as the means of man's return to God, this is not simply taking a position on a particular topic, but entering into a perspective which, by stressing the divine participations in mystery, illuminates

---

[64] *Epp.* ccli (*PL*, CCXI, 516): ". . . novum volumen ex eis compactum, et in scolis solemniter legitur, et in foro venaliter exponitur, applaudente coetu notariorum, qui in conscribendis opusculis suspectis, et laborem suum gaudent imminui, et mercedem augeri. Vae duo predicta sunt, et ecce restat tertium vae: facultates quas liberales appellant, amissa libertate pristina, in tantam servitutem devocantur, ut comatuli adolescentes eorum magisteria impudenter usurpent, et in cathedra seniorum sedeant imperbes; et qui nondum norunt esse discipuli, laborant ut nominentur magistri. Conscribunt et ipsi summulas suas pluribus salivis effluentes et madidas philosophorum sale nec conditas. Omissis regulis artium abjectisque libris authenticis, artificum muscas inanium verborum sophismatibus suis, tanquam aranearum tendiculis includunt." (When a new volume has been put together by them, it is both solemnly read out in the schools and commercially displayed in the market-place, to the delight of the guild of scribes who, as the ones who wrote out copies of these wretched little books, are pleased to see their work lessen and their income increase. This is a double woe, yet there remains a third: the so-called liberal faculties, their original liberty having been lost, are so captivated by ambition that, like dandified adolescents, they impudently usurp the magisterial dignity and, though beardless youths, they take over the chairs of their elders; not yet knowing how to be disciples, they strive for the title of master. They too write their little *summae* which are soaked and overflowing with rich juices but lack the salt of the philosophers. Dropping the rules of the arts and discarding the works of authorities, with their sophistries of empty words they catch imaginary flies in fancied spider-webs.)

[65] *Introd. ad theol.* (*PL*, CLXXVIII, 981): "Tria sunt, ut arbitror, in quibus humanae salutis summa consistit: fides videlicet, charitas et sacramentum."

the entire field of theology. The history of the different outlines of the *summae* is one of the most important chapters in the history of theology itself; its first task is to discern the language used in the treatises, as well as all the joints and hinges of their construction. The uniformity imposed by the success of the *Sentences* of Peter Lombard could not last, especially before the demands of a more organic vision of the goals of theology. St. Thomas, dissatisfied on several counts with the structure of the commentaries found in the *Sentences*, composed a *summa*. From the twelfth century, in the work of a single master, Alan of Lille, the *Summa* and the *Regulae,* so different in conception and structure, give a striking example of the crucial importance of systematizing in theology. The plan of the *summa* of William of Auxerre is full of significance for the complex of problems of his time.

A New Era: from Monastic Theology to Scholastic Theology

The new forms used in theological literature by the masters, to speak only of the rational device of the *quaestio* and the construction of the *summa* while ignoring their contents and purposes, have brought us far from the works of the cloisters and their theologians who, working within the institutional and spiritual framework of the monastic life, embroidered upon the word of God, the *sacra pagina*, according to their particular purposes. Moving from monastic theology to scholastic theology, we have passed into a new age.

The monastic *collatio* had a long history, and it would be incorrect to see it as restricted to a single literary genre, for was it not its law to have no form—like the conversation between a father and his children? It was not, however, by any means the only organic expression of the reading and meditation of scripture in the monastery; for from the twelfth century, besides the treatises of Anselm of Canterbury, writings that we would say transcend literature, there are the various forms of sermons, of which the masterpieces came of course from St. Bernard. The Cistercian abbot had another form and another tone from that of the Cluniac, if only as a personal reaction against the emerging scholastic exegesis. The changes undergone by William of Saint-Thierry, who went over to Cîteaux, give clear proof of this.[66] But however varied, monastic reading was firmly tied to the monastic ideal. This ideal was seen in each of the operations by which the monastic reading developed: reading, meditation, prayer (or contemplation), terms to which one must not deny technical significance despite the varied meanings given them in the heady atmosphere of the monastery. Peter the Venerable (died 1156) is, even in his conservatism, an eminent witness not only of these spiritual experiences but of their carefully considered expression.[67] A close comparison with the analysis of Richard of Saint-Victor would show clearly his differences of accent and of categories. There would be even more of a contrast with the masters who preached, such as Peter Lombard, Peter Comestor, Maurice of Sully, Stephen Langton—those who had become pastors teaching people through the word of God.[68]

If one were to characterize the *lectio* of the master, in contrast to the *collatio* of the monk,[69] one could say that it was before anything

---

[66] Cf. P. Dumontier, *Saint Bernard et la Bible* (Bruges-Paris, 1953), esp. the index of terminology.

[67] On the history and use of these categories, cf. E. C. Butler, *Western Mysticism*, 2nd ed. (London, 1927). It is noteworthy that Hugh of Saint-Victor *Didascalicon* vi.13 (Buttimer, p. 130; Taylor, p. 151), in taking up these same categories in his educational program, finally, after a lengthy discussion on *lectio*, arrives at *meditatio*, only to announce that he is not going to discuss it since there would be too much to say about this "res enim valde subtilis et simul jucunda" (thing truly subtle and at the same time delightful.) John of Salisbury also gave up this monastic cliché in his *Metalogicon* i.24 (Webb, p. 53; McGarry, p. 65): "Qui ad philosophiam aspirat, apprehendat lectionem, doctrinam, et meditationem." (One who aspires to become a philosopher should therefore apply himself to reading, doctrine, and meditation.) These substitutions and gradual changes are highly significant.

[68] Among so many examples, Ghellinck, *Mouvement*, p. 175, points out the transformation of the methods and goals of exegetical exposition by contrasting the sermons of Geoffrey Babion with those of Peter Comestor.

[69] The masters also held *collationes* beginning in the twelfth century. Cf. John of Salisbury *Metalogicon* i.24 (Webb, p. 56; McGarry, p. 68). But the word was to have several meanings: (1) the old monastic meaning, still used by Abelard *Monita ad Astrolabium* (*PL*, CLXXVIII, 1759–66): "Lectio sacra minus, sed plus collatio prodest; haec petit ut quaeras, quod petis illa docet." (Sacred reading is less profitable than the "collation," for the former asks that you question but the latter teaches what you ask;) cf. Hugh of Saint-Victor *De arca Noe morali* prol. (*PL*, CLXXVI, 617); (2) *collatio* also referred to a pious exhortation delivered at a school; cf. John of Salisbury in the passage

else an exegesis; i.e., an interpretation attempting to explore the objective substance of a text, whatever the subjective needs or the results obtained. For thus the organized scholarly transmission of revelation demanded it; this is why it had to develop sooner or later into a science, moving further and further away from the personal and affective character of religious witness. The word of God was treated as an "object," given, to be certain, within the context of the faith, but apart from one's own fervor and experience. The repugnance of Rupert towards the new schools, in contrast to the *schola Christi*, originated only more or less consciously, but vigorously, in the impersonality of the reading style of the masters. And it is true that the works of his adversary Anselm of Laon, however valuable, had none of the animation of the sacred commentaries of the abbot of Deutz and his kind. The *Sentences* of Peter Lombard would have provoked a similar outrage in Rupert. Scholastic objectivity robbed the traditional *meditatio* of its ends and of its dynamism. Even with Richard of Saint-Victor, whose intellectual vigor was irresistible, theological reason remained objectively communicable as it was. The pressure of faith, the light of grace were certainly everywhere present, but scientifically new—for the benefit of scientific lucidity. The *summae* were the masterpieces of this lucidity.

Within this objectivity there were widely divergent intellectual trends. The masters of the twelfth century, employing Neoplatonic metaphysics based on Augustine or on pseudo-Dionysius, maintained a more spontaneously religious orientation than their successors, who were equipped with Aristotle as their guide to reason and eventually also their guide to an understanding of nature and of man himself. The intervention of this new guide caused great tension, this time within scholasticism. The causes of this tension and its effects on the history of Christian thought are well known. Yet however divergent,

---

cited above; this usage passed into the regulations of the University of Paris in the thirteenth century; (3) *collatio* had a technical meaning in philosophy, referring to a type of reasoning; cf. M.-D. Chenu, "Collectio, collatio: note de lexicographie philosophique médiévale," *RSPT*, XVI (1927), 435–46; and (4) *collatio* also referred to the working procedure of a student exercise practised at Chartres, according to John of Salisbury, again in the passage cited above, where he uses the term in two different senses on the same page; cf. *Metalogicon* iii.10 (Webb, p. 163; McGarry, p. 200).

the scholastic theology of the masters always responded to other needs and took other forms than did the monastic *collatio*. It would be overlooking these needs and dissolving these forms to attribute them to differences of temperament.

At the heart of this difference, as shown by the origins of the *quaestio*, there was, in the service of an *intellectus fidei*, the search for causes and reasons. And this is the point upon which Rupert's faith gagged; to look for reasons was to lack respect for God who spoke. The only reason—if we must employ this all-too-human, in any case non-scriptural, word—was the good pleasure of God. And thus only a single-minded reference to God had value, without any of these secondary causes introduced by our earthly reason whose terms failed in their pretensions to signify. Rupert asked why men would drink out of mere cisterns when already they had the living fountain of Christ.[70]

Naturalism was the crime of the masters, according to William of Saint-Thierry and William of Saint-Jacques, whether in elaborating a critique of divine names, or in applying to the acts of God the terminology of human psychology, or in reducing the evangelical virtues to the categories of the philosophers. A false intoxication, the intransigent Gerhoh of Reichersberg called it, taking up the theme of *sobria ebrietas*; such an intoxication detracts sober readers of scripture from God's real meaning.[71] When Master Alexander entered the Abbey of Jumièges in 1180, he once again built up that famous monastery's school which had declined badly. A former master in the schools of Paris, he did not divert the school of Jumièges from its traditions, though he did procure some of the principal products of the new style for its library: Peter Comestor's *Historia scholastica*, an expression of the new historical reading of the Bible; Alan of Lille's *Ars fidei*, an expression of the new theology; Simon of Tournai's *Expositio symboli*, a critique of the great Augustinian theme of

---

[70] Cf. above, n. 6.

[71] *De gloria et honore Filii hominis* Ep. dedic. (*PL*, CXCIV, 1074–5): "Si autem lectores ebrii, scolastico potius quam theologico vino ultra modum potati offenduntur in scriptis meis, ignoscendum est illis." (If, however, intoxicated readers, having drunk scholastic rather than theological wine beyond measure, are scandalized in my writings, they ought to overlook it.)

divine ideas.[72] Cîteaux, it should be said, was one of the milieux in which the works of pseudo-Dionysius as translated by John the Scot were widely circulated. But such infiltrations, however valuable and significant, resulted from a concern for mystical theophany and not out of any interest in the metaphysical structures of Greek theology. The followers of Gilbert of La Porrée, on the other hand, masters par excellence in theology, so neutralized suspicion and attacks that, following the example of their master, they became the leading practitioners of rational method.[73]

Profanae novitates (I Tim. 6:20)—their innovations were doubly suspect: as innovations and as profane in origin. They desacralized the *sacra pagina*. Peter of Blois got himself sat upon by a prior, the superior of some of his friends, for introducing materials and procedures of profane disciplines into an exhortation to the prior's colleagues.[74] Peter was berated for presenting the word of God as in a school and not as in a monastic chapter. To be sure the monks had cultivated and made magnificent use of the seven secular arts; but only after purging them of their arrogant ways and, according to the current image, reducing them to handmaids.[75] They had constructed

---

[72] Cf. M.-D. Chenu, "Culture et théologie à Jumièges après l'ère féodale," *Jumièges: Congrès scientifique du XIIIe centenaire* (Rouen, 1954), pp. 775–81; also, P. Delhaye, "Alexandre de Jumièges," *Ibid.*, p. 785.

[73] Cf. M.-D. Chenu, "Un essai de méthode théologique au XIIe siècle," *RSPT*, XXIV (1935), pp. 258–67.

[74] *Epp.* viii (*PL*, CCVII, 21–24).

[75] Cf. Ghellinck, *Mouvement*, pp. 93–96, on the program of the seven arts. A typical statement is that by Rupert of Deutz *De Trinitate et operibus ejus,* "De operibus Spiritus Sancti" vii.10 (*PL*, CLXVII, 1763–4): "Ingressae sunt ergo septem artes liberales tanquam famulae in sacrum et reverendum dominae suae triclinium, et quasi de triviis licentiosis ad districtum et severum verbi Dei magisterium dispositae et assidere jussae sunt. Vagabantur enim prius per circuitum, lascivae, garrulae et verbosae puellulae, nihil operantes, sed curiosae agentes solummodo." (Thus the seven liberal arts like servant wenches came prying into the sacred and state banquet chamber of their mistress and, as if checked in their wanton ways and disciplined under the annoyed and strict surveillance of the word of God, were ordered to sit down; previously they had wandered all about like obscene, chattering, verbose girls, doing nothing except acting out of indiscrete curiosity.) Once again, the holy zest of Rupert is seen at work; but it relies wholly upon imagery that was universally accepted in both form and meaning. When applied to philosophy and to reason, this imagery was evidently no longer valid; and the masters stripped it of all cogency and worth.

an ideal humanism where faith remained sovereign lady and her worldly adornments glorified her without compromising her. Reasons and categories, on the other hand, failed to respect her purity and, by their very complexity, could not respect her in the way the seven arts had been made to do. By their methodological autonomy, the rational and categorical approaches developed even more than did Abelard's dialectic a curiosity that dissolved all mystery. A tract falsely attributed to Alexander of Jumièges carried the title: *De praescientia Dei contra curiosos* (*On God's Foreknowledge, against the Meddlesome*). The syllogism had no place in the school of Christ, according to Rupert, only a clear-sighted and loving adoration. And the venerable abbot of Saint-Rémy, Peter of Celle, with emotion reminded his friend John of Salisbury, that great and intelligent reader of Aristotle, that the determination of questions could be expected to take place only in "the school of Christ."[76]

Monastic theology found a further source of growth within the sacralized world fashioned by the forms of monastic worship. Cosmic realities were transformed through liturgical symbolism just as historical realities were transformed by liturgical allegory. In each case, the prime matter, nature or history, was transfigured into something sacred by a mental transport free of the constraint imposed by the objective laws of the physical universe. The world in which the monks lived was nothing but a symbolic cosmos; scripture entered into theology only as interpreted in the liturgy. The *collatio* remained always an element in the machinery of the divine office. The masters of Saint-Victor reacted against this, by trying to construct in its place a symbolism based exclusively on history.

Monastic allegorization of nature and history was the literary and

---

[76] *Epp.* i.73 (*PL*, CCII, 520): "O beata schola, ubi Christus docet corda nostra verbo virtutis suae, ubi sine studio et lectione apprehendimus quomodo debeamus aeternaliter beate vivere! Non emitur ibi liber, non redimitur magister scriptorum, nulla circumventio disputationis, nulla sophismatum intricatio, plana omnium questionum determinatio, plana universarum rationum et argumentationum apprehensio." (O blessed school, where Christ teaches our hearts by the word of his virtue, where we learn without studying and reading how we ought to live blessed lives eternally! No book has to be bought there, the master of the scriptorium does not get paid, there is no onslaught in disputations, no weaving of sophistries; it is free of passing judgment on all questions, free from involvement in all reasoning and argument.)

exegetical reflection of a mode of life entirely subordinated to an eschatological perspective sacred beyond the movements of time and the operation of causes on earth. The pseudo-Dionysian anagogy, by its "analogy," dealt sparingly with the physical reality of the cosmos; but despite the infiltrations of Greek thought, the Roman Gregory remained the master of monastic exegesis and theology. The monk led an other-worldly life in this world. This pervasive theme colored his way of thought as well as his behavior, his understanding of scripture as of the universe, his conception of the church as of earthly kingdoms.[77] The Benedictine world order, in the view of Friedrich Heer, was and remains the spiritual alphabet of European culture.[78]

In such a perspective, theological projects developed under the inspiration and in the climate of spiritual quietude (*otium*), a term much loved and characteristically used, but best seen as the expression of an interior law. Not that they failed to appreciate the stringent demands of the exercises of *lectio-meditatio*, but they insisted that these were free of external involvements, were without any concern for social—even apostolic—utility. It was purely contemplative theology, at leisure to turn towards God (*vacare Deo*) in a mystical sabbath where the labors of the week were all over. The activity of reason, too, gave priority to the tranquility of the soul. In such activity, as in others, the monk imitated the heavenly life on earth. His theology was an anticipation of paradise where all dialectic would be ludicrous, where wisdom would absorb all science, even sacred science.

On this ground the *claustrales* (cloistered monks) asserted in many ways and with vehemence the radical originality of the revealed truth, irreducible to the laws of the human mind, just as any Christian event could not be placed on equal footing with the data that written history provides: *Divina scriptura non subjacet regulis Donati* (Divine scripture is not subject to the rules of Donatus). The masters risked treating scripture simply as another problem, a major one of course but, like all the rest, subject to their abstract categories: the

---

[77] Cf. texts presented and commented upon by J. Leclercq, *La vie parfaite; points de vue sur l'essence de l'état religieux* (Turnhout-Paris, 1948); also L. Bouyer, *Le sens de la vie monastique* (Turnhout-Paris, 1950).

[78] "L'héritage Europe," *Dieu vivant*, XXVII (1955), 32.

category of "nature" includes the human nature of Christ; that of "virtue" embraces the spiritual *habitus*; "matter and form" comprehend the sacramental symbol: "essence" subsumes that of God; etc. The risk came from deliberately confronting mystery through those elements, those *rationes*, which mystery can supposedly possess in common with natural phenomena and the workings of the mind. The masters would have to work incessantly at their effort to isolate the supereminence of the divine truths. We have seen with what resources, from the end of the twelfth century, they undertook to formulate the laws and methods of this eminence. The *claustrales* were not obliged to formulate and use an analogical method in order to appreciate the transcendence of mystery. They thought and lived at once in mystery, within the framework of biblical images and on their various tropological levels, just as while still on earth they lived the monastic life within the foreimage of the celestial city. This was admirable theophany.[79] Rupert was the best witness of it. It was the theophany indeed of scripture and of its divine events, by which God displayed his will to men in human history. The monks had no desire to transform this theophany into a rational theodicy sorting out the divine attributes.[80]

Were monastic and scholastic theology really disparate? Certain quarrels, by underscoring the possible points of rupture, with respect to both institutions and methods, would make one think so—as would perhaps also the manner in which they have been intentionally discussed here. But the radical evolutionism of Anselm of Havelberg which so shocked Rupert did not preempt theology any more than it did existing institutions. The development of diverse trends should not be allowed to obscure the strong connections among these various strains of the *intellectus fidei*. One could certainly agree with the masters in rejecting the Gregorian idea of a humanity which, created as a substitute for the fallen angels, was defined on earth by heavenly

---

[79] The term "theophany," which is not Gregorian, became current in monastic circles during the latter part of the twelfth century. See Chenu, *TDS*, chap. 13, "Orientale Lumen," pp. 304–5.

[80] While presented in an extremely personal treatment of both thought and style, this is still the basic line of St. Bernard's theology. Cf. among others, E. Kleinedam, "Wissen, Wissenschaft, Theologie bei Bernhard von Clairvaux," *Bernhard von Clairvaux Mönch und Mystiker* (Wiesbaden, 1955), pp. 128–67.

standards. This was a classic theme of monastic theology, St. Bernard's included, according to which the terrestrial components of the church, of man, of nature, of reason were only incidental and symbolic.[81] But the autonomy of reason, man, and nature in the new humanism of the twelfth century did not disrupt either the unity of the faith in theology or the unity of the church as an institution. Faith and church provided several different abodes: monastic, scholastic, canonical, apostolic. The continuity of these modes can be observed along any line of development, whether in history, speculation, allegorization, contemplation. The great theme of the silence of God, or of God's seclusion from the world, or of the divine self-sufficiency, was certainly not weakened by the Platonic metaphysics of the One. Traditional trinitarian contemplation on the divine appropriations of power, wisdom, and goodness (*potentia, sapientia, bonitas*) was again found in Abelard and Hugh of Saint-Victor without having lost any of its biblical inspiration. Experimental description of the virtues at Cluny and at Cîteaux strengthened the new categories taken over from the secular psychologists and moralists.

Likewise the primacy of scripture was not overthrown. When Hugh of Saint-Victor constructed his theological *De sacramentis*, it is not as if he subordinated scriptural texts to a system in which they would be nothing more than the instruments of his theological reasoning. Scripture remained always the goal of his theological enterprise. The summa *De sacramentis* was intended, according to its own preface, as an intermediate and reasoned step between the initial historical reading (*historica lectio*) of the Bible and the supreme doctrinal penetration of scripture, "the second level of learning, which is found in (doctrinal) allegory" (*secunda eruditio, quae in allegoria [doctrinali] est.*)[82]

Rather than speak of continuity in this development, we ought better to say coexistence, and always a fruitful coexistence at that. Monastic theology was not an outmoded, downgraded item. It expressed, as did the *ordo monasticus* itself, permanent values for the

---

[81] Cf. Chenu, *TDS*, chap. 2, "Cur homo?", pp. 52–61.
[82] Cf. G. Paré, A. Brunet, P. Tremblay, *La renaissance du XIIe siècle* (Paris-Ottawa, 1933), p. 264.

church and for all of humanity. Men would take notice of this when the masters themselves would one day slip by their self-satisfaction into a decadent state, content, as professors, to be theorists about God instead of active theologians (the contrast was made by Gregory IX), content to construct their splendid systems without tending to their own vital roots in the scriptural, patristic, and monastic soil. Gregory IX was right to address the masters at Paris who gloried in their young university with a solemn warning, telling them not to profane their sacred wisdom in vain ostentation, "transposing by profane innovations the terms defined by the fathers."[83]

Anselm and Abelard were the creators of scholasticism. This all-too-simple cliché voiced by historians has the merit at least of pointing out, in these protagonists, the two opposed but vital and delicately balanced components of the school. Anselm was the finest product of monastic theology. He went beyond it in fact, in method and structure, even in procedure—for example, his writings lacked the affectation of scriptural citations—a genius who defies classification. Master Abelard obviously did not live at the monastery of Bec, yet the dialectic of his *Sic et non* and the conceptualism which fed upon it blended with the *rationes necessariae* of Anselm into a potentially rich collaboration of curiosity and contemplation, out of which the science of theology in fact developed during the thirteenth century.

The statues of Reims would have been out of place in the tympanum at Vézelay, no less than the masters would have been in monastic cloisters. But the two Christendoms of feudal Vézelay and of urban Reims, each with its own understanding of faith and mode of expression, formed part of a single church.

---

[83] Gregory IX to the "reigning masters in theology" at Paris, July 7, 1228, in *CUP*, I, 114–15 (#59): ". . . quidam apud vos spiritu vanitatis ut uter distenti positos a patribus terminos prophana transferre satagunt novitate. . . ." Cf. M.-D. Chenu, "Vocabulaire biblique et vocabulaire théologique," *NRT*, LXXIV (1952), 1029–41.

9

Tradition and Progress

Like dwarfs standing on the
shoulders of giants, we see
farther than they.

BERNARD OF CHARTRES

"**B**UT I SHALL not pass over silently the fact that certain people, supposedly out of reverence for the church fathers, will not try their hand at anything left undone by them; they say they don't want to presume to go beyond their venerable predecessors. But having thus covered up for their inertia, they dawdle about lazily and deride, ridicule, and mock the industriousness shown by others in the quest and discovery of truth. But he who dwells in heaven shall ridicule them; the Lord shall mock them." So writes Richard of Saint-Victor in introducing his commentary on the vision of Ezekiel, a favorite text for patristic exegesis, of which St. Gregory was hitherto the uncontested master.[1]

This lively indignation on the part of the Victorine scholar of course betrays his own personal curiosity, constantly stimulated by the difficulties of the biblical text, the insufficiencies of traditional interpretations, and his passion for theological understanding. But such a bitter statement also presupposes the existence of people whose mental rigidity was stifling this very sort of healthy curiosity about faith. In fact there is an abundance of texts from around this time,

---

[1] *In visionem Ezechielis* prol. (*PL*, CXCVI, 527): "Sed nec illud tacite praetereo, quod quidam quasi ob reverentiam Patrum nolunt ab illis omissa attentare, ne videantur aliquid ultra majores praesumere. Sed inertiae suae ejusmodi velamen habentes, otio torpent et aliorum industriam in veritatis investigatione et inventione derident, subsannant, exsufflant. Sed qui habitat in coelis irridebit eos, et Dominus subsannabit eos." [Cf. Smalley, p. 108.]

the 1160's, which testify to a climate of fierce resistance to such curiosity. In the preface to his *Sentences*, Robert of Melun poured out at length his conservative protest:

Moreover, a new type of teaching has lately appeared, or rather a childish way of prating has gained inordinate popularity among certain men who hunt only for the leaves that cover up the fruit.[2]

Those who are busy teaching this way seem not to know and not to want others to know the things they pride themselves on teaching. Or perhaps they are anxious to be thought to teach new and bizarre things; I say this because by their weird and disgusting newness of terminology they do not fear to divulge what they hope.[3]

Stephen of Tournai, bishop between 1192 and 1203, wrote to the pope denouncing unequivocally the novelties of an enticing and specious theology. Consistent in his sharp vigilance, he also criticized the public disputes of the masters and opposed the new communal institutions:

Scriptural studies have lapsed into a state of confusion in our time, for students applaud nothing but novelties and the masters are more intent on glory than doctrine; everywhere they draw up new and modern little summaries and supporting commentaries on theology, and with these they lull, hold, and deceive their listeners, as if the works of the sacred fathers did not still suffice.[4]

---

[2] [The meaning of this phrase is an open question among scholars. Franz Bliemetzrieder, "Robert von Melun und die Schule Anselms von Laon," *ZKG*, LIII (1934), 139, 152, argues that Robert was alluding to Abelard's attack on his own master, Anselm of Laon, in the *Historia calamitatum* iii (*PL*, CLXXVIII, 123; Muckle, p. 20): "Arbor ejus tota in foliis aspicientibus a longe conspicua videbatur, sed propinquantibus, et diligentius intuentibus infructuosa reperiebatur." (His tree appeared thick with foliage to those who looked at it from far away, but those who approached it to look closely found it fruitless.) Cf. Smalley, pp. 73–74.]

[3] *Sententie* praef. (Martin, I, 4): "Est vero preter hec novum docendi genus nuper exortum, immo puerile recitandi studium, populari favore quorundam folia fructum tegentia querentium immoderate elevatum." *Ibid.*, p. 38: "Qui ergo in hoc modo docendi occupantur, nec scire nec sciri velle videntur ea que se docere gloriantur. Aut forsitan nova et inaudita estimari docere exoptant, eo quod inaudita et detestabili quadam verborum novitate quid in voto contineant divulgare non formidant."

[4] *Epp.* ccli (*PL*, CCXI, 517): "Lapsa sunt apud nos in confusionis officinam sacrarum studia litterarum, dum et discipuli solis novitatibus applaudunt, et magistri gloriae potius invigilant quam doctrinae, novas recentesque summulas et commentaria firmantia super theologia passim conscribunt, quibus auditores suos demulceant, detineant, decipiant, quasi nondum sufficerint sanctorum opuscula patrum." Cf. above, p. 299, n. 64.

In the field of philosophy and the sciences, Adelard of Bath had protested against the congenital vice of his contemporaries who rejected every new discovery and obliged him to camouflage the presentation of his research under pseudonyms or under the name of some Muslim scholar.

> This generation has an innate vice, namely, that it can accept nothing which has been discovered by contemporaries; as a consequence, when I wish to publish something I myself have discovered, I ascribe it to someone else, saying: "A certain man not I, has said. . . ."[5]

When we look back upon the spiritual and doctrinal currents described in the foregoing chapters, we can readily see how certain minds could have reacted as they did. A pretentious devotion to tradition precluded their perceiving the resources for renewal which lay within that tradition. And their reactionary stance in turn only sets in sharper relief the vigor of the new spiritual and doctrinal currents. If the masters were systematizing the content of the word of God, first in *quaestiones* and then in organized *summae*, it is because they believed this theological understanding integral to the faith, against those who apprehended dangers from men's pretensions to such understanding. If the expanded lists of authoritative passages from the fathers, which already incorporated critical perception of disagreements among these authorities, of their *sic et non*, now introduced besides, disruptive elements from the vision and mentality of the Greeks, one could anticipate the anxiety of those people accustomed to the fixed positions and coherence of Latin theology. If the evangelical awakening and scriptural literalism raised doubts about certain heavy-handed forms of allegory as well as about certain institutional orthodoxies, it was to be expected that, given their sociological conditioning, some very fine people would be apprehensive about innovations that tended towards such questionable breaks with the past. All this helps explain those immediate reactions, not yet fixed in theories, that showed a revealing hypersensitivity to the many manifestations of "renaissance," in which, to the amazement of all who

---

[5] *Quaest. nat.* prol. (Müller, p. 1): "Habet enim haec generatio ingenitum vitium, ut nihil, quod a modernis reperiatur, putet esse recipiendum. Unde fit, ut si quando inventum proprium publicare voluerim, personae id alienae imponens inquam: 'Quidam dixit, non ego.' "

were convinced that the world was getting old, the new youthfulness of the gospel mingled with the discovery of ancient reason.

The Partisans of Progress

It was not some fit of peevishness brought on by the peculiar difficulties of the vision of Ezekiel that caused Richard of Saint-Victor to react as he did in the passage cited above; the passage is consistent with his whole outlook. He said elsewhere: "I have said these things on account of those who accept nothing but what they have gotten from the fathers."[6] Furthermore, the passage reflects the reform of scriptural studies at Saint-Victor, where Andrew articulated the new principles, boldly claiming, despite his modest language, the right of perpetual discovery (*inventio*) within the most confidently held faith. He brought up the example of St. Jerome in one of his best wrought pieces of writing, stylistically and substantively:

If Jerome had judged it idle, rash, or presumptuous to expend enthusiasm and work for the sake of investigating the truth of the scriptures after the fathers had taken such great care to elaborate upon them, then never would that wise, industrious, and good man, who kept in mind that it is written: "Make good use of your time," have worked so hard on this task or have spent his whole life at it. For he surely knew, that learned man knew—he knew, I say, and he knew best—how obscure truth is, how deep it lies buried, how far from mortal sight it has plunged into the depths, how it will admit only a very few, by how much work it is reached, how practically no one ever succeeds, how it is dug out with difficulty and then only bit by bit. . . . Careful search can find it, but only in such a way that careful search can find still more. No one can bring out all of it but ferrets it out in bits and pieces and, when all is said and done, in vain. While fathers and forebears discovered it, more remained for sons and descendants to find. While it is always sought, more always remains to be sought. While it is always being found, more always remains to be found. Therefore, just because our forebears gave themselves over to the search for truth through studying and expounding sacred scripture, there is nothing dishonorable or presumptuous or wrong or idle or superfluous about us lesser men devoting ourselves to that same search.[7]

---

[6] *Expos. tabernaculi foederis* i (*PL*, CXCVI, 211): "Haec propter illos dicta sunt qui nihil acceptant nisi quod ab antiquissimis patribus acceperunt."

[7] *In Isaiam* prol. (MS Paris Mazarine 175, fol. 40; cited by Smalley, pp. 378–9): "Si otiosum vel temerarium vel presumptuosum esse post patres, qui explicandis evigilaverunt scripturis, ei rei veritatis investigande gratia studium

Moreover, Rupert of Deutz himself, the master of monastic exegesis in the first half of the twelfth century, having to reply to the same critics, claimed the same right to discover the truth without being charged with contempt or presumption towards the work of the ancients.

But someone will say: What those far better and no less holy and learned men discovered and wrote is already quite enough. It is wrong, it is rash to add anything to what was said by the renowned and catholic fathers, and thus to make readers sick by swelling the multitude of commentaries.

To which I say: The broad domain of the sacred scriptures surely belongs to all the confessors of Christ, and the freedom of investigating them cannot by right be denied anyone, provided that, the faith remaining unharmed, he say or write what he feels. For indeed who can be properly indignant when, after the fathers before them dug one or two holes, their sons and heirs dig yet more by their own labor in their common property?[8]

Moreover, once the criticism of authorities had been introduced, even if it was for the sake of harmonizing them, the possibility of

---

et operam adhibere iudicaret, nunquam vir sapiens, industrius, et bonus, et qui bene meminisset scriptum esse: 'Tempori parce,' tantam huic studio operam impenderet, totamque in eo etatem consumeret. Novit certe, novit vir eruditus, novit, inquam, et optime novit quam abstrusa sit veritas, quam alte subsederit, quam procul a mortalium oculis se in profundum demerserit, quam paucissimos admiserit, quanto labore ad eam penetratur, a quam paucis vel potius nullis ad eam pervenitur, quam difficiliter et minutatim eruitur. . . . Sic a diligenter querentibus invenitur, ut item si diligenter quesita fuerit inveniatur. Nemini tota contingit; particulatim, et ut ita dictum sit, frustratim eruitur. Sic eam invenerunt parentes et avi, ut nepotibus et filiis superesset quod invenirent. Sic semper queritur, ut semper supersit quod queratur. Sic semper invenitur, ut semper supersit quod inveniatur. Non est ergo quippiam derogare, non est presumere, non est perperam agere, non est otiosum vel superfluitas, quia majores nostri in sancti expositione eloquii veritatis indagationi vacaverunt, eiusdem investigationi in scripturarum explanatione nos minores invigilare. . . ."

[8] *In Apoc.* prol. (*PL*, CLXIX, 826): "Sed dicet aliquis: Jam satis est quod alii meliores et sanctiores nihilominus et doctiores invenerunt atque scripserunt. Illicitum est, temerarium est, adjicere quidpiam ad ea quae a nominatis catholicisque patribus dicta sunt, atque ita fastidium legentibus facere, augendo multitudinem commentariorum.

"Ad haec inquam: Nimirum sanctarum spatiosus ager scripturarum omnibus Christi confessoribus communis est, et tractandi illas nulli jure negare potest licentia, dummodo, salva fide, quod sentit dicat aut scribat. Quis namque recte indignetur eo quod in eadem possessione post unum aut duos puteos quos foderunt patres praecedentes, plures proprio fodiant labore filii succedentes."

progressing beyond passive acceptance of them was suggested. The proliferation of florilegia, their didactic manipulation in the schools, the rival interpretations of texts with ill-defined implications—all these things tended increasingly to impose the principle of progress. Each of the fathers was situated, delimited, and characterized, with the effect of making his authority only relative. Augustine himself, despite the universality of his teachings and his stature, was brought into question.[9] The newly introduced Greek writings exerted an influence of which men were to become increasingly aware, from the incrimination of Gilbert of La Porrée for his "profane innovations"[10] to the troubled conflicts among the masters at the beginning of the thirteenth century concerning the "innovations" of John the Scot.[11]

---

[9] Thus already Rupert of Deutz had written in the dedicatory letter (*PL*, CLXIX, 202) which precedes his commentary on the Gospel of St. John, a text on which Augustine was the supreme and unchallenged expert: "Quia vox christianae legis et organum catholicae fidei, pater Augustinus, vocali atque dulci evangelium Joannis tractatu declamavit, reprehensionem vel derogationem illius esse somniant quod idem evangelium, idest ipsum Dei verbum, post tantum doctorem ruminare praesumpsi, multumque indignantur quasi novo homini, quod antiquae nobilitati inserere vel etiam praeferre per superbiae spiritum ausus sim. Ego autem testem me habere confido Deum in animam meam." (Since that voice of Christian law and spokesman for the catholic faith, Father Augustine, held forth on the Gospel of John in graceful homilies, they foolishly regard it as reprehensible or derogatory towards him that I have presumed to work over the same gospel, nothing less than the word of God, after such a learned man; and they are angered because, as they think, I have dared out of pride to arrogate to an upstart a task for which only the noble ancients were fit. However, I am confident that I have God for a witness in my soul.) And, to those who denounced him for having abandoned an opinion of Augustine, he wrote in his commentary *Super quaedam capitula regulae divi Benedicti abbatis* i (*PL*, CLXX, 496): "Ejus rei necessitas me compulit ut dicerem non esse in canone scripta beati Augustini, non esse illi[s] per omnia confidendum sicut libris canonicis. . . . At illi me ex hoc diffamare ceperunt, tanquam haereticum, qui dixissem non esse in canone beatum Augustinum." (Necessity compels me to say that the writings of St. Augustine are not part of the canon, that they are not to be trusted in all matters as are the canonical books. . . . Moreover, they have begun to denounce me as a heretic for saying that St. Augustine was not canonical.)

[10] Cf. John of Salisbury *Historia pontificalis* viii (Chibnall, pp. 15–19) and Otto of Freising *Gesta Frederici* i. 54 (Simson, pp. 75–77; Mierow-Emery, pp. 89–90).

[11] Letter of Honorius III (*CUP*, I, 107, #50): "Quia igitur idem liber, sicut accepimus, in nonnullis monasteriis et aliis locis habetur, et nonnulli claustrales et viri scolastici novitatum forte plus quam expediat amatores, se studiosius occupant dicti libri, gloriosum reputantes ignotas proferre sen-

"Innovation" in these cases evidently meant not recent doctrines but doctrines not customarily encountered in one's education.

The same susceptibility to Greek influence marked Anselm of Havelberg's work concerning not the interpretation of scripture but the very life of the church in its progressive movement through time. Anselm imbued both his analysis of institutions and his doctrinal investigations with this idea of historical progress. And both this analysis and this doctrinal investigation were perfectly consistent with his life and his religious involvement, outside the monastic tradition, with the regular canons. They find expression not only in occasional, odd reflections, but in statements integral to a total vision of the divine economy, "from the just man Abel right up to the last of the elect," neatly organized and framed by relating the principal stages in the history of salvation to the three persons of the Trinity.

Stages in the progress and renewal of Christendom could thus be observed in the succession of Christian institutions. Already Honorius of Autun had discerned five ages in the church, just as there had been in the Old Testament; these corresponded to the roles played successively by the apostles, the martyrs, the fathers, the monks, and antiChrist. Historians began to use the foundation-dates of the orders as turning points in history.[12] The unforeseen forms which, towards the end of the twelfth century, the apostolic movement came rapidly to assume as it sought equilibrium encouraged this type of historical awareness and, at the same time, an explicit reliance upon the role of the Holy Spirit, the same who formerly inspired the fathers. We have described the proliferation of the apostolic movement, from the multiform institution of the regular canons and the founding of the "new and strange" mendicant orders,[13] to those sects foundering in

---

tentias, cum apostolus profanas novitates doceat evitare. . . ." (Since therefore the same book [the *De divisione naturae* by John the Scot], as we have learned, is found in some monasteries and other places, and not a few monks and scholars, far more enamoured of novelties than they should be, concern themselves too assiduously with the said book, thinking it wonderful to put forward strange and unknown ideas whereas the Apostle teaches us to avoid profane new things.)

[12] Cf. J. Spörl, "Das Alte und das Neue im Mittelalter," *HJ*, L (1930) pp. 297–341, 498–524, esp. 336–41. [For Honorius, see *PL*, CLXXII, 351.]

[13] Anon. *Ex annalibus normannis*, ad annum 1215 (*MGH, Scriptores*, XXVI, 516): "Isti duo ordines cum magno gaudio propter conversacionis

heresy which were to be called "of the new spirit" (*de novo spiritu*). Hadewych of Antwerp gave candid witness to the influence of this new spirit at the start of the Beguine movement early in the thirteenth century. While Bishop Fulk of Toulouse marvelled at the Beguines but the Benedictine Walter of Coincy ridiculed them, Hadewych in her song announced the new springtime of a renewed life.[14]

In the schools this renewal was manifested in the classic quarrel between the ancients and the moderns; it was the moderns of the twelfth century who furnished the West with the first substantial episode in this recurrent rivalry.[15] Antiquity had supplied the original clichés of this permanent conflict of the generations; and it is curious to find these arguments, either for or against the good old times, among medieval men so tied to their classical models. There is a song in the *Carmina Burana* which gives perfect expression of these commonplaces lamenting the times and the decadent world: young people no longer want to learn anything; culture is fading; the world is upside down; the blind are leading the blind—into a pit; birds quit the nest before they know how to fly; stableboys pass themselves off as knights, etc. The church fathers—Gregory, Jerome, Augustine, and Benedict the father of the monks—can all be found at the alehouse, or in court, or at the fish market. Mary no longer likes the contemplative life, Martha no longer the active. Leah is sterile. Rachel's eyes are red from tears. Cato frequents the stews, and Lucretia has become

---

novitatem, ab ecclesia et populo sunt recepti, et ubique cerperunt praedicare nomen Christi. Ad quorum ordines multi nobilium et juvenum sophistarum, propter novitatem insolitam, transierunt, in tantum quod in pauco tempore terram repleverunt." (These two orders [the Franciscans and Dominicans] were received by the church and the people with great joy because of the newness of their way of life, and everywhere they began to preach the name of Christ. Many noble and educated young men came to these orders attracted by their strange freshness, so that within a short time they covered the earth.)

[14] The French translator of the poems of Hadewych has called attention to the author's predilection for the word "new," which he associates with the name which this sect "of the new spirit" adopted in Swabia: Hadewych of Antwerp, *Poèmes des Béguines*, tr. J.-B. Porion (Paris, 1954), esp. pp. 62, 109.

[15] This is said without prejudice against the age of the Carolingian renaissance. The poet Walafrid Strabo (died 849) spoke of his own times as "the modern age" (*saeculum modernum*); *MGH, Poetae latini aevi Carolini*, II, 271.

a whore.[16] On the other hand, Joseph of Exeter, in the introduction to his Trojan epic, undertook, as Horace had once done, the ardent defense of the young against their elders; and John of Hanville, like Ovid, rejoiced at being a modern.[17]

And so it went also in philosophy. We still employ today the distinction between the old and the new logic, between which the literary and doctrinal frontier of modern times shifts variously as texts and methods are discovered up to the middle of the thirteenth century. It was the same with the rise of grammar, poetics, jurisprudence, ethics, and metaphysics. Peter Elias was the modern who between 1140 and 1150 introduced the speculative categories of Aristotle into grammar in place of the traditional descriptive method of Priscian. Geoffrey of Vinsauf between 1208 and 1213 based the laws of his *Poetria nova* on the *Ars* written by the "modern" Matthew of Vendôme before 1175, and on the poems of Walter of Châtillon, who flourished about 1180. Alan of Lille in his *Anticlaudianus* criticized

---

[16] One of the *Carmina Burana* begins thus:
> Florebat olim studium,
> Nunc vertitur in tedium;
> Iam scire diu viguit,
> Sed ludere prevaluit.

> (Study did thrive in days of yore,
> But now is thought to be a bore;
> For long was knowledge highly prized,
> Now only play is not despised.)

A. Hilka and O. Schumann, eds., *Carmina Burana*, vol. 1: *Die moralisch-satirischen Dichtungen* (Heidelberg, 1930), pp. 7–8. For a résumé and further references, see E. R. Curtius, *European Literature and the Latin Middle Ages*, tr. W. R. Trask (London, 1953), pp. 94–95; for a discussion of the theme of the ancients against the moderns in the twelfth century, see *ibid.*, pp. 251–5. Curtius comments (*ibid.*, pp. 254–5): "The contrast between the 'modern' present and Pagan-Christian Antiquity was felt by no century so strongly as by the twelfth. . . . We find in the period none of those philosophico-religious speculations upon a *vita nova* in which Burdach wished to see the seed of the Italian Renaissance. But we do find a clear consciousness of the turn of an era. More precisely: of the dawn of *the* new era, compared with which *everything* earlier is 'old'—Horace's poetics, the Digests, philosophy—and old in the same sense as the Old Testament."

[17] Joseph of Exeter *De bello troiano* i.15,23 (London, 1825); cf. *Horace Epp.* ii.1.76–89. John of Hanville *Architrenius* i in Thomas Wright, ed., *The Anglo-Latin Satirical Poets and Epigrammists of the Twelfth Century* (London, 1872), I, 242; cf. Ovid *Ars amandi* iii.121.

the crudity displayed by the moderns in their new poetics, as contrasted with the humanism of the ancient poets.[18] In his *Doctrinale* of 1199, Alexander of Villedieu actually rejected as "ancient" the norms of the tonic accent. Textual commentators turned away from the old methods of literary analysis in order to use the categories of the four causes, made fashionable by the philosophers. According to Conrad of Hirsau in his *Dialogus super Auctores:* "In works of criticism the ancients required seven topics to be discussed: the author, the title of the work, the type of poem, the intention of the writer, the order and then the number of books, and the explanation; but the moderns judge that only four things need to be inquired into: the matter of the work, the intention of the writer, the final cause, and under what part of philosophy the work is to be placed."[19] Like moralists of all ages, Walter of Châtillon complained, "We moderns ignore the path trodden by the ancients."[20]

But it was in theology itself that the term "modern" had the widest use and significance, since, from the first appearance of "master" as a professional title in the schools, "modern" was attached to it to distinguish the medieval teachers from the ancient authorities. Manegold of Lautenbach, who died in the first decade of the twelfth century, was considered the master of the modern masters;[21] the *Liber pancrisis* was among the first to collect, alongside statements by the fathers, the opinions of such "modern masters" as William of Champeaux, Ivo of Chartres, and the brothers Anselm and Ralph of Laon.[22]

By definition and by the shift of generations, however, the moderns

---

[18] Prol. (*PL,* CCX, 487).

[19] R.B.C. Huygens, ed. (Collection Latomus, XVII [Berchem-Brussels, 1955]), p. 19: ". . . in libris explanandis vii antiqui requirebant, auctorem, titulum operis, carminis qualitatem, scribentis intentionem, ordinem, numerum librorum, explanationem. sed moderni iiii requirenda censuerunt, operis materiam, scribentis intentionem, finalem causam et cui parti philosophie subponatur quod scribitur."

[20] "Nescimus vestigia veterum moderni," in Karl Strecker, ed., *Moralisch-satirische Gedichte Walters von Chatillon* (Heidelberg, 1929), p. 97.

[21] Anon. Mellicensis *De script. eccl.* cv (*PL,* CCXIII, 981): "Manegoldus presbyter modernorum magister magistrorum." (Manegold the priest, master of the modern masters.)

[22] MS Troyes 425. Cf. O. Lottin, "Un nouveau témoin du *Liber Pancrisis,*" *RTAM,* XXIII (1956), 114–8.

became in their turn the ancients: the glossators of Peter Lombard, the epitome of the modern masters, soon directed against him the opinions of the moderns.[23]

For after all there is nothing which is in itself modern; and modernity, materially speaking, is a mobile value. Walter Map with notable ingenuity computed the period of time during which one remained modern. He figured it to be about a century; during this period, which is the outside limit of man's survival, the recent past remains still present in people's memories. He observed, however, that antiquity remains prestigious from generation to generation and that at all times modernity has been suspect, always on the edge of disfavor until the day when the halo of antiquity would rehabilitate the former moderns.[24]

---

[23] Thus, for example, the glossator of MS Luxemburg, Nat. lat. 65, *In III Sent.*, d.32, c.4, n.154: "Satis probavit magister, quod Christus in illo triduo fuit homo. Sed modernis creditur qui dicunt, quod non fuit homo hoc corpus, sed cadaver" (The master proved to his own satisfaction that Christ during those three days in the tomb was a man. But credence is given the moderns who say that this body was not a man but a cadaver); or *In IV Sent.*, d.2, c.6, n.22: "Hic dicunt moderni, quod omnes baptizati a Johanne sunt denuo baptizati" (The moderns say that all who were baptized by John were baptized a second time); or *In IV Sent.*, d.40, c.2, n.365: "Moderni contrahunt in quinto gradu" (The moderns contract marriage in the fifth degree of relationship); all cited in A. Landgraf, "Frühscholastische Abkürzungen der Sentenzen des Lombarden," *Studia mediaevalia in honorem admodum reverendi Patris Raymundi Josephi Martin* (Bruges, 1948), pp. 197–8.

[24] Walter Map *De nugis curialium* (*Anecdota Oxoniensia*, Medieval and Modern Series, Part XIV, ed. M. R. James [Oxford, 1914], p. 59): "Nostris hec sunt orta temporibus. Nostra dico tempora modernitatem hanc, horum scilicet centum annorum curriculum, cuius adhuc nunc ultime partes extant, cuius tocius in his que notabilia sunt satis est recens et manifesta memoria, cum adhuc aliqui supersint centennes, et infiniti filii qui ex patrum et avorum relacionibus certissime teneant que non viderunt. Centum annos qui effluxerunt dico nostram modernitatem. . . ." (It is in our times that these things have arisen. By "our times" I mean this modern period, the course of the last hundred years now just approaching completion, and the memory of whose notable events is relatively fresh and clear, for there are still some centenarians alive, and there are very many sons who possess, by the narration of their fathers and grandfathers, distinct knowledge about things they did not actually see. I say that the hundred years that have just run out constitute our "modern times"); and *ibid.*, p. 158: "Scio quid fiet post me. Cum enim putuerim, tum primo sal accipiet, totusque sibi supplebitur decessu meo defectus, et in remotissima posteritate mihi faciet auctoritatem antiquitas, quod tunc ut nunc vetustum cuprum preferetur auro novello. . . . Omnibus seculis sua displicuit modernitas, et quevis etas a prima preteritam sibi pretulit." (I know what

The Partisans of Tradition

To relieve his irritability, to denounce Peter Lombard after working on Abelard and Gilbert of La Porrée, Gerhoh of Reichersberg
could not have given his pamphlet a title better suited to his taste
than *Liber de novitatibus hujus temporis* (*The Book of Present-Day
Novelties*), 1156.[25] For him, newness was in itself worthy of condemnation; and the invitation to silence which Alexander III addressed to him in the midst of praises (letters of March 22, 1164, to
Gerhoh himself and to his superior, the archbishop of Salzburg)[26]
did not cool his ardor.

Denunciation of this damnable newness had led Odo of Tournai
(died 1116) to reject the direct interpretation of Porphyry and of
Aristotle, as against the traditional commentaries of the ancients, in
particular of Boethius.[27]

"Avoid new, profane forms of speech"[28]—this precept of St. Paul
was apparently the decisive scriptural authority for establishing the
value of tradition against innovation. Its enunciation here was aimed
not simply at doctrine but specifically at certain terms. Alan of Lille

---

will happen after I die. When I have decayed, only then will I be savored; all
my defects will be made up for by my death; in the furthest posterity antiquity
will render me authoritative, for then as now, old copper will be preferred to
new gold. . . . Every age has found its own modernity displeasing, and every
age after the first has preferred a past age to itself.) [For an English translation,
differing in detail from the above, see M. R. James, *Walter Map's "De Nugis
Curialium"* (Cymmrodorion Record Series, No. 9 [London, 1923]), pp. 64–
65, 171.]

[25] *MGH, Libelli de lite*, III, 288–306.

[26] *Regesta Pontificum Romanorum*, ed. P. Jaffé and W. Wattenbach, 2 vols.
(Leipzig, 1885–8), II, 179 (nos. 11011, 11012); texts in *PL*, CC, 288–9.

[27] Reported by Hermann, historian at Saint-Martin of Tournai (*PL*,
CLXXX, 42): ". . . qui nihil aliud quaerentes nisi ut dicantur sapientes, in
Porphyrii Aristotelisque libris magis volunt legi suam adinventitiam novitatem,
quam Boethii caeterorumque antiquorum expositionem" (those who, seeking
nothing but that they should be called learned, prefer that their own trumped-
up novelties upon the books of Porphyry and Aristotle be read instead of the
exposition by Boethius and all the other ancients).

[28] [I Tim. 6:20: "O Timothee depositum custodi devitans profanas vocum
novitates et oppositiones falsi nominis scientiae." (O Timothy, guard what
has been entrusted to you. Avoid new, profane forms of speech and contra-
dictions of what is falsely called knowledge.)]

made it a basic rule of his theological work.[29] The author of the *Ysagoge in theologiam* (*Introduction to Theology*), a follower of Abelard writing around 1150, insisted at length on the "form of words":

> Since in that supreme wisdom concerned with divine matters there is no place for fake commentation or ostentatious novelty, you ought to prefer a work that brings together old and widely known authorities to one that trades on the new and unexpected. We know of certain people . . . who now make bold assertions based on no authority whatever, now claim impossible texts as their authorities after altering words as they please. Yet sacred science will eject from its sanctuary not only erroneous opinions but also the inauthentic form of words. . . . For he who works to replace the ideas of the ancients with his own verbal novelties is trying to diminish the authority of their teaching.[30]

John the Scot posed a serious problem as much by his language as by his opinions, and certain of his terms became a sure sign of heresy.[31] The anonymous *Liber de vera philosophia* brought the term *novitas* into play against the "Sabellian" errors of the Latins on the Trinity.[32] William of Saint-Thierry rejected the philosophy of Wil-

---

[29] *Regulae caelestis iuris* xxxiv (*PL*, CCX, 637): "Omnis sermo theologicus debet esse . . . usitatus . . . quia profanas verborum novitates ecclesia devitat." (Every theological term ought to be . . . current . . . because the church shuns new, profane forms of speech.) Cf. *De planctu naturae* (*PL*, CCX, 452).

[30] Prol. (Landgraf, p. 64): "Sed quoniam in hac divinorum summa sophia falso commenticio et ostentatorie novitati nullus est locus, tractatum potius vetera dissipata contrahentem quam novum aliquod inopinatumve cudentem expectare debes. Videmus enim nonnullos . . . modo inaudita nulloque auctoritatis presidio nixa edicere, modo iam dicta infanda verborum commutatione sibi arrogare. Divina vero pagina non solum opiniones erroneas, verum etiam inauthenticorum formam verborum a suo eliminat sacrario. . . . Doctrine enim sue auctoritatem nititur demere, qui veterum rationes verborum novitate laborat effere."

[31] Cf. the reaction of William of Saint-Thierry before the *inusitatum vocabulum* (unusual term) which he attributes to John the Scot: *Disputatio catholicorum patrum adversus dogmata Petri Abaelardi* iii (*PL*, CLXXX, 322): "Quod autem temporalitatis hujus cursum vocat involucrum, Joannem Scotum sequitur, qui frequentius hoc inusitato vocabulo usus, et ipse pro sua subtilitate de haeresi notatus est." (Moreover, in referring to the course of time as an *involucrum* [envelope], he [Abelard] follows John the Scot, who used this unusual term rather frequently and is known as a heretic for his subtlety.)

[32] Prol. (Paul Fournier, ed., "Un adversaire inconnu de S. Bernard et de Pierre Lombard," *BEC*, XLVII [1886], 394–417): "Ex quo ceperunt hujusmodi novitates crebescere. . . . Videbatur enim sibi istud verbum ('Quidquid

liam of Conches, this *philosophia nova* with its *novitatum vanitates* (vainglorious novelties), and he piled up epithets accusing Abelard of innovations.[33]

To press the point of this Pauline precept, traditionalist biblical scholars sometimes attacked the masters whose technical vocabulary was patently novel and who transgressed outside those scriptural frontiers "beyond which no citizen of the community of theologians is permitted to pass."[34] This was an important but subtle critique: it would work to restrain the indiscriminate posing of "undisciplined questions" (*indisciplinatas quaestiones*—an expression employed by Alexander III at the Council of Sens in 1164 concerning the christological debates and which would reappear frequently in pontifical directives)[35] but it also had the effect, in certain milieux, of raising suspicion against the theological masters with their rational categories, and even, under the aegis of the Pauline text, of robbing theological

---

est in Deo, Deus est') esse causa et origo fere omnium novitatum, ex quibus videbatur haeresis sabelliana proculdubio ressuscitari." (According to [the Council of Reims, 1148], innovations of this kind were beginning to proliferate. . . . for it seemed to the council that the expression ['Whatever is in God, is God'] was the cause and start of nearly all these innovations out of which in turn the Sabellian heresy was doubtless being revived.) Cf. P. Fournier, "Joachim de Flore et le *Liber de vera philosophia*," *RHLR*, IV (1899), 3–32.

[33] William of Saint-Thierry *De erroribus Guillelmi de Conchis* (*PL*, CLXXX, 333): "Etiam post theologiam Petri Abaelardi, Guillelmus de Conchis novam affert philosophiam, confirmans et multiplicans quaecumque ille dixit, et impudentius addens adhuc de suo plurima, quae ille non dixit. Cujus novitatum vanitates. . . ." (Moreover, after the theology of Peter Abelard, William of Conches produced a new philosophy, confirming and strengthening whatever the former had said, and with greater impudence adding to it much of his own which Abelard had not said. His [William's] vainglorious novelties.) And against Abelard in a letter to St. Bernard (*PL*, CLXXXII, 531): "Petrus enim Abaelardus iterum nova docet, nova scribit; et libri ejus transeunt maria, transiliunt Alpes; et novae ejus sententiae de fide, et nova dogmata per provincias et regna deferuntur, celebriter praedicantur et libere defenduntur: in tantum ut in curia romana dicantur habere auctoritatem." (For again Peter Abelard teaches new things, writes new things; and his books cross the seas and leap over the Alps; and his new opinions on the faith and new teachings are dispersed through provinces and kingdoms; they are preached with acclaim and freely defended, so much so that they are said to carry authority at the Roman curia.)

[34] Alan of Lille *Summa* prol. (Glorieux, p. 120): "ultra quos nemini qui civis theologicus est concedatur progressus."

[35] Cf. *Annales reicherspergenses* (*MGH, Scriptores*, XVII, 471).

studies of their verbal richness. The "innovators" were rationalists; at the basis of the alleged errors of Gilbert, and behind the reservations provoked by the conceptual arguments, was the charge that secular methods were being introduced. Monastic theology, which was pursued as a part of an inner religious experience and which found its home in the atmosphere of the cloister, in fact refused to break verbal contact with the sacred text. On the institutional level, moreover, had not Cluny already treated as "innovators" the reformers of Cîteaux, those very ones who were so sensitive to the light from the East?[36]

Dynamic Tradition

The most conservative among these theologians and administrators were not unwilling now and then to accept these new developments or, in the words of the parable, to bring forth from their treasures new things as well as old (Matt. 13:52). In developing a thesis concerning the incarnation against a certain Folmar, Gerhoh of Reichersberg wrote, "Since every learned scribe in the heavenly kingdom is like a householder who brings forth from his treasure both new things and old, let us add to the testimonies of our predecessors new testimonies written in our times."[37] The *Ysagoge*, so careful to avoid inauthentic terms, grouped together as designations of the divinity both Christian and pagan terms: Son and νοῦς (mind), Spirit and

---

[36] Cf. the letter of Cardinal Matthew of Albano, former prior of Saint-Martin-des-Champs, to the abbots assembled at Reims, published in U. Berlière, *Documents inédits pour servir à l'histoire ecclésiastique de la Belgique*, I (Maredsous, 1894), pp. 94–102: "Quae est nova lex? Quae est ista nova doctrina? Unde ista nova doctrina? Unde ista nova regula? Unde ista, si auderem dicere, nova praesumptio et inaudita?" (Now what is this new law? What is this new doctrine? Where does this new doctrine come from? Where does this new rule come from? Where, if I may ask, does this new and unheard of presumption come from?) Other conservative spokesmen were Robert of Torigny *De immutatione monachorum* i (*PL*, CCII, 1309), and Ordericus Vitalis *Hist. eccles.* viii.25, xiii.4 (*PL*, CLXXXVIII, 642–6, 935–6), listed as viii.26, xiii.13 in *The Ecclesiastical History of England and Normandy*, tr. T. Forester, 4 vols. (London, 1854–6), III, 39–48, IV, 131–3.

[37] *Liber de gloria filii hominis* xvi.10 (*PL*, CXCIV, 1131): "Quoniam omnis scriba doctus similis est in regno caelorum patrifamilias qui profert de thesauro suo nova et vetera, veterum testimoniis addamus nova temporibus nostris edita."

world soul.[38] Stephen of Tournai accepted the new classifications of the sacraments but with some reservation: ". . . if you can stand the new terminology" (*si vocabulorum novitatem non abhorres*).[39] Alan of Lille did not consider himself unfaithful to the precept of St. Paul when defining the rules of theology according to Gilbertine terms and principles.

In the field of trinitarian theology, where the creation of new terms such as *persona, hypostasis,* and *subsistentia* was a patent fact—it had been inevitable, potentially dangerous, but also beneficial—the pseudo-Hugh presented observations based on history, on method, and on doctrine:

> It is asked whether all terminological innovations are to be avoided.
> Reply: No, because they are not all profane, for example the Christian term *homoousia* (same substance); *mandatum novum* (new order), *testamentum novum* (new testament), and *canticum novum* (new song) refer to innovations which are not profane but holy and religious. The use of the term *hypostasis,* however, constituted a profane novelty in the time of the heretics, who applied it to either a person or a substance, in order to deceive the unlettered. But use of that word does not any longer constitute a profane novelty because the word has been restricted to signifying persons. Therefore one could now easily grant that the Trinity consists of three hypostases, and not one. Such a statement could not have been made without qualification when the word still retained several meanings.[40]

The most questionable terms lost their ambiguity precisely because of the hard work of theologians and thus became useful instruments

---

[38] *Ysagoge in theologiam* iii (Landgraf, pp. 257–8).

[39] *Die Summa des Stephanus Toracensis über das Decretum Gratiani,* ed. J. F. von Schulte (Giessen, 1891), p. 260.

[40] Pseudo-Hugh of Saint-Victor *Quaest. in Epp. Pauli,* I ad Tim., q. 38 (*PL,* CLXXV, 602): "Quaeritur an omnes vocum novitates sint vitandae. Solutio. Non, quia non omnes sunt profanae, ut hoc ipsum nomen christianum *homoousia,* mandatum *novum,* et testamentum *novum,* et canticum *novum,* novitates vocant non profanas, sed sacras et religioni congruentes. *Hypostasis* autem tempore haereticorum notabat profanam novitatem, quo nomine haeretici utebantur, nunc in significatione personae, nunc in significatione substantiae, ad deceptionem simplicium. . . . Nunc autem hoc vocabulum non notat profanam novitatem, quia redactum est ad significationem personae. Unde concedimus modo simpliciter trinitatem esse tres hypostases, et non unam, quod non erat concedendum sine determinatione olim, quando adhuc retinebat multiplicem significationem." Richard of Saint-Victor in his *De trin.* iv.4 (*PL,* CXCVI, 932) called to mind St. Jerome's opinion that when the term *hypostasis* was new, it was tainted with poison (*veneni suspicio*).

for the solution of new problems. The term *persona* is the leading instance of this, for it became universally understood and settled, not only that the term was legitimate, but that it had a definition, even though it was variously elaborated. Instead of *subsistentia*, which was henceforth currently used, Richard of Saint-Victor preferred less learned terms; yet he did not object to its use by specialists.[41] Everyone was weighing, correcting, distinguishing, and defining these innovations in terminology (*novitates vocum*).

To the extent that the masters analyzed the most highly qualified authorities and, on the other hand, organized the heritage of revelation into conceptual schemes, they were led to work out the laws of vital continuity of their developing faith so that, in the tradition of Abelard, they reconciled St. Paul's rejection of "new profane forms of speech" and "the new and the old" of the parable.

Peter of Blois, replying to invidious critics, declared that it was his frequenting of the ancients which had led him, like an industrious bee, to give force and style to traditional doctrine within an organic structure. "We are like dwarfs standing on the shoulders of giants; thanks to them, we see farther than they: busying ourselves with the treatises written by the ancients, we take their choice thoughts, buried by age and the neglect of men, and raise them, as it were, from death to renewed life."[42]

Dwarfs mounted on the shoulders of giants: the image is packed with meaning. No one will be surprised to learn that it was Bernard of Chartres who in the first third of the century put it into circulation.[43]

---

[41] *Ibid.*, 933: "Nomen personae in ore omnium, etiam rusticorum, versatur; nomen vero subsistentiae nec ab omnibus saltem litteratis agnoscitur." (The noun 'person' is regularly found in the mouths of all, even of peasants, whereas the term 'subsistence' is not even recognized by all literate persons.)

[42] *Epp.*, 92 (*PL*, CCV, 290): "Nos quasi nani super gigantium humeros sumus, quorum beneficio longius quam ipsi, speculamur, dum antiquorum tractatibus inhaerentes elegantiores eorum sententias, quas vetustas aboleverat, hominumve neglectus, quasi jam mortuas in quamdam novitatem essentiae suscitamus."

[43] John of Salisbury *Metalogicon* iii.4 (Webb, p. 136; McGarry, p. 167): "Dicebat Bernardus Carnotensis nos esse quasi nanos gigantium humeris insidentes, ut possimus plura eis et remotiora videre." (Bernard of Chartres said that we are like dwarfs standing on the shoulders of giants, so that we are able to see more and farther than they.) Cf. R. Klibansky, "Standing on the Shoulders of Giants," *Isis*, XXVI (1936), pp. 147–9.

The image suggests the progress of civilization; it expresses, as well, the law of tradition and progress among theologians.

"It ought not be judged reprehensible if human institutions sometimes adapt to changing times, especially when urgent necessity or obvious utility demands it. God himself often changed in the New Testament what he had established in the Old."[44] We have observed a steady balance, generally speaking, between doctrinal and institutional developments. This decree of the Fourth Lateran Council, Canon 50, dealing with a rather modest issue—removing certain obstacles to marriage—intentionally elaborated a broad principle; and its subsequent incorporation in the Decretals assured it a still broader significance.[45] The statement, moreover, acknowledges not only the fact of a change in the times, but also the purely religious perception of the progressive working out in history of God's plan, as Anselm of Havelberg had already understood it.

The Fourth Lateran Council, in the wide variety of its interventions and decisions and even of its reactions, testified to this dynamic tradition—a dynamic tradition finally stabilized by the perception that the integrity of the faith was not jeopardized by the rational bases of its theological formulations, by reconciling the refurbished monastic institutions with the amazing vigor of the new apostolic movements, and by holding the inviolable constitution of the church in tension with the sociological forms arising within a changing Christendom.

Against the doctrinal confusion and spiritual anarchy of certain evangelical groups, the council articulated clearly, by doctrine, legislation, and administrative reform, the essential sacramental structure and apostolic constitution of the church. The prelates, many of them from the Roman aristocracy, haunted by memories of the Roman commune of Arnold of Brescia, and responsive to the prestige of the monastic order, were cautious about the new apostolic formations

---

[44] Mansi, XXII, 1035: "Non debet reprehensibile judicari, si secundum varietatem temporum statuta quandoque varientur humana, praesertim cum urgens necessitas vel evidens utilitas id exposcit, quoniam ipse Deus, ex his quae in veteri testamento statuerat, nonnulla mutavit in novo."

[45] *Decretal.* lib. 4, tit. 14, c.8 (Friedberg, II, 703–4).

and forbade the founding of new orders.[46] But at that very moment, Innocent III, resisting the pressure of those prelates, upheld Francis of Assisi and the preachers of Dominic in their evangelical enterprise.[47]

With discipline in view, the council established laws governing the sacraments, especially penance and the eucharist, which were to be administered by each parish priest within his parochial jurisdiction. Yet at the same time, voluntary fraternities were encouraged and organized. These democratic organizations, independent of the parishes but related to the communes, and delicately placed between independence and institutional control, were supposed to head off popular heresies.

Strongly Mediterranean in composition in the absence not only of the Greeks but also of the German prelates, the council was much under the influence of Rome, of imperial and papal Rome, while at the same time purposely defiant towards Constantinople and actively concerned with directing a crusade against Islam. But this was also the moment when Latin Christendom was engaging in a major missionary effort: to the Slavs, to Asia, to Islam itself. Teams were being formed at the University of Paris; John of Matha founded an order for the redemption of captives with the approval of Innocent III; Minors and Preachers by the hundreds went off in all directions.

In theology, it is true, the Latins triumphed. The exaltation of Peter Lombard was surely in the first place a declaration of his orthodoxy against his adversaries; but it implied also, in this instance, a

---

[46] Can. XIII: *De novis religionibus prohibitis* (Mansi, XXII, 1002–3).

[47] Cf. among others the aggravated testimony of the monk Matthew Paris *Chron. maj. (MGH, Scriptores*, XXXVIII, 248): ". . . spretis beatissimi Benedicti pleni spiritu omnium sanctorum et magnifici Augustini disciplinis, contra statutum concilii sub gloriosae memoriae Innocentio III celebrati, tot viri litterati ad inauditos ordines subito convolarunt" (spurning the discipline of the most holy Benedict, who was filled with the spirit of all saints, and of the magnificent Augustine, and defying the statute of the council held under Innocent III of glorious memory, many educated men rushed into these unheard of orders). He calls attention in his *Hist. Anglorum (MGH, Scriptores,* XXXVIII, 397) to the rise of the new orders with the connivance of Pope Innocent (*favente papa Innocento*).

consecration of his theology, the Augustinianism and Latin forms of which would bar subsequent incursions by the Greeks.

From on high, Innocent III dominated this evolution towards equilibrium. Himself a great feudal lord, he extended his authority audaciously yet prudently to embrace the apostolic groups, the same which, in their evangelical liberty, had emancipated themselves from the feudal structures of monasticism and the episcopacy. Imbued for his own part with traditional spirituality, witness his *De contemptu mundi*, Innocent was receptive to the spirit of St. Francis and the projects of St. Dominic; his vision of the Lateran, threatened with collapse yet held up by the divine envoy from Assisi, expressed perfectly his thought and program.

Both his teaching and his action were rooted in feudal principles, in the imperial myth of the two powers, and in the idea of a papacy that was heir to the Roman Empire. Yet when the French had gained their victory over the German Empire at Bouvines in 1214 ("the greatest political event of the thirteenth century," according to Jacques Pirenne),[48] Innocent broke the political traditions of the Holy See, not without some risks, by consenting to the temporal independence of the young monarchies and pledging himself to the new Christendom that was emerging from the age of theocracy.[49] It would be pointless to argue for a systematic evolution in Innocent III's political outlook.[50] More would be gained by comparing him with his contemporary, Philip Augustus, so very modern in many respects, even though he still thought in feudal terms. Yet Innocent presided over, governed, and inspired a church which, with the twelfth-century crises behind it, now entered upon the most glorious century of its history filled with evangelical ardor, confident of reason's place in theology, and with its political power in decline. The year 1215, year

---

[48] *The Tides of History*, tr. L. Edwards (London, 1963), II, 147.

[49] Cf. Friedrich Kempf, *Papsttum und Kaisertum bei Innocenz III. Die geistigen und rechtlichen Grundlagen seiner Thronstreitpolitik, MHP*, XIX (Rome, 1954).

[50] Cf. Edouard Jordan, *L'Allemagne et l'Italie aux 12e et 13e siècles* (Paris, 1939), p. 170: "This great politician (Innocent III) hardly intended—far from it—to do all the things that he did."

of the Fourth Lateran Council, witnessed the first legislation on the University of Paris in the statute promulgated by the papal legate Robert of Courçon; it also witnessed the public approbation of the friars. Here are two innovations which define authentically the progress made by the church in the midst of the thousand years of the "Middle" Age.

Abbreviations

1. Periodicals, Series, Reference Works, and Collections of Sources

AHDL	*Archives d'histoire doctrinale et littéraire du moyen-âge*
ALKG	*Archiv für Literatur- und Kirchengeschichte*
ARSP	*Archiv für Rechts- und Sozialphilosophie*
ASOC	*Analecta Sacri Ordinis Cisterciensis*
BEC	*Bibliothèque de l'École des Chartes*
BGPM	*Beiträge zur Geschichte der Philosophie und Theologie des Mittelalters*
CSEL	*Corpus scriptorum ecclesiasticorum latinorum*
CUP	H. Denifle and E. Chatelain, eds., *Chartularium universitatis parisiensis*, 4 vols. (Paris, 1889–97).
DHGE	*Dictionnaire d'histoire et de géographie ecclésiastiques*
DTC	*Dictionnaire de théologie catholique*
GCFI	*Giornale critico della filosofia italiana*
HF	*Recueil des historiens des Gaules et de la France*, 24 vols. (Paris, 1738–1904).
HJ	*Historisches Jahrbuch*
MGH	*Monumenta Germaniae Historica*
MHP	*Miscellanea Historiae Pontificiae*
MIOG	*Mitteilungen des Instituts für österreichische Geschichtsforschung*
MP	*Modern Philology*
MRS	*Mediaeval and Renaissance Studies*

MS	*Mediaeval Studies*
MSR	*Mélanges de science religieuse*
NRT	*Nouvelle revue théologique*
PG	J.-P. Migne, *Patrologiae cursus completus, series graeca*, 162 vols., with Latin translation (Paris, 1857–66).
PL	J.-P. Migne, *Patrologiae cursus completus, series latina*, 221 vols. (Paris, 1844–64).
RH	*Revue historique*
RHE	*Revue d'histoire ecclésiastique*
RHEF	*Revue d'histoire de l'église de France*
RHLR	*Revue d'histoire et de littérature religieuses*
RHPR	*Revue d'histoire et de philosophie religieuses*
RHR	*Revue de l'histoire des religions*
RIFD	*Rivista internazionale di filosofia del diritto*
RLM	*Revue liturgique et monastique*
RSPT	*Revue des sciences philosophiques et théologiques*
Rech. SR	*Recherches de science religieuse*
RSR	*Revue des sciences religieuses*
RTAM	*Recherches de théologie ancienne et médiévale*
Schol.	*Scholastik*
Spec.	*Speculum*
Trad.	*Traditio*
ZKG	*Zeitschrift für Kirchengeschichte*
ZKT	*Zeitschrift für katholische Theologie*
ZRG	*Zeitschrift für Rechtsgeschichte*

2. Authors, Editors, and Translators

Aquinas, *Opera omnia*	Thomas Aquinas, *Opera omnia*, ed. G. M. Allodi, 25 vols. (Parma, 1852–73; photo reprint: New York, 1948–50).

Aquinas, *Summa*	Thomas Aquinas, *The Summa theologica,* tr. Fathers of the English Dominican Province, 22 vols. (New York, 1911–25).
Aquinas, *S. Gent.*	Thomas Aquinas, *The Summa Contra Gentiles,* tr. the English Dominican Fathers from the Latest Leonine edition, 4 vols. (London, 1924–9)
Barach-Wrobel	Bernard Sylvester, *De mundi universitate libri duo sive megacosmus et microcosmus,* ed. C. S. Barach and J. Wrobel (Innsbruck, 1876).
Bloch	M. Bloch, *Feudal Society,* tr. L. A. Manyon, 2 vols. (Chicago, 1964).
Buttimer	Hugh of St. Victor, *Didascalicon de studio legendi,* ed. C. H. Buttimer (Washington, 1939).
Chenu, *St. Thomas*	M.-D. Chenu, *Toward Understanding St. Thomas,* tr. A. M. Landry and D. Hughes (Chicago, 1964).
Chenu, *TDS*	M.-D. Chenu, *La théologie au douzième siècle* (Paris, 1957).
Chibnall	John of Salisbury, *Memoirs of the Papal Court,* tr. M. Chibnall (London, 1956).
CSMV	Hugh of St. Victor, *Selected Spiritual Writings,* tr. by a religious of the Community of St. Mary the Virgin (London, 1962).
Deferrari	*Hugh of Saint Victor: On the Sacraments of the Christian Faith,* tr. R. P. Deferrari (Cambridge, Mass., 1951).
Delhaye	P. Delhaye, *Godefroy de Saint-Victor: Microcosmos,* 2 vols. (Lille, 1951), vol. 1: Texte, vol. 2: *Etude théologique.*
Dickinson	John of Salisbury, *The Statesman's Book, Being the Fourth, Fifth, and Sixth Books, and Selections from the Seventh and Eighth Books of the Policraticus,* tr. J. Dickinson (New York, 1927).
Diehl	Ernst Diehl, ed., *Procli Diadochi in Platonis Timaeum commentaria,* 3 vols. (Leipzig, 1903–6).
Faral	E. Faral, *Les arts poétiques du XIIᵉ et du XIIIᵉ siècles* (Paris, 1923).
Festugière	A.-J. Festugière, *La révélation d'Hermès Trismegiste,* 4 vols. (Paris, 1944–54).

333

Friedberg	E. Friedberg, *Corpus juris canonici,* 2 vols. (Leipzig, 1888–92).
Ghellinck, *Essor*	J. de Ghellinck, *L'essor de la littérature latine au XIIe siècle,* 2nd ed. (Brussels, 1955).
Ghellinck, *Mouvement*	J. de Ghellinck, *Le mouvement théologique du XIIe siècle,* 2nd ed. (Brussels, 1948).
Glorieux	P. Glorieux, ed., "La Somme *Quoniam homines* d'Alain de Lille," *AHDL,* XX (1953), 113–364.
Gollancz	Berechiah, ben Natronai, Nakdan, *Dodi Ve-nechdi, Uncle and Nephew;* to which is added the first English translation of Adelard of Bath's *Quaestiones Naturales,* ed. and tr. H. Gollancz (London, 1920).
Gregory	T. Gregory, *Anima mundi: la filosofia di Guglielmo di Conches e la scuola di Chartres* (Florence, 1955).
Grundmann	H. Grundmann, *Religiöse Bewegungen im Mittelalter,* 2nd ed. (Hildesheim, 1961).
Haring	N. M. Haring, ed., "The *Eulogium ad Alexandrum Papam tertium* of John of Cornwall," *MS,* XIII (1951), 253–300.
Haskins, *Renaissance*	C. H. Haskins, *The Renaissance of the Twelfth Century* (Cambridge, Mass., 1927).
Haskins, *Studies*	C. H. Haskins, *Studies in the History of Medieval Science,* 2nd ed. (Cambridge, Mass., 1927).
Jeauneau	Édouard Jeauneau, *Guillaume de Conches, Glosae super Platonem. Texte critique avec introduction, notes et tables.* (Paris, 1965).
Lammers-Schmidt	Otto of Freising, *Chronica sive historia de duabus civitatibus,* ed. W. Lammers and A. Schmidt (Berlin, 1960).
Landgraf	A. Landgraf, ed., *Écrits théologiques de l'école d'Abélard* (Louvain, 1934).
Larkin	P. Mandonnet and M.-H. Vicaire, *St. Dominic and His Work,* tr. M. B. Larkin (St. Louis, 1944).
Lefèvre	Yves Lefèvre, *L'Elucidarium et les lucidaires. Contribution, par l'histoire d'un texte, à l'histoire des croyances religieuses en France au moyen âge* (Paris, 1954) [text, pp. 359 ff.].

Mandonnet	P. Mandonnet and M.-H. Vicaire, *Saint Dominique. L'idée, l'homme et l'oeuvre,* 2 vols. (Paris, 1938).
Mansi	J. D. Mansi, ed., *Sacrorum conciliorum nova et amplissima collectio,* 31 vols. (Florence-Venice, 1759–98).
Martin	Robert of Melun, *Sententie,* ed. R.-M. Martin and R. M. Gallet, 2 vols. (Louvain, 1947–52).
McGarry	*The Metalogicon of John of Salisbury,* tr. D. D. McGarry (Berkeley, 1962).
Mierow	Otto of Freising, *The Two Cities, A Chronicle of World History to the Year 1146 A.D.,* tr. C. C. Mierow (New York, 1928).
Mierow-Emery	Otto of Freising, *The Deeds of Frederick Barbarossa,* tr. C. C. Mierow and R. Emory (New York, 1953).
Muckle	*The Story of Abelard's Adversities,* tr. J. T. Muckle (Toronto, 1954).
Müller	M. Müller, ed., *Die Quaestiones naturales des Adelardus von Bath, BGPM,* XXX, ii (1934).
Mullach	F. Mullach, ed., *Fragmenta philosophorum graecorum,* II (Paris, 1881).
Paré	G. Paré, *Les idées et les lettres au XIIIᵉ siècle: Le Roman de la Rose* (Montreal, 1947).
Parent	J.-M. Parent, *La doctrine de la création dans l'école de Chartres* (Paris, 1938).
Pike	John of Salisbury, *Frivolities of Courtiers and Footprints of Philosophers, Being the First, Second, and Third Books, and Selections from the Seventh and Eighth Books of the Policraticus,* tr. J. B. Pike (Minneapolis, 1938).
Prou	Maurice Prou, ed., *Raoul Glaber, Les cinq livres de ses histoires (900–1044)* (Paris, 1886).
R. de Lage	G. Raynaud de Lage, *Alain de Lille, Poète du XIIᵉ siècle* (Montreal-Paris, 1951).
Riedel	Bernard Sylvester, *Commentarium super sex libros Eneidos Vergilii,* ed. G. Riedel (Greifswald, 1924).
Simson	Otto of Freising, *Gesta Frederici I imperatoris,* ed. B. de Simson (Hannover, 1912).

Smalley

B. Smalley, *The Study of the Bible in the Middle Ages* (Oxford, 1952).

Taylor

The Didascalicon of Hugh of St. Victor, tr. J. Taylor (New York, 1961).

Webb, *Metalogicon*

John of Salisbury, *Metalogicon libri IV,* ed. C. C. J. Webb (Oxford, 1929).

Webb, *Policraticus*

John of Salisbury, *Policraticus, sive de nugis curialium et vestigiis philosophorum libri VIII,* ed. C. C. J. Webb, 2 vols. (Oxford, 1909).

Willner

H. Willner, ed., *Des Adelard von Bath Traktat, De eodem et diverso, BGPM,* IV (Münster, 1903).

Wrobel

Johannes Wrobel, ed., *Platonis Timæus interprete Chalcido cum eiusdem commentario* (Leipzig, 1876).

Index

Abelard, Peter: xvii, xviii, xix, 15, 27, 44, 57, 62, 65, 67n*31*, 69, 70–71, 102, 103, 172, 173, 202, 237, 273, 274, 280, 284, 290, 299, 308, 309, 323, 326; distinction between natural forces and divine activity, 16; *De dialectica*, 51n*1*; *Expositio in Hexaemeron*, 16n*34*; *Historia calamitatum meum*, 219n*35*, 290n *49*, 311n*2*; *Introductio ad theologiam*, 22n*46*, 70n*40*, 71n*42*, 172n*22*, 299n*65*; *Monita ad Astrolabium*, 301n*69*; *Theologia christiana*, 51n*1*, 57n*14*, 71n*40*, 172n*22*

Abraham, 180

Absalom of Saint-Victor, 10

Adalbero of Laon: *Carmen ad Robertum regem francorum*, 264n*42*

Adam, 180, 184

Adam of Dryburgh: *Epist. ad Praemonstr.*, 7n*12*; *De tripartito tabernaculo*, 267n*47*; *De triplici sanctae Ecclesiae statu*, 184n*47*, 268n*50*

Adamek, J.: *Vom römischen Endreich der mittelalterlichen Bibelerklärung*, 186n*51*

Adelard of Bath: 65, 87; defense of science against intellectual authoritarianism, 13; *Astrolabium*, 13n*27*; *De eodem et diverso*, 50n*1*, 65; *Liber prestigiorum Thebidis secundum Ptolemeum et Hermetem*, 87n*64*; *Quaestiones naturales*, 13, 312n*5*

Adhémar of Chabannes, 178

Adhémar of Saint-Ruf: *Commentarium in Boetii de Trinitate*, 293n*53*

Alan of Lille: 16, 18–19, 28, 31–32, 33, 37, 45, 47, 49–50, 54, 57, 61, 65, 89, 96, 99, 100, 102, 108, 119, 131, 132, 139n*73*, 296, 322, 325; allegorizing of, 113, 117, 141, 144; commentaries on, 92; corporeal and incorporeal, participating in divine goodness, 25–26; myth, 70–71, 71n*43*; naturalism of, 20, 27, 47, 48, 161, 162, 233; Neoplatonism of, 31n*32*, 50, 89; Platonism of, 96; *translatio* in, 139n*73*; *Anticlaudianus*, 28n*57*, 92, 109n*25*, 318, 319n*18*; *De arte seu articulis catholicae fidei*, 45n*96*, 279n*30*, 280, 303; *Contra haer.*, 26n*49*, 251n*15*, 281; *Distinctiones*, 20n*42*, 32n*70*, 136n*69*; *Elucid. in Cant. cant.*, 136n*71*; *Liber sententiarum*, 113n *36*; *De planctu Naturae*, 18ff, 19nn*38, 39*, 27, 48n*102*, 71n*41*, 78–79n*56*, 99n*1*, 100n*2*, 141, 144, 322n*29*; *Regulae caelestis iuris*, 37n*82*, 48n*101*, 54nn*7, 8*, 80n*58*, 281, 290, 296, 300, 322n*29*; *Rhythmus alter*, 117n*43*; *De sex alis Cheribim*, 144n*85*; *Summa 'Quoniam homines,'* 57n*13*, 60, 88, 140, 300, 296n*58*, 323n*34*; *Summa*

Works: divine and natural, 41; of man as artisan, 40–41

World: "mirror" of God, 116; origin of, in Platonism, 56, 68; "philosophy of the world," 47; problem for Christian, 36, 38, 47; as a whole, 67–68, 67n33

World soul: *See* Soul

Ysagoge in theol., 322n30, 324, 325n38